BLUE GUIDE

FLORENCE

Alta Macadam

Somerset Books • London
WW Norton • New York

Blue Guide Florence
Ninth edition

Published by Blue Guides Limited, a Somerset Books Company
49–51 Causton St, London SW1P 4AT
www.blueguides.com
'Blue Guide' is a registered trademark

ISBN 1–905131–02–X

A CIP catalogue record of this book is available from the British Library.

Published in the United States of America by
WW Norton and Company, Inc.
500 Fifth Avenue, New York, NY 10110
USA ISBN 0–393–32731–0

Cover photographs: Top: Detail of *The Birth of St John the Baptist* (1486–90)
by Domenico Ghirlandaio,
in Santa Maria Novella (Bridgeman Picture Library).
Bottom: Ponte Vecchio (Corbis Royalty Free Photograph).
Title page: Detail of a stained glass window showing the emblem of Florence,
photo: Monica Larner

All other acknowledgements, photo credits and copyright information are given
on p. 400, which forms part of this copyright page.

CONTENTS

THE GUIDE

THE WALKS

PRACTICAL INFORMATION

About the author

Alta Macadam has been a writer of Blue Guides since 1970. She lives with her Italian family in Florence, where she has been associated with the Bargello museum, the Alinari photo archive, Harvard University at Villa I Tatti, and New York University at Villa La Pietra. Her *Americans in Florence* was published by Giunti in Florence in 2003. As author of the Blue Guides to Rome, Venice, Tuscany and Umbria, she travels extensively in Italy every year to revise new editions of the books.

HIGHLIGHTS
OF FLORENCE

Romanesque buildings

The Baptistery is the most important early building in the city, and the classical geo-metrical design of its exterior is repeated in the beautiful 11th-century façade of San Miniato. The little church of Santi Apostoli has a lovely early basilican interior.

Renaissance works

The masterpiece of the Florentine Renaissance and the city's most visible landmark is the dome of the Duomo, designed by Brunelleschi. Other works by this important architect include the portico of the Spedale degli Innocenti, the Pazzi Chapel and the Old Sacristy in San Lorenzo, as well as the churches of San Lorenzo and Santo Spirito. Lorenzo Ghiberti's east doors of the Baptistery, with their relief sculptures of Old Testament scenes, along with Masaccio's frescoes in the Brancacci Chapel (Santa Maria del Carmine) are two more key works of the early Renaissance. Leon Battista Alberti, the great theorist and architect of the Renaissance, was born in Florence. He designed the façade of Santa Maria Novella as well as (almost certainly) that of Palazzo Rucellai, and the exquisite little Cappella del Santo Sepolcro.

Museums

The Uffizi is one of the great museums of the world, and contains the most important collection of paintings in Italy; it is now particularly famous for its works by Botticelli. The Galleria Palatina, in the huge Palazzo Pitti, contains masterpieces by Raphael, Titian and Rubens. The Bargello has an important collection of Renaissance sculpture, including numerous works by Donatello. The Galleria dell'Accademia houses Michelangelo's famous *David*, as well as other works by him.

Small museums

The city also has numerous smaller (and less crowded) museums of exceptional inter-est: the Museo dell'Opera del Duomo (sculpture), the Casa Buonarroti (works by Michelangelo), and the Museo di San Marco (paintings and frescoes by Fra' Angelico) being the main three.

Palaces

Many palaces in Florence have fine façades and handsome courtyards (although the interiors are often inaccessible). The best are Palazzo Medici-Riccardi, Palazzo Pitti and Palazzo Strozzi, as well as Palazzo Antinori and Palazzo Rucellai. Streets with par-ticularly handsome palaces include Via Tornabuoni and Borgo degli Albizi.

Sculpture

For centuries, it was the custom in Florence to erect sculptures in the main squares (*piazze*) or on the exterior of buildings. Some of these works have now had to be restored, moved and placed under cover, and replaced *in situ* with copies. There are numerous important sculptures (by Donatello, Cellini and Giambologna) in the central Piazza della Signoria and under the Loggia della Signoria. The exterior of Orsanmichele is decorated with statues in niches, including three by Lorenzo Ghiberti, and others by Donatello, Nanni di Banco and Verrocchio. The originals are currently being restored. Piazza Santissima Annunziata also has an equestrian statue (of Grand Duke Ferdinando I) by Giambologna.

The best collection of sculpture in Florence is to be found in the Bargello museum. The Museo dell'Opera del Duomo and the Galleria dell'Accademia are also famous for their sculpture. Roman masterpieces which formed part of the Medici collections are kept in the Tribuna and corridors of the Uffizi, and there is some very fine Etruscan and Roman sculpture in the Museo Archeologico. Garden statuary can be seen in the Boboli Gardens as well as the Medici villas in the environs (notably Villa di Castello).

Frescoes

Florence has a great number of frescoed chapels and cloisters. Those dating from the 14th century include the chapels in Santa Croce (two by Giotto, and others by Agnolo and Taddeo Gaddi, Maso di Banco and Giovanni da Milano), the Strozzi Chapel in Santa Maria Novella (Nardo di Cione), and the sacristy of San Miniato (Spinello Aretino). Renaissance frescoes include those in the sanctuary of Santa Maria Novella and the Sassetti Chapel in Santa Trìnita by Domenico Ghirlandaio, the chapel in Palazzo Medici-Riccardi by Benozzo Gozzoli, the convent of San Marco by Fra' Angelico, and the Chapel of Filippo Strozzi in Santa Maria Novella by Filippino Lippi. 16th-century works include the frescoes in the atrium of Santissima Annunziata (Andrea del Sarto, Franciabigio, Rosso Fiorentino, Pontormo), the Capponi Chapel in Santa Felicita by Pontormo, and the Cappella di Eleonora in Palazzo Vecchio by Bronzino. The reception rooms in Palazzo Pitti were frescoed in the 17th century by Pietro da Cortona.

Cenacoli

Numerous convents in Florence have refectories with a depiction of the *Last Supper* (*cenacolo*) in fresco. Some of the best examples are by Taddeo Gaddi (Santa Croce), Orcagna (Santo Spirito), Domenico Ghirlandaio (Ognissanti and San Marco), Andrea del Castagno (Sant'Apollonia), Andrea del Sarto (San Salvi) and Alessandro Allori (Santa Maria Novella).

Cloisters

The beautiful cloisters of Florence provide some of the city's most peaceful spots. They include Brunelleschi's cloister at Santa Croce, and those attached to San Lorenzo and Santa Maria Maddalena dei Pazzi. Other lovely cloisters have frescoed lunettes: Santa Maria Novella (Paolo Uccello), the Badia Fiorentina (early 15th-century frescoes in the Chiostro degli Aranci), Santissima Annunziata (Chiostro dei Morti, with the

Madonna del Sacco by Andrea del Sarto), Ognissanti (Jacopo Ligozzi and Giovanni da San Giovanni), and San Marco (17th-century lunettes in the Chiostro di Sant'Antonino).

Environs of Florence

The most interesting place in the environs of Florence is Fiesole. Beautiful country walks can be taken in this district, and towards Maiano and Settignano. There are also a number of Medici villas open to the public, including the Villa di Castello and Villa della Petraia.

Views of the city

The best view of the city is from the Forte di Belvedere. Piazzale Michelangelo, below San Miniato, provides a famous panoramic view, though San Miniato itself affords an even better—and more peaceful—vantage point. The city and its surrounding hills can also be appreciated from the tops of the Duomo and campanile. The tall building of Orsanmichele provides a fine view of the city centre. The Corridoio Vasariano affords delightful glimpses of the river and there are also good views from the Boboli Gardens. Via di Bellosguardo also has splendid views back towards Florence. The roads up to Fiesole all give excellent views of the city, as does the hill of San Francesco above Fiesole.

THE FLORENTINE
RENAISSANCE

by Nigel McGilchrist

The Origins of Florentine Art

'A painting is a window looking onto the world', wrote Alberti in 1436. We take this so completely for granted today that it is easy to forget that the idea of a picture coherently and realistically describing the world around us was born in Florence in the early 1400s. Or rather, it was re-born in Florence for the first time since the end of the Roman Empire. Florence, as her name so happily implies, embodies the very flowering of a new European art. Within her walls were born the individuals and the ideas which were to shape the nature of our modern visual sensibility. Certainly Florence could not have achieved what she did without the roots and the tree of Italian art as a whole; but Florence remains the flower of that tree, in particular in the 1400s when her pre-eminence was uncontested anywhere in Italy, or even in Europe. The fact that so many figures of genius who have become household names well beyond the shores of Italy and of Europe—Giotto, Dante, Petrarch, Donatello, Masaccio, Botticelli, Leonardo da Vinci, Michelangelo, Galileo, Macchiavelli—should all have come from or worked in this small and hitherto insignificant town in the space of little more than 300 years—is not only statistically extraordinary, but it requires some kind of explanation. So also does the fact that, after Michelangelo's death in 1564, Florence produced no artists of comparable stature ever again, and indeed she all but vanishes from the pages of art history books.

In this way Florence appears like a blazing comet in the artistic firmament in the 14th and 15th centuries, and just as dramatically disappears at the end of the 16th century. For the visitor this means that the city, in marked contrast to Rome, presents itself as an architectural and artistic unity, a complete expression of one particular period and spirit. This spirit we commonly call the Renaissance. It was a conscious re-birth or 're-naissance' of the principles of ancient Roman and Greek thinking, and the art of the city cannot be understood except by reference to that ever-present emulation of, and desire to exceed, the achievements of Antiquity. We think of the Florentine Renaissance as principally an artistic revolution: revolution it certainly was, but it was as much about science—about optics, geometry and anatomy, in particular—as it was about art. It just happens that in Florence, that scientific thinking was linked to visual expression. Hence the unforgettable physical beauty of this tiny city and its disproportionate wealth of monuments and pictures.

Florentine art begins, as so often, with money. Ancient Roman Florence was perhaps only a quarter of the size of Pompeii, and would have remained comparably insignificant, had it not begun in the 12th century to play an important role in the continent's wool trade. Wool was always needed for clothing and was a big industry in medieval Europe. The raw material was produced in Northern Europe, but was processed, dyed and carded in a number of centres in the Mediterranean, of which Florence became one of the foremost. This was a lucrative business, and it made a small group of Florentine families immensely rich. That wealth, however, might never have had the determining influence it was to have on European art, had not some of those families begun, in the 13th century, to use their wealth for banking and for making substantial loans, both locally and internationally. The gold florin, named after the city, was minted from 1252 onwards and became an internationally recognised coinage. The wealthy banking families of Florence became steadily wealthier. But there was one moral issue that gnawed at their sophisticated, Christian consciences. Banking was based on usury, and usury was a sin—a deadly sin, furthermore, that might jeopardise the comfort of their souls after death. One way of atoning for this was to underwrite fine buildings for the Church, and to commission sculptures, murals and altarpieces to the greater glory of God. It is, of course, difficult to know exactly how much early Florentine art is a product of this desire to atone for the sin of usury; but its influence as an idea was undoubtedly far-reaching, and the great families who patronised the artists of Florence in the 1300s and 1400s soon realised as well that their artistic—and highly visible—commissions could also be fruitful vehicles for propaganda and personal glorification. The fertile soil for an artistic revolution was thus created, and in that soil, around the year 1400, a remarkable group of free-thinking and curious minds found an ideal environment for intellectual and artistic growth.

What happened in the miracle of the Florentine Quattrocento (15th century) did not appear from nowhere, and we need first to look for its roots in the previous hundred and fifty years.

The Duecento and Trecento

A remarkably stubborn tradition has seen a figure by the name of Cenni di Peppi (c. 1240–1302) or 'Cimabue' (about whom we know little that is certain) as the first exponent of a style in painting that we can begin to call distinctively Florentine. We can see what this refers to by looking at a great work, probably by this master, in the cloisters of the Florentine Church of Santa Croce. This unexpectedly moving (although much damaged) processional crucifix (see p. 242) is created in a tradition which descended from Byzantine religious painting. But if we look at it carefully we see that, although it is rhythmically stylized and rigorously icon-like in appearance, it nonetheless reveals an attention to modelling and a quality of pathos and drama which is essentially alien to the spirit of Byzantine art. And if we imagine the huge cross-shaped panel held high above a surging procession in the streets of the town, we can begin to see the purpose of that pathos. We have our first intimation also of how important and recurrent the processional element is going to be in the greatest Florentine art.

This new and sculptural tendency in the creations of Cimabue was intently felt and perceived by his greatest pupil, Giotto (c. 1267–1337). The anecdotal version of the relationship between this master and pupil of genius is delightfully told by Giorgio

Vasari, who in 1550 published his famous *Lives of the most excellent Painters, Sculptors and Architects*, one of the first modern pieces of art-historical writing. Giotto took that hint of drama and human pathos which he found in Cimabue and fashioned it into his own inimitable visual language. In almost the first room of the Uffizi Gallery you have the opportunity to compare these two painters side by side in the two strikingly similar paintings of the Madonna enthroned (*see p. 88*): the *Santa Trìnita Madonna*, generally attributed to Cimabue, and the *Ognissanti Madonna*, attributed to Giotto. Several things distinguish Giotto's work from his master's: the pared-down simplicity of Giotto's version; the coherence and unity of its design; the awakening humanity of the faces; and the new, weighty solidity of the figures. It was these characteristics that opened the way to generations of later Italian and European painting. Masaccio was to learn these lessons, and Piero della Francesca and Michelangelo, too, amongst the many artists who came to study and to draw in front of the works of Giotto.

Though Giotto's masterpiece, the Scrovegni Chapel, is in Padua, his works can be found elsewhere in Florence—principally in the (rather damaged) murals of the Bardi and Peruzzi Chapels in Santa Croce. The design of the graceful campanile of Florence cathedral is also his.

Was Giotto then really the founding spirit of the Italian Renaissance? The answer is complicated by the fact that perhaps a whole generation of potential artists who immediately followed him was virtually eliminated by repeated outbreaks of the plague in the middle of the 14th century. Florence suffered terribly, both economically and demographically, and, in concomitance, the momentum of Giotto's artistic revolution seems to falter. The 14th century, or Trecento, may have been a period of lost potential, but nonetheless it was one of a productivity of a high technical quality. In its pantheon of lesser known artists, two families of painters stand out: the di Cione (Andrea, always called 'Orcagna', and his brothers Nardo and Jacopo), and the Gaddi (Taddeo, the father, and Agnolo, the son). Outside the Uffizi Gallery, the works of these accomplished artists are to be found in the two magnificent and spacious churches of the preaching orders which mark the western and eastern extremities of Medieval Florence: Santa Maria Novella of the Dominicans, and Santa Croce of the Franciscans.

To the eyes of the uninitiated the religious works and altarpieces of the 14th century can appear to have an unwelcome sameness to them. This impression is not helped by museums which exhibit these beautiful, but often damaged, works side by side, spreadeagled and pinned uncomfortably to the walls under a harsh and uncompromising light, like patients in a hospital ward. We owe it to the works themselves to undo this damage, and in our mind's eye to set them once again on the quiet altars in dark churches for which they were originally created, with the light of candles or oil-lamps in front of them, giving a tender and deep illumination to their gold backgrounds and jewel-like colours. Nor should we ever forget that many people in the 14th century might have seen no more than three or four paintings in a whole lifetime: they would therefore have given them the time and the concentration that we no longer have, and would have appreciated above all else the fineness of their execution.

It must also be remembered that much of the city's creative energy in the 1300s was concentrated solely on its greatest project: the cathedral of Santa Maria del Fiore. The vastness and the grandeur of this project were an expression of the wealth and optimism of Florence at this period. But it risked overshooting in its optimism, and would in fact have done so had it not been saved by the scientific brilliance of the following generation. In designing one of the largest churches in existence, the architects had left themselves with a seemingly insoluble problem: the octagonal drum on which the final dome was to be placed was just over 43 metres in diameter—a distance too great to construct the wooden jig, or 'centring' as it is called, which was necessary for the construction of any solid dome. To Florence's humiliation in the eyes of her neighbours, work on the Duomo stopped, and the building had no dome. It needed a new generation and a radically new and different way of thinking to solve this problem. That solution was to be typical of the mentality and the genius of the Quattrocento.

The Quattrocento

One of the things that had most astonished contemporaries about Giotto's pictorial art, was its uncanny ability (as it seemed to them) to give a convincing sense both of human emotion and of spatial reality. What they were observing was not only a change in artistic practice; it was a fundamental change in human thinking. Whereas Byzantine and medieval religious art aimed always to take the gaze of human devotion up and away from the sordid parenthesis of earthly life to an unchanging and golden eternity where emotion and descriptive reality had no place, suddenly, with Giotto, the direction was being reversed and the scenes of spiritual life were being brought down to the world of human reality, put into an earthly setting, given physical depth and weight, and imbued with human feeling. In other words, instead of striving to raise human devotion to the level of the sacred, the sacred was brought down to the level of the human. Many had sensed the beginning of this change in Giotto, but none was to absorb its lesson so completely and so deeply as a young 20 year-old painter, working 100 years after Giotto, by the name of Tommaso di Mone, known as Masaccio (1401–28).

Florentine art—and the achievements of Donatello, Piero della Francesca and Michelangelo, all of whom studied his work in these places—cannot be understood without visiting the church of Santa Maria Novella to see Masaccio's fresco of the *Trinity*, or the Brancacci Chapel in the church of Santa Maria del Carmine, where Masaccio worked, after 1423, on a cycle of frescos depicting the life of St Peter and other biblical scenes. All those lessons learnt from Giotto are there: the sheer reduction to the essential elements, the clear narrative urgency, the concentrated sculptural forms, and the careful proportion of figure to space. But there is much else that is new: a genuine concern for convincing anatomy and physical presence (see *St Peter Baptising*), for the accurate evocation of three-dimensional space and the grouping of figures in space (see *The Tribute Money*), and a completely new and unflinching sense of human drama (see the electrifying *Expulsion of Adam and Eve from Paradise*). These paintings are amongst the most ground-breaking works in the history of Western art, and no visit to Florence should overlook them. Though Masaccio's works in the Brancacci Chapel are alongside the work of other painters—Masolino, 18 years his elder, and Filippino Lippi, who carried on Masaccio's work after his untimely death at the age of 27—Masaccio's style is so irreducibly different and individual, that it is not hard for even the first-time visitor to distinguish those elements painted by him. Indeed it is very instructive to attempt to do so.

In an altogether gentler and less dramatic way, the Dominican friar Fra' Angelico (1387–1455) had also learnt much from Giotto's example. His works can be found in many locations in the city, but the greatest concentration is in the ex-Convent of San Marco, which today functions partly as a museum dedicated to the painter. Here one gets a full sense of the jewel-like brilliance of his works—as if they were illuminated manuscripts enlarged upon panels or walls. Everywhere we look, we find a simplicity and clarity of form learnt from Giotto; but it is Fra' Angelico's delight in clear colour—the characteristic coral pinks and pale blues—that is unforgettable and which, together with the often intricate work in gold on the surface of many of his paintings, imparts a radiance which is far from the spirit of Masaccio's more austere world.

Fra' Angelico loved colour; for Masaccio, it was an afterthought. Fra' Angelico enjoyed extraneous detail; Masaccio rigorously banished it. There is a linear grace and instinctive draughtsmanship in Fra' Angelico; in Masaccio all line is subordinated instead to a powerful sense of volume and sculptural weight. The two painters are completely different. There were, in the end, only a few in Florence who followed Fra' Angelico's instincts—most notably Benozzo Gozzoli (c. 1421–97), whose exquisite and tapestry-like pageant of the *Procession of the Magi to Bethlehem* decorates the walls of a tiny chapel in Palazzo Medici-Riccardi; and, greatest of all, Sandro Botticelli. The mainstream of Florentine painting, however, felt the irresistible influence of Masaccio right down to the time of Michelangelo who, as a young man, must have sat and sketched in the Brancacci Chapel, and never forgot the lessons he learnt there.

Masaccio shows how sculpture and sculptural instincts are never far from the surface in Florentine painting. His contemporary and friend Donatello (1386–1466) was one of the greatest and most versatile sculptors of all time, and it is impossible to say which of the two artists influenced the other more deeply. The sheer scope of Donatello's visual language is astonishing: sometimes solemn, as in the *St George* from Orsanmichele; sometimes riotous, as in the dancing putti and the dissolved architectural divisions of his cantoria for the Duomo, now in the Museo dell'Opera del Duomo; sometimes sensual and elegiac, as in the bronze *David* of the Bargello, one of the first wholly nude pieces to be sculpted in Europe since Antiquity; sometime terrifying, as in the haggard *Mary Magdalen* in the Museo dell'Opera del Duomo; but always profoundly idiosyncratic, technically faultless, and pushing the very limits of conventional taste in his treatment of subject matter.

We know that Masaccio, the painter, Donatello, the sculptor, Brunelleschi, the engineer, and Leon Battista Alberti, the theorist were all close friends; all of them in turn were acquainted with Lorenzo Ghiberti, Luca della Robbia, Paolo Uccello, Piero della

Francesca, and so forth. But the complexity of human relationships is such that their closeness to one another gave rise at the same time to a cross-fertilization of ideas and skills, and also to a powerful competitiveness. These two together were an irresistible force, increasing the critical mass and driving forward the achievements of Florentine art. As in Periclean Athens, or late 19th-century Paris, the sheer density of contact—friendly and competitive—within a group of artists, coupled with the possibility of unstinting financial support, gave rise to a ferment of activity that was to change European art for ever.

The city itself contributed to the momentum of invention by instituting public competitions for designs for new doors for the Baptistery (1401 and 1425), and for the completion of the cathedral's cupola (1418). Lorenzo Ghiberti (1378–1455), a stranger perhaps to modesty but an artist and metalworker of incomparable technical prowess, won both the competitions for the Baptistery doors. When we compare his far bolder second series of 1425 (those created for the east door) with the first series begun in 1403 (on the north entrance), we can see how clearly he has absorbed the influence of Donatello in the intervening years. And it was Donatello, in turn, who had accompanied the person whom Ghiberti had most notably defeated in the 1401 competition, Filippo Brunelleschi (1377–1446), on a journey to Rome immediately after the competition results had been announced. That journey, undertaken together, was to teach both artists an immense amount, as they came in contact with the wealth of buildings and sculpture still visible in Rome. It was Brunelleschi's meticulous study of the Pantheon and its dome that would help him understand how to solve the problem of the construction of a dome for Florence's cathedral. His solution had many brilliant aspects; but most importantly it involved throwing away the received idea of a single, vertical 'centring' for the dome, and using instead a one-level, horizontal centring, which rose *pari passu* with the dome's construction, and was dismantled and reconstructed, therefore, with each successive completed ring. The lateral thinking involved, the willingness to return to first principles, to learn from Antiquity, and to embrace new solutions was typical of Florentine ingeniousness and originality: it was to make Brunelleschi the hero of his city.

No painter or sculptor or architect in Florence in the mid 15th century could remain wholly unaffected by these developments. In some, this became almost obsessive, as in Paolo Uccello's desire to master perspective illusion at all costs in his whimsical, idiosyncratic paintings (as in *The Battle of San Romano* in the Uffizi, and the *Flood* in the cloister of Santa Maria Novella); or in Andrea del Castagno's emulation of Masaccio's sculptural qualities in the severe and sinewy figures of his brooding *Last Supper*, painted in the Refectory of Sant'Apollonia. But perhaps no one assimilated all the lessons together so intelligently nor harmonized them so completely as one painter, born in rural Tuscany but who worked in Florence and who expresses almost better than any the quintessence of Florentine painting—the thoughtful and taciturn Piero della Francesca (c. 1420–92). In him we find the gravity and clarity of Giotto, the limpid colour of Fra' Angelico, the sculptural weight of Masaccio, and the clear logical design of Brunelleschi—all transfigured by a bright Florentine light which once seen can never be forgotten. There is no sentiment in Piero's works, only a profound thoughtfulness.

One of the only artists who remains largely untouched by this lofty Florentine severity was Sandro Filipepi, known as Botticelli (1445–1510), who seems—almost thankfully—to be travelling in a different flight-corridor from all the others. To stand in the Botticelli room in the Uffizi Gallery between his two huge paintings, the *Birth of Venus* and the *Primavera*, is one of the happiest experiences that great painting can offer. Nowhere in Florence does painting so closely resemble music. The pictures can be appreciated simply for their consummate beauty and decorative splendour: but that should not blind us to the fact that they are also complex philosophical expositions. The *Primavera*, for example, is an effortless disquisition on the relationships between different kinds of love, and of the passage of love through the human sphere as it evolves from the earthly passion of a coming spring on the right-hand side of the picture, and is transmuted into a sublime and platonic love, above the clouds which are gently stirred by Hermes's *caduceus* in the top left of the picture. Commissioned for one of the young, rising stars of the Medici family, these paintings give us an intimation of the rarefied and subtle ideas that circulated in the philosophical soirées of Florence's aristocracy.

Botticelli's dalliance with that sophisticated world was always fragile, however. In the autumn of his very productive life, he fell—if we are to believe what Vasari tells us—under the spell of the terrifying preaching of Girolamo Savonarola. In thrall to Savonarola's fundamentalist rejection of the vanity of Florentine society, legend has it that Botticelli consigned many of his paintings and drawings to the flames. True or not, it is certainly the case that Florence was deeply shaken by the Savonarola episode (*see p. 73*). But in the aftermath of this cultural earthquake a new generation of artists, in every way as great as the one before, was waiting to emerge.

The Cinquecento

The image of David, the young boy who slew the giant Goliath, had always been dear to the Florentine imagination as a symbol of the tiny and virtuous republic of Florence in its struggle against the monolithic forces at its borders—the Papal States of Rome, and the Duchy of Milan. For this reason, sculptures of David recur frequently throughout early Florentine art. In January of 1504, a committee was convened to decide where the latest and greatest David yet should be placed in the city. On the committee sat Leonardo da Vinci, Botticelli, Perugino, Andrea della Robbia and Filippino Lippi—amongst a total of 30 distinguished artists. The David in question had been sculpted by Michelangelo Buonarroti from a huge block of marble that had been taking up space in the cathedral workshops ever since an earlier project on it had been abandoned.

Michelangelo (1475–1564) was only 26 at the time he received the commission for *David*, and 29 when he completed it. The *David* he had sculpted was triumphantly nude, brooding and vast, when compared with Donatello's winsome version of almost a century earlier: he stands in a pose sacred to the aesthetic of ancient Greek and

Roman statuary—neither walking, nor standing. His magnificent profile conceals a new and more troubled spirit—one in which a restlessness and grandeur have replaced the human ease and human scale of the art of the early Renaissance. Alongside a surviving preparatory sketch for this *David*, we find a few curious words written by the artist: these have often (perhaps fancifully) been interpreted as implying that Michelangelo saw the *David* as his bid to slay his own personal Goliath, namely Leonardo da Vinci (1452–1519), who, over 20 years his elder, was then the prince of artists in Florence. True or not, this hypothesis evokes an important fact: that these two giant spirits, so different from one another and yet so similar in many ways, dominate the psychic landscape of early 16th century Florence in a way that leaves little space for the other artists of the age.

Leonardo was agnostic; Michelangelo, a devout believer. Leonardo appears to have been gregarious, humorous, good-looking, if not a little vain; Michelangelo was combative, short, sinewy, unnaturally serious and solitary, and gave little thought to outward appearance. The physical and material fascinated Leonardo; the invisible and abstract fascinated Michelangelo. Leonardo's curiosity knew no limits as he turned his brilliant mind to every aspect of the world around him: Michelangelo returned again and again with increasing intensity to the same few artistic passions. Yet both had a prodigious capacity for work; both had a profoundly introverted and thoughtful nature; both were perfectionists with a persistent tendency to leave projects unfinished. The very fact that we are here making these comments about their personalities is another indication of the changing status of the artist in the Renaissance: the artist is no longer the anonymous artisan, but a complex figure whose passions and idiosyncrasies are inextricable from his creations. With the coming of the Renaissance, psychology and art are no longer separable.

Leonardo is today a strangely invisible presence in the city: in part because his greatest paintings are elsewhere, and in part because so much of Leonardo's achievement was in his writings. On his death he left few more than a dozen pictures which we can safely say are his. Of these, not all are finished, many have been cut down, and most would now be unrecognisable to Leonardo because of changes which have occurred in the oil medium with which he so relentlessly experimented in his search for perfection. But to look closely at the surface of any one of his paintings is to witness something miraculous. The transparency, subtlety and perceptible depth of the paint surface can be compared only with the very finest Flemish masters. It is all peculiarly un-Florentine. None of this could have been possible without the new medium of oil which Leonardo tried unstintingly to master. And in this he could not have been further from the technique of Michelangelo.

Michelangelo was first and foremost a sculptor and architect, and this is apparent even in his paintings, where there are vigorous and confident hatching strokes, as he uses his brush like a chisel. He never enjoyed painting; he found it a torment, and complained that he had been dragged to Rome with a 'halter about my neck' to paint the Sistine Chapel for the pope. It is instructive to look at his *Pietà* in the Museo dell'Opera del Duomo, which was intended to mark his own tomb in the cathedral.

It is left unfinished like the majority of his sculptures, but was given some semblance of completeness by his pupil, Tiberio Calcagni, after Michelangelo himself had abandoned the piece and smashed part of it in rage at the appearance of a fault line in the marble, at a point when much of the preliminary work had already been done. The vivacity of the claw-chisel strokes with which Michelangelo delicately draws out the form of Christ's torso and of the face pressed against his mother's, as if in a pen and ink drawing, is astonising, and forms a fascinating comparison with the flat and pedestrian strokes of his pupil's work on the head and the leathery face of Mary Magdalen. Michelangelo's passion for his material made the stone become a sensitive, obedient and living substance, completely at one with his intentions.

To understand Michelangelo's architectural genius, we must turn to the Biblioteca Laurenziana, the library commissioned by Giuliano de' Medici (Pope Clement VII) and built according to Michelangelo's design. The justly famous vestibule which precedes the library reading-room is one of the most extraordinary spaces in the history of Western architecture. The vocabulary of architectural elements it contains is precisely what we might find in a serene and perfectly proportioned interior by Brunelleschi: likewise, the sober white colour and the grey *pietra serena*. But that vocabulary no longer expresses the meanings we expect of it: it has become, with Michelangelo, a highly original, dense and allusive poem. Architecture is often at its greatest when it succeeds in surprising us: and everything in this small space does just that. The proportions confound us; the elements of construction seem iconoclastically to do the opposite of what is expected of them, and, in the midst of it all, the staircase bursts out into the space before us like a flow of lava that cannot even be contained by its railings—more a piece of sculpture than of architecture, made of turbulent oval shapes and strange volutes. But then we enter the library itself, and order, serenity and enlightenment return. The contrast is total. But Michelangelo reserves just one last twist: the block of grey *pietra serena* that forms the pediment over the door at the far end of the reading-room is traversed diagonally by a minute and perfect line of some natural, white, geological impurity. This time Michelangelo has not raged at the defect as he did with the *Pietà*, but has exalted it. It is the master's finest punctuation mark: never had a humble imperfection become such a brilliant protagonist.

After Michelangelo

Michelangelo's death in 1564 left the artistic community of Florence in a stall. His presence had been so monumental, and his ability and pre-eminence in all fields so total, that life after Michelangelo was hard for the Florentines to contemplate. To any artist living at that time, Michelangelo had always been there, always revered and endlessly producing works of genius for as long as could be remembered. How then were they to proceed now that he was gone? What direction to follow? But the story does not just end there: Michelangelo was more directly involved in the crisis which was effectively to end—or at least drastically to shorten—Florence's artistic future. He deliberately turned his back on the one important technical revolution which was to carry painting forward into the next four centuries: the development of oil-painting, as against egg-tempera and fresco technique. This inconspicuous but far-reaching technical revolution was to transform both art and the artist, and to give them a new life. It liberated the artist from his studio of assistants, it freed him to paint in front of nature, it gave him new territories of possibility in the description of light and surface, and the creation of mood and colour, and, when combined with the canvas support currently being developed in Venice, it allowed works to travel easily and be seen in places they could never have reached before. The potential of oil as a medium had captivated the far-sighted Leonardo; but he was now gone from Florence for good. Oil paintings from Flanders, too, had come to Florence and caused a sensation. Michelangelo had even seen them. People held their breath to hear what the great master's opinion might be. And it was this:

> ...that it was all very well, and could bring tears to the eyes of the devout, but these were mostly women, young girls, clerics, nuns and gentlefolk without much understanding for the true harmony of art.

Michelangelo had spoken, and, to all intents and purposes, oil-painting was now dead in the water in Florence. And as Florence stalled, the artists of Venice embraced the new technique, and forged ahead evolving a new kind of painting that was to shape and influence virtually all European art for the next 300 hundred years, and which was to make Florentine painting suddenly look remote and archaic. Titian was a contemporary of Michelangelo: he said himself that he had no desire to emulate Michelangelo's greatness for fear of being judged by those high standards. But history has proven him to be a painter of a far greater influence than Michelangelo, showing the way forward to later generations of artists. Michelangelo, whose greatness is no less unimpeachable, was to become instead the closing chapter in the story of a city that had once led the world.

The story ends, ironically, with the person who first wrote it down. Giorgio Vasari (1511–74) came as a young man to Florence from his native Arezzo. He idolized and was eventually befriended by Michelangelo. He was a not indifferent painter, in technical terms, and an architect of genuine brilliance, designing what is for the visitor one of the most memorable buildings in Florence, the Uffizi, appropriately now the home to the firmament of Florentine painting which Vasari so admired and did so much to promote. Fifteen hundred years earlier, Plutarch had paid eloquent tribute to the city of Athens in a series of *Lives* of the personalities that had made her great. But both Plutarch's and Vasari's *Lives*, brimming as they are with urbanity and insight, are fundamentally autumnal works of profound nostalgia. By their very urge to look back and describe the greatness in words, they close the wide arc of time in which their cities' greatness was incarnate instead in monuments and deeds and wondrous works of art.

HISTORICAL SKETCH

by Charles Freeman

There will always be mystery at the heart of the history of Florence. How could a city that prided itself on its republican principles come to be ruled by one of the most famous hereditary dynasties Europe has ever known? How did a commercially-minded city also become the centre of revolutionary new approaches to art and ideas? Great wealth is often the enemy of good taste, but the patrons of Florence—its guilds, the Church or its great families—commissioned brilliantly executed works of art which are still regarded as masterpieces today. Less visible, but just as fascinating, are the intellectual and literary achievements of the Florentines. Dante's *Divine Comedy*, his journey to the next world, represents the peak of medieval Christendom; Petrarch introduces the new age of humanism, taken up in the city by a host of penetrating scholars, historians and political thinkers who defined an ideology of republican greatness which harked back to Athens and Rome. All this in a city which was continually ravaged by internal faction, devastated by floods and plagues, and at war with its neighbours.

The difficulty for the historian lies in exposing the complexity of the city's history, teasing out the nuances of political control as exercised by its most successful family, the Medici, noting how works of art, remarkable in their quality, gained much of their resonance from the places they were displayed, sensing how even the most revolutionary work drew on ancient levels of meaning, both Christian and pagan. In the opulently decorated Sala dei Gigli (Hall of Lilies) in the Palazzo Vecchio (*see p. 81*), San Zenobio, a 4th-century bishop of the city, is portrayed alongside six heroes of the Roman Republic, while Dante and Petrarch are shown on the connecting doors. Heroes from three distinct periods of history interact in a triumphant expression of republicanism just at a time when the city appeared dominated by the wealth and influence of one family, the Medici. The essence of the Florence of the 15th century is concealed under so many layers of meaning that it often seems irrecoverable.

It was Jacob Burkhardt who defined this outburst of energy as the Renaissance, and its intellectual driving force as humanism (*The Civilization of the Renaissance in Italy*, first German edition, 1860). He assumed a stagnant Middle Ages which was swept away by the vigour of a Renaissance—but this dramatic cultural break proved difficult for later historians to locate. Even the most enterprising and innovative 'Renaissance' societies remained rooted in medieval faith, while other 'Renaissances' appeared from earlier centuries (the 12th century in France, for instance), and in other parts of Europe outside Italy, such as Flanders and Paris, Burkhardt's Italian Renaissance of the 14th–16th centuries risked being stifled under a blanket of scholarly caveats.

Yet to enter Florence's Piazza Santissima Annunziata and be confronted by Brunelleschi's Ospedale degli Innocenti (*see p. 166*), or to mount the stairway of the monastery of San Marco and emerge face to face with Fra' Angelico's *Annunciation*, soon dissolves scholarly inhibitions. Donatello's *David* (now in the Bargello, *see p. 219*) is a biblical subject undressed as a pagan classical hero, with a sensuality and frivolity which is alien to both. Across the river in the Brancacci Chapel of Santa Maria del Carmine (*see p. 273*), Masaccio's Adam and Eve howl with a desolation no medieval Last Judgement achieves. All these works were created at the same period, the first half of the 15th century, and were revolutionary in their own terms. They demand an explanation. That explanation lies partly in the city's origins—or at least in how Florence defined those origins.

The Roman city

Florence was founded as a Roman colony, *Florentia*, 'the place of flowers', by Julius Caesar in 59 BC. A colony was a defensive settlement of Roman citizens, often made up of ex-soldiers, which was planted on a strategically important route. In *Florentia*'s case this was at the crossing of the Arno by the Via Cassia, one of the roads which radiated northwards from Rome. In the long centuries of Roman peace, *Florentia* grew prosperous from road and river traffic, and became the administrative capital of Tuscia. Like other cities of Italy, Florence adopted Christianity in the 4th century and its earliest patron saint was Reparata, a martyr from Palestine.

The emergence of the Comune

Florence suffered from the collapse of the Roman Empire and the tortuous wars between the invading forces of Byzantines, Goths and Lombards that pulled Italy into the Dark Ages. The city became part of the kingdom of Lombardy, which was finally overthrown by the Frankish king Charlemagne. Charlemagne was created Holy Roman Emperor by Pope Leo III in 800. As heirs to the Lombards, and in Charlemagne's eyes to the Roman Empire itself, Charlemagne and his successors claimed sovereignty over northern Italy, and so Florence was technically under imperial control. With the emperors based far north of the Alps, however, it was the papacy that exercised more immediate influence over the Italian cities, and for centuries rivalry between popes and emperors formed the backdrop to Italian politics. The most important development, however, was the slow revival of Mediterranean trade, of which the Italian cities took every advantage. The expansion of Florence was at first hindered by her remoteness from the seas and isolation from the major land routes which ran north along the coast, but from the 11th century there was a growing Mediterranean demand for cloth. The waters of the Arno, which narrowed at Florence, were ideal for washing and fulling wool, and the countryside had a surplus of labour. Florence's weakness was a lack of good local supply, but this stimulated the rise of enterprising merchant companies who would travel as far as Flanders and England in search of the raw material, and then sell the finished cloth throughout the Mediterranean. In order to cover the time lapse between buying raw materials and selling them as finished goods, credit arrangements were needed, and thus the Florentines developed a banking network. The city's gold currency, the florin, first minted in 1252, became the most stable and widespread currency in Europe. By 1300, Florentine family firms such as those of the Bardi and Peruzzi were the richest of the continent, and the road north from Rome now ran through Florence. The demand for labour was so powerful that the city's population doubled, from around 50,000 to 100,000 between 1200 and 1300.

Florence's political history was much less happy. A formidable early ruler, Matilda, Countess of Tuscia, gave the city its independence in 1115, and this allowed a communal government to become established—in whose survival the emperors acquiesced. The city was to be ruled by a council of a hundred men. Yet there were heavy pressures on the early commune. Florence was repeatedly caught up in the rivalries between popes and emperors, while the neighbouring coastal cities of Pisa and Lucca, as well as Siena to the south, resisted its growth. Warfare was a continual strain on resources, although Florence gradually extended its territory into the countryside, absorbing its smaller towns and citadels as it did so. Most of its leading families, some of noble origins, some more humble, had migrated from the countryside to take advantage of the growing economic opportunities in the city, but competition between them was fierce. 13th-century Florence was dominated by the rivalry between the Guelphs and the Ghibellines. In origin the Ghibellines were supporters of the Holy Roman Emperor, anti-papal, and drawn from the nobility. The Guelphs were more from the merchant classes, and supported the pope against the emperor. These distinctions became blurred as the factions became more self-serving; even when the Guelphs finally triumphed, they soon split into Black and White Guelph factions, with the two sides largely reflecting family rivalries.

Forms of government

This turmoil encouraged the search for political stability. One device, used in other cities in the same period, was the appointment of a *podestà*, a chief magistrate, from outside the city for a period of a year. The first, from Lombardy, arrived in 1207. By the middle of the century, however, another political force, *il popolo*, the people of the city, was asserting itself. *Il popolo* was a shifting concept. It might genuinely be the people of the city meeting in open session, but it could also be a small oligarchy of families, claiming to be the representatives of the people. In 1250 a determined, and genuinely popular, rising of the *popolo* in Florence drove out the *podestà*, banned the nobles from government and established a *capitano del popolo* to defend its interests. He was set up in a fortress-like structure in the centre of the city, which still remains as the Bargello (so called after the title of the city's chief of police in the 16th century). The new regime (known as the *primo popolo*) lasted only until it was discredited by a dramatic defeat of Florence at Montaperti by Siena in 1260. The city was spared destruction, but the richer families regained control. A more successful reassertion of the *popolo* took place in the 1280s, when a new city government was installed (the *secondo popolo*). This was made up of six (later eight) priors, each representing a district of the city and chosen by lot for two months' service. In order to impose better order on the streets a *gonfaloniere di giustizia* was appointed, with a militia of 1,000. These nine officials were collectively known as the Signoria (literally 'magistracy'), and were housed in the imposing Palazzo della Signoria (now Palazzo Vecchio), begun in the 1290s in a space left vacant by the expulsion of a defeated family. The Palazzo's tower came to symbolise the dominance of the republican government over the nobility, many of whom were now excluded from politics under the so-called Ordinances of Justice of 1293 (ordinances which it was the specific duty of the *gonfaloniere* to enforce).

An important requirement of the new constitution was that the priors had to be members of one of the leading guilds, thus tying the government of the city to its commercial interests. The guilds were fundamental to the economic and social structure of the city, and they were graded according to their importance. Among the leading guilds the Lana represented all the activities involved in the manufacture of wool, the Calimala the importers of cloth (to be reworked or redyed in the city), the Cambio the bankers, and the guild of Por Santa Maria the silk weavers. Notaries and lawyers had their own guild as did the doctors and apothecaries. These major guilds were supplemented by a host of minor ones, including shoemakers, bakers and builders, 72 in all by 1301, though only the 21 major guilds could provide priors. (Exactly which guilds could supply priors shifted with time depending on whether conservative or popular groups held power.) The guilds looked after the needs of their own members, carried out charitable works and took responsibility for major buildings in the city.

The fourteenth century

Florence was no more settled in the 14th century than it had been in the 13th. Just to list the disasters is to emphasise the extraordinary resilience of the Florentine people. The century started with a great fire (1304). In 1333 a massive flood swept away all the city's bridges (it is the replacement of the Ponte Vecchio, constructed in 1345, which survives today). Then the Bardi and Peruzzi family banks, which had lent heavily to the English king Edward III, were driven into bankruptcy when the king defaulted on the debt, and this failure rippled through Florence's economy. Just two years later, in 1348, the Black Death swept through the city, killing perhaps half its inhabitants. Wars with Siena, Pisa, Lucca and, between 1375–78, with the papacy, added to the strain on the city, while in 1378 the discontent of the wool workers (the Ciompi) led to a major uprising in which the government was temporarily overthrown by the rioters. The reaction led to the renewed dominance of the greater guilds in government, and the century ended more successfully when an invasion by the Duke of Milan, Gian Galeazzo Visconti, which appeared to be on the brink of success, collapsed in 1402 with his death from plague. In 1406 Florence finally gained control of Pisa, and with the city its own outlet to the sea.

The disasters of the century also mask the extraordinary shift in economic power. The loss of half the city's population in the 13th century meant, in fact, that wealth was consolidated among the survivors. A similar contraction in the rest of Europe led to an increase in demand for luxury goods, which the sophisticated Florentine merchants were able to meet. Soon the skills of many cloth workers were being diverted into the making of silk, the city's most successful new industry of the 15th century. A mass of commodities, from slaves to spices, were picked up on the trade routes and sold alongside these staples. The shock of the Bardi and Peruzzi bankruptcies led to more efficient methods of managing credit, and the merchant families of Florence remained the most resourceful of all players on the international stage. In Venice easy access to the sea and the confident architecture of the city emphasise its openness to the outside world. In Florence the narrow streets and the heavy fortress-palaces give the impression of defensiveness, and it is difficult for the visitor today to appreciate the extent of the city's international reach and its ruthless exploitation of new markets, whether in Spain and Portugal, Antwerp and Bruges, Rhodes and Jerusalem and—after the fall of Constantinople in 1453—the triumphant Ottoman Empire. A typical Florentine firm may have had 25 overseas branches across the Mediterranean and northern Europe.

In the 14th century something in the mood of the city changed. In his *Divine Comedy*, written after his expulsion from the city in 1302, when the Black Guelphs ousted the White, Florence's greatest poet Dante Alighieri takes a journey through Hell and then ascends through Purgatory to Heaven, where, accompanied by his beloved Beatrice, he comes to realise that only through the acceptance of God's love and divine order can peace be found on a troubled earth. This is a medieval world view. In the 1350s, after the Black Death, another Florentine, Giovanni Boccaccio, sets the tales of his *Decameron* among a group of survivors who are determined to enjoy life on earth. Socially confident, the women virtuous but at ease with their male companions, they approach the world with no illusions, and would certainly not assume any divine solution to its troubles. They live in a city which is shifting from the functional in its building—as shown in the walls, administrative buildings and churches of the 13th century—to display. The greatest painter of the day, Giotto, provided the frescoes of the chapels of the Bardi and Peruzzi in Santa Croce (in the 1330s, before their bankruptcy) and then went on to design the graceful campanile of the cathedral. The Signoria commissioned the elegant Loggia della Signoria in 1376 as a reception area for visiting dignitaries and the public swearing-in of officials. One of the strangest buildings of the city was also put in hand. The city needed a grain market backed by a permanent store of grain for emergencies. The store was to be built on the site of an oratory to St Michael, on one of whose pillars there was a miracle-working image of the Virgin. The shrine (surmounted by an awesome tabernacle of 1355 by Andrea Orcagna), store and market are combined in the massive Orsanmichele (*see p. 62*), whose exterior was covered with statues provided by the guilds in the early 15th century.

The rise of Humanism

The readiness to spend the city's wealth on its glorification was now given impetus by an intellectual revolution. The catalyst was Francesco Petrarch (1304–74). Petrarch came from a Florentine family which had been exiled at the same time as Dante, and almost all his life was spent outside Florence. He had a passion for ancient texts, and through them he rediscovered Latin as spoken and written by major classical authors such as Cicero and Virgil. The texts he and other scholars accumulated dealt with law, oratory, history and moral philosophy, and their study gave birth to the movement known as humanism. In Florence, humanism was given focus by the city's official representative on formal occasions, its chancellor Coluccio Salutati (chancellor 1375–1406). A scholar in his own right, Salutati wove the republican language of ancient Rome, its sense of moral purpose and suspicion of tyranny, into an ideology of Florentine republicanism. He also invited a Greek scholar, Manuel Chrysoloras, to the city to teach Greek. Soon Florence was a centre of scholarship, with Greek texts being read for the first time in the west for a thousand years, and many being translated into Ciceronian Latin. Coluccio's successor as chancellor, Leonardo Bruni (1370–1444), was another fine scholar who rewrote the history of the city to make it appear as if it was one long story of resistance to tyranny. His *Laudatio* (1403), a panegyric of Florence, in which he compares the city to ancient Rome, struck a chord with his fellow citizens. and he was honoured by a fine Renaissance tomb in Santa Croce (*see p. 237*), where he lies with his *History of the Florentine People* on his chest. To be able to speak and write Latin was now essential for any man of status, and the ancient virtues of sobriety and civic responsibility were absorbed with the studied texts.

By the early 15th century, therefore, a combination of wealth, intense civic pride and commitment to the glorification of Florence through patronage made the city the intellectual and artistic capital of Italy. Patronage flowed through many channels: the city itself, its guilds, the Church and wealthy individuals. It was set within an atmosphere of intense competition, of which the contest for the Baptistery doors, sponsored by the guild of the Calimala, is the most celebrated (*see p. 49*). Such competition between patrons for artists and between artists for patronage helped liberate architecture, painting, sculpture and a host of minor crafts from conventional themes. The classical world, revived and brought into the core of Florentine republican ideology, must have provided its own inspiration as a pinnacle of excellence which, alone among its rivals, the city might meet. Florence not only absorbed the achievements of the classical past; it transformed them into something radically new.

The dominance of the Medici

The family which best symbolises the achievement of Renaissance Florence is the Medici. This is partly because they retained their influence so successfully over most of the 15th century—a consummate achievement for any family in faction-torn Florence. Then, in the 16th century, they transformed themselves into a dynasty which was to rule Florence for 200 years. Yet their position was never so dominant or assured as outsiders believed it to be. What is remarkable about Florence in the 15th century is the range of families who prospered. This was the great age of palace building. In 1470, 35 palaces are recorded as under construction, and more were to follow. The forbidding exteriors concealed large open courtyards (an innovation for domestic buildings) and public audience rooms for the display of the family. Politics was now turned inwards. The Signoria and the committees which supported it remained as the public face of the city, while control over them was manipulated behind palace façades.

Giovanni di Bicci de' Medici (1360–1429), the founder of his family's pre-eminence in the city, was a merchant and banker rather than a politician. It was his conservative investment policies (including the purchase of property inside Florence and farmland outside it) and his shrewd building up of contacts which led to a steady accumulation of wealth. In 1410 one of his contacts Baldassare Cossa, became Antipope (if only temporarily, as John XXIII) and the Medici took over the papal finances. Returns of over 30 per cent a year were possible, and Rome now provided half the Medici income. Even when Cossa was deposed and failed to repay a large loan, Giovanni did not desert him and this added to the Medici reputation for loyalty and trustworthiness. (In fact, Giovanni paid for Cossa's fine tomb in the Baptistery, *see p. 52*). Within Florence itself, Giovanni was cautious. He did hold office, as *gonfaloniere*, in 1421 and served on other committees. He put in hand the rebuilding of the family church of San Lorenzo but was never a great patron of the arts. On major political issues he carefully sided himself with the lesser guilds, supporting, for instance, the *catasto*, a tax system which demanded more from the rich who had to declare all their assets. He died popular and respected.

Giovanni was from the last generation of wealthy Florentines not to know Latin. His son, Cosimo (1389–1464), was already forty when his father died, and educated in the new humanism. He was also a man of exceptional political shrewdness. He revealed little of his personality or his thoughts, but he understood the city's deep distrust of any form of tyranny. When Brunelleschi offered to build him a vast new palace, he opted for a more modest, though still substantial, building. One of his protégés, Marsilio Ficino, was given the task of providing the first Latin translations of the Greek philosopher Plato, and this led to a revival of Platonism in the intellectual circles of the city.

As a politician Cosimo worked carefully behind the scenes. What appeared to be a disaster, his exile at the hands of the Albizi family in 1433, became a triumph when he re-entered the city to general rejoicing in 1434. Occasionally, as in 1458, when he was threatened with unrest, he risked calling an assembly of the *popolo* to consolidate his control over the constitution, but he preferred the steady winning over of his rivals through his wealth or patronage. He would use his allies to restrain or exile enemies and so presented the image of a settled and well governed state to the outside world. A major diplomatic coup was the holding of the Council of Florence, an important meeting of the Eastern and Western Churches under the auspices of Pope Eugenius IV, in the city, in 1439. Cosimo had himself elected *gonfaloniere* so that he could personally welcome the pope, the Eastern emperor, and other dignitaries on behalf of the city. Hardly had the Council's business finished than Florence achieved a major victory over the Milanese at Anghiari in 1440, which further boosted Cosimo's position. Many were tempted to compare him with Octavian, later the Roman emperor Augustus—even to the extent of spreading a myth that Florence had been founded by Octavian rather than Julius Caesar. The titles given to Cosimo—*princeps*, 'first citizen', and, after his death, *pater patriae*, 'father of the fatherland'—had, in fact, been used of Augustus fourteen hundred years earlier.

Cosimo died in his bed in 1464, still without any formal title, but undoubtedly the leading citizen of the city. Despite massive spending, the fortunes of the family were intact, and in 1466 were boosted through being awarded, by the papacy, the lucrative monopoly on the alum mines in papal territory (alum was a mineral salt used to fix dyes into cloth). Cosimo's son, Piero il Gottoso (the Gouty), maintained Medici control of Florence, and when he died in 1469 his twenty-year-old son Lorenzo was in place to carry on the Medici name and fortunes. In fact, Lorenzo was immediately approached by a delegation of citizens asking him 'to take charge' of the city.

Despite his youth, Lorenzo was already skilled in the exercise of power. He had visited Milan, Venice and Rome on official business and his wife, Clarice Orsini, came from one of the most ancient and aristocratic families of Rome. He was energetic, intelligent and had a charisma which transcended an ugly face. He was deeply schooled in humanist values. He had been taught Greek by Marsilio Ficino himself, and was attracted like his grandfather to the philosophy of Plato. In fact, he felt at home with intellectuals. One of his circle, the poet Angelo Poliziano (1454–94), was such an erudite classicist that many of his emendations to corrupt Greek manuscripts are still accepted as correct by scholars today. Another intimate, Pico della Mirandola (1463–94), was one of the first Christians to master Hebrew in depth. This role of cultural patron went hand in hand with a solid grip of the government of Florence. Political business was often referred to Lorenzo directly.

While Lorenzo appeared to be successfully fulfilling the ambiguous role of *princeps* in a city which detested tyranny, not all his fellow citizens were ready to acquiesce in his influence. In 1478, he was lucky to escape with his life when a plot to assassinate him (the Pazzi Conspiracy) almost succeeded (*see p. 241*). However, the backlash was easy to exploit. Lorenzo issued a medal to commemorate his survival and basked in the period of comparative stability which followed. Lorenzo played his own part in keeping the peace. He intervened to thwart the ambitions of Naples against Florence and engineered an alliance with Florence's old enemy, Milan, which he was able to use against the papacy, Venice and Naples if they threatened him. He turned around his relationship with the papacy so successfully that in 1489 he was able to persuade Pope Innocent VII to make his son Giovanni a cardinal at the tender age of thirteen.

Behind the façade, however, things were not so secure. The Medici fortune was being eroded by economic uncertainty and unwise investments. Lorenzo was not a good businessman, and his manager, Sassetti, despite the glorious frescoes in his family chapel in Santa Trìnita (*see p. 206*), was less astute than he might have been, and all but bankrupted the firm. When Lorenzo died, aged only 43, in 1492, his son Piero no longer had the capital to secure goodwill with largesse as Lorenzo had done so successfully. A much weaker character than his predecessors, Piero also alienated the Signoria through his arrogant behaviour, losing all remaining support when he surrendered some of Florence's possessions to the French king Charles VIII, who had invaded Italy in 1494. An outraged populace drove out the Medici and their palace was sacked. Donatello's *David*, which had been commissioned by Cosimo as a mark of the family's commitment, real or imagined, to republicanism (David symbolising the plucky resistance of humble Florence to the surrounding tyrannical Goliaths), was repositioned in the Piazza della Signoria.

Troubled times and the emergence of the Duchy, 1494–1570

Charles VIII's invasion introduced a period of intense instability in Italy. The Dominican monk Girolamo Savonarola (*see p. 73*), whose influence had been growing in Lorenzo's reign, played on his support among the poorer classes of the city to pro-

THE MEDICI FAMILY

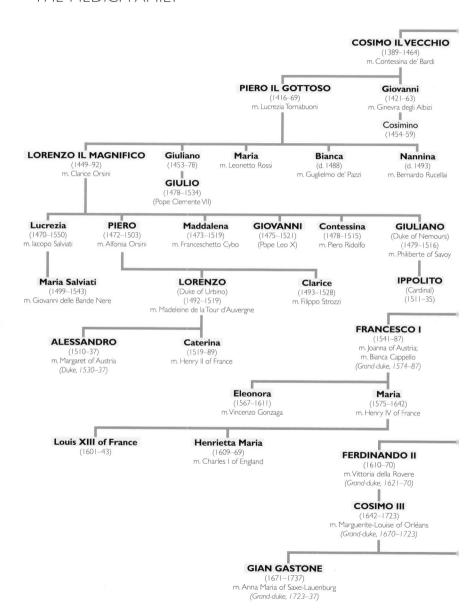

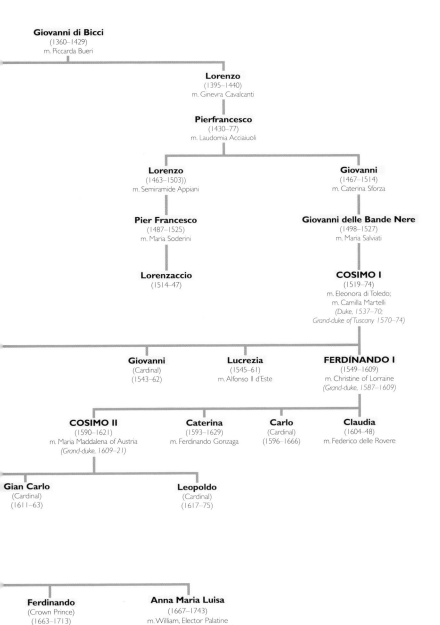

Giovanni di Bicci
(1360–1429)
m. Piccarda Bueri

Lorenzo
(1395–1440)
m. Ginevra Cavalcanti

Pierfrancesco
(1430–77)
m. Laudomia Acciaiuoli

Lorenzo
(1463–1503))
m. Semiramide Appiani

Giovanni
(1467–1514)
m. Caterina Sforza

Pier Francesco
(1487–1525)
m. Maria Soderini

Giovanni delle Bande Nere
(1498–1527)
m. Maria Salviati

Lorenzaccio
(1514–47)

COSIMO I
(1519–74)
m. Eleonora di Toledo;
m. Camilla Martelli
(Duke, 1537–70;
Grand-duke of Tuscany 1570–74)

Giovanni
(Cardinal)
(1543–62)

Lucrezia
(1545–61)
m. Alfonso II d'Este

FERDÍNANDO I
(1549–1609)
m. Christine of Lorraine
(Grand-duke, 1587–1609)

COSIMO II
(1590–1621)
m. Maria Maddalena of Austria
(Grand-duke, 1609–21)

Caterina
(1593–1629)
m. Ferdinando Gonzaga

Carlo
(Cardinal)
(1596–1666)

Claudia
(1604–48)
m. Federico delle Rovere

Gian Carlo
(Cardinal)
(1611–63)

Leopoldo
(Cardinal)
(1617–75)

Ferdinando
(Crown Prince)
(1663–1713)

Anna Maria Luisa
(1667–1743)
m. William, Elector Palatine

claim a popular republic which was also a city of God. An elected Grand Council of a thousand members was to be set up to act as a restraint on the Signoria, but the new government turned against the spirit of Renaissance humanism and instituted a reign of puritanism. The backlash eventually led to the burning of Savonarola for heresy. Italy, meanwhile, was in turmoil. There were fresh French invasions in 1499 and 1515, and the Spanish invaded southern Italy in 1512. Then the powerful Habsburg monarch Charles V, elected Holy Roman Emperor in 1519, made his own entrance, and in 1527 his undisciplined troops sacked Rome. While the Medici pope Clement VII cowered in his stronghold, Florence erupted in yet another pro-republican revolt. Pope Clement elected to come to terms with Charles, whose status as emperor in Italy he endorsed. A deal was then done by which Charles would help restore the Medici to Florence, and the imperial troops surrounded the city. After an appalling ten-month siege in which half the city's population may have died of hunger or disease, Florence capitulated. An illegitimate great-grandson of Lorenzo the Magnificent, Alessandro de' Medici, was imposed on the city with the title of Duke (1531), and his position was further secured by his marriage to Charles V's own illegitimate daughter, Margaret.

The city was now under imperial control, but when Alessandro was murdered in 1537, in a sordid conspiracy which even members of his own family supported, the city attempted to reassert its independence by asking a distant cousin of Alessandro, Cosimo de' Medici (who traced his lineage back to Cosimo il Vecchio's brother, Lorenzo), to be head of government. Cosimo had no support outside the city, but fought off his rivals and consolidated himself so successfully that eventually both pope and then emperor accepted him as Duke of Florence. In theory this was not an overthrow of the republic, but Cosimo tightened his grip. An important symbolic move was made in 1540 when he transferred his headquarters from the Medici palace to the Palazzo della Signoria (Palazzo Vecchio) itself. Further success came after Cosimo's only military adventure ended with the conquest of Florence's old rival Siena in 1557. The increasing splendour of Cosimo's position was marked by the adoption of the Palazzo Pitti for ceremonial occasions and the creation of a fine set of administrative offices, the Uffizi, which soon became a gallery for the family's art collection. In 1570 the pope created Cosimo Grand Duke of Tuscany, and this was the title the Medici were to hold, as a hereditary dynasty, until 1737.

The Medici dukes and the decline of Florence

Florence's economy after 1600 went into decline as economic vitality passed to northern Europe, and Mediterranean trade was superseded by the new routes across the Atlantic. While the city was still producing 30,000 pieces of cloth in the 1570s, by 1610 that figure stood at only 10,000 and was only half as many by 1650. This decline was typical of Italy as a whole, and marked a shift towards agriculture as the core of the economy and the strengthening of ancient feudal custom. In Florence the grand dukes, few of whom were outstanding personalities, presided over a provincial kingdom where court life was more important than entrepreneurship, and where it was land rather than a vault full of gold florins which now gave status. As with many such states (Venice provides a comparable example), inner decay was masked by extravagant display. The dukes searched for their brides on the European stage—Austria, France and Italy—and each was welcomed to Florence with pageants and feasting.

The story of the Medici grand dukes could, in fact, be told through the embellishment of the Palazzo Pitti and the care, nurture and display of their fabulous collection of art (see pp. 111–138). The palace was extended and extensively remodelled over three centuries by the Medici dukes, the Dukes of Lorraine, Napoleon and Vittorio Emanuele II, the first king of a united Italy, whose royal palace it briefly became. The Medici collection, enhanced by Raphaels and Titians from Urbino brought in by the marriage of Ferdinando II (Grand Duke 1621–70), was displayed here and in the Uffizi, where the Tribuna became the home to the family's classical sculpture (the Venus de' Medici was the highlight of many a Grand Tour). After so much care had been lavished on collection and display, it seems fitting that the sister of the last grand duke, Anna Maria Luisa, heiress of her childless brother and thus of all his property and art, would bequeath it on her death in 1743 to the House of Lorraine, which was to rule the city, on condition that it remained in Florence 'for the ornament of the state, the utility of the public and in order to attract the attention of foreigners'.

However, to pass on too quickly is also to miss some important developments. Cosimo's son and successor, Francesco, (grand duke 1574–87) deserves to be remembered for championing Tuscan as the purest form of Italian. However, it was in his reign, and with his acquiescence, that Spain became the dominant influence in Tuscany as in much of the rest of Italy. The independence of Florence, so vigorously asserted by Cosimo I, was lost. Francesco's brother, Ferdinando I (grand duke (1587–1609) was an effective ruler at a time when the city was still prosperous. The strength of his position is emphasised by Giambologna's equestrian statue of him in the Piazza Santissima Annunziata (1608), the first self-glorifying statue any ruler of Florence dared to erect in his own lifetime. Ferdinando's young and short-lived son, Cosimo II (grand duke 1609 –21), can be remembered for his patronage of Galileo: he appointed the great scientist Philosopher and Mathematician to the Court for life after Galileo shrewdly named the moons of Jupiter which he had discovered, 'the Medicean stars'. His successor Ferdinando II (grand duke 1621–70) continued the patronage, even if he was unable to prevent Galileo's eventual condemnation by the Vatican. His successor, Cosimo III (grand duke 1670–1723), spent much of his long life in a state of pious gloom (the nakedness of Michelangelo's David was concealed under a tarpaulin), the population of his city shrinking to only 42,000 as grass began to grow on the streets and buildings to fall inwards. With Cosimo's childless son Gian Gastone the dynasty came to an end in 1737. By now an untaxed but influential Church, a feudal system of land ownership and a stagnant industrial sector combined to make Tuscany a backwater.

Then the Duchy had some luck. Gian Gastone had secured a promise that the duchy (which was still under the nominal control of the Holy Roman Emperors) would remain an independent state on his death. The Spanish Bourbons tried to impose their own grand duke, but the European powers assigned Tuscany to the House of Lorraine, cousins of the Austrian Habsburgs. The first Lorraine grand duke, Francis (later Holy

Roman Emperor Francis I), spent little time in Florence, but through his regents he set in hand desperately needed reforms. The power of the Church and the feudal aristocracy was challenged, trade was liberalised and the state debt reorganised. More was to come. Under his successor, his son Peter Leopold, Tuscany moved to the forefront of the Italian Enlightenment. The ramshackle state administration and bureaucracy was overhauled, the vast landed wealth of the Church redistributed, and an attempt made to create a class of small landholders. An enlightened penal code which outlawed the death penalty and torture was promulgated in 1787. However, the duchy remained miserably poor, and there was no social group of sufficient maturity to sustain the reformed state. By the time Peter Leopold succeeded to the title of Holy Roman Emperor in 1790, and installed his son Ferdinand as Grand Duke Ferdinand III of Tuscany, there was severe unrest in the city.

Then came the whirlwind of the French Revolution, followed by Napoleon's conquests of Italy in the late 1790s. Tuscany briefly became the (independent) Kingdom of Etruria, before Napoleon absorbed it back into his reconstituted Italy, with his sister Elisa as its grand duchess. She prepared the Palazzo Pitti for her brother by building an exquisite Neoclassical bathroom for him—but he never came. Instead, many of Florence's finest works of art were moved to Paris to glorify the Louvre. Fortunately they were restored to the city, together with Ferdinand III, who ruled peaceably until his death in 1824.

One effect of Napoleon's reorganisation of Italy was to stimulate a nationalist reaction. In Florence this is manifested by Canova's monument to the 18th-century poet Vittorio Alfieri in Santa Croce (*see p. 237*). A personification of Italy mourns the poet—and the spirit of the monument entirely reflects the spirit of the times. It was not that the last Grand Duke of Tuscany, Ferdinand's son Leopold, was inadequate. He conscientiously drained marshes and modernised parts of the city, but he represented a foreign power—Austria—at a time when a vocal minority of Italians were looking towards unification and self-government. Even though Tuscany's prime minister Fossombroni was unsure whether Florence under the House of Savoy would enjoy more autonomy than it did under distant Vienna, Leopold's rule could not last. In 1859, the machinations of Camillo Cavour, the first minister of the Kingdom of Savoy, saw Tuscany swept into the newly unified Italian state. Leopold left Florence without a struggle. Cavour and his king, Vittorio Emanuele, entered the city to some enthusiasm. Florence was even to serve as the capital of the new Italy between 1865 and 1871.

By the second half of the 19th century Florence was being recreated in the European—and above all the British—imagination as the centre of the Renaissance. Art lovers, romantics and self-improvers, all in search of cultural enlightenment, took advantage of the new railway system to reach the city. The process has been cumulative, so that any visit to the city today is defined almost as much by the massed groups being led from one icon to the next as by the city and its treasures themselves. It is perhaps the visitor who breaks out and explores for him or herself who most learns to appreciate what Florence has to offer.

Heads of the Medici family, de facto leaders in Florence

Cosimo il Vecchio (*Pater Patriae*)	1434–64
Piero di Cosimo (*il Gottoso*; the Gouty)	1464–69
Lorenzo (*il Magnifico*; the Magnificent)	1469–92
Piero di Lorenzo (*il Fatuo*; the Unlucky)	1492–94

[Republic 1494–1512]

Giovanni (later Pope Leo X)	1512–13
Giuliano, Duke of Nemours	1513
Lorenzo, Duke of Urbino	1513–19
Giulio (later Pope Clement VII)	1519–23
Ippolito	1523–27

[Republic 1527–30]

Alessandro	1531–32

Dukes of Florence

Alessandro	1532–37
Cosimo	1537–70

Grand Dukes of Tuscany

Cosimo I	1570–74
Francesco	1574–87
Ferdinando I	1587–1609
Cosimo II	1609–21
Ferdinando II	1621–70
Cosimo III	1670–1723
Gian Gastone	1723–37

Lorraine Grand Dukes

Francis (Franz Stephan of Lorraine)	1737–65
Peter Leopold (later Holy Roman Emperor Leopold II)	1765–90
Ferdinand III	1791–99

[Napoleonic interlude 1799–1814]

Ferdinand III	1814–24
Leopold II	1824–59

FURTHER READING

History and general

Studies of the Medici family include *The Government of Florence under the Medici, 1434–94* by Nicolai Rubinstein (1968); *Florence and the Medici* by J.R. Hale (1977); *The Last Medici* by Harold Acton (1932, reprinted 1980); *The Rise and Fall of the House of Medici* by Christopher Hibbert (1974) and *The Medici: Godfathers of the Renaissance* (paperback edition 2005) by Paul Strathern.

General books include *Florence, a Travellers' Companion* (1986) by Harold Acton and Edward Chaney; *Florence: Biography of a City* (1993, reissued 2004) by Christopher Hibbert; *The City of Florence: Historical Vistas and Present Sightings* by R.W.B. Lewis (1995) and *Florence: a Portrait* (1996) by Michael Levey. *Hawkwood, Diabolical Englishman* (2004) by Frances Stonor Saunders is a biography of the life and times of the famous *condottiere*.

Art historical works

Classic accounts of the Renaissance include Jacob Burckhardt's *The Civilisation of the Renaissance in Italy* (1860, reprinted 1965) and Walter Pater's *The Renaissance* (1873, reprinted 1967). There is also *Renaissance Florence* by Gene Brucker (1969).

Bernard Berenson wrote pioneering studies of Florentine art including *The Italian Painters of the Renaissance* (1930, and many subsequent editions). John Pope-Hennessy also wrote numerous monographs on Renaissance artists (including Donatello, Luca della Robbia, Cellini, Fra' Angelico and Paolo Uccello) as well as general studies on Florentine sculpture.

Other useful studies of the Renaissance include Charles Avery's *Florentine Renaissance Sculpture* (1970); Michael Levey's *Early Renaissance* (1967) and *High Renaissance* (1975); Howard Hibbard's *Michelangelo* (1978); and Mary Hollingsworth's *Patronage in Renaissance Italy* (1994). *Brunelleschi's Dome* (2000) by Ross King is an interesting study of Brunelleschi's life and the construction of the dome of the cathedral.

Guidebooks

Old guides which are still of great interest include John Ruskin, *Mornings in Florence* (1873); Susan and Joanna Horner, *Walks in Florence* (1877); Grant Allen, *Historical Guide to Florence* (1897); Augustus Hare, *Florence* (1904); Janet Ross, *Florentine Palaces and Their Stories* (1905); Arnold Bennett, *Florentine Journal* (1910, republished in 1967); E.V. Lucas, *A Wanderer in Florence* (1912); and works by Edward Hutton, *Country Walks about Florence* (1926), *Florence and Northern Tuscany* (c. 1926) and *Florence* (new edition 1966).

Literature

Literature from the 19th and 20th centuries with a Florentine background includes *Romola* by George Eliot (1863, and numerous subsequent editions); the poetry of

Robert Browning and Elizabeth Barrett Browning; short stories by Henry James (*Madonna of the Future*, 1879) and Vernon Lee (*Il Cassone Nuziale*); Anthony Trollope's novel *He Knew he was Right* (1869). John Keats' 'Isabella, or the Pot of Basil' (1820) is based on a story by Boccaccio. Shelley wrote his 'Ode to the West Wind' in Florence in 1819. William Blundall Spence described the activities of art dealers in Florence in *The Lions of Florence* (1852). There are also descriptions of Florence in W.D. Howells' *Indian Summer* (1886) and D.H. Lawrence's *Aaron's Rod* (1933).

Recent books set in Florence include the numerous crime stories by Magdalene Nabb, such as *Death of a Dutchman* and *The Marshall and the Murderer* (1980s), Robert Hellenga's *The Sixteen Pleasures* (1994), Penelope Fitzgerald's *Innocence* (1986), and *Galileo's Daughter* by Dava Sobel (1999), a novel based on translations of the fascinating letters written by daughter to father. A useful general book is *Florence: a Literary Companion* by Francis King (1991).

Memoirs

Memoirs by Florentine residents include Iris Origo, *Images and Shadows* (1970); Harold Acton, *Memoirs of an Aesthete* (1948); and Nicky Mariano, *Forty Years with Berenson* (1966). *Paradise of Exiles* (1974) and *The Divine Country: The British in Tuscany 1372–1980* (1982), both by Olive Hamilton, describe the foreign residents of Florence.

THE DUOMO & BAPTISTERY

THE DUOMO

The Duomo, the cathedral dedicated to the Madonna of Florence, Santa Maria del Fiore, fills Piazza del Duomo making a full view of the huge building difficult in the confined space. It produces a memorable effect of massive grandeur, especially when seen from its southern flank, lightened by the colour and pattern of its distinctive marble walls (white from Carrara, green from Prato, and red from the Maremma). The famous dome, one of the masterpieces of the Renaissance, rises to the height of the surrounding hills (from which it is nearly always visible), holding sway over the whole city.

History of the Duomo

The early Christian church dedicated to the Palestinian saint Reparata is thought to have been founded in the 6th–7th centuries, or possibly earlier. It was reconstructed several times in the Romanesque period. Considerable remains of this church survive beneath the present cathedral (*see below*). The Bishop's seat, formerly at San Lorenzo (*see p. 180*) is thought to have been transferred here in the late 7th century. By the 13th century, a new and larger cathedral was deemed necessary. In 1294, Arnolfo di Cambio was appointed architect, and it is not known precisely how far building had progressed by the time of his death in the first decade of the 14th century. In 1331, the Arte della Lana (guild of wool merchants) assumed responsibility for the cathedral works and Giotto was appointed *capomaestro* (director of works). He began the Campanile in 1334. It was not until 1355 that work was resumed again on the cathedral itself, this time by Francesco Talenti. It seems he followed Arnolfo's original design of a vaulted basilica with a domed octagon flanked by three polygonal tribunes. During the 14th century numerous other architects, including Orcagna, joined Talenti, and the octagonal drum was practically completed by 1417. The construction of the cupola had for long been recognized as a major technical problem. A competition was held and Brunelleschi and Ghiberti were appointed jointly to the task in 1418. Brunelleschi soon took full responsibility for the work and the dome was finished up to the base of the lantern by 1436 when Pope Eugenius IV consecrated the cathedral.

The Dome

The majestic dome or cupola (1420–36), the greatest of all Brunelleschi's works, is a feat of engineering skill. It was the first dome to be projected without the need for a wooden supporting frame to sustain the vault during construction. This was possible partly because the upper section was built in brick (rather than the heavier sandstone used in the rest of the structure) in consecutive rings in horizontal courses, bonded together in a vertical herring-bone pattern. However, the exact construction technique used by Brunelleschi has still not been satisfactorily explained. The dome was the largest and highest of its time. Its pointed shape was probably determined by the octagonal drum which already existed over the crossing and from which the eight marble ribs ascend to the lantern. The cupola has two concentric shells, the octagonal vaults of which are evident both on the exterior and interior of the building. This facilitated construction and lessened the weight; the outer shell is thinner than the inner shell. Some of the apparatus invented by Brunelleschi which was used during the building of the dome can be seen in a store room on the ascent of the dome (*see p. 45*), and in the Museo dell'Opera del Duomo (*see p. 58*). Since 1980, detailed long-term studies have been carried out by a special commission to establish whether the stability of the cupola is in danger. The weight of the dome had caused cracks in the drum by the mid 17th century, and the structure is now being observed using a sophisticated system of monitors.

On the completion of the cupola, Brunelleschi was subjected to another competition, as his ability to crown it with a lantern was brought into question. It was begun a few months before the architect's death in 1446, and the work was continued by his

friend Michelozzo. Brunelleschi also designed the four small decorative exedrae with niches which he placed around the octagonal drum between the three domed tribunes. In the late 1460s, Verrocchio placed the bronze ball and cross on the summit. This left only the brickwork on the upper part of the drum at the base of the dome still uncovered: a competition was held in 1507 for the execution of a balustrade here and projects were submitted by the leading artists of the day—but when Baccio d'Agnolo began the construction of a balcony (to a design by Giuliano da Sangallo) on the southeast side, work was soon halted when Michelangelo (who had himself taken part in the competition) declared that it reminded him of a cricket's cage. The rest of the brickwork remains bare to this day.

The Exterior

The building of the cathedral was begun on the south side, where the decorative pattern of the marble can be seen to full advantage. The doors were adorned with 14th-century sculptures, the most elaborate of which, the Porta della Mandorla, is on the north side. It takes its name from the almond-shaped frame around the *Assumption of the Virgin* by Nanni di Banco (c. 1418–20), a sculptor who was at work for the Opera del Duomo at the same time as Donatello. The lower part, dating from 1391–1405, had an important influence on early Renaissance sculpture. In the lunette is an *Annunciation* in mosaic added by the Ghirlandaio brothers at the end of the century.

The old façade, erected to a third of its projected height by 1420, was demolished in 1587–88 (the sculptures are preserved in the Museo dell'Opera del Duomo, *see p. 56*). It was only in 1876 that it was decided to erect a new façade to a conservative neo-Gothic design by Emilio de Fabris, funded by public subscription (with conspicuous contributions from the foreign community resident in Florence, including Frederick Stibbert and Paolo Demidoff). Some of the best-known artists of the day worked on the elaborate decoration, including Giovanni Dupré and Tito Sarrocchi. The great American novelist Henry James, who often stayed in Florence, attended the ball at Palazzo Vecchio to celebrate the new façade, and he joined the historical cavalcade which processed through the streets in splendid 15th-century costumes to the unveiling.

The Interior

Open 10–5; Sun and holidays 1.30–5. The Duomo is entered from a door in the main façade: the entrance and exit gates are electronically monitored so that no more than 800 people are inside the building at any one time. Excavations of Santa Reparata open 10–5 except Sun and holidays. Every year on 8 September the roof and galleries are opened to the public.

The Gothic interior is somewhat bare and chilly after the warm colour of the exterior, whose splendour it cannot match. The huge grey stone arches of the nave reach the clerestory beneath an elaborate sculptured balcony. The massive pilasters which support the stone vault have unusual composite capitals. The beautiful stained glass windows date mostly from 1434–45, and are among the most important works of their kind in Italy. Three dark tribunes with a Gothic coronet of chapels surround the huge dome. The fine marble pavement dates from 1526–1660.

Monuments in the Nave

A West wall: The mosaic of the *Coronation of the Virgin* was attributed by Vasari in the 16th century to an otherwise unknown artist called Gaddo Gaddi. It seems likely he also worked on the Baptistery mosaics, and that this mosaic (c. 1290) was originally in the old cathedral of Santa Reparata. Ghiberti designed the three round stained-glass windows. The 16th-century frescoes of the angel musicians are by Santi di Tito. The huge clock uses the *hora italica* method of counting the hours—the last hour of the day (XXIIII) ends at sunset or Ave Maria (a system used in Italy until the 18th century). Paolo Uccello decorated it and painted the four heads of prophets in 1443. The recomposed tomb of Antonio d'Orso, Bishop of Florence (d. 1321) by Tino da Camaino, includes a fine statue.

B Bust of Brunelleschi: Memorial bust in a medallion probably taken from Brunelleschi's death mask. It is by his adopted son Buggiano (1446).

C Bust of Giotto: A similar monument to the above, commissioned by the Opera del Duomo. The idealized bust (1490) is by Benedetto da Maiano, with an inscription by the scholar-poet and friend of Lorenzo the Magnificent Angelo Poliziano.

D Bust of Marsilio Ficino: Commemorative bust by Andrea Ferrucci (1521) of the famous Neoplatonist philosopher and friend of Cosimo il Vecchio (1433–99). Ficino—who claimed that Cosimo had taught him as much as Plato—went on to become the mentor of Cosimo's grandson Lorenzo the Magnificent. The beautiful stained glass window, with six saints (1394–95), was designed by Agnolo Gaddi.

E The Dome and Sanctuary: Above the octagon the great dome soars to a height of 91m. The fresco of the *Last Judgement* (1572–79, *pictured on p. 44*) is by Vasari and Federico Zuccari. The 15th-century stained glass in the round windows of the drum is described on p. 45. Against the piers of the octagon stand eight 16th-century statues of Apostles.

The marble sanctuary was part of a grandiose project begun in 1547 by Baccio Bandinelli, who had been appointed head of the Opera del Duomo in 1540 by Cosimo I. It included some 300 reliefs but was never finished.

F Michelino's Dante: The painting of *Dante with the Divina Commedia which Illuminates Florence* is one of the few works known by Domenico di Michelino (1465): it is particularly interesting as it shows the drum of the cupola before it was faced with marble.

G Condottieri Memorials: These two splendid frescoes of equestrian statues, executed to look like funerary monuments, commemorate two famous *condottieri*, Sir John Hawkwood (by Paolo Uccello, 1436) and Niccolò da Tolentino (by Andrea del Castagno, 1456). Hawkwood was born in England, and came to Italy as captain of

THE DUOMO

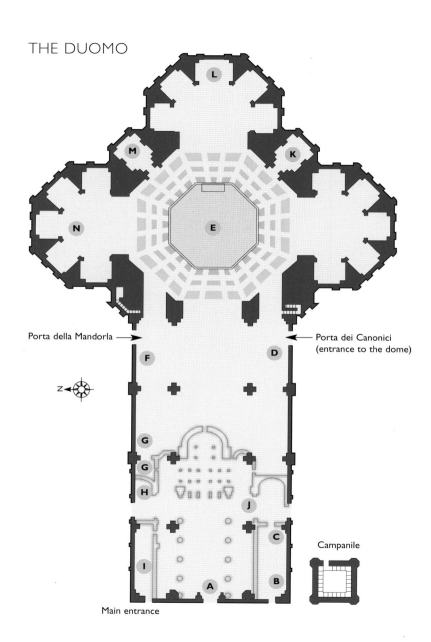

Porta della Mandorla →

← Porta dei Canonici
(entrance to the dome)

Campanile

Main entrance

a band of mercenaries in 1362. From 1377 onwards, as Captain of the Florentine army, he became one of the most famous *condottieri* in Italy, known as 'Giovanni Acuto'. In 1432 Niccolò da Tolentino led the Florentine army against Siena at the Battle of San Romano: although the outcome was in fact indecisive, the Florentines considered it their victory and a painting of it in three episodes was commissioned by the Medici a few years later from Paolo Uccello (*see p. 91*).

H Bust of Antonio Squarcialupi: Portrait bust by Benedetto da Maiano (1490). Born in 1416, Squarcialupi was cathedral organist from 1432 until his death in 1480. He was also a composer, and although none of his music has survived, his name is particularly famous since he left a manuscript at the Biblioteca Laurenziana (the 'Squarcialupi Codex') which represents the most important collection of 14th-century Italian secular music. The epigraph is thought to be by Poliziano (*see p. 149*).

I The Prophet Joshua: This sculpture (traditionally thought to be a portrait of the humanist friend of Cosimo il Vecchio, Poggio Bracciolini) is attributed to Donatello, and was probably destined for a niche in the Campanile.

J Santa Reparata: Steps lead down to the excavations of the ancient cathedral of Santa Reparata, uncovered in 1965–74 (*for opening times see p. 40*). At the bottom of the stairs to the left—now disturbed by a bookshop—the simple tomb-slab of Brunelleschi can be seen beyond a grille; the slab was found here in 1972. The architect of the cupola was the only Florentine granted the privilege of burial in Santa Maria del Fiore.

The complicated excavations (*admission fee*) include Roman edifices on which the early Christian church was built, a fine mosaic pavement from the earliest church (the precise plan of which is not known), and remains of the pre-Romanesque reconstruction and the Romanesque edifice with its five apses. Finds from the excavations include the gilded bronze sword and spurs of a magistrate of the city, Giovanni de' Medici (whose tomb also survives here), Roman sculpture and paving tiles, Romanesque architectural fragments, majolica and unglazed pottery from earth fills and tombs dating from the construction of the present cathedral (1296–1375), and fresco fragments.

The East End

NB: The sanctuary is the only part of the east end of the church open to visitors. Most of the rest is reserved for private worship. Each of the three apses is divided into five chapels with stained glass windows designed by Lorenzo Ghiberti.

K The South Sacristy: Above the entrance is a large lunette of the *Ascension* in enamelled terracotta by Luca della Robbia.

L The Central Apse: The east chapel has two graceful kneeling angels carved by Luca della Robbia. Beneath the altar is a bronze reliquary urn by Lorenzo

Vasari and Zuccari's fresco of the *Last Judgement*, in the cupola of the Duomo.

Ghiberti, carved with exquisite bas-reliefs.

M The North Sacristy: Over the door is fine relief, again by della Robbia, of the *Resurrection*. This was his earliest important work (1442) in enamelled terracotta. The iconographical composition was copied by later artists. The doors were Luca's only work in bronze (1446–67); he was assisted by Michelozzo and Maso di Bartolomeo. It was in this sacristy that Lorenzo the Magnificent took refuge on the day of the Pazzi Conspiracy (*see p. 241*) in 1478; he was saved, but his brother Giuliano was murdered.

The interior has fine intarsia cupboards dating from 1436–45 by a group of artists including Lo Scheggia, Antonio Manetti, and (end wall) Giuliano da Maiano (1463–65).

N Left Apse: In the pavement is Toscanelli's huge gnomon (1475) for solar observations (related to a window in the lantern of the cupola). Toscanelli, a famous scientist, mathematician and geographer, discussed his calculations concerning perspective with his friend Brunelleschi. In the second chapel from the right, there is a dossal of the *Madonna and Child with Four Saints*, and, on the back, the *Annunciation,* with four more saints. This is attributed to the hand of Giotto (probably with the intervention of his *bottega*).

Inside the Dome

The dome (entrance from Porta dei Canonici; marked on the plan on p. 42) can be climbed 8.30–6.20; first Sat of the month 8.30–3; other Sats 8.30–5; closed Sun and holidays.

The climb (463 steps) is not as difficult as you might expect, and is highly recommended (except for those who suffer from claustrophobia). It follows a labyrinth of corridors, steps and spiral staircases (used by the builders of the cupola) as far as the lantern at the top of the dome. As you ascend, you can admire and appreciate the dome's structure (*described on p. 38*). The views of the inside of the cathedral from the two balconies around the drum, and of the city from the small windows and from the lantern, are stunning.

Beyond the ticket desk steps ascend inside one of the piers, and a window at the end of a short corridor frames a view of the top of Palazzo Vecchio. The steps emerge inside one of the small exedrae which Brunelleschi added beneath the drum. Here are displayed some of the original (or reconstructed) devices—including winches and iron supports—used in the construction and maintenance of the dome (also labelled in English). From here a spiral staircase continues up. A corridor emerges on the balcony which encircles the octagonal drum, providing a splendid view of the inside of the cathedral, and of the late-16th-century frescoes by Vasari and Federico Zuccari which cover the dome. When Brunelleschi was commissioned to construct the cupola, the cathedral was already built to this point: from here you can appreciate the huge space (45.5m in diameter) which the architect was required to vault. The seven beautiful stained glass windows in the roundels were designed in 1443–45 by Paolo Uccello (*Nativity* and *Resurrection*); Andrea del Castagno (*Deposition*); Donatello (*Coronation of the Virgin*); Ghiberti (*Ascension, Prayer in the Garden* and *Presentation in the Temple*).

The balcony is followed for part of its length to another corridor which leads to the base of the double dome, the curve of which can be seen clearly. The ascent continues and now becomes more arduous because the steps are used by visitors going up and coming down. It passes between the two shells by means of short corridors and flights of steps, and small windows frame views of the monuments of the city. The distinctive herring-bone pattern of the bricks, used at intervals in the construction of the dome, is clearly visible here, as well as the transverse arches which strengthened the structure. On the right, a steep flight of steps (one way up) scales the uppermost part of the inner dome. Another short flight of steps continues out onto the lantern, beautifully carved in marble. The mighty marble ribs which decorate the exterior of the dome can be appreciated from here.

The view from this point (91m) embraces the city. The most conspicuous buildings include (right to left): the campanile, Palazzo Strozzi and the church of the Carmine in the distance; Santo Spirito with its dome and campanile and the huge Palazzo Pitti, and (nearer) the tall Orsanmichele. At the foot of the cathedral is a group of small medieval houses and towers. The Forte di Belvedere can be seen in the distance on its hill behind Palazzo Vecchio, the Uffizi and the Loggia della Signoria. Farther left is the Badia with its tall tower, and the Bargello, the marble façade of Santa Croce with its campanile, and, across the Arno, San Miniato. Beyond the arcaded façade of the hospital of Santa Maria Nuova rises the green dome of the Synagogue. The straight Via dei Servi leads to Santissima Annunziata, to the right of which are the extensive buildings of the Innocenti, and nearer at hand the octagonal rotunda of Santa Maria degli Angeli, also by Brunelleschi. In the distance rises the hill of Fiesole. The long façade of Palazzo Medici-Riccardi on Via Cavour can be seen in front of the tall iron roof of the 19th-century market beside the domed church of San Lorenzo and the Biblioteca Laurenziana. Near the station is Santa Maria Novella with its cloisters and campanile.

Another flight of steps is taken on the way down to scale the inner dome and then, at first, the same route is taken on the descent. A spiral staircase continues down to emerge on the lower balcony round the drum overlooking the interior of the cathedral. A corridor leads off it (with a view from the window of the green market building of San Lorenzo) and then a spiral staircase continues down to an exedra beneath the drum which is used to store casts of statues. The exit is from the Porta della Mandorla.

BRUNELLESCHI'S PERSPECTIVE EXPERIMENT

In the eyes of his fellow-citizens, Brunelleschi had something of the magician: and never more so than when he stood on the steps in front of the west doors of the Duomo to demonstrate his perfect-perspective instrument in 1425. Since the time of Giotto, painting had been feeling its way towards a coherent system of perspective, namely the rendering of a perfect illusion of three-dimensional space on a two-dimensional surface: but the matter was only resolved—for the first time in history—by Brunelleschi's invention. This consisted of a polished mirror, a painted panel and a metal bar holding the two at a predetermined distance from each other. The viewer squinted through a pin-hole in the back of a panel, on which was painted a coherently drawn, mirror-image perspective depiction (on a scale of 1:75) of the view of the Piazza and the Baptistery as seen from the Duomo doors. As the viewer looked through the hole, he saw this depiction reflected in the mirror held in front by the metal arm. The mirror could be raised and the viewer would see the Piazza itself; or it could be left in position so that he saw Brunelleschi's image in the mirror. If the two were identical and indistinguishable, then Brunelleschi had proved his point: that there is one, and only one, coherent and exact way to represent 3D space in two dimensions. The experiment was a classically pragmatic way of proving a complex point of optics and geometry. Its principles were later meticulously explained by Alberti, in his essay *Della Pittura* of 1436. What it shows better than anything, however, is how deeply underpinned by science were the developments of the Florentine Renaissance. N.McG.

Brunelleschi's dome as seen from the Campanile.

THE CAMPANILE

Open 8.30–7.30; T: 055 230 2885.

The Campanile (the cathedral bell-tower, nearly 85m high) was one of the most admired buildings in Florence up until the 19th century: its wonderful effect was perhaps diminished when the elaborate façade of the Duomo was constructed beside it (and in the same style) at the end of the 19th century.

The Campanile was begun by Giotto in 1334 when, as the most distinguished Florentine artist, he was appointed city architect. It was continued by Andrea Pisano (1343), and completed by Francesco Talenti in 1348–59. It is built of the same coloured marbles as the Duomo, in similar patterns, in an extremely well-proportioned design. Between the various storeys are horizontal bands of green, white, and pink inlay. The lowest storey bears two rows of bas-reliefs, copies of the originals in the Museo dell'Opera (*see p. 58*). The lowest rows are contemporary with the building, and some of them are thought to have been designed by Giotto. They were executed by Andrea Pisano and illustrate the *Creation of Man*, and the *Arts and Industries*. Five reliefs on the north face were added by Luca della Robbia. The upper register has reliefs by pupils of Andrea Pisano. The niches in the row on the second storey contain casts of the statues of prophets and sibyls (1415–36) by Donatello and others, also removed to the Museo dell'Opera (*see p. 57*). There are two storeys above, each with a pair of beautiful double-arched windows in each side, followed by the highest storey, with large and triple-arched openings, and the cornice.

The **ascent of the bell-tower** by 414 steps is interesting for its succession of views of the Duomo, the Baptistery, and the rest of the city. Although lower than the cupola, the climb is steeper. The third and fourth storeys, with their Gothic windows, overlook the Duomo and the Baptistery. The terracotta pots along the roof of the aisle of the Duomo serve to protect the building from the direct fall of rainwater from the gutters. On the Campanile's highest storey, with its beautiful slender windows, the modern bells can be seen hanging above the original ones (the Apostolica bell, displayed on a platform, dates from the beginning of the 15th century). Steep steps continue to emerge beside the simple tiled roof above the cornice.

The splendid panorama of the city includes (right to left): Piazza della Repubblica, with Palazzo Strozzi behind and the Carmine in the distance. Farther left is Santo Spirito; then Palazzo Pitti with the Boboli Gardens stretching as far as the Forte di Belvedere on its hill. Nearer at hand rises the tall Orsanmichele. Farther left is the Loggia della Signoria beside Palazzo Vecchio and the Uffizi. The Badia is marked by its tall bell-tower next to the Bargello. Beyond Santa Croce, the Synagogue can be seen just to the right of the cupola. On the other side of the dome, the long, straight Via Ricasoli leads out of the city towards the hills of Fiesole in the distance. On the parallel Via Cavour stands Palazzo Medici-Riccardi. The huge 19th-century market building is near San Lorenzo with its dome and the large church of Santa Maria Novella can be seen beside the railway station.

THE BAPTISTERY
Map p. 397, B2

Open 12–6.30; Sun and holidays 8.30–1.30.

The Baptistery of San Giovanni is one of the oldest and most revered buildings in Florence, and has always held a special place in the city's history. Interestingly enough, even today the date of its foundation is uncertain, although it is documented by 897. It is now generally considered to have been built in the 6th or 7th century, or even as early as the 4th–5th century. We know that it was reconsecrated in 1059, when for a period it served as the cathedral of Florence. In Dante's time it was thought to have Roman origins: in later centuries, Florentines, intent on emphasizing the city's glorious past, were quick to support this claim, and it was this building that was chosen for adornment at the very beginning of the 'Renaissance' (art historians often take the date of the competition won by Lorenzo Ghiberti—which was held in 1401 to decide which of the greatest artists of the day should provide it with a second set of bronze doors—as a convenient date to mark the birth of that great artistic movement). Two trial panels from that competition, submitted by Ghiberti and Brunelleschi, are displayed in the Bargello museum (*see p. 221*).

The Exterior

The Baptistery is an octagonal building of centralised plan derived from Byzantine models, with an exceptionally large dome. The classical geometrical decoration of the exterior was carried out in the 11th–13th centuries using precious marbles (white from Luni, a Roman city in Liguria, just across the northern border of Tuscany, and green from nearby Prato), all at the expense of the Arte di Calimala, the most important guild (representing cloth-importers) in the medieval city. The design became a prototype for numerous Tuscan Romanesque religious buildings (including, in Florence, Santa Maria Novella and San Miniato al Monte). Both the rectangular scarsella which replaced a semicircular apse, and the white pyramidal roof which conceals the cupola, are particularly unusual architectural features, probably also dating from the 13th century (although the lantern which crowns the building was made in the 12th century). The building is famous for its three sets of gilded bronze doors at its three entrances.

The Doors

South Door

Now used as an exit, this door was made by Andrea Pisano in 1336: a few years later he took over from Giotto as architect of the Campanile close by (where he also worked on its sculpted decoration). The door has 28 panels containing very fine reliefs enclosed in Gothic quatrefoil frames. They illustrate the history of St John the Baptist and the theological and cardinal Virtues (faith, hope and charity, and prudence, fortitude, temperance and justice). It was at first erected at the main entrance facing the Duomo, but in the 15th century it was moved to its present position to make way for Lorenzo Ghiberti's new door (*see below*), and the elaborate decorations of the bronze frame were added by Lorenzo's son Vittorio. Over the doorway are bronze figures of the Baptist, the executioner and Salome, by the Mannerist sculptor Vincenzo Danti (1571).

North Door
The door now used as the entrance, by Lorenzo Ghiberti (1403–24), is again divided into 28 panels, and the Gothic frames are copied from the earlier Pisano doors. A chronological sequence of the scenes from the life of Christ begins on the left-hand door on the third panel from the bottom and runs left to right towards the top. The two lower registers depict the Evangelists and Doctors of the Church. Ghiberti's self-portrait appears in the fifth head from the top of the left door (middle band), wearing an elaborate hat. The exquisite decoration of the frame is also by Ghiberti. The bronze statues (1506–11) above the door of St John the Baptist preaching, the Levite and the Pharisee are by Francesco Rustici: according to Vasari, Leonardo da Vinci was responsible for the design of this three-figure group.

East Door
This is the most celebrated work of Lorenzo Ghiberti, and it took him most of his life to complete it (1425–52). Michelangelo is said to have called it the 'Gate of Paradise'. The ten separate panels contain reliefs of scriptural subjects, the design of which probably owes something to Ghiberti's contact with the humanists. The artist was assisted by Michelozzo, Benozzo Gozzoli and others. The pictorial reliefs, no longer restricted to a Gothic frame, depict each episode with great conciseness. They are exquisitely carved, with scenes in low relief extending far into the background. The use of perspective here is of great importance, and typical of the new Renaissance concept of art. They were cast nearby—a plaque at no. 1 Via Bufalini (*map p. 397, C1*) marks the site of Ghiberti's workshop.

A copy of the door made from casts taken in 1948 was installed here in 1990 and the original panels have been exhibited inside the Museo dell'Opera del Duomo after their restoration. The subjects (*for a full description see pp. 54–56*), from the top downwards, starting with the left panel, are as follows:

1. The Creation and Expulsion from Paradise.
2. Noah's Sacrifice and Drunkenness;
3. Esau and Jacob.
4. Moses Receiving the Tablets of Stone.
5. David and the Battle with the Philistines.
6. Cain and Abel.
7. Abraham and the Angels and the Sacrifice of Isaac.
8. Joseph Sold and Recognized by his Brothers.
9. Joshua and the Fall of Jericho.
10. Solomon and the Queen of Sheba.

Moses Receiving the Tablets of Stone (detail), from the east door of the Baptistery.

Surrounding the reliefs are 24 very fine statuettes of prophets and sibyls, and 24 medallions with portraits of Ghiberti himself (the fourth from the top in the middle row on the left) and his principal contemporaries.

The splendid bronze door-frame is also by Ghiberti. Above the door the sculptural group of the *Baptism of Christ*, begun by Andrea Sansovino in 1505 and finished later in the century by Vincenzo Danti (with an angel added by Innocenzo Spinazzi in the 18th century), is a cast of the original now in the Museo dell'Opera del Duomo.

The two porphyry columns here, which were formerly free-standing between the Baptistery and the Duomo, seem to have been given to Florence by grateful Pisans for help in vanquishing the Saracens in the Balearic Islands in the early 12th century. But the tale is told that they turned out to be (intentionally?) unsound and therefore couldn't be used as architectural elements: proof of the age-old rivalry between the two Tuscan cities. Perhaps instead they were simply bought back from the islands as booty by the Florentines and set up here in civic pride. In any case it is known that the war carriage which flew the flag of the Comune and bore an altar, and which led the Florentines into battle during the Middle Ages, was kept inside the Baptistery and her soldiers' battle cry was 'for San Giovanni'. St John the Baptist is also the patron saint of Florence and was proudly displayed on the gold florin first minted in the early 13th century.

The Interior

The lovely old marble interior (at present entered by the north door) has huge granite columns from a Roman building with gilded Corinthian capitals below a cornice and a gallery with divided windows. The walls are in panels of white marble divided by bands of black, in the dichromatic style of the exterior. As the floor shows, the centre of the building used to be occupied by a huge octagonal font. Dante mentions this (*Inferno*, Canto XIX) in a passage in which he recalls saving a boy from drowning in it, and it is at this point in the poem that he makes his famous reference to '*mio bel San Giovanni*', illustrating what a significant place the building held in the great Florentine poet's mind. Indeed, towards the end of *Paradiso* (Canto XXV), when he speculates on the possibility that his poem might one day be recognised by his detractors in Florence and that on its account he might be allowed to return from exile to his beloved city, he imagines an occasion on which he might be crowned with the poet's laurels here at the font where he had been baptised.

The font was dismantled in 1576 and around the present Gothic font the oldest part of the splendid **mosaic pavement** (begun in 1209) can be seen. Made out of square tesserae, and contemporary with the lovely pavement in San Miniato (*see p. 284*), it includes geometrical designs, oriental motifs and the signs of the Zodiac. Beside the handsome high altar (13th century; reconstructed) is an elaborate 14th century paschal candlestick. To the right is the **tomb of the antipope John XXIII**. When Baldassare Cossa was elected pope during the Great Schism in 1410, he helped Giovanni di Bicci de' Medici (father of Cosimo il Vecchio) become a papal banker. But he was expelled from Rome by imperial troops and fled to Florence in 1413 before being deposed by the Council of Constance and imprisoned. Through his Florentine connections he was finally released in 1419 and returned to Florence, but died in the same year. Giovanni di Bicci was an executor of his will and, since the pope had asked to be buried in the Baptistery, it was he who in 1424 commissioned Donatello and Michelozzo to design the funerary monument. It is one of the earliest Renaissance tombs in the city, and apart from the exquisite carving, it is especially remarkable for the way it is inserted into a narrow space between two huge Roman columns, in no way disturbing the architectural harmony of the building. Michelozzo was later to introduce a beautiful Renaissance structure at the very centre of the Romanesque church of San Miniato, again demonstrating the extreme sensibility of the great Renaissance artists to the artistic masterpieces of previous centuries. It is usually thought that it was Donatello who sculpted the bronze effigy of the pope himself. On the left of the apse are two late-Roman sarcophagi adapted as tombs (one showing a wild boar hunt and the other, adapted as the tomb of a bishop in 1230, with scenes of Roman life).

The **mosaics in the vault,** the only mosaic cycle which exists in Florence, are remarkably well preserved (and superbly lit). The earliest (c. 1225) are in the scarsella above the altar; they are signed by the monk 'Iacopo' (Talenti), a contemporary of St Francis, who was influenced by Roman or Venetian mosaicists. The little vault is decorated with an elaborate wheel with the figures of the prophets, which surround the Agnus Dei. This is supported by four caryatids kneeling on Corinthian capitals. On either side are the Virgin and *St John the Baptist Enthroned*. On the first arch are half-figures of saints flanking a striking image of the Baptist, and on the intrados of the outer arch a frieze of saints in niches. The outer face is decorated with vine tendrils. Work on the mosaics of the main dome was well advanced by 1271, but probably continued into the 14th century. The graceful decoration around the lantern includes early Christian symbols surrounded by a band of angels. Lower down is a broad band with full-length figures of angels in pairs and the Baptist between seraphim. On the three sections nearest to the altar is the *Last Judgement* with a huge figure of Christ (8m high) in a central tondo. The remaining section of the cupola is divided into four bands: the inner one, beneath the frieze of angels, has scenes from Genesis (beginning over the north entrance door) with the *Creation*; the second band, the *Story of Joseph*; the third band, the *Story of Christ*; and the lowest band, the *Story of St John the Baptist*. All the scenes are divided by mosaic columns of different designs. The marble rectangular frames at the base of the dome contain mosaic saints. It is not known with certainty which Florentine artists were responsible for the design of the mosaics, but most scholars now agree that Cimabue, the greatest artist of the 13th century, was not directly involved.

Piazza San Giovanni

Beside the Baptistery is the Pillar of St Zenobius, erected in the 14th century to commemorate an elm which came into leaf here when the body of the bishop saint (died c. 430) was moved from San Lorenzo to Santa Reparata in the 9th century. In the piazza, at no. 7, is the ancient little Casa dell'Opera di San Giovanni, with a copy in the lunette of a statuette of St John by Michelozzo (the original is in the Bargello). The medieval courtyard survives. This was the headquarters of the office responsible for the maintenance of the Baptistery; it is at present being restored as a reception centre for visitors.

MUSEO DELL'OPERA DEL DUOMO
Map p. 397, C2

Open 9.30–7.30, Sun and holidays 9–1; T: 055 230 2885.
Behind the east end of the Duomo, at no. 9 Piazza del Duomo, is the entrance to the Museo dell'Opera del Duomo in a building which has been the seat of the Opera del Duomo (responsible for the maintenance of the cathedral) since the beginning of the 15th century. The museum, first opened in 1891, contains numerous masterpieces of sculpture from the Baptistery, Duomo and Campanile, and successfully illustrates the complicated histories of all these buildings. It also has very fine works by Donatello and Luca della Robbia. When the exhibition space is expanded into the former theatre next door, Michelangelo's *Pietà* and the Ghiberti doors will be moved and the present arrangement altered. Highlights are described below.

Ground Floor

Panels from the Baptistery Doors
In the courtyard, recently covered with a glass roof, are displayed eight restored gilded bronze panels by Lorenzo Ghiberti removed from the east door of the Baptistery (*see p. 50*; the remaining two will be housed here when restoration work on them has been completed). They are masterpieces of the early Renaissance and it took Ghiberti 22 years to complete them. Each panel describes in continuous narrative various episodes from Old Testament stories:

The Creation and the Story of Adam and Eve: This is perhaps the most beautiful of them all, showing the *Creation of Adam*, the *Creation of Eve*, the *Fall* (in a wood full of birds), and the *Expulsion from Paradise*. The human figures are extraordinarily elegant, and the numerous graceful angels add particular charm to the scenes.

The Story of Jacob and Esau: Set in an elegant arched building. Some of the scenes are difficult to interpret, but pride of place is given to an elegant group of four serving women in the left foreground. Isaac is shown with his eldest son Esau (accompanied by two dogs) and Rebecca with her favourite younger son Jacob who, in another scene, disguised by the kid on his shoulders, kneels in front of his blind father to receive his blessing. Rebecca is also shown in her bed chamber and (at the top right) kneeling before God the Father, and Esau leaving for the hunt is carved in low relief.

The Story of Benjamin and Joseph: The scene takes place in front of a circular building where the Egyptians are emptying sacks of grain. At the top of the panel Joseph is seen saved from the well to be sold by his brothers into slavery to the Ishmaelites. In the left foreground are Joseph's brothers opening their sacks to find, to their despair, Joseph's silver chalice. In the background, Joseph is embracing his youngest brother Benjamin. In the right foreground, a camel is being loaded with sacks while Joseph leaves his brothers, on their way back to their father. Another scene in low relief at the top of the panel shows Joseph revealing his identity to his brothers.

The Meeting of Solomon and the Queen of Sheba (detail).

Saul with David and Goliath: This panel shows the battle between Saul (in his war chariot) leading the men of Israel against the Philistines. At the bottom of the panel, David cuts off Goliath's head with a sword, after the giant has fallen 'upon his face to the earth' having been killed by a stone from David's sling. In the background can be seen a group of women rejoicing as they come out of the city to meet Saul and David bearing the head of Goliath.

The story of Cain and Abel: Here we see the elderly Adam and Eve sitting in front of their hut with their children Cain and Abel. Below are two distinct scenes with Abel tending his flock of sheep and Cain tilling the soil with the help of two oxen. At the top of the panel the brothers are then depicted sacrificing a lamb and the fruits of the land to the Lord, who shows his preference for Abel's offering. Then Cain, in anger, is shown killing Abel, and in the last scene the Lord appears to Cain beside a stream asking him where his brother is and Cain replies, 'I know not; am I my brother's keeper?'

Moses Receiving the Tablets of Stone: This panel shows a large crowd beside the Red Sea and their encampment in a group of exquisite trees. The crowd looks up to Mount Sinai on which Moses is seen receiving the Law on the Tablets of Stone from God the Father, who is accompanied by a glory of beautiful angels. Just below Moses his brother Aaron kneels in wonder.

The Meeting of Solomon and the Queen of Sheba: The scene takes place in a splendid vaulted hall filled with a large crowd of people.

Abraham and the Angels and the Sacrifice of Isaac: In front to the left Abraham kneels before three angels (one of whom is God the Father disguised) while his wife Sarah is shown leaving their tent. Above a group of beautiful tall trees is the scene of the sacrifice of Isaac (the subject of the trial reliefs submitted for this commission by Brunelleschi and Ghiberti, now in the Bargello, *see p. 221*). Abraham's two servants who wait below with the mule may be a reference to the intimate friendship between the brothers Isaac and Ishmael.

Sculptures from the Duomo façade
A large hall displays sculptures from the Duomo's old façade (never completed), designed by Arnolfo di Cambio and demolished in 1587. The facsimile displayed here of a drawing by Bernardino Poccetti of the old façade made shortly before its demolition is the most detailed illustration of it to have survived. On the long wall are numerous sculptures by Arnolfo di Cambio and his *bottega*. Arnolfo was the architect of the Duomo, but died soon after building had begun: he also carried out a lot of work in other parts of Italy including Siena, Rome and Orvieto. His sculptures include a seated *Madonna and Child* (a somewhat enigmatic work with striking glass eyes), flanked by St Reparata, St Zenobius, the *Madonna of the Nativity* (shown lying on her side; displayed on the upper part of the wall), and (at the end of the room) Boniface VIII. On the other long wall are the four seated Evangelists, including St John the Evangelist (dating from 1408), interesting as Donatello's first large-scale statue. The upper part of the body is elongated to compensate for its raised position. The other three Evangelists, still Gothic in spirit, are by his less skilled contemporaries, Nanni di Banco, Niccolò di Pietro Lamberti, and Bernardo Ciuffagni whose work can also be seen at Orsanmichele. These were added to the lower part of the façade in the early 15th century.

Works from inside the Duomo
Another room displays 13th–15th-century paintings, including a processional painting of St Agatha with an icon of the saint, Byzantine in spirit, dating from c. 1270 by an unknown master named after this work (the painting on the other side of the panel dates from the 14th century). St Agatha was venerated in Florence as protectress from fires and this icon would have been carried through the streets on her feast day (5 February). The very fine marble panels from the choir of the Duomo by Baccio Bandinelli and Giovanni Bandini (1547) representing prophets, apostles and nude male pagan figures, are beautifully carved.

Michelangelo's Pietà
This beautiful late work, carved when Michelangelo was almost eighty years old, is
displayed on the stair landing. It was intended for Michelangelo's own tomb which
was to have been in the basilica of Santa Maria Maggiore in Rome. According to
Vasari, the head of Nicodemus is a self-portrait. Dissatisfied with his work, the sculptor destroyed the arm and left leg of Christ, and his pupil, Tiberio Calcagni, restored
the arm and finished the figure of Mary Magdalen. The sculpture was brought to
Florence by Grand Duke Cosimo III for the crypt of San Lorenzo, and then from 1721
it was exhibited in the Duomo.

First Floor

The Della Robbia and Donatello cantorie
The first room is dominated by these two famous works, made in the 1430s by Luca
della Robbia and Donatello, probably as organ lofts rather than singing galleries (*cantorie*) to go above the two sacristy doors in the Duomo. The one on the left, by Luca
della Robbia, was his first important commission, and is his masterpiece. The original
panels are displayed beneath the reconstructed cantoria. As the inscription indicates,
the charming sculptured panels illustrate Psalm 150 (*Praise the Lord! Praise God in his
sanctuary; praise him in his mighty firmament! Praise him for his mighty deeds; praise him
according to his surpassing greatness! Praise him with trumpet sound; praise him with lute
and harp! Praise him with tambourine and dance; praise him with strings and pipe! Praise
him with clanging cymbals; praise him with loud clashing cymbals! Let everything that
breathes praise the Lord!*). The children (some of them drawn from classical models),
dancing, singing or playing musical instruments, are exquisitely carved within a beautiful architectural framework. Donatello's cantoria, opposite, provides a striking contrast, with a frieze of running putti against a background of coloured inlay.

Statues from the Campanile
Around the walls of the same room are the 16 statues from the four sides of the
Campanile (*see p. 48*). When they were removed they were already very ruinous, and
for this reason they are not all easy to attribute. The earliest ones by Nino and Andrea
Pisano date from after 1337; others are attributed to their contemporary Maso di Banco
and the early-15th-century sculptor Nanni di Bartolo, but the most important are those
by Donatello. *Jeremiah* is one of his most remarkable marble sculptures with a striking
portrait head (at present being restored). *Habakkuk* was one of the sculptor's most
admired works and the subject of Vasari's story that Donatello was found one day in his
studio looking intensely at *Habakkuk* and commanding him to talk. It has always been
nicknamed '*lo Zuccone*' or big-head, and the form of the skull indicates that the sculptor almost certainly used a life model, perhaps a disabled man: it may be that Donatello
wished to suggest that wisdom, a gift from God, is in no way connected to one's physical aspect. Donatello also sculpted the *Abraham and Isaac* (a two-figure group), and
probably also the head of *Jonah* (sometimes identified as St John the Baptist).

Bas-reliefs from the Campanile

In an adjoining room the original bas-reliefs removed from the two lower registers of the Campanile are exhibited. The lower row, which date from the early 14th century, are charming works by Andrea Pisano (some perhaps designed by Giotto); they illustrate the Creation of Man, and the Arts and Industries. Starting on the entrance wall: *Creation of Adam*, *Creation of Eve*, *Labours of Adam and Eve*, *Jabal* (the Pastoral life), *Jubal* (Music), *Tubalcain* (the Smith), *Noah*, *Gionitus* (Astronomy), *The Arts of Building, Medicine, Hunting, Weaving, Phoroneus the Lawgiver, Daedalus, Navigation, Hercules and Cacus, Agriculture, Theatrica, Architecture, Phidias* (Sculpture), *Apelles* (Painting). The last five reliefs (on the right wall) were made in 1437–39 by Luca della Robbia to fill the frames on the north face of the Campanile: *Grammar*, *Philosophy*, *Orpheus* (representing Poetry or Rhetoric), *Arithmetic* and *Astrology* (with the figure of Pythagoras). The upper row of smaller reliefs by pupils of Pisano, illustrate the seven Planets, the Virtues and the Liberal Arts, and the lunette of the *Madonna and Child* formerly over a door of the Campanile is by Andrea Pisano, who also carved the exquisite statuettes of the Redeemer and Santa Reparata exhibited here.

Donatello's Mary Magdalen and the Altar of St John the Baptist

Donatello's famous sculpture, displayed in a room on the other side of the cantoria room, stood formerly in the Baptistery, and is thought to be a late work (c. 1454). The dramatic wooden statue shows the penitent Magdalen as an old toothless woman with only her long hair covering her nakedness and her palsied hands seeming to shake as she attempts to join them in prayer. At the other end of the room is the magnificent altar of silver-gilt, also from the Baptistery, a Gothic work by Florentine goldsmiths, begun in 1366 and finished in the 15th century, illustrating the history of St John the Baptist. It includes a statuette of the Baptist by Michelozzo, a relief of the *Birth of the Baptist* by Antonio Pollaiolo (on the left flank) and the *Beheading of the Baptist* by Verrocchio (on the right flank), and a Cross (1457–59). The 27 needlework panels with scenes from the life of St John the Baptist formerly decorated vestments made for the Baptistery. These are exquisite works by the craftsmen of the Arte di Calimala (cloth importers' guild) made in 1466–87 to a design by Antonio Pollaiolo. This technique known as *or nué* is created by using minute stitches in coloured silk thread over a backing of silk core wrapped in beaten (or Japanese) gold, which produces a unique effect, with particularly subtle shading and modelling (and these panels are recognised as being the best examples known of this type of needlework).

The construction of the dome

In a corridor scaffolding and tools reconstruct a building site thought to be similar to that set up by Brunelleschi when working on the dome of the cathedral. The apparatus which may have been used in the construction of the cupola (or in its maintenance), including pulleys, ropes, tackle, hoists and technical instruments, is displayed here. It was found in a storeroom at the foot of the cupola, together with Brunelleschi's original brick moulds. At the end is a wooden model of the lantern thought to have been made by Brunelleschi as his (winning) entry in the competition of 1436, as well as the architect's death mask. When the shutters are open there is a view of the dome from the window.

AROUND PIAZZA DEL DUOMO

From the corner of Piazza del Duomo (by Via del Proconsolo), there is a good view of the cathedral and dome. The piazza follows the curve of the east end of the Duomo. The 16th-century **Palazzo Strozzi-Niccolini** bears a 19th-century plaque and bust of Donatello since it stands on the site of a house where the sculptor had his studio. Nos 5 and 3 in the piazza are restored medieval houses decorated with coats of arms (some of them put up in 1390), and a pretty top-floor loggia. In Via dei Servi (at the end of which can be seen Piazza Santissima Annunziata with the equestrian statue of the Grand Duke Ferdinando I) is the **church of San Michelino** (*map p. 397, C1*; its full name is San Michele Visdomini), which was demolished in 1363 in order to make way for the east end of the Duomo, and, incredibly enough, reconstructed on this site a few years later. It is of ancient foundation and is known to have been enlarged by the Visdomini family in the 11th century. Inside, on the right side is a *Holy Family* (commissioned in 1518 by Francesco Pucci) by Pontormo. The other altarpieces are by painters who were at work in the late 16th century (Empoli, Poppi, and Passignano). The 18th-century vault fresco in the crossing showing the *Fall of Satan* is by Niccolò Lapi. At the east end are interesting 14th-century frescoes and *sinopie* attributed to Spinello Aretino, and a 14th-century wood Crucifix.

On the south side of Piazza del Duomo ambulances are usually parked in waiting outside the **Misericordia**, a charitable institution which gives free help to those in need. The Order, founded by St Peter Martyr in 1244, moved to this site in 1576 from the Bigallo across the road. In the Middle Ages, the brotherhood was particularly active during the plague years, when it gave medical care to the poor and attended to their burial. The lay confraternity continues its remarkable work with about 2,500 volunteers, who up until this day have always worn distinctive black capes with hoods, although from 2005 these will have to be replaced by the standard uniform for those who work in emergency services. The cape is recorded in Pietro Annigoni's painting (1970) outside the entrance of a member of the confraternity carrying a sick person.

The main door leads into the busy Sala di Compagnia which preserves its old-fashioned cupboards and furniture. On the end wall is a seated statue of the *Madonna and Child* by Benedetto da Maiano (left by him to the Bigallo; finished by Battista Lorenzi in 1575). The two kneeling statues of angels are by Giovanni della Robbia. The pretty little Oratory (entered to the left of the main door), decorated in the 17th century, contains a very fine marble statue of St Sebastian by Benedetto da Maiano which is said to have influenced the early work of Michelangelo. This was left unfinished by Benedetto in his studio nearby (on the corner of Via dei Servi and Via del Castellaccio) where he had been at work on many fine sculptures since 1480, and was also bequeathed by the sculptor to the Bigallo. The enamelled terracotta altarpiece by Andrea della Robbia was commissioned by Francesco Sassetti for his chapel in the Badia Fiesolana.

The small Gothic **Loggia del Bigallo** was built for the Misericordia in 1351–58 probably by Alberto Arnoldi, who also worked as architect on the Duomo, and carved the reliefs and the lunette of the *Madonna and Child* (1361) above the door into the Oratory (facing the Baptistery). The Compagnia del Bigallo, founded in 1245, and involved, like the Misericordia, in charitable works, moved to this seat in 1425 when the two confraternities were merged. Lost and abandoned children were exhibited beneath the loggia for three days before being consigned to foster-mothers. The three 14th-century statues in tabernacles high up on the façade came from the Bigallo's former headquarters near Orsanmichele.

The **Museo del Bigallo** is the smallest museum in the city and one of the most charming (*opening times are erratic, although officially they are 10–6 except Tues; Tel: 055 215 440*). It preserves most of the works of art commissioned by the Misericordia and the Bigallo over the centuries from Florentine artists. These include the *Madonna of the Misericordia* by an artist in the circle of Bernardo Daddi, a fresco which dates from 1342 and includes the earliest known view of Florence, with the marble Baptistery prominent in the centre near the incomplete Campanile and façade of the Duomo. A small portable triptych, dated 1333, is one of Bernardo Daddi's most important early works. The beautiful *Madonna of Humility* with two angels is by Domenico di Michelino (1359–64), and the tondo of the *Madonna and Saints*, in a lovely contemporary frame, is by Jacopo del Sellaio. The 13th-century painted Crucifix is attributed to the Maestro del Bigallo, who takes his name from this work.

There are some interesting, quiet, narrow streets which preserve their old paving off the south side of Piazza del Duomo. The narrow Via del Campanile (*map p. 397, B2*) leads to Via della Canonica, where a building with wooden *sporti* is used as offices by the Opera del Duomo, and meetings of the Cathedral Chapter have been held in the little piazza here since 1680. On the corner with Via dello Studio is the 13th-century Palazzo Tedaldini, and a low building here with a cast of the relief of the stonemasons' and carpenters' guild on Orsanmichele (*see p. 63*), is used as a workshop by the stonemasons of the Opera del Duomo, who can usually be seen at work here. Over the centuries the stonework of the exterior of the Duomo has had to be constantly renewed in order to preserve it against the elements, a task which continues to this day. Via dello Studio, which has medieval ground-floor arches and a doorway surmounted by a pretty della Robbian lunette, slopes gently downwards to the Duomo providing a particularly good view of the cupola. In the little Piazza Sant'Elisabetta is the ancient round Torre La Pagliazza, which was used as a prison in the 13th–14th centuries, but was sadly over-restored in 1988 for use as a hotel. In Via delle Oche the 14th-century Palazzo Visdomini preserves its tower.

PIAZZA DELLA REPUBBLICA & ORSANMICHELE

Between the Baptistery and the Campanile, the straight Via de' Calzaiuoli leads due south towards Piazza della Signoria. On the line of a Roman road, this was the main thoroughfare of the medieval city, linking the Duomo to Palazzo Vecchio, and passing the guildhall of Orsanmichele. Although many of the shops on the ground floors of the buildings still have arches, the street was transformed when it was widened in the 1840s: it is still the busiest pedestrian street in the city.

PIAZZA DELLA REPUBBLICA
Map p. 397, B2

Piazza della Repubblica lies on the site of the Roman forum. It was laid out at the end of the 19th century after the ruthless demolition of many medieval buildings in the Mercato Vecchio, the old commercial centre, and part of the Ghetto (created in 1571, this extended from the north side of the present square to Via de' Pecori). Much criticized at the time, the Piazza remains a disappointing intrusion into Florence's historic centre, with its sombre colonnades, triumphal arch, and undistinguished buildings .

The piazza has several large cafés with tables outside, including the Giubbe Rosse, a famous meeting place in the early 1900s of writers and artists (including the poet Eugenio Montale and the writer Italo Svevo, widely thought to have been the inspiration for Joyce's Leopold Bloom). The arcades are brightened up on Thursdays when a flower and plant market is set up. In the bar of the Cinema Gambrinus is an encaustic allegorical painting (1948) by Giovanni Colacicchi (1900–92), a figurative painter and member of the Giubbe Rosse circle, whose work is full of light, and who was part of the artistic movement now known as the Italian Novecento.

'The old centre of the city, restored to new life from centuries of gloom'. Vainglorious inscription in the 19th-century Piazza della Repubblica.

ORSANMICHELE
Map p. 397, B3

The tall, rectangular Orsanmichele bears little resemblance to a church, although it is consecrated as such and is on the site of San Michele ad Hortum, founded in the 9th century (but destroyed in 1239). It is thought that a grain market was erected here c. 1290 by Arnolfo di Cambio, but burnt down in 1304. The present building was also built as a market by Francesco Talenti, one of the architects of the Duomo, in 1337, but its arcades were enclosed only a few decades later by huge three-light Gothic windows. These, in turn, were bricked up shortly after they were finished (but their superb tracery can still be seen). The upper storey, completed in 1404, was intended as a granary, but housed archives for contracts and wills after 1569. It is now a museum.

THE FLORENTINE GUILDS

The seven Arti Maggiori, or Greater Guilds, took control of the government of the city at the end of the 13th century and their regime, known as the *secondo popolo*, lasted for nearly a century. Bankers, professional men and merchants in the most important trades were members of these greater guilds, which were the Calimala (the premier guild, named from the street where the wholesale cloth importers had their warehouses), the Giudici e notai (judges and notaries), the Cambio (bankers), the Lana (woollen-cloth merchants and manufacturers), the Por Santa Maria (named after the street which led to the workshops of the silk-cloth industry), the Medici e speziali (physicians and apothecaries, the guild to which painters belonged), and the Vaiai e pellicciai (furriers). The Arti Minori, created in the 13th century, represented shopkeepers and skilled artisans. Guild members were required to maintain a high standard in their work, and carry out specific duties and respect their obligations to other members. In the early 15th century, most of the public works in the city were commissioned by the guilds, and many important buildings were put in their charge (the cathedral itself was the responsibility of the Arte della Lana from 1331 onwards). The guilds competed with each other in spending vast sums of money on buildings and their embellishment in order to add to their prestige.

The Statues on the Exterior

The decoration of the exterior of Orsanmichele was undertaken by the guilds, who commissioned statues of their patron saints from the best artists of the age to fill the canopied niches. The statues are an impressive testimony to the skill of Florentine sculptors over a period of some 200 years. Restoration of the 14 statues and their beautiful niches (which was begun in 1984) is almost finished, and all but two of the statues have now been replaced by copies (the originals are kept in a museum in the hall above. Since this is not at present regularly open to the public, the statues have been described in full here). The description of the tabernacles, and the guilds to whom they belonged, begins on the side facing Via de' Calzaiuoli, and goes round to the right.

Calimala (wholesale cloth importers): Tabernacle and *St John the Baptist* (1413–16) by Lorenzo Ghiberti (signed on the cloak). This was the first life-size statue of the Renaissance to be cast in bronze. It is the largest statue made for Orsanmichele and is still very Gothic in spirit (the niche is at present empty).

Tribunale di Mercanzia (beyond the church door, this was the merchants' court, where guild matters were adjudicated): The bronze group of the *Incredulity of St Thomas* (1473–83) is a superb work by Verrocchio, Leonardo da Vinci's master, who (like his pupil) was both a sculptor and painter. The tabernacle was commissioned earlier by the Parte Guelfa; it is the work of Donatello, and formerly contained his *St Louis of Toulouse*, now in the Museo dell'Opera di Santa Croce (*see p. 242*). Above is the round stemma of the Mercanzia in enamelled terracotta by Luca della Robbia (1463).

Giudici e Notai (judges and notaries): Tabernacle by Niccolò di Pietro Lamberti (1403–06), with a bronze statue of *St Luke* (1583–1601) by Giambologna.

Beccai (butchers): *St Peter* (c. 1425) is generally attributed to Bernardo Ciuffagni, but some scholars think it could be by the more famous sculptors Brunelleschi or even Donatello. The fine della Robbian stemma was made in 1858.

Conciapelli (tanners): Tabernacle and *St Philip* (c. 1410–12) by Nanni di Banco.

Maestri di Pietrai e di Legname (stonemasons and carpenters, the guild to which architects and sculptors belonged): Tabernacle and statues of four soldier saints (the *Quattro Santi Coronati*) are the masterpiece of Nanni di Banco (c. 1409–16/17), modelled on antique Roman statues. The relief, by the same artist, illustrates the work of the guild. Above is their stemma in inlaid terracotta by Luca della Robbia.

Armaiuoli (or Corazzai e Spadai; armourers): *St George* by Donatello (c. 1415–17). The marble statue was removed to the Bargello in 1891 and replaced here by a bronze copy in 1892. The exquisite bas-relief is also now in the Bargello.

Cambio (bankers): Tabernacle and bronze statue of *St Matthew* (1419–22), by Lorenzo Ghiberti (the niche is at present empty).

Lanaiuoli (wool manufacturers and clothiers; beyond the door): Bronze *St Stephen* by Lorenzo Ghiberti (1427–28).

Maniscalchi (farriers): *St Eligius* (c. 1417–21), and bas-relief of the saint in a smithy by Nanni di Banco.

Linaiuoli e Rigattieri (linen merchants and used-clothes' dealers): *St Mark*

(1411–13) by Donatello, still showing Gothic influence.

Pellicciai (furriers): *St James the Greater*, with a bas-relief of his beheading attributed to Niccolò di Pietro Lamberti (c. 1422), also with Gothic elements.

Medici e Speziali (physicians and apothecaries): Gothic tabernacle attributed to Simone Talenti (1399), with a *Madonna and Child* (the *Madonna della Rosa*) thought to be the work of Pietro di Giovanni Tedesco (c. 1400), but is also thought by some scholars to be the work of Niccolò di Pietro Lamberti or Simone Ferrucci. It is in a better state of preservation than the other statues since it was moved in 1628 to the inside of the church (but then replaced in the exterior niche in 1925). Above, stemma by Luca della Robbia.

Setaiuoli e Orafi (silkweavers and goldsmiths): *St John the Evangelist*, bronze statue by Baccio da Montelupo (1515).

The Interior

The church (*closed for restoration*) is a dark rectangular hall, divided into two aisles by two massive pillars. Two altars are set at one end on a raised platform. The vaults and central and side pilasters are decorated with frescoes of patron saints painted in the late 14th or early 15th century by Tuscan artists. The fine Gothic stained glass windows include one showing *St Jacob Among the Shepherds* designed by Lorenzo Monaco.

The Gothic tabernacle by Andrea Orcagna (1349–59) is a masterpiece of the decorative arts, ornamented with marble and coloured glass, as well as with reliefs and statuettes. This is the only important sculptural work by this artist, who was also a painter and architect. Around the base are reliefs of the life of the Virgin (including, in front, the *Marriage of the Virgin* and the *Annunciation*). Behind the altar is an elaborate sculptured relief of the *Transition and Assumption of the Virgin*. A beautiful frame of carved angels encloses a painting on the altar of the Madonna by Bernardo Daddi. On the other altar is the *Madonna and Child with St Anne*, a statue by Francesco da Sangallo (1522). The fresco in the vault above shows St Anne holding a 'model' of Florence (with the Baptistery prominent).

Museo di Orsanmichele

At present closed for restoration but normally open daily on request at Orsanmichele at 9, 10 and 11, except the first and last Mon of the month; T: 055 265 171.

This museum, on the upper floors of Orsanmichele, is entered from Palazzo dell'Arte della Lana by an overhead walkway built in 1569 to give access to the archives formerly housed here. A large Gothic hall with fine brick vaulting exhibits the splendid restored marble and bronze statues from the niches outside (*described above*). A steep, modern flight of stairs leads up to another Gothic hall with a fine wooden roof, which houses very damaged stone statuettes of saints and prophets dating from the late 14th century, removed from the exterior of the building. There are splendid views from the windows.

WALK ONE

AROUND ORSANMICHELE

This walk takes in interesting medieval buildings in the centre of the city around Orsanmichele, many of them once guild headquarters. This was also an area of markets, one of which survives to this day.

Palazzo dell'Arte della Lana, next door to Orsanmichele, was built in 1308 by the Guild of Wool Merchants, but arbitrarily restored in 1905. The Arte della Lana represented the most important Florentine industry which was responsible for the city's economic growth in the 13th century (it has been estimated that a third of the population was employed in the woollen cloth industry in the 13th and 14th centuries). Among the *stemme* on the building is that of the guild, the Agnus Dei. At the base of the tower is the little oratory of Santa Maria della Tromba (late 14th century), one of the largest of the many tabernacles in the city, moved here when the Mercato Vecchio was destroyed (*see p. 61*). Behind the neo-Gothic grille is an early 14th-century painting of the *Madonna Enthroned*, by Jacopo del Casentino and, in the lunette, the *Coronation of the Virgin* added by Niccolò di Pietro Gerini later in the same century. On Via Calimala, where a shop has remains of early frescoes, is the 13th-century Torre Compiobbesi.

At no. 4 Via Orsanmichele is **Palazzo dell'Arte dei Beccai**, built c. 1415, the headquarters of the Butchers' Guild until 1534; their stemma (a goat) can be seen high up on the façade. It is now the seat of the Accademia delle Arti del Disegno, and admission to the interior is usually granted on written application (it houses two works by Pontormo and a bronze bust of Michelangelo by Daniele da Volterra).

On the other side of Orsanmichele, on the corner where Via dell'Arte della Lana crosses Via Lamberti, is the site of the **first headquarters of the Medici bank**, set up in 1397 by Giovanni di Bicci, father of Cosimo il Vecchio. It was Giovanni who founded the family fortune which enabled his descendants to excel in Florence as politicians and patrons of the arts. Close by is the **Mercato Nuovo**, which, although it has been the site of a market since the beginning of the 11th century, was so-named to distinguish it from the Mercato Vecchio which dated from even earlier. The loggia was erected by Cosimo I in 1547–51 when it was used principally for the sale of silk and gold. It is still a busy market-place, and usually good value (*open daily in summer; closed Mon and Sun in winter*), almost exclusively frequented by visitors, for leather goods, scarves, gloves, bags and souvenirs. It is still sometimes called the 'straw-market' by English-speaking visitors (since it was famous for the sale of straw work in the 20th century), but it is always known to Florentines humorously as '*Il Porcellino*' (the piglet), after the well-loved statue of a massive seated wild boar, whose snout has been kept polished by generations of admirers. This bronze was copied by Pietro Tacca around 1612 from an antique statue (based on a Hellenistic original in the Uffizi); he added the delightful base with numerous plants and animals (which is now replaced by a copy). Coins thrown into the fountain are collected and given to charity. On the building opposite is a tabernacle with a painting of the *Madonna and Child* by Giovanni Colacicchi (1953).

On Via Porta Rossa (so-named since at least the beginning of the 13th century) is **Palazzo Davanzati**, now the Museo della Casa Fiorentina Antica, and the best surviving example of a medieval nobleman's house in Florence (despite numerous restorations), particularly interesting as an illustration of Florentine life in the Middle Ages. Serious structural problems, however, have meant that the entire palace has had to be closed, except for the spacious vaulted entrance hall, which runs the whole width of the building and was used as a loggia for family ceremonies, and later as shops. The palace was built in the mid-14th century by the Davizzi family and became the property of Bernardo Davanzati, a successful merchant and scholar, in 1578. It remained in his family until the end of the 19th century. In 1904 the palace was bought by the antiquarian and art dealer Elia Volpi, who restored it and recreated, with the help of skilled artisans, the interior of a medieval Florentine house. The antiques from his private museum here were later sold to various museums around the world (in a famous sale in 1916, much of the contents went to American buyers). It

helped form the taste of foreigners in furnishing their houses in the early 20th century, and the last successful sale of its contents was held in 1929. The Italian state purchased the house in 1951. Interesting graffiti and drawings referring to contemporary events (1441–1516) have been found on many of the walls.

The typical 14th-century façade consists of three storeys above large arches on the ground floor. The proportions have been altered by the loggia at the top, which was added in the 16th century and probably replaced battlements. The ironwork is interesting, and includes brackets which carry diagonal poles across the windows. These were used to hang out the washing, suspend birdcages, or for the hangings which decorated the façade on special occasions. The huge Davanzati coat of arms dates from the 16th century; it was brought from another family house close by.

The interior is of great interest for its architecture and contemporary wall-paintings, which are rare examples of a decorative form typical of 14th-century houses. Until the museum reopens, a few of the contents are displayed in the entrance hall. These include pieces of restored furniture, the painted wood cupboard (a Sienese work of the 16th century) which stored the family weapons, a charming series of hand-warmers in the form of shoes (18th century), a case of 15th-century bas-reliefs, the family tree of the Davanzati, painted in the 17th century, detached 15th-century frescoes from the courtyard, and a 15th-century terracotta *Madonna Annunciate*.

At the end of the street is the **Palazzo Bartolini-Salimbeni** (now the Albergo Porta Rossa), with wrought-iron lanterns and a projecting upper storey supported on stone *sporti*. The palace was built by the Bartolini-Salimbeni in the early 16th century (their heraldic emblems decorate the façade), and the hotel opened here in the mid-19th century. It has preserved its Art Nouveau decorations, including colourful stained glass.

In a little piazza near the other end of Via Porta Rossa is **Palazzo di Parte Guelfa**. This was built as the official residence of the captains of the Guelph party in the 13th century. The Parte Guelfa was a political and military organization which supported the pope and virtually controlled the government of the city from c. 1267 until 1376. The famous feud between the Guelphs and Ghibellines (who took the side of the Holy Roman Emperor) coloured much of the history of the city during the Middle Ages (*see also p. 22*). Beneath the crenellations is a row of *stemme* and a tall Gothic window. The outside stair was modified by Vasari, who added the pretty little terrace and corner loggia. In the 15th century the palace was enlarged by Brunelleschi, who built a fine hall, the windows of which can still be seen. The restored interior is rarely open. The other buildings in the piazza include Palazzo Giandonati, dating from the 14th century, with two arches on the ground floor, and the 15th-century Palazzo Canacci (no. 3) with grisaille decoration and a fine loggia (heavily restored at the beginning of the 20th century). On the third side of the square is the rough façade of the former church of Santa Maria Sovraporta (once used as a fire station, and now a library). The Cappella di San Bartolomeo here (1345–52) preserves interesting frescoes high up in the vault, including a fragment of a townscape. A narrow lane leads past Brunelleschi's handsome extension to Palazzo di Parte Guelfa into **Via delle Terme**, a pretty medieval street, which takes its name from the Roman baths which were in this area. The back of the medieval portion of Palazzo di Parte Guelfa and a number of medieval tower houses can be seen from here. A series of ancient lanes known as *chiassi* connect this street with Borgo Santi Apostoli towards the river (*described on p. 261*). The palace at no. 9 has a Renaissance courtyard and there is a medieval tower at no. 13 (red). At no. 17 an unusually small house survives, just one storey high, above two wide arches.

Via di Capaccio leads off Via delle Terme back to the Mercato Nuovo past the **Palazzo dell'Arte della Seta** (no. 3). This was established as the headquarters of the guild of the silk-cloth industry at the end of the 14th century. It still bears its beautiful stemma encircled by cherubs, in the style of Donatello.

PIAZZA DELLA SIGNORIA & PALAZZO VECCHIO

PIAZZA DELLA SIGNORIA
Map p. 397, B3

Dominated by Palazzo Vecchio, the town hall, this great square has been the political centre of the city since the Middle Ages. Here the Signoria (the magistrate and priors who ruled the city) would, in moments of crisis from the 13th century onwards, call a *parlamento*, or an assembly of Florentine citizens. It was the scene of public ceremonies, but also a gathering place in times of trouble. The history of the square has followed that of Palazzo Vecchio itself. The area at the foot of the palace was laid out as Piazza del Popolo in 1307. During the 14th century, houses were demolished nearby in order to expand the size of the piazza. By 1385, when it was paved and heavy traffic was banned, it had nearly reached its present dimensions. In the life of the city today, the piazza is still the focus of public celebrations and political demonstrations, although it is always crowded with tourists as well as Florentines.

Remains of Roman baths as well as traces of the south wall of the Roman colony, founded in 30 BC, and an early Christian basilica were found during excavations here in the 1980s. Subsequent controversial restoration work was carried out on the 18th-century paving of the piazza in 1991, when the old paving stones were taken up and new ones laid. The destruction of the old pavement has caused permanent damage to the appearance of the square.

A number of narrow medieval lanes still survive leading out of the piazza, including Chiasso dei Baroncelli with the 14th-century Palazzo Benini Formichi, and Via Calimaruzza, where the most powerful guild in Florence, the guild of wholesale cloth importers (the Arte di Calimala), set up their headquarters in the late 14th century (their stemma, an eagle holding a bale of cloth in its talons, can still be seen at no. 2a).

Sculptures in the Piazza

In front of Palazzo Vecchio stands a **replica of Michelangelo's *David***. The huge statue was commissioned by the city of Florence in 1501 and set up here in 1504 as a political symbol representing the victory of republicanism over tyranny. When it was unveiled, it was heralded as a masterpiece and at once established Michelangelo as the greatest Florentine artist of his age. The original was removed to the Accademia in 1873 (*see pp. 161 & 162*).

In 1534 Michelangelo left Florence for Rome never to return to his native city, and it was in this same year that the colossal statue of *Hercules and Cacus* here was sculpted by Baccio Bandinelli, in a disastrous attempt to imitate the *David*. All the defects of this two-figure group were pointed out by Cellini to Cosimo I in the presence of the

Ammannati's Neptune Fountain (1560–75).

sculptor, but despite its failure Bandinelli, under the secure patronage of the Medici grand duke and in the absence of Michelangelo, quickly became the most important sculptor in Florence and remained unrivalled for some two decades (his most successful works were carried out for the Opera del Duomo). He also carved one of the bizarre statues here between the two colossal figures (the other is by his pupil Vincenzo de' Rossi).

Farther to the left, in front of the palace, is a copy of the statue of *Judith and Holofernes* by Donatello; the original is inside the Palazzo Vecchio (*see p. 81*). It was the first of all the statues to be installed in the piazza, after its confiscation from Palazzo Medici following the family's expulsion in 1494. Beyond a copy of Donatello's *Marzocco*, the heraldic lion of Florence (the original is in the Bargello, *see p. 218*), is the **Neptune Fountain** (1560–75). The colossal flaccid figure of Neptune is always known to Florentines as *il Biancone* (the white giant). It was carved from a block of marble which, despite the opposition of Cellini, was first offered to Bandinelli and on his death to Ammannati. In the more successful and elegant bronze groups on the basin, Ammannati was assisted by other sculptors, including Giambologna.

The porphyry disc with an inscription in the pavement in front of the fountain marks the spot where Savonarola was burnt at the stake on 23 May 1498 (*see p. 73*).

On a line with the statues across the front of Palazzo Vecchio is a beautiful bronze **equestrian monument to Cosimo I** by Giambologna (1595; *pictured opposite*). It was commissioned by the grand duke's son Ferdinando I, and on the base are scenes of Cosimo's coronation and conquest of Siena. The horse's head is particularly fine. Behind the statue is the building where the Tribunale di Mercanzia (or Merchants' Court) was installed in 1359. Founded in 1308, guild matters were discussed here. Palazzo Uguccioni (no. 7) has an unusual but handsome façade of 1550, sometimes thought to be on a design by Michelangelo, and adorned with a bust of Cosimo I.

LOGGIA DELLA SIGNORIA

The Loggia della Signoria is also known as Loggia dei Lanzi after the *Lanzichenecchi* (bodyguards) of Cosimo I who were stationed here. Its three beautiful lofty arches, semicircular in form, break free from Gothic shapes and anticipate the Renaissance. It was intended not only as an ornament to the square but also for use by government officials during public ceremonies. It was built in 1376–82 by Simone Talenti, son of the architect Francesco, with the help of Benci di Cione, but the design is probably by the more famous architect Orcagna. In the spandrels are seven marble statues of Virtues (1384–89) against a blue-enamelled ground, designed by Agnolo Gaddi. It is thought that the head of *Faith* was probably substituted by Donatello, after the original fell to the ground. The columns are decorated with (worn) statuettes and lions' heads, and have composite capitals; there are two elaborate corbels on the back wall.

Monument to Cosimo I by Giambologna (1595).

Perseus (1554) by Benvenuto Cellini.

Cellini's magnificent bronze **Perseus**, in which Perseus exhibits the Medusa's severed head, was commissioned by Cosimo I in 1545; it is considered Cellini's masterpiece. It was his last public commission and took him nine years to complete: afterwards Bandinelli was favoured by the grand dukes and Cellini retired to write his *Autobiography*. Here he provides a graphic description of the difficulties he encountered while casting the *Perseus* (during which time his studio caught fire and he retired to bed with a fever). He saved the situation at the last moment by seizing all his pewter plates and bowls and throwing them into the melting-pot. It is known that his studio was at no. 59 Via della Pergola (*map p. 399, E2*), and this was where he died in 1571.

The elaborate pedestal (replaced by a copy; the original is in the Bargello, *see p. 218*), using classical motifs, incorporates bronze statuettes and a bas-relief of Perseus rescuing Andromeda.

Giambologna's three-figure group of the **Rape of the Sabines** was commissioned by Francesco I for this position in 1583. The elaborate serpentine composition is designed to be seen from every angle. Giambologna, a Flemish sculptor who came to live in the city in the mid 16th century, had a fundamental influence on the course of Florentine Mannerist sculpture, and this statue in particular was much praised by his contemporaries. The other statues were all placed here in the 18th century when the loggia was first used as an open-air museum of sculpture. The lions at the entrance (the one on the left a Roman work and the one on the right made in the late 16th century) and the Roman statues (2nd century AD) along the back wall came from the Villa Medici in Rome. *Ajax with the Body of Patroclus* is a Roman copy of a Greek original of 240 BC, which entered the Medici collections in 1570 (restored in the 17th and 19th centuries). *Hercules and the Centaur* is by Giambologna, with Pietro Francavilla, and the *Rape of Polyxena* is by Pio Fedi (1866).

GIROLAMO SAVONAROLA

Girolamo Savonarola (1452–98), born in Ferrara, became a Dominican friar in Bologna. In 1489 he took up residence in Florence, and was appointed prior of San Marco just two years later. He was famous for his eloquence as a preacher, and in his dramatic sermons—which he declared were divinely inspired—he denounced 'immoral luxuries' and advocated a return to simple Christian principles. It was Cosimo il Vecchio who had claimed that 'you cannot govern a state with paternosters'. Savonarola maintained that there was no other way for a state to be governed. His advocation of theocracy and his fierce puritan streak made him unpalatable to many, but he had a wide following as his congregations show (his sermons had to be held in the Duomo as the only church large enough to hold them).

Portrait of Savonarola with the attributes of the Dominican saint Peter Martyr.

He was also a learned theologian, admired by the Florentine humanists, including Pico della Mirandola and Poliziano. Botticelli was one of the Renaissance artists probably influenced by him, and Michelangelo is said to have commented as an old man that he could still hear the friar's voice ringing in his ears. Although Savonarola had been critical of Lorenzo the Magnificent, it seems Lorenzo called him to his death-bed in order to receive his blessing. But Savonarola remained an enemy of the Medici, and his address to the Great Council in 1496 did much to strengthen republican zeal in the government of the city. The Borgia pope Alexander VI finally managed to excommunicate him, however, and he was then accused by the Florentine government of attempting to organize a political party. Denounced for heresy and treason, he was hanged and burned, together with two of his companions, in Piazza della Signoria, where, at his instigation only a few years earlier, bonfires had been lit to destroy profane books and works of art. Every year, on 23 May, a ceremony is held here in his memory by those who consider him a martyr. As was the case with his 15th-century followers and opponents, he still arouses particularly strong feelings amongst historians today.

PALAZZO VECCHIO

Open 9–7; Thurs, Sun and holidays 9–2; T: 055 276 8224. Reduction for those aged 18–25 and over 65, and further reduction for children; family tickets also available. Combined ticket with the Brancacci Chapel valid 3 months. Room numbers given below refer to the plans in the text. 'Secret' itineraries (percorsi segreti) are shown on guided tours (booking advised; T: 055 276 8224), and there is a little children's museum (Museo dei Ragazzi) open Sat–Sun (booking also advised). There are usually two entrances open, one on Via de' Gondi and the other on Piazza della Signoria.

History of Palazzo Vecchio

Palazzo Vecchio, also known as Palazzo della Signoria, was the medieval Palazzo del Popolo and is still the town hall of Florence. The palace stands on part of the site of the Roman theatre of Florence built in the 1st century AD. The *priori* (the governing magistrates of the city) lived here during their two months' tenure of office in the government of the medieval city. In times of trouble the bell in the tower, called the Martinella, summoned citizens to *parlamento* in the square below (the bell was restored in 2004 and now rings out again at dawn, midday and dusk). In 1433, Cosimo il Vecchio was imprisoned in the Alberghetto in the tower before being (temporarily) exiled. The building became known as Palazzo della Signoria during the Republican governments of the 15th century, and alterations were carried out inside by Michelozzo, Giuliano and Benedetto da Maiano and Domenico Ghirlandaio. At the end of the century, after the expulsion of the Medici, the huge Salone dei Cinquecento was built by Cronaca to house the Great Council.

One of the most significant moments in the history of the palace occurred in 1540 when Cosimo I moved here from the private Medici palace in Via Larga (now Via Cavour). Vasari and later Buontalenti were called in by the early Medici dukes to redecorate the building, now called Palazzo Ducale, and to extend it at the back without, however, altering the exterior aspect on Piazza della Signoria. It became known as Palazzo Vecchio only after 1549 when the Medici grand dukes took up residence in Palazzo Pitti. The Provisional Governments of united Italy in 1848 and 1859 met here, and from 1865 to 1871 it housed the Chamber of Deputies and the Foreign Ministry when Florence was capital of the Kingdom of Italy. Since 1872 it has been the seat of the municipal government.

The Exterior

Palazzo Vecchio is an imposing fortress-palace built in *pietra forte* on a trapezoidal plan, to a design traditionally attributed to Arnolfo di Cambio (1299–1302). The façade has remained virtually unchanged, with its graceful divided windows and a battlemented gallery. It became the prototype of many other *palazzi comunali* in Tuscany. Until the 15th century it was the tallest edifice in the city; the tower (1310), asymmetrically placed, is 95m high.

The flank of the building on Piazza della Signoria includes the battlemented 14th-century nucleus of the palace, the unfinished exterior of the Salone dei Cinquecento, with a hipped roof and marble window, and the handsome façade added by Buontalenti in Via de' Gondi. The 16th-century additions at the back of the building on Via dei Leoni incorporate medieval houses. On Via della Ninna parts of the 14th-century masonry can be seen, and extensions of various dates (the three large windows high up, with two smaller ones below, belong to the 15th-century Salone dei Cinquecento).

Above the main entrance is a frieze dedicated to Cristo Re with the monogram of Christ flanked by the two symbolic lions of Florence, set up in 1529.

The Interior

Ground Floor

The courtyard (Cortile) was reconstructed by Michelozzo in 1453, and the elaborate decorations were added in 1565 by Giorgio Vasari to celebrate the marriage between Francesco, son of Cosimo I, and Joanna of Austria. The columns were covered with stucco and the vaults and walls painted with grotesques and views of Austrian cities. The fountain designed by Vasari bears a copy of Verrocchio's charming little *Putto Holding a Dolphin* (c. 1470), a bronze made for a fountain at the Medici villa at Careggi. The original is preserved inside the palace (*see below*).

In the adjoining courtyard (with the ticket office and bookshop) can be seen the 15th-century weather-vane with the *Marzocco* lion, which was removed from the top of the tower in 1981 (when it was replaced by a copy), near a fragment of the original terracotta pavement in herring-bone style.

In the large rectangular Sala d'Arme, the only room on this floor which survives from the 14th-century structure, exhibitions are held. The rest of the ground floor is taken up with local government offices. The monumental grand staircase by Vasari ascends in a theatrical double flight to the first floor (there is also a lift).

First Floor

(1) Salone dei Cinquecento: This immense hall (53.5m x 22m, and 18m high) was built by Cronaca in 1495 for the meetings of the new legislative body, the Consiglio Maggiore of the Republic, which represented the aristocratic character of the new regime. Leonardo da Vinci was commissioned in 1503 by the government to decorate one of the two long walls with a huge mural representing the Florentine victory over Milan at Anghiari in 1440. He experimented, without success, with a new technique of mural painting, and completed only a fragment of the work before leaving Florence for Milan in 1506. It is not known whether this had disappeared by the middle of the 16th century or was destroyed by order of Cosimo I to make way for the new decorations. Michelangelo was asked to do a similar composition on the opposite wall, representing the battle of Cascina between Florence and Pisa in 1364, but he only completed the cartoon before being called to Rome by Julius II. The cartoons of both works and the fragment painted by Leonardo were frequently copied and studied by contemporary painters before they were lost (a copy survives in the Sala di Ester, *see below*).

The room was transformed and heightened by Vasari in 1563–65 when the present decoration was carried out in celebration of Cosimo I. The iconographical scheme was devised by Vasari's friend, the prior of the Spedale degli Innocenti, Vincenzo Borghini, who was an outstanding figure in 16th-century Florence and counsellor to Cosimo on artistic and literary matters. He was later to provide the ceremonial procedure for Cosimo's funeral as he

PALAZZO VECCHIO
(FIRST FLOOR)

Stairs up to 2nd floor

1 Salone dei Cinquecento
2 Udienza
3 Studiolo
4 Sala di Leone X
5 Sala dei Dugento

Stairs from ground floor

had for that of Michelangelo. In the centre of the magnificent ceiling is the *Apotheosis of the Duke* surrounded by the *stemme* of the guilds. The other panels, by Vasari and his workshop (including Giovanni Stradano, Jacopo Zucchi and Giovanni Battista Naldini), represent *Allegories of the Cities of Tuscany under Florentine Dominion*, the *Foundations and Early Growth of Florence*, and the *Victories over Siena and Pisa* (1554–55 and 1496–1509 respectively). On the walls are huge frescoes by the same artists illustrating three more episodes in the wars with Pisa (entrance wall) and Siena. The narrow triangular section of the ceiling (produced by the irregular plan of the building) above the raised Udienza was filled in with putti and self-portraits of Vasari's assistants who worked on the ceiling.

Michelangelo's *Victory* **A** is a strongly knit, two-figure group, probably intended for a niche in the tomb of Julius II in Rome. It was presented to Cosimo I by Michelangelo's nephew in 1565 and set up here by Vasari as a celebration of the victory of Cosimo I over Siena. The serpentine form of the principal figure was frequently copied by later Mannerist sculptors.

Giambologna's original plaster model for *Virtue overcoming Vice* (or '*Florence victorious over Pisa*') **B** was commissioned as a pendant to Michelangelo's *Victory* (the marble is in the Bargello).

The 16th-century statues around the walls **C** represent the *Labours of Hercules*, and are the best works of Vincenzo de' Rossi, pupil of Bandinelli (*see pp. 69–70*).

(2) **Udienza:** This raised chamber contains statues of distinguished members of the Medici family: Cosimo I, Giovanni delle Bande Nere, Leo X (seated), Duke Alessandro, Clement VII (crowning the emperor Charles V), and Francesco I. Many of them, dressed as Romans, are by Baccio Bandinelli. On the wall opposite the Udienza are antique Roman statues.

(3) **The Studiolo:** This tiny study, reached by an inconspicuous door in the entrance wall, is a charming, windowless room also created by Vasari and his school in 1570–75 with the help of Vincenzo Borghini, for Cosimo's son Francesco I. Entirely decorated with paintings and bronze statuettes, it celebrates Francesco's interest in the natural sciences and alchemy, and is a masterpiece of Florentine Mannerist decoration, on a much smaller scale than the Salone dei Cinquecento and hence much easier to appreciate.

The present entrance from the Salone was opened later and unfortunately it can now only be seen from the doorway. The original entrance from the private rooms of the dukes is used in one of the *percorsi segreti* of the palace (*see p. 84*) when the interior of the Studiolo is shown to the public.

The lower row of paintings conceal cupboards in which Francesco kept his treasures. On the barrel vault, by Il Poppi, are allegories of the four elements and portraits by Bronzino of Francesco's parents, Cosimo I and Eleonora di Toledo. The four walls each symbolize one of the four elements with paintings and bronzes by the leading artists of the day (including Vincenzo Danti, Santi di Tito, Alessandro Allori, Giambologna, and Bartolomeo Ammannati).

(4) **Sala di Leone X:** This is the first of a suite of well preserved rooms known as the Quartiere di Leone X. They were decorated by Vasari and assistants (including Giovanni Stradano) in 1555–62 for Cosimo I, to illustrate the political history of the Medici family. Only this first room, the Sala di Leone X, is regularly open to the public; the others are used as mayoral offices. The paintings on the walls and ceiling illustrate the life of Cardinal Giovanni de' Medici, son of Lorenzo the Magnificent and later Pope Leo X. The red-and-white terracotta pavement survives, as well as the fireplace designed by Ammannati.

Second Floor

Stairs decorated with pretty grotesques lead up to the second floor, past an interesting fresco (c. 1558) by Giovanni Stradano of the fireworks in Piazza della Signoria celebrating the festival of St John the Baptist (*see p. 363*). At the top of the stairs on the left are the Quartiere degli Elementi, where the walls and ceilings are decorated with complicated allegories of the elements and classical divinities, again intended as a glorification of the Medici, and also by Vasari and assistants. Some of the ceilings are finely carved and the red-and-white terracotta floors survive. There are also a few 17th-century cabinets decorated with tortoiseshell and *pietre dure*.

(5) Sala degli Elementi: From this room, which illustrates the four elements, there is a good view of the Forte di Belvedere on the skyline and the top of the tribune above the Uffizi building.

(6) Scrittoio di Calliope: This is where Cosimo kept his precious treasures including miniatures, coins and statuettes. It has a charming ceiling painting of Calliope by Vasari. The late-16th-century stained-glass window by Walter of Antwerp is the only one of this date to survive in the palace.

(7) Terrazza di Giunone: This little space was formerly open on three sides and surrounded by a hanging garden, but it was enclosed in the 19th century. This is where Verrocchio's *Putto with a Dolphin* is displayed, the original removed from the courtyard below. Beyond, a little room with *grottesche* decorations has a view of Santa Croce and the hill of San Miniato.

(8) Terrazza di Saturno: This room was sadly reduced in size in the 19th century. Beyond the delicately carved eaves, the fine view of Florence includes (on the extreme right) the Corridoio Vasariano running from Palazzo Vecchio to the Uffizi, and beneath it can be seen the side of the Loggia della Signoria; farther left is the back of the Uffizi building with the lantern of the Tribuna, the Kaffeehaus in the trees of the Boboli Gardens, Forte di Belvedere on the skyline, and on the extreme left San Miniato and the façade and campanile of Santa Croce.

(9) Cappella di Eleonora: Returning through the Sala degli Elementi you come to a balcony which leads across the end of the Sala dei Cinquecento, providing a splendid view of the huge hall. The following rooms form part of the Quartiere di Eleonora di Toledo, the apartments of the wife of Cosimo I. The chapel was decorated by Bronzino in 1540–45, and is one of his most important and original works. On the vault, divided by festoons, are *St Francis Receiving the Stigmata*, *St Jerome*, *St John the Evangelist on Patmos*, and *St Michael the Archangel*. On the walls are episodes from the *life of Moses*, which may have a symbolic reference to Cosimo I. The original altarpiece of the *Lamentation* by Bronzino was sent by Cosimo to France, so the artist was asked to replace it with the present replica.

(10) The Sala di Ester: This and the rooms adjoining it were decorated by

PALAZZO VECCHIO
(SECOND FLOOR)

Stairs from 1st floor

5   Sala degli Elementi
6   Scrittoio di Calliope
7   Terrazza di Giunone
8   Terrazza di Saturno
9   Cappella di Eleonora
10 Sala di Ester
11 Sala di Gualdrada
12 Cappella della Signoria
13 Sala d'Udienza
14 Sala dei Gigli
15 Cancelleria
16 Sala dei Carte Geografiche
17 See 'Percorsi Segreti', p. 84

Stairs back to 1st floor

Vasari and assistants at the same time as the other suites of rooms. The Sala di Ester has a pretty frieze of putti intertwined in the letters of the name of Eleonora. A painting of 1557 shows the lost fragment of the *Battle of Anghiari* by Leonardo (*see p. 76*), probably the best copy that has survived.

(11) Sala di Gualdrada: The frieze at the top of the wall shows charming views of festivals in Florence, and a cabinet in *pietre dure* and mother of pearl with mythological scenes.

The passage running from this room leads to the older rooms of the palace, and has remains of the old 14th-century polychrome ceiling and parts of the ancient tower. It contains a copy of the death mask of Dante.

(12) Cappella della Signoria (or dei Priori; 1511–14): A chapel decorated by Ridolfo del Ghirlandaio, including an

Annunciation with a view of the church of Santissima Annunziata in the background (before the addition of the portico).

(13) Sala d'Udienza: Audience chamber with a superb gilded 15th-century ceiling by Giuliano da Maiano and assistants. The huge mural paintings illustrate stories from the life of the Roman hero Marco Camillus and were added c. 1545–48 by Francesco Salviati; they are one of the major works by this typically Mannerist painter. From the windows can be seen Orsanmichele, the Campanile and the Duomo, and the two towers of the Badia Fiorentina and the Bargello. Above the door from the chapel, designed by Baccio d'Agnolo, is a dedication to Christ (1529). The other doorway, crowned by a statue of *Justice*, is by Benedetto and Giuliano da Maiano. The intarsia doors, with figures of Dante and Petrarch, are also by Giuliano.

(14) Sala dei Gigli: This room takes its name from the fleurs-de-lys of the French house of Anjou—the golden lilies on a blue ground painted in 1490 on the walls, and the carved lilies on the magnificent coffered ceiling. The other face of the doorway has a statue of the *Young St John the Baptist* and putti by Benedetto and Giuliano da Maiano. The well preserved fresco by Giuliano's friend Domenico Ghirlandaio dates from 1482 and was to have been part of a series commissioned for this room but never carried out. A celebration of the Florentine Republic, it shows Florence's patron saint Zenobius enthroned between Saints Stephen and Lawrence, in an open loggia behind which there is

a glimpse of the Duomo. The two lions of Florence hold the flags of the '*popolo*' and the '*comune*' (the fresco was damaged in the late 16th century when the marble doorway was constructed). Above is a painted relief sculpture of the *Madonna and Child* with two angels on a 'mosaic' ground. The two other lunettes show six heroes of ancient Rome.

Here, since its restoration, is displayed Donatello's bronze *Judith and Holofernes*, removed from Piazza della Signoria. One of his last and most sophisticated works (c. 1455), it was commissioned by the Medici and used as a fountain (the holes for the water can be seen in the cushion) in the garden of their palace. On their expulsion from the city in 1495, it was expropriated by the government and placed under the Loggia della Signoria with an inscription warning against tyrants. From the windows there is a superb view of the cupola and campanile of the Duomo as well as the towers of the Badia Fiorentina and the Bargello.

(15) Cancelleria: A window of the old palace serves as a doorway into this chamber, built in 1511 and used as an office by Niccolò Machiavelli during his term as government secretary (*see p.* 83). He is commemorated here with a fine bust (16th century) and a painting by Santi di Tito. Also preserved here is the stone bas-relief of *St George and the Dragon* (c. 1260) which used to decorate Porta San Giorgio, an old gate in the walls of Florence.

(16) Sala delle Carte Geografiche: This was decorated in 1563–65 with a fine ceiling and wooden cupboards, on the presses of which 57 maps illustrated the then-known world with a remarkable degree of accuracy. Of great scientific and historical interest, they were painted by Fra' Egnazio Danti for Cosimo I and completed by Stefano Bonsignori (1585) for Francesco I. The map on the left of the entrance shows the British Isles. The huge globe in the centre was also designed by Danti.

THE MEDICI AT PALAZZO VECCHIO

Cosimo I (duke 1537–70; grand duke 1570–74)

Cosimo became duke in 1537, following the murder of his cousin Alessandro. Even though both pope and emperor had combined forces to see the Medici reinstated seven years before, Cosimo managed to keep the Tuscan state free from any more outside interference during his long reign, and brought the subject cities of Tuscany firmly under Florentine rule. In 1540 he left the Medici palace and moved into Palazzo della Signoria to assert his position publicly as leader of the government. Cosimo was, all in all, an enlightened despot who commissioned works of art and architecture to embellish Florence as well as to glorify his own name. Various suites of rooms in the palace were decorated by Vasari, culminating in the 1560s with the decoration of the huge Salone dei Cinquecento which celebrates the rule of Cosimo through elaborate allegories. In 1549 Cosimo's wife, Eleonora di Toledo, used part of her immense fortune to buy the even grander Palazzo Pitti, which became the official seat of the Medici dynasty.

Francesco I (grand duke 1574–87)

Francesco was an introvert and a chemist and alchemist, little interested in affairs of state. He had an unhappy, loveless first marriage to Joanna of Austria, and conducted a long liaison with Bianca Cappello, a beautiful Venetian girl who had fled to Florence with her husband at the age of 15. Medici protection saved her from her family's ireful revenge. When Joanna died, in 1578, Francesco married Bianca scarcely two months later.

Francesco made much use of the Mannerist architect Bernardo Buontalenti (who earned the sobriquet 'delle Girandole' from the whirling pyrotechnics he created for his patrons' masques), and commissioned a number of works from Giambologna including the famous *Rape of the Sabines* in the Loggia della Signoria. He also built two of the most beautiful small rooms in Florence, the Tribuna in the Uffizi and the Studiolo in Palazzo Vecchio. It was Francesco who invented the idea of making mosaics out of *pietre dure*, so founding a craft which was successfully practised for centuries in Florence. But perhaps his greatest achievement was to assemble all the family pictures and antiquities in the Uffizi, thus inaugurating the idea of keeping together the Medici treasures in an art gallery in the city. He died without male heirs and was succeeded by his brother Ferdinando.

NICCOLÒ MACHIAVELLI

Niccolò Machiavelli (1469–1527) is famous as the author of *The Prince*, probably the most celebrated treatise on governance and statecraft ever written. The
son of a Tuscan lawyer, he first came to prominence during the republican period of 1494–1512, when his talents were spotted by the ruling magistrate (*gonfaloniere*) Piero Soderini, who took charge of the republic's affairs after the execution of Savonarola. Soderini made Machiavelli secretary of the Council of Ten,
and used him for diplomatic missions, relying greatly on his reports. He was also
influenced by Machiavelli's ideas on how the republic should be administrated
and defended. Machiavelli proposed doing away with the *condottiere* system,
which had shown itself to be costly and ineffective (for *condottieri* too often
placed their own interests above those of the states they served) and introduc-
ing a Florentine militia. When Pope Julius II called upon the states of Italy to
help him drive out the French, Soderini—who, advised by Machiavelli, had
always steered a pro-French course—demurred. Enraged, the pope's Holy
League sent an army marching on Florence, intent on restoring the Medici, who
would institute a regime more amenable to the pope's demands. Soderini
resigned, and went into exile. Machiavelli was removed from office, and the
Medici were restored. A few months later Machiavelli was arrested on conspiracy charges. Certainly innocent, he was subsequently released, and retired to the
country to write. He completed *The Prince* in 1514, drawing on the turbulent
political experiences of his own lifetime to paint a portrait of how strong and
lasting government should be achieved. He also produced numerous historical
studies, and some plays, the best known of which is *La Mandragola*, which was
performed for Pope Leo X (Giovanni de' Medici) in 1519. Though the Medici
never restored Machiavelli to public office, Giulio de' Medici (later Pope
Clement VII) did commission him to write a history of Florence. Machiavelli
died, leaving a wife and six children in near poverty, in 1527.

Collezione Loeser and Sala dei Dugento

Stairs lead down from outside the Sala dei Gigli towards the exit, passing a mezzanine
floor in which four rooms display the Collezione Loeser, left to the city in 1928 by the
distinguished American connoisseur and collector, Charles Loeser, who came to live in
Florence in 1907. The masterpiece of the collection is the *Portrait of Laura Battiferri*, wife
of Bartolomeo Ammannati, one of Bronzino's most sophisticated portraits. Other works
of art include a *Portrait of Ludovico Martelli* attributed to Pontormo, a Crucifix dating
from 1290, a *Madonna and Child* by Pietro Lorenzetti, a tondo of the *Madonna and Child
with the Young St John* by Alonso Berruguete, and the *Passion of Christ*, a very unusual
painting by Piero di Cosimo. The sculptures include a marble angel by Tino da Camaino
(from the Bishop Orso monument in the Duomo), two statuettes of angels by Jacopo

Sansovino, a head of Cosimo I by Vincenzo de' Rossi, a bronze statuette of Autumn by Benvenuto Cellini, a small bronze *Hercules and the Hydra* by Giambologna, a bronze horse, and two battle scenes in terracotta by Gianfrancesco Rustici.

The stairs continue down to a vestibule (the coved ceiling of which has painted grotesque decorations) outside the Sala dei Dugento (*usually closed to the public; no 5 on the plan on p. 77*), where the town council meets. The name is derived from the council of 200 citizens who used to meet here. The room was reconstructed in 1472–77 by Benedetto and Giuliano da Maiano, who also executed the magnificent wood ceiling.

The 'Percorsi Segreti'
To take one of the guided 'secret itineraries' of the palazzo, it is best to book in advance.
The first itinerary follows the staircase known as the Scala del Duca d'Atene, built in 1342 by Walter de Brienne—known as the Duke of Athens—who held absolute power in the city for one year before his expulsion by popular uprising. The entrance is through the small door beside the entrance to the palace in Via della Ninna, and in the first little room the original wall of the back of Arnolfo's building can be seen. The secret staircase, partly spiral, built inside the later wall leads up to the first floor into a room which was later part of Cosimo I's private apartment.

Visitors on the second itinerary are taken into the Studiolo (*see p. 78*) through its original entrance, and up the small staircase to the Tesoretto, the richly decorated tiny private study of Cosimo I, preserved intact from 1562 with stuccoes, vault frescoes, a marble and *pietra serena* floor, and the original cupboards which used to house Cosimo's treasures.

Another itinerary includes a room (*marked 17 on the plan on p. 80*) which contains a sculpted relief showing Palazzo Vecchio and a detached 14th-century fresco illustrating the expulsion of the Duke of Athens. From the balcony above the Salone dei Cinquecento a staircase leads up to the remarkable roof of the Salone, where the complicated system of rafters and beams can be seen which support both the roof and the paintings of the ceiling.

The Museo dei Ragazzi
The Children's Museum (*booking advisable*) is a project which uses parts of the palace not otherwise open to the public to illustrate certain historical periods, or to explain architectural principles or scientific theories to teenage children. It includes a laboratory in which children can experiment with models which explain the rules of perspective, in a room at the top of the palace with very fine views of the Duomo. There is also a laboratory where fresco technique is explained. Another part of the museum includes a theatre workshop where representations of the Medici court of Cosimo I and Eleonora di Toledo are held and children can dress up in costumes of the period. There is a theatre workshop on the mezzanine floor, and on the ground floor, off the entrance courtyard, in the Sala di Bia e Garzia, named after two of the children of Cosimo and Eleonora, there are games for younger children (aged 3–6).

GALLERIA DEGLI UFFIZI

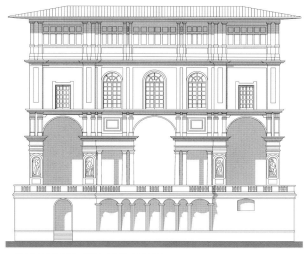

PALAZZO DEGLI UFFIZI: ARNO FAÇADE

Open Tues–Sat 8.30–6.50; summer 8.30–9; T: 055 238 8651. Booking service (T: 055 294 883, Mon–Fri 8.30–6.30; Sat 9–12), highly recommended to avoid the infamous queue. You pick up your ticket five or ten minutes before the booked time (and pay an extra booking fee). Reductions for EU students between 18 and 25. The Corridoio Vasariano (ticket includes entrance to the Uffizi and Boboli Gardens) and Collezione Contini-Bonacossi (free) by appointment only; T: 055 265 4321.

The massive Palazzo degli Uffizi extends from Piazza della Signoria to the Arno. Houses were demolished to create this long, narrow site next to Palazzo Vecchio, and Vasari was commissioned by Cosimo I to erect a building here to serve as government offices (*uffici*, hence 'uffizi'). The unusual U-shaped building with a short façade on the river front was begun in 1560 and completed, according to Vasari's design, after his death in 1574 by Alfonso Parigi the Elder and Bernardo Buontalenti (who also made provision for an art gallery here for Francesco I). Resting on unstable sandy ground, it is a feat of engineering skill. The use of iron to reinforce the building permitted extraordinary technical solutions during its construction, and allowed for the remarkably large number of apertures. A long arcade supports three upper storeys pierced by numerous windows and a loggia in *pietra serena*. In the niches of the pilasters are statues of illustrious Tuscans made in 1842–56 by the leading sculptors of the day, including Lorenzo Bartolini, Giovanni Dupré and Pio Fedi. The building now houses the famous Galleria degli Uffizi, the most important collection of paintings in Italy and one of the great art collections of the world.

History of the Uffizi Collection

The origins of the collection go back to the Medici grand duke Cosimo I, and the galleries were enlarged and the collection augmented by his son Francesco I. The Medici dynasty continued to add numerous works of art in the following centuries: Ferdinando I transferred sculptures here from the Villa Medici in Rome; Ferdinando II, who married Vittoria della Rovere, inherited paintings by Raphael, Titian and Piero della Francesca from Francesco Maria della Rovere of Urbino; and Cardinal Leopoldo began the collection of drawings and self-portraits. The last of the Medici, Anna Maria Luisa (d. 1743), widow of the Elector Palatine, settled her inheritance on the people of Florence through a family pact (1737). The huge collection was partly broken up during the 19th century when much of the sculpture went to the Bargello and other material was transferred to the Museo Archeologico. In the 20th century many paintings removed from Florentine churches found a home in the gallery, which was partly redesigned for them in the 1950s by the well-known Tuscan architect Giovanni Michelucci and the Venetian architect Carlo Scarpa, who redesigned a number of important museums in Italy.

Since the Archivio di Stato was moved from the building in 1989, plans have been underway to expand the gallery in stages. The rooms on the third floor will probably remain more or less as they are, while in 2004 the *piano nobile* was partially opened to display works by Caravaggio and his school and provide a route to the new exit from the gallery at the back of the building in Piazza de' Castellani (where a huge projecting roof designed by the Japanese architect Arata Isozaki, already criticized for its gigantic proportions, is also planned). Alterations are expected to take until at least 2006, when the exhibition space will be more than doubled and about 3,000 paintings will be displayed (instead of the present 1,000). At the same time, it will be possible to house 1,500 visitors simultaneously (over twice the number at present permitted).

In 1993, the gallery was damaged by a bomb placed in a car (by the Mafia) in Via Lambertesca, which killed five people and injured 29. There was severe structural damage to the first part of the Corridoio Vasariano and the rooms off the west corridor. About 90 works of art were damaged, but they have been (or are being) carefully restored, including three paintings (two by Bartolomeo Manfredi and one by Gherardo delle Notti) which were almost totally destroyed.

Planning your Visit

The gallery tends to be extremely crowded with tour groups, but is usually more peaceful in the early morning, over lunchtime and in the late afternoon. Automatic signals on the ground floor provide information about expected waiting time if there is a queue (a maximum of 660 people are allowed into the gallery at any one time). It is too much to try to see the entire collection in one day; the first rooms (up to Room 15) include the major works of the Florentine Renaissance; the later rooms can be combined in a second visit.

The collection is arranged chronologically by schools. The following description includes only some of the most important paintings and sculptures (the most important artists or works are given in bold). Many of the paintings have superb contemporary frames. The labelling of the works is kept to a minimum, and the lighting is very poor in the earlier rooms. Round red labels indicate the date a work was restored.

The Gallery

Ground Floor

A series of large rooms, once occupied by law courts and then by the state archives, now house ticket offices (separate one for pre-booked visits), a large specialised bookshop, and cloakrooms. Tickets are shown at the foot of the grand staircase, just beyond which there are lifts, officially reserved for the staff, but which can usually be used on request if you are on your own.

The staircase, lined with antique busts and statues, leads up past part of the huge theatre built into the building by Buontalenti for Francesco I in 1586–89. Over the central door is a bust of the grand duke attributed to Giambologna. On the left the old entrance now serves as the entrance to the Prints and Drawings Room (*open to scholars with special permission, 9–1*). The collection is one of the finest in the world and is particularly rich in Renaissance and Mannerist works. Exhibitions are held periodically.

Third Floor: East Corridor

At the top of the stairs are ten **busts of the Medici** from Lorenzo the Magnificent to the last grand duke, including one by Giambologna (Cosimo I) and two by Giovanni Battista Foggini. Tickets are checked in the vestibule, which contains antique sculpture including a statue of Augustus and two dogs—well-preserved Greek works.

Beyond is the east corridor of the long U-shaped gallery with its vault painted with grotesques in 1581 by Alessandro Allori. Although the splendid tapestries which used to hang on the walls have been removed for conservation reasons, the corridor is arranged with portraits and antique sculpture (all of them well labelled with diagrams) more or less as it was in the 16th century. At the top of the walls is a series of **portraits of famous men**, commissioned by the Medici in 1552–89 from the otherwise little known Cristofano dell'Altissimo. They are copies of a series of portraits which had been collected by the historian Paolo Giovio, who died in 1552. At intervals between them are hung portraits of members of the Medici dynasty in the 15th and 16th centuries, beginning at the short north end of the corridor with a portrait of Giovanni di Bicci de' Medici, founder of the dynasty, by Alessandro Allori. Both series of paintings are continued right round the walls of all three corridors.

The superb collection of **antique sculptures** (mostly Hellenistic works dating from around 325–31 BC) collected by Cosimo I and augmented by his sons Francesco and Ferdinando, was first arranged in this corridor (and provided with an inventory) in 1595–97. The statue of *Hercules and a Centaur*, which has been at the end of the first corridor since that time, is a Roman copy of a Hellenistic original, but with numerous restorations: the Hercules was restored in 1579 (only the feet are original), and the tail, head and upper part of the torso of the centaur were remade by Giovanni Battista

Caccini ten years later. The portrait busts include one known (erroneously) as *Augustus* and one of Agrippa (the heads are original, but the busts are probably by Caccini), considered the founders of Rome; these were given to Lorenzo the Magnificent in Rome by Pope Sixtus IV and bought back to Florence to decorate Palazzo Medici.

On the window wall, the statue of the so-called *Mercury* or *Hermes* was formerly in the Cortile del Belvedere in the Vatican and was moved to Florence in 1536, when it was displayed in the Sala delle Nicchie in Palazzo Pitti. The hat, arms and base are all restorations, and it in fact represents a young man or satyr (and is a replica of a work by the famous Greek sculptor Praxiteles).

The Rooms off the East Corridor

Room 1: The **antique Roman sculptures** here clearly influenced Florentine Renaissance sculptors and include a circular altar with reliefs showing the *Sacrifice of Iphigenia* (late 2nd century BC), a basalt torso, a Roman copy of a bronze statue by Polyclitus, and a marble torso, which is an original Greek work dating from the 2nd century BC.

Room 2: This provides a fitting introduction to the painting galleries illustrating Tuscan painting of the 13th century. Three huge paintings of the *Madonna Enthroned* (known as the *Maestà*) dominate the room. On the right, the *Madonna in Maestà* by **Cimabue** (c. 1285), painted for the church of Santa Trìnita, marks a final development of the Byzantine style of painting, where a decorative sense still predominates. On the left is another exquisite version of this subject, the *Rucellai Madonna* by **Duccio di Buoninsegna**, commissioned by the Laudesi confraternity in 1285 for their chapel in Santa Maria Novella. Between the 17th and 18th centuries it was put in the Rucellai Chapel (hence the name) in the same church, and has been housed in the Uffizi since 1948. It was painted on five planks of poplar wood 4.5m high

and c. 60–65cm wide. Since the wood was unseasoned, huge cracks formed, but the painting was beautifully restored in 1990 when the splendid blue mantle of the Virgin was discovered beneath a layer of over-painting from the 17th century. The frame, with painted roundels, is original. The painting was traditionally attributed to Cimabue, but is now recognized as the work of the younger Sienese artist Duccio, who is known to have worked in Cimabue's studio.

The *Madonna in Maestà* by **Giotto**, painted some 25 years later for the church of Ognissanti, has a sense of realism which had never been achieved in medieval painting or by Giotto's master Cimabue. The figure of the Madonna has acquired a new monumentality, and she is set in a more clearly defined space. This is considered one of the masterpieces of a painter whose work heralded a new era in Western painting. Giotto also painted the polyptych which is displayed here of the *Madonna and Four Saints* for the Badia Fiorentina.

Room 3: This room displays 14th-century **Sienese painting**, which flourished at this period under the influence of Duccio. His greatest follower was

Simone Martini whose charming *Annunciation* (1333) dominates the room. The Gothic elegance of the Madonna and annunciatory angel set against a rich gold ground makes this one of the masterpieces of 14th-century Tuscan painting, and one of the most memorable paintings in the gallery. It is the only major work by Simone in Florence (painted for the Duomo of Siena, it was moved here by the Tuscan grand duke in 1799). It is signed by Simone and his brother-in-law Lippo Memmi, who may have painted the lateral saints. The neo-Gothic frame was added in 1900. The small *Madonna and Child* exhibited on the same wall, by Andrea Vanni, clearly shows the influence of Simone.

The brothers **Pietro and Ambrogio Lorenzetti**, also important protagonists of the Sienese school, are represented here in a number of fine works: the *Presentation in the Temple* (1342), four *Scenes from the Life of St Nicholas*, and a triptych reassembled when the central panel was left to the Uffizi by Bernard Berenson in 1959, are all by Ambrogio, while the panels of a dossal with the story of the *Blessed Umiltà* and the *Madonna in Glory*, signed and dated 1340, are both by Pietro.

Room 4: Florentine painting of the 14th century. *Deposition* (from the church of San Remigio) attributed to Giottino, a painter otherwise little known, and who has affinities with Giotto's most gifted pupils Maso di Banco and Giovanni da Milano. Giovanni is represented here with panels of saints, martyrs and virgins. There are also works by **Bernardo Daddi** (including a triptych and a tiny portable altar), as well as **Orcagna**, and his brothers, Nardo and Jacopo di Cione, all of whom left numerous works in the city. The elegant *Dossal of Santa Cecilia*, by an unknown master who takes his name from this work, is another beautiful piece.

Rooms 5 and 6: These are in fact one room, and illustrate the **International Gothic** style. The monk known as **Lorenzo Monaco** is represented by two superb altarpieces: the large *Coronation of the Virgin* (1413) and the *Adoration of the Magi*. His wonderful colouring and graceful, elongated figures make him one of the greatest artists of this period. His focus is often on the depiction of the human figure leaving the landscape behind (as can be seen in the *Adoration of the Magi*, an abstraction of rocks and unreal buildings seemingly there to add yet more colour to the work). The central angel (playing the organ) in the *Coronation* was carefully painted in 1998 to cover a hole when the altarpiece was restored. The other important painter of this period was **Gentile da Fabriano**. He was born in the Marche but moved to Florence in 1420 at the invitation of Palla Strozzi, who commissioned the richly decorated *Adoration of the Magi* (at the other end of the room) in 1423, in which the horses' bridles and the brocaded costumes, as well as the crowns worn by the Kings, are highlighted in gold. This famous work has a charming, fairy-tale quality and numerous delightful details, including the animals and the servant bending down to take off one of the king's spurs, and the two graceful serving ladies behind the Madonna

GALLERIA DEGLI UFFIZI

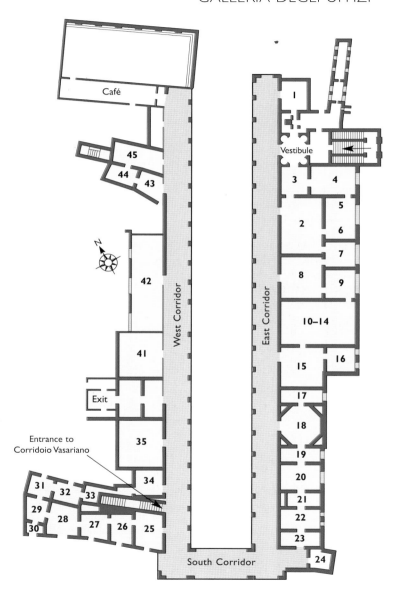

Café

45
44
43

42

41

Exit

35

Entrance to
Corridoio Vasariano

34

31
32
33
29
30
28
27
26
25

West Corridor

East Corridor

South Corridor

Vestibule

1

3   4
5
2   6
7
8   9

10–14

16
15

17
18
19
20
21
22
23
24

examining one of the Kings' gifts. The predella is also exquisitely painted, with a beautiful scene set in a grove of orange trees showing the *Flight into Egypt*. Gentile also painted the *Mary Magdalen, St Nicholas of Bari, St John and St George* in 1425 (formerly part of a polyptych), all of them sumptuously dressed and standing on a decorated pavement.

The window in this room affords a good view of the top of Santa Croce and the hill of San Miniato.

Room 7: Early 15th-century paintings representing the **early Renaissance**. The *Battle of San Romano* is an amusing exercise in perspective by **Paolo Uccello**. Together with its companions, now in the Louvre and the National Gallery, London, it decorated Lorenzo the Magnificent's bedroom in Palazzo Medici-Riccardi in 1492. It celebrates the battle in which the Florentines were victorious over the Sienese. The most important elements in the painting are the horses and lances. By the window is the famous diptych by **Piero della Francesca**, with the portraits of Federico da Montefeltro and his duchess, Battista Sforza, in profile against a superb detailed landscape in a transparent light stretching into the far distance. On the reverse are their allegorical triumphs in a rarefied atmosphere with another wonderful landscape. These exquisite works, profoundly humanist in spirit, were painted in Urbino c. 1465 in celebration of this famous Renaissance prince, always depicted in profile since he lost his right eye in a tournament.

The *Madonna Enthroned with Saints Francis, John the Baptist, Zenobius and Lucy* by **Domenico Veneziano** is one of the few known works by this artist, who was born in Venice but moved to Florence where he lived until his death in 1461. It is painted in beautiful soft colours in a Renaissance setting, and is one of the loveliest altarpieces of this familiar subject in Florence (the figure of St Lucy recalls the style of Piero della Francesca, who was Domenico's pupil). The *Madonna and Child with St Anne* was painted by **Masolino**, but Masaccio is thought to have added the Madonna and Child to his master's painting, which has, however, been otherwise completely repainted. The tiny painting of the *Madonna and Child* (with the Madonna tickling the Child's chin) is an undocumented work attributed to Masaccio. Also here are two works by **Fra' Angelico**, including a lovely *Coronation of the Virgin*.

Room 8: This contains paintings by **Filippo Lippi** and his son Filippino. The best works here by Filippo Lippi are perhaps the predella of the *Barbadori Altarpiece* (the rest of the altarpiece is now in the Louvre), which has a remarkable sense of space, and the *Madonna and Child with Two Angels* (c. 1465), with a particularly beautiful Madonna, justly one of his most famous works. There are also two paintings of the *Adoration of the Child*, a crowded *Coronation of the Virgin*, and a *Madonna Enthroned with Saints* by him. **Filippino Lippi** is represented by a lovely *Adoration of the Child* and two large altarpieces (*Madonna and Saints* painted for the Sala degli Otto in Palazzo Vecchio, and the *Adoration of the Magi*). Another *Madonna and Child with Saints* and an *Annunciation* are by Alesso Baldovinetti.

In the corridor outside, on the window wall, is a statue of a dancing girl, formerly identified as Pomona, the Roman goddess of tree-fruits, now thought to be an allegory of Autumn (the head is a restoration). Five other similar statues are known and it is possible that one of them could have influenced Botticelli when he painted the figure of Flora in his *Primavera*.

Room 9: The altarpiece of *Saints Vincent, James and Eustace* by **Antonio Pollaiolo** is one of his best works. The three saints, full of character, are splendidly dressed with rich costumes and stand on a terrace behind which can be glimpsed an open landscape. It was painted for the Chapel of the Cardinal of Portugal in the church of San Miniato, where it has been replaced by a copy. Antonio is also thought to have painted the famous *Portrait of a Lady in Profile*, a charming girl in Renaissance dress. The *Portrait of Galeazzo Maria Sforza* is now usually attributed to his younger brother Piero. The seven paintings of the theological and cardinal virtues are also by the Pollaiolo brothers except for *Fortitude*, which is an early work by Botticelli. In the case are four exquisite small panels, two of them by Antonio Pollaiolo showing the *Labours of Hercules*, and two by **Botticelli** illustrating *Judith Returning from the Camp of Holofernes* and the *Discovery of the Decapitated Holofernes in his Tent* (c. 1470). These last two are among the most exquisite works in the gallery. The very fine portrait of a *Young Man in a Red Hat* is by an unknown artist (usually attributed to Filippino Lippi).

Rooms 10–14: These rooms have been converted into one huge space and the rafters of the stage of the old Medici theatre (*see p. 87*) exposed. This is now home to **Botticelli's masterpieces**, which include both religious and mythological subjects. The *Primavera* is one of his most important and most famous pictures. It was painted probably c. 1478 for Lorenzo di Pierfrancesco de' Medici, Lorenzo the Magnificent's younger cousin. An allegory of Spring, which was the season which began the year in 15th-century Florence, it is thought to have been inspired by a work of Poliziano, although its precise significance is still debated. There is a rhythmical contact between the figures, who are placed in a meadow of flowers within a dark orange grove, the Garden of Hesperides of classical myth. To the right, Zephyr chases Flora and transforms her into Spring, who is shown bedecked with flowers. In the centre Venus stands with Cupid above her, and beyond the beautiful group of the Three Graces united in dance, is the figure of Mercury (perhaps an idealized portrait of Lorenzo the Magnificent). The work is richly painted on panels of poplar wood. The varnishes which had been added in various restorations were removed in 1982, and the painting was cleaned to restore its original appearance. The botanical details which were revealed include a variety of spring flowers, most of which can still be seen today growing in Lorenzo di Pierfrancesco's Villa of Castello (*see p. 312*).

Sandro Botticelli: *Judith Returning from the Camp of Holofernes* (c. 1470).

SANDRO BOTTICELLI

Botticelli (1446–1510) was one of most important and most original painters of the Italian Renaissance, greatly admired in his lifetime. He fell into oblivion soon after his death, however, and was only 'rediscovered' by the Anglo-American community living in Florence at the end of the 19th and beginning of the 20th centuries. John Ruskin, Walter Pater, Dante Gabriel Rossetti, Herbert Percy Horne and Ezra Pound all wrote about him with great enthusiasm. In 1870, Walter Pater noted that 'the peculiar character of Botticelli is the result of a blending in him of a sympathy for humanity in its uncertain condition, its attractiveness, its investiture at rarer moments in a character of loveliness and energy, with his consciousness of the shadow upon it of the great things from which it shrinks, and that this conveys into his work somewhat more than painting usually attains of the true complexion of humanity'. In 1881, Dante Gabriel Rossetti wrote a poem entitled 'Spring by Sandro Botticelli':

> ... the Graces circling near,
> Neath bower-linked arch of white arms glorified:
> And with those feathered feet which hovering glide
> O'er Spring's brief bloom, Hermes the harbinger.

The *Birth of Venus* is perhaps the most famous of all Botticelli's works. It was probably also painted for Lorenzo di Pierfrancesco and hung in the Medici villa of Castello. The pagan subject is taken from a poem by Poliziano and illustrates Zephyr and Chloris blowing Venus ashore while Hora, her fluttering dress decorated with cornflowers and daisies, hurries to cover her nakedness. The elegant figures are painted with a remarkable lightness of touch in a decorative linear design. The classical nude figure of Venus balances on the edge of a beautiful scallop shell as it floats ashore. A strong wind blows through this harmonious Graeco-Roman world.

The splendid religious works by Botticelli in the room include two *tondi* of the Madonna (the *Madonna of the Magnificat* and the *Madonna of the Pomegranate*), the *Madonna of the Rose Garden* and the *Madonna of the Loggia*. Of the three fine altarpieces painted for Florentine churches, the *Madonna and Saints* from Sant'Ambrogio is the earliest and is particularly lovely, with a beautiful *Mary Magdalen*. The *Coronation of the Virgin* (from San Marco), which has recently been restored, has a charming circle of angels in the sky and a delightful predella. The late *Annunciation* shows an extraordinary spiritual bond between the two figures. The relatively small *Adoration of the Magi* has an unusual setting but the Holy Family is relegated to the back of the painting and the interest lies above all in the portraits of the Medici courtiers who are depicted as the Kings and their entourage. Giuliano de'

Medici (or possibly Lorenzo the Magnificent), lost in thought, is dressed in black and red on the right and Botticelli himself is shown in a self-portrait (dressed in a yellow cloak) on the extreme right. The standing figure by the horse's head on the left may be Lorenzo the Magnificent next to the poets Poliziano and Pico della Mirandola (who were with Lorenzo on his deathbed). The kneeling 'Magus' in black represents Cosimo il Vecchio, and the one dressed in red, his son Piero il Gottoso.

Botticelli's skill as a portrait painter is also shown in the *Portrait of a Man in a Red Hat*, a very fine and well restored painting of an unknown sitter who is holding a medal of Cosimo il Vecchio. The subject of the small, elaborate painting entitled *Calumny* (painted after 1487) is taken from the ancient Greek writer Lucian's account of a picture by Apelles described in Alberti's treatise on painting. The *Pallas and the Centaur* was probably intended as a moral or political allegory, the significance of which has been much discussed. Pallas, whose clothes are decorated with Lorenzo's emblem, is shown taming the centaur, and it may be that Pallas represents Florence or Lorenzo the Magnificent, and the centaur—half-man and half-beast—represents disorder and barbarism. Another interpretation is that Pallas symbolises Humility or Prudence, restraining Pride. The tiny painting of *St Augustine in his Cell* is one of a number of pictures Botticelli painted of this saint. Here he is shown busy writing, with discarded sheets of paper littering the floor at his feet.

The huge triptych of the *Adoration of the Shepherds* was commissioned by the Medici agent in Bruges, Tommaso Portinari from **Hugo van der Goes**. It was shipped back to Florence in 1475 for his family chapel in Sant'Egidio. On the wings are saints and members of the Portinari family. It includes exquisitely painted details such as the still life in the foreground showing two vases of flowers and a sheaf of wheat, and the charming portraits of the two Portinari boys. The painting had an important influence on contemporary Florentine artists.

Also in this room are three good works by Michelangelo's master **Domenico Ghirlandaio**: two beautiful altarpieces of the *Madonna Enthroned with Saints*, one with a lovely vase of flowers on a carpet, four delightful angels and orange trees behind the balustrade, and a tondo of the *Adoration of the Magi* with a pretty landscape (1487).

Room 15: Here are displayed the early Florentine works of **Leonardo da Vinci** and the paintings of his master, Verrocchio. Leonardo da Vinci's *Adoration of the Magi* (1481) is a huge, crowded composition, remarkable for its figure studies and unusual iconography. The painting was left unfinished when Leonardo left Florence for Milan; it remains in its preparatory stage of chiaroscuro drawn in a red earth pigment. His *Annunciation* was painted in Verrocchio's studio. The extent of the master's intervention is unclear: it is thought that he was probably responsible for the design, for the figure of the Madonna and for the classical sarcophagus. **Verrocchio**'s *Baptism of Christ* was begun c. 1470. According to Vasari, the angel on the left was painted by the young Leonardo.

Leonardo da Vinci: *Adoration of the Magi* (1481).

The *Crucifix* by **Luca Signorelli** is one of his most remarkable paintings: Mary Magdalen is shown at the foot of the Cross with a dramatic, strong, dark figure of Christ; while in the background scenes of the Crucifixion are set in a desolate landscape against a light ground. The botanical details are also exquisitely painted. The *Trinity with the Madonna and Saints* is also by Signorelli. There are also four works by the Umbrian painter **Perugino**: *Madonna with Saints Sebastian and John* (the figure of St Sebastian is particularly beautiful),

Pietà, Crucifix with Saints and *Christ in the Garden*.

Room 16: This room is the Sala delle Carte Geografiche and its walls are painted with **maps of Tuscany** by Stefano Bonsignori. A charming painting of the *Three Archangels* by Francesco Botticini is exhibited here, and some fine Roman sarcophagi.

In the corridor, by the entrance to the Tribuna (Room 18), is a male statue in Parian and rare black marble. Known as the *Ares Borghese*, it is a Roman copy of an Attic original, with restored arms and head).

Room 18: The beautiful octagonal **Tribuna**, inspired by classical models, was designed by Bernardo Buontalenti for Francesco I (1584) to display the most valuable objects in the Medici collection. It has a mother-of-pearl dome and a fine pavement in *pietre dure*. It formerly had only one entrance, from the corridor. Now, unfortunately, you are obliged to visit it from a walkway, and so it is impossible to examine the works in the centre of the room. The octagonal table is a masterpiece of *pietre dure*, made in the Florence Opificio between 1633 and 1649 (to a design by Bernardino Poccetti and Jacopo Ligozzi). The magnificent cabinet in ebony and *pietre dure* belonged to Ferdinando II and dates from c. 1650. Since the 17th century, the room has contained the most important **classical sculptures** owned by the Medici, the most famous of which is the *Medici Venus* (*see box overleaf*) probably a Greek marble copy (made around the 1st century BC) of the *Aphrodite of Cnidos* by Praxiteles. The so-called *Arrotino* ('Knife-grinder') is now thought to represent a Scythian preparing to flay Marsyas, as part of a group of Apollo and Marsyas. It is the only surviving replica of an original by the school of Pergamon (3rd or 2nd century BC), and it was purchased by Cosimo I in 1558 on Vasari's advice. It is of extremely high quality (and has had very few restorations). The group of *Wrestlers* is a much-restored copy of a bronze original from the school of Pergamon, of which no other replicas are known (though only the two torsos are original). The moment of victory in the contest was signalled when the winner was able to place his knee on his opponent's back. The *Dancing Faun* is a beautifully restored work and the *Apollino* (Young Apollo) is derived from an Apollo by Praxiteles.

Around the walls are a remarkable series of distinguished court portraits, many of them of the family of Cosimo I commissioned from **Bronzino**. These include Cosimo himself, dressed in armour, and his wife Eleonora di Toledo with their son Giovanni, a very fine portrait which speaks eloquently of its period. There is another portrait of Giovanni as a very young child, and portraits of Cosimo's other son Francesco as a boy, and of his daughter Isabella, a vivacious and accomplished girl, strangled by her husband after he discovered her adultery. The two well-known idealized portraits of Cosimo's famous ancestors Lorenzo the Magnificent and Cosimo il Vecchio are by Vasari and Pontormo (who was Bronzino's master). Other splendid portraits here by Bronzino of unknown sitters include a *Portrait of a Man*, an intellectual typical of his time, and a portrait of a girl with a book. *Bartolomeo* and *Lucrezia Panciatichi* are also by this artist. The (framed) fresco of Bianca Cappello, the second wife of Francesco I, is by Alessandro Allori. Although the arrangement of the room has changed over the centuries, the paintings of a *Girl with a Book of Petrarch* by Andrea del Sarto, the *Madonna and Child with the Young St John* by Pontormo, and the *Young St John the Baptist in the Desert* by Raphael (and his *bottega*) have all hung here since 1589.

THE MEDICI VENUS

The Tribuna was for centuries the central attraction of the Uffizi, and most high-ly prized among all its treasures was the *Medici Venus*. It is one of six important classical statues which had been acquired by Cardinal Ferdinando de' Medici, and which were brought from the Villa Medici in Rome in 1677–80 by Cosimo III. It is signed by 'Cleomenes, son of Apollodorus', and was probably made in Rome in the first century BC. Whether it is a copy of a Greek original is uncer-tain. During the Grand Tour of Italy in the 18th century—when Florence was one of the principal destinations and classical works were much in vogue—the *Medici Venus* was renowned for her beauty, and was possibly the most famous work of art in Florence. Numerous travellers left records of their admiration, including Goethe in 1740 and Edward Gibbon in 1764. Queen Charlotte, wife of George III, commissioned Johan Zoffany to paint a conversation piece of the room in 1772. From this time on, no more replicas were allowed to be made of the statue since there were fears that it would be damaged. It was one of the greatest trophies seized by Napoleon and taken to Paris, but returned here in 1816 (in the interim it was 'replaced' by another statue of Venus, especially com-missioned by Napoleon from Canova, and which is now in the Galleria Palatina in Palazzo Pitti). In the early 19th century, Hazlitt, Leigh Hunt, Byron and Shelley all left enthusiastic descriptions of the statue. Byron writes of it in *Childe Harold* in ecstatic terms ('the veil of heaven is half undrawn').

In the later 19th century, however, the *Medici Venus* found her admirers falling away, and she was eclipsed by her rival, the *Venus de Milo* (discovered in 1820).

Room 17: The little Sala dell' Ermafrodito, decorated with small bronzes, is named after the statue of a sleeping hermaphrodite, a copy of a Greek original of the 2nd century BC.

Room 19: Rooms 19–23 have ceilings decorated with grotesques and views of Florence carried out in 1588. Room 19 contains four portraits by **Perugino**, among them a *Young Boy* and *Francesco delle Opere*, a Florentine artisan who was the brother of a friend of Perugino's. There are also are two beautiful *tondi* by **Luca Signorelli** of the *Madonna and Child*, one with allegorical figures in the background which clearly influenced Michelangelo. The portrait of Evangelista Scappi is by Francesco Francia and the half-length figure of St Sebastian by Lorenzo Costa. The *Crucifixion* by Marco Palmezzano shows the influence of Giovanni Bellini. *The Annunciation*, with a lovely landscape beyond the loggia, and the remarkable female nude *Venus* are both interesting works by Lorenzo di Credi. *Perseus Liberating Andromeda*, an unusual mythological scene, is by Piero di Cosimo.

Room 20: Works by German artists. **Dürer** painted the *Adoration of the Magi* in 1504 after a visit to Italy. The *Portrait of the Artist's Father* is Dürer's first known work, painted when he was 19. The two bearded heads of the Apostles St James and St Philip are also by him. **Lucas Cranach the Elder** is represented by two fine portraits of Martin Luther, whose Protestant cause he supported (the smaller one shows him with Filippo Melantone, and the other with his wife Katherina Bore). Cranach also painted the tiny *St George* and the two full-length figures of Adam and Eve (showing the influence of Dürer). The portrait of Cranach (formerly thought to be a self-portrait) was painted by his son, Lucas Cranach the Younger. There is also a fine *Portrait of a Boy* by the Netherlandish painter Joos van Cleve.

Room 21: The Venetian School. Paintings by **Giovanni Bellini** include a *Sacred Allegory* (removed for restoration), an exquisite painting of uncertain meaning, infused with an exalted humanist quality, and *Lamentation over the Dead Christ*, an unfinished painting left at the chiaroscuro stage. The other key painter of the Venetian Renaissance, **Giorgione**, is represented with the *Judgement of Solomon* and its companion piece the *Infant Moses Brought to Pharaoh*, showing the influence of Bellini. They are exhibited on either side of a splendid *Knight in Armour with his Page*, traditionally thought to be a portrait of the Venetian *condottiere* Gattamelata, by an unknown Venetian painter, but often attributed to Giorgione. The two large figures, usually identified as a prophet and sibyl, are attributed to Vittore Carpaccio.

Room 22: Fine portraits by Flemish and German artists. The series of five superb male portraits by **Hans Memling** exhibited on one wall, are mostly of unidentified sitters, except for the one of Benedetto di Tommaso Portinari, Memling's Italian patron. Portraits by **Hans Holbein the Younger** include a *Self-portrait*, and *Sir Richard Southwell* (1536), which was given by Thomas Howard, Earl of Arundel, to Cosimo II in 1620. The supposed portrait of Thomas More is now thought to be a work by the school of Holbein. The double *Portrait of a Man and his Wife* is by Joos van Cleve the Elder, and the *Adoration of the Magi* by Gerard David.

Room 23: Works by northern Italian artists, including three very fine works by **Mantegna**: a small triptych of the *Adoration of the Magi*, *Circumcision* and *Ascension*, exquisitely painted and preserving its beautiful frame; a remarkable portrait thought to show Cardinal Carlo de' Medici; and the tiny *Madonna delle Cave*. The *Leda* is the best-known copy of a lost painting by Leonardo da Vinci. Another Leonardesque work is the small painting of *Narcissus* by Giovanni Antonio Boltraffio. The small *Portrait of a Gypsy Girl* is by Boccaccio Boccaccino. On another wall are three good works by the Emilian artist Correggio: a tiny *Madonna in Glory*; the *Rest on the Flight* and *Madonna in Adoration of the Child*.

Room 24: The Collection of Miniatures (15th–18th century) is exhibited in this little oval room (only visible through the doorway) designed in 1781.

Third Floor: South Corridor

The short south corridor has a wonderful view of Florence. Across the river, on the extreme left, is San Miniato with its campanile on the skyline and the Forte di Belvedere. In the other direction, beyond the Uffizi building, is Palazzo Vecchio and the cupola of the Duomo. At the far end of the corridor you can see the tiled roof of the Corridoio Vasariano leading away from the Uffizi to Ponte Vecchio. The Arno flows downstream beneath Ponte Santa Trinita and the bridges beyond. On the south bank the dome and campanile of Santo Spirito are prominent, and further downstream the dome of San Frediano in Cestello is visible.

Some fine pieces of **ancient sculpture** are arranged in the south corridor. Outside Room 24 the *Sleeping Cupid* is a 16th-century copy in black basalt of a Hellenistic original. At the end of the east corridor there is a Roman copy—made in the 1st century AD—of the famous original of an athlete carrying a spear (the *Doryophorus*) by the Greek master Polyclitus. On the window wall looking towards Palazzo Vecchio are Roman statues of *Demeter* (the copy of a Hellenistic original), *Leda* (restored by Giovanni Battista Foggini); *Eros and Psyche*; and *Apollo* (a copy of a Greek original by Praxiteles). In the centre of the south corridor is a fragment of a she-wolf in porphyry, a Roman copy of a 5th-century Greek original made at the time of the emperor Hadrian. In the corner (overlooking the Arno), the beautiful *Colossal Head* in Greek marble is probably a late Hellenistic original (one of the few in the whole gallery) of a triton (river god). It was long thought to represent Alexander the Great dying; as the only portrait of the emperor known until 1780, it was considered extremely important, and in the 16th and 17th centuries was one of the most frequently copied works in the whole gallery. It was restored in 1795 (including part of the hair and the nose).

Third Floor: West Corridor

At the beginning of the west corridor there are two gruesome statues of the satyr Marsyas, hung up and ready to be flayed by Apollo, both Roman copies of Hellenistic originals of the 3rd or 2nd century BC. The one in red marble was, according to Vasari, restored by Verrocchio, but the upper part of the torso is now thought to be the work of Mino da Fiesole. It is known that it belonged to Lorenzo the Magnificent who kept it by the back entrance to Palazzo Medici in Via dei Ginori. The one opposite, which was formerly in the Capranica collection, entered the Uffizi in 1780.

The Rooms off the West Corridor

Room 25: Opposite the entrance is the famous *Tondo Doni of the Holy Family* by **Michelangelo**, his only finished tempera painting. It was painted for the marriage of Agnolo Doni with Maddalena Strozzi (1504–05), when the artist was 30 years old. Although owing much to Signorelli (*see Room 19*), it breaks with traditional representations of this familiar subject and signals a new moment in High Renaissance painting, pointing the way to the Sistine Chapel frescoes. The splendid contemporary frame is by Domenico del Tasso. *The Portrait of a Lady* ('la Monaca di Leonardo') is a beautiful work now thought to be by Ridolfo del Ghirlandaio. Also here are works by Fra' Bartolomeo, Mariotto Albertinelli (*Visitation*) and Francesco Granacci.

Room 26: Masterpieces by **Raphael**. *Leo X with Giulio de' Medici and Luigi de' Rossi* was painted shortly before the artist's death, and is one of his most powerful portrait groups; it was to have a great influence on Titian. The first Medici pope (son of Lorenzo the Magnificent) is shown with his two cousins whom he created cardinals: Giulio de' Medici later went on to become Pope Clement VII. The painting was commissioned by Leo X in Rome in 1518, so that it could be sent to Florence on the occasion of the wedding of Leo's brother Giuliano, Duke of Nemours, with Philiberte of Savoy, since the Pope was unable to attend. The various shades of red are extremely effective and all three prelates express their self-assurance through their attitudes of proud independence. The *Portrait of Julius II* is usually thought to be a replica of a painting of the same subject in the National Gallery in London. The *Madonna del Cardellino* ('Madonna of the Goldfinch'), is one of Raphael's most famous sacred works. Painted for the marriage of the artist's friend, Lorenzo Nasi, it was shattered by an earthquake in 1547, but carefully repaired by the owner, although it remains in a very ruined state (it is at present being restored). Raphael's *Self-portrait*, in a lovely frame, is painted with a remarkable freshness of touch. The *Portrait of a Young Man* (formerly thought to be Francesco Maria della Rovere) is also by Raphael, but other portraits here are now only attributed to him (including the man once thought to represent Perugino). Other very fine portraits by lesser-known artists include *Pietro Carnesecchi* by Domenico Puligo and *Young Man with Gloves* by Franciabigio. The *Madonna of the Harpies* (named after the carvings on the throne) is by Andrea del Sarto.

Room 27: Florentine Mannerism. **Rosso Fiorentino** is particularly well represented with a *Madonna and Saints* and two portraits, three of the few surviving Florentine works by the painter who went on to be court artist to Francis I at Fontainebleau. The geometrical forms of the nudes in the foreground of his *Moses Defending the Children of Jethro* (possibly a fragment) display a very original and modern tendency. There is a self-conscious denial of spatial depth and naturalistic proportions in order to emphasize the drama of the scene and the virtuosity of the painter. There are also good works by **Pontormo** including the *Portrait of Maria Salviati*, widow of Giovanni delle Bande Nere (father of Cosimo I) and the *Martyrdom of St Maurice and the Eleven Thousand Martyrs*. His *Supper at Emmaus* (1525), painted for the Certosa del Galluzzo, is an uncharacteristic work (above the head of Christ is a surrealist symbol of God the Father). The portrait of the musician Francesco dell'Ajolle, formerly thought to be by Pontormo, is now attributed to the less well known painter Pier Francesco di Jacopo Foschi. The *Holy Family* which belonged to the Panciatichi is by Bronzino.

Room 28: Some of the finest works by **Titian** include the *Venus of Urbino*, which was commissioned by Guidobaldo della Rovere, later duke of Urbino, in 1538. It is one of the most beautiful nudes ever painted and has had a profound influence on subsequent European painting. *Flora* is another masterpiece by Titian, a seductive, exquisite portrait of a girl with beautiful hair, holding roses in her hand. The male portrait is known as the *Sick Man*. Other superb portraits by Titian here are Eleonora Gonzaga, Duchess of Urbino, in a splendid dress, and her husband Francesco Maria della Rovere, wearing armour; a Knight of Malta, charged with religious fervour; and Bishop Ludovico Beccadelli. The portrait of Pope Sixtus IV in profile, although full of character (and in bad condition) shows the intervention of Titian's *bottega*.

The *Death of Adonis* is a very fine work by the Venetian artist Sebastiano del Piombo. Beyond an autumnal landscape there are views of Palazzo Ducale and the Piazzetta in Venice. Sebastiano also painted the beautiful *Portrait of a Lady* (formerly called *La Fornarina*). Three works by another northern artist, Palma Vecchio, are also exhibited here.

Rooms 29 and 30: The *Madonna dal collo lungo* ('Madonna with the long Neck') by **Parmigianino** (1534–36) is a work of extreme refinement and originality, typical of the Mannerist style. Also here are works by Dosso Dossi, another representative of the Emilian school, and Room 30 has small works by his contemporary Garofalo.

Room 31: Works by the great Venetian painter **Paolo Veronese** include the *Annunciation*, designed around a perspective device in the centre of the picture. The work is delicately painted in simple colours, in contrast to the rich golden hues of the figure of St Barbara in the *Holy Family with St Barbara*, a work of the artist's maturity. When the curtains are open, the window in this room offers a good view of Palazzo Vecchio, the Duomo and the top of Orsanmichele.

Room 32: *Leda and the Swan* is a good work by another great Venetian painter, **Tintoretto**, with the fine nude figure of Leda and her pretty serving girl; he also painted the portrait of his contemporary Jacopo Sansovino, the Tuscan architect and sculptor who built many fine buildings in Venice.

Room 33: 16th-century works by **French artists**. The tiny equestrian *Portrait of Francis I of France* is by the court painter François Clouet. It was probably brought to Florence in 1589 by Christine of Lorraine, wife of Ferdinando I. The amusing painting of *Two Women in the Bath* is by the late 16th-century School of Fontainebleau. The *Christ Appearing to St Mary Magdalen* is by Lavinia Fontana, one of the few women painters represented in the gallery.

Room 34: Lorenzo Lotto and the 16th-century Lombard school. Small works by **Lorenzo Lotto** include the fine *Head of a Young Boy* and *Holy Family with Saints*. Another remarkable portrait (in poor condition) in this room is that of an old

Titian: *Flora* (c. 1515).

man with long grey hair, thought to represent Teofilo Folengo, by an unknown 16th-century painter. Fine portraits by **Giovanni Battista Moroni** include *Count Pietro Secco Suardi* (1563), a full-length standing portrait and a *Man with a Book*. The *Female Nude* is an extraordinary work, very unusual for its period since it lacks any mythological references, attributed to Bernardino Licino.

Room 35: Works by Federico Barocci including the *Madonna del Popolo*, a delightful crowded composition, a *Noli me tangere*, and a portrait of Francesco Maria della Rovere.

Room 41: In the corridor here (on the window wall) is a *Wounded Warrior*, kneeling, now recognized as a **Greek original of the 5th century** BC (only the shield and arms have been restored). The head is antique but comes from another statue of a barbarian. The 'leather' armour is extremely delicately carved. Nearby are displayed a seated *Apollo* and, opposite, *Ganymede*, both of them Roman copies of Hellenistic originals.

Room 41 itself contains fine works by **Rubens**. These include; *Henri IV Entering Paris*, *Henri IV at Ivry*, two huge paintings comprising the first part of a cycle depicting the king's history, and the *Triumphal Entry of Ferdinand of Austria into Antwerp*; *Portrait of Isabella Brandt*; and an equestrian portrait of Philip IV of Spain. Works by van Dyck include *Margaret of Lorraine*, an equestrian portrait of the Emperor Charles V, *Suttermans's Mother* and *John of Montfort*. There is also a portrait of Galileo by Suttermans.

Room 42: Called the Niobe Room, this was designed by Gaspare Maria Paoletti and Zanobi del Rosso in 1771–79 and it has a gilded stucco vault. It was built to house the statues forming a group of *Niobe and her Children*, found in a vineyard near the Lateran in 1583, and bought to Florence in 1775 from the

Villa Medici in Rome. These are Roman copies of **Greek originals of the school of Skopas** (early 4th century BC), but many of the figures are badly restored and others do not belong to the group (the lying figure of Niobe is in different marble). On the end wall, to the right, is Niobe herself with one of her children, and on the opposite wall is a statue of a pedagogue. The horse, probably part of a group of the *Dioscuri*, was found offshore near Rome, and the tail and legs are restorations. The room was beautifully restored after serious bomb damage in 1993 (*see p. 86*). The view includes the top of the dome and campanile of Santo Spirito on the left, with the trees of Bellosguardo on the skyline.

Room 43: Closed for rearrangement.

Room 44: Three splendid works by **Rembrandt**: *Self-portrait*, *Portrait of an Old Man* and *Self-portrait as an Old Man*. Also here are Dutch and Flemish works including Jan Steen's *Lunch-party* and a fine landscape by Jacob Ruysdael.

Room 45: 18th-century paintings. The Venetian school is represented by Piazzetta (*Susannah and the Elders*), Giovanni Battista Tiepolo, Francesco Guardi and Canaletto. Among the French and Spanish portraits are two of children by Chardin, two of Maria Theresa by Francisco Goya; *Vittorio Alfieri and The Countess of Albany* by Françoise Xavier Fabre, and *Maria Adelaide of France in Turkish Costume*, by Etienne Liotard.

Leaving the West Corridor

At the end of the west corridor is exhibited a copy by Baccio Bandinelli of the famous Hellenistic work praised by Pliny, representing Laocoön and his sons in the coils of the serpents (now in the Vatican). Also in this part of the corridor is a sculpted boar (a copy of a Hellenistic original), the model for the Porcellino in the Mercato Nuovo. The Roman statue of a Nereid on a sea-horse is a copy of a Hellenistic original, and, opposite, the standing veiled female statue dates from the 2nd century AD.

The **Café** has tables on the roof terrace of the Loggia della Signoria, from which there is a splendid view over Piazza della Signoria beyond the buildings of the city to the hills of Fiesole.

A long flight of stairs descends from the west corridor to the piano nobile and the exit. In the west corridor on the piano nobile is the huge marble *Medici Vase*, a neo-Attic work acquired by Lorenzo de' Medici, and two 16th-century bronze statues: *Mars* by Bartolomeo Ammannati, and *Silenus and the Young Bacchus* by the little known sculptor Jacopo del Duca. Beyond is a room with three famous works by **Caravaggio**: *The Sacrifice of Isaac*, *Young Bacchus*, and *Medusa Head* (painted on a shield). Also here are paintings by Artemisia Gentileschi. The next room contains works by Bartolomeo Manfredi, one of them acquired in 1994 after the Mafia bomb attack on the Uffizi when Manfredi's *Concert* was blown to pieces. There are fine works (including a charming *Adoration of Christ*) by Gherardo delle Notti, all of which had to be restored after the bomb attack. More works by the school of Caravaggio are displayed in the adjoining room and in the last room are three works by Guido Reni, including *St Andrea Corsini* (a recent acquisition). Stairs continue down to the new exit at the back of the building.

The Corridoio Vasariano

The Corridoio Vasariano can usually be visited on certain days of the week and in the summer and autumn, but only by previous appointment (T: 055 265 4321). Groups are accompanied on a two-and-a-half-hour tour (known as the 'Percorso del Principe', starting from the Salone dei Cinquecento in Palazzo Vecchio and finishing in the Boboli Gardens). There are long-term plans to open it regularly so that visitors can get directly from the Uffizi to the Pitti, and to empty it of its paintings (which will be rehung on the first floor of the Uffizi).

The Corridoio Vasariano was built by Vasari in five months to celebrate the marriage of Francesco de' Medici and Joanna of Austria in 1565, and provides unique views of the city. Nearly a kilometre long, its purpose was to connect Palazzo Vecchio via the Uffizi and Ponte Vecchio with the new residence of the Medici dukes at Palazzo Pitti, in the form of a private covered passageway. This was particularly convenient in wet weather, and it was sometimes used as a nursery for the children of the grand dukes. Since it has no steps, elderly or infirm members of the family were wheeled along it in basket chairs. Paintings were first hung here in the 19th century when the Savoy royalty put up their family portraits, and later in the century it was used as a deposit for the Uffizi. Since the early years of the 20th century, the Uffizi's celebrated collection of self-portraits has been hung here.

Stairs (*see plan on p. 90*) lead down from a door in the west corridor of the Uffizi to two rooms which have been restored since they were severely damaged by the bomb explosion in 1993. To the right is the entrance to the corridor proper. Here, displayed by regional schools, are 17th-century works including *Susannah and the Elders* by Guido Reni, the *Sleeping Endymion* by Guercino, and a *Portrait of Cardinal Leopoldo de' Medici* by Baciccio.

The **collection of self-portraits** begins on the bridge itself. It was started by Cardinal Leopoldo in the 17th century. Having acquired the self-portraits of Guercino and Pietro da Cortona, he went on to collect some 80 artists' and other portraits in his lifetime. The collection continued to be augmented in the following centuries up to the present day (only a selection is at present on display). The self-portrait of Vasari is hung opposite a charming large painting by Jacopo da Empoli, formerly in the chapel of the goldsmiths, showing St Eligius, their protector. The self-portraits are arranged chronologically and include works by Agnolo Gaddi (with Taddeo and Gaddo Gaddi), Andrea del Sarto (two self-portraits, one in fresco on a tile), Baccio Bandinelli, Alessandro Allori, Beccafumi, Bronzino, Perino del Vaga, Santi di Tito, Cristofano Allori, Giovanni da San Giovanni (painted on a tile) and Cigoli. The self-portraits on the left wall include works by Jacopo Bassano, Titian, Niccolò Cassana, Rosalba Carriera, Domenico Parodi, Sofonisba Anguissola, Carlo Dolci and Correggio.

Beyond the centre of Ponte Vecchio, on the right wall, are Federico and Taddeo Zuccari, Lorenzo Bernini, and Pietro da Cortona. On the left wall are Agostino and Annibale Carracci, Salvatore Rosa, Luca Giordano, and Pompeo Batoni.

On the further side of the Arno the corridor skirts the Torre di Mannelli and the display of self-portraits continues with 16th–18th-century foreign works by Pourbus, Rubens, Gerard Dou, Suttermans, Rembrandt, van Dyck, Zoffany, Velázquez, and Callot. British painters represented include Peter Lely, Sir Godfrey Kneller, James Northcote, George Romney and Sir Joshua Reynolds.

The corridor now descends past a window overlooking the interior of Santa Felicita. Here are displayed miniature portraits including works by Giovanna Garzoni, self-portraits by Pourbus and Lavinia Fontana, and works attributed to Holbein, van Dyck and Samuel Cowper. Also here is a delightful series of miniature portraits of the Medici dynasty (from Giovanni di Bicci to Cosimo I) by Bronzino and his *bottega*.

The last section of self-portraits has 19th- and 20th-century works (the Italians on the left wall and the foreign schools opposite). British and French artists represented include Ingres, Delacroix, Corot, Jacques Louis David, Mengs, Holman Hunt, Frederic Leighton, George Frederic Watts, Alma-Tadema, John Everett Millais, Benjamin Constant, John Singer Sargent and Fantin-Latour, as well as the Russian-born painter Chagall. On the left wall: Francesco Hayez, Silvestro Lega, Giovanni Fattori, Giacomo Balla, Carlo Levi, Gino Severini and Renato Guttuso.

In the last section of the corridor are 17th- and 18th-century family portraits of members of the Medici and Lorraine dynasties, including some by Santi di Tito and Francesco Furini. The colossal *Head of Zeus* is from a 4th- or 3rd-century BC original.

A door leads down to the exit through the Boboli Gardens.

Palazzo della Zecca

Adjoining the side of the Loggia della Signoria, the ground floor of Palazzo della Zecca, with its well protected windows, is incorporated into the Uffizi building. The famous gold florins, first issued in 1252, were minted here; they became the standard gold coin of Europe. The Sala delle Reali Poste here, built as a post office in 1866, is a fine hall with a huge skylight supported on a cast-iron framework. It is used for exhibitions. At the end of Via Lambertesca is the Porta delle Suppliche, added after 1574 by Buontalenti and surmounted by a bust of Francesco I, the masterpiece of Giovanni Bandini.

The Contini-Bonacossi Collection

Since 1998, this collection has been housed in ten rooms in a wing of the second floor of the Uffizi building; the entrance is in Via Lambertesca (*admission only by booking in advance; T: 055 265 4321, for a maximum of 20 people at a time*).

It is a choice collection made by Alessandro Contini-Bonacossi (with the advice of Roberto Longhi) and contains Italian and Spanish paintings as well as 15th–17th-century majolica and furniture. Works by artists not already represented in the Uffizi were favoured. Contini-Bonacossi died intestate, and much of the collection was sold by the family after 1960, but they ceded this part of the collection to the state in 1974. The paintings have frames typical of the 1920s. Some of the rooms have pretty 18th-century decorations.

Among the best works are a *Madonna and Child* by Duccio; a well-preserved altarpiece of *St John the Baptist with Stories from his Life* by Giovanni del Biondo; the *Madonna della Neve*, painted for the cathedral of Siena by Sassetta; two panels with *Scenes from the Life of St Nicholas* by Paolo Veneziano and a fresco from the castle of Trebbio showing the *Madonna and Child with Angels and Saints and Two Children of the Pazzi Family* by Andrea del Castagno. There are also fine Venetian and Spanish works.

MUSEO DI STORIA DELLA SCIENZA
Map p. 397, B4

Open winter 9.30–5, Tues 9.30–1, closed Sun except for the second Sun of the month, 10–1; summer 9.30–5, Tues and Sat 9.30–1, closed Sun; T: 055 265311. Library open to students.

Towards the Arno, in Piazza dei Giudici (with a view of the tower of Palazzo Vecchio), stands Palazzo Castellani, a fine medieval palace named after its owners in the 14th century, an important Florentine family whose wealth was based on the cloth trade. It now contains the Museo di Storia della Scienza, with its well displayed collection of scientific instruments from the Medici and Lorraine grand-ducal collections, illustrating the history of science.

Since the days of the Medici dynasty Florence has held an extremely important place not only in the arts but also in the history of science. A large part of this collection was owned by the Medici grand dukes, and the Museum of Physics and Natural Sciences, directed by Felice Fontana and opened in 1775 by Grand Duke Peter Leopold, was moved here in 1929. A brief guide (also in English) is given to visitors, and excellent handlists with more detailed information (also available in English) can be borrowed from the custodians on each floor. The museum is beautifully kept and extremely well run. The custodians will demonstrate some of the models in Rooms IV, VI and VII for groups.

First Floor

Mathematical and astronomical instruments include an Arab globe made c. 1080 showing the constellations; 10th–16th-century astrolabes, quadrants and sundials; and compasses (mostly 17th-century), including a pair from the 16th century traditionally thought to have been used by Michelangelo.

Many of the mathematical instruments are 16th-century pieces brought to Florence from Germany by Prince Mattias, brother of Ferdinando II, in 1635. There are also the nautical instruments invented and used by Sir Robert Dudley, Duke of Northumberland (1574–1649). He left England for Italy in 1605, became a naval engineer and administered the port of Livorno for Ferdinando II. The calculator was invented by the British diplomat Sir Samuel Morland in 1666.

Room III has compasses, quadrants, a celestial globe, an armillary sphere made in Tuscany in the 16th century and an astrolabe, traditionally associated with Galileo, and attributed to Egnazio Danti. There is also a pair of compasses used by Vincenzo Viviani, Galileo's disciple. Room IV is devoted entirely to Galileo. The lens (cracked by the scientist himself before he presented it to Ferdinando II) which Galileo used to discover the four largest moons of Jupiter—Galileo named them the 'Medicean stars'—is displayed here. The pair of compasses and lodestones (of natural magnetic rock) were probably also used by the scientist. The bones of his right middle finger were removed from his tomb when his remains were transferred to the church of Santa Croce. The models of Galileo's inventions, made in the 18th century by order of Grand Duke Peter Leopold, include a water pump and an instrument for measuring the acceleration of gravity.

Highlights in the following rooms include two telescopes made by Galileo, and others by his pupil Evangelista Torricelli (1608–47), as well as a superb display of globes around a huge Ptolemaic armillary sphere (showing the movements of celestial bodies) built by Antonio Santucci in 1588, and glass made for the Accademia del Cimento, an experimental academy founded by Cardinal Leopoldo de' Medici in 1657.

Second Floor

The Lorraine Scientific Collections are displayed on this floor, including numerous exhibits related to Peter Leopold, grand duke in 1765–90. There are exhibits illustrating the origins of the mechanical clock, from the invention of the escapement device c. 1330 to the first mechanical pendulum clock invented in 1640 by Galileo. A clock designed for Palazzo Vecchio in 1510 by Lorenzo della Volpaia shows the movement of the planets. The development of the electric current and electromagnetism is illustrated with reference to Leopoldo Nobili (1784–1835) and, more famously, Alessandro Volta (1745–1827), inventor of the 'voltaic pile', ancestor of the modern battery, for which invention he was ennobled by Napoleon. The unit of electrical potential, the volt, is named after him. There are also wax and terracotta anatomical models made in Florence for use in obstetrics, as well as displays showing the origins of modern chemistry in Florence, with exhibits relating to the 18th-century naturalists Felice Fontana and Giovanni Fabbroni. The desk used by Peter Leopold for his chemical experiments is also preserved.

GALILEO GALILEI

Galileo (1564–1642) was born in Pisa, and lived and died in Florence. He perfected the telescope, and discovered the four satellites of Jupiter in 1610. He was appointed Professor of Mathematics at Pisa University by Cardinal Ferdinando de' Medici (later grand duke), and then took up a chair at Padua University from 1592 to 1610, where he attracted pupils from all over Europe. He stayed in the Villa Medici (on the site of the Villa Demidoff at Pratolino) in 1605–06 as tutor to the future Cosimo II. In 1632, he published a defence of the Copernican theory of astronomy. He was condemned by the Inquisition in 1633 in Rome for his contention that the Earth was not at the centre of the Universe, but through the good offices of Grand Duke Ferdinando II he avoided imprisonment, and spent the latter part of his life in Florence, where he died in 1642. He bought a house for his son Vincenzio on Costa San Giorgio and lived, practically as a prisoner, at Villa il Gioiello in Pian de' Giullari (see p. 303), under the protection of the grand duke. Although infirm and almost blind, he wrote some of his most important tracts here and was visited by Evangelista Torricelli, Vincenzo Viviani, Thomas Hobbes and possibly also Milton. On his death he was not allowed a Christian burial: it was not until 1737 that his remains were permitted to be transferred to Santa Croce and a monument was set up to him in the church (see p. 239). He was later honoured by Grand Duke Leopold II when he erected the tribuna in the museum known as La Specola (see p. 279) in Galileo's memory in 1841. Eventually, in 1992, the Pope announced the rehabilitation of Galileo and cancelled the condemnation imposed on him in 1633.

PALAZZO PITTI
& THE BOBOLI GARDENS

PALAZZO PITTI
Map p. 398, C4

The ticket office is on the far right side of the façade. Times and tickets vary for the different museums and the royal apartments, and are attached to each museum description. A ticket for the Galleria Palatina includes admission to the Appartamenti Reali. There is a separate ticket for the Galleria d'Arte Moderna and the Galleria del Costume. A third ticket provides admission to the Museo degli Argenti and Boboli Gardens. It is well worth buying the combined ticket for all the museums and Boboli Gardens valid for three consecutive days, although this is not available when exhibitions are on. Information and reservations, T: 055 294 883 (Mon–Fri 8.30–6.30, Sat 8.30–12.30).

Off the courtyard are a museum shop, café, cloakroom, toilets (there are more toilets, usually much less busy, in the Galleria d'Arte Moderna), and lifts for the Galleria Palatina and the Museo d'Arte Moderna and Galleria del Costume.

History of the Palace

Palazzo Pitti was built by the merchant Luca Pitti as an effective demonstration of his wealth and power to his rivals the Medici. The majestic golden-coloured palace is built in huge, rough-hewn blocks of stone in different sizes. Its design is attributed to Brunelleschi, although building began c. 1457, after his death. Luca Fancelli is known to have worked on the building, but it is generally considered that another architect, whose name is unknown, was also involved. The palace remained incomplete on the death of Luca Pitti in 1472; by then it consisted of the seven central bays with three doorways. Houses were demolished to create the piazza in front of the palace. The site, on the slope of a hillside, was chosen to make the palace even more imposing. Bartolommeo Ammannati took up work on the building c. 1560 and converted the two side doors of the façade into elaborate ground-floor windows. These were then copied after 1616 by Giulio and Alfonso Parigi the Younger, when they enlarged the façade to its present colossal dimensions (possibly following an original design). The two rondos (wings) were added later: the one on the right was built sometime after 1760, and the one on the left (known as the Rondo di Bacco) in the 19th century (it incorporates a small theatre, now used for lectures).

In 1549, the palace was bought by Eleonora di Toledo, wife of Cosimo I. It became the official seat of the Medici dynasty of grand dukes after Cosimo I moved here from Palazzo Vecchio (to which he connected the Pitti by means of the Corridoio Vasariano, *see p. 105*). The various ruling families of Florence continued to occupy the palace, or part of it, until 1919, when Vittorio Emanuele III presented it to the state. Behind the palace are the superb Boboli Gardens designed for Cosimo I.

Silvestro Lega: *Walk in the Garden*, in the Galleria d'Arte Moderna.

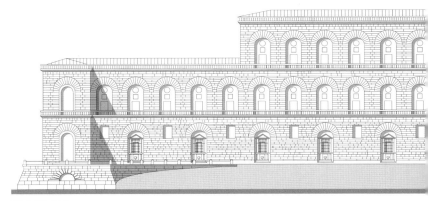

PALAZZO PITTI

THE MUSEUMS IN PALAZZO PITTI

The palace contains the apartments used for four centuries by the grand dukes and rulers of Florence and Tuscany, as well as the works of art acquired by them. It houses a number of important museums, including the Galleria Palatina, with one of the finest collections of paintings in Italy; the Museo degli Argenti; and the Galleria d'Arte Moderna. The state apartments used by the Medici and Lorraine grand dukes, and later by the royal house of Savoy, have been beautifully restored to their appearance of 1911. The winter apartments on the top floor of the palace are sometimes open, as are other suites of rooms used in various seasons, and the attic floor known as the 'Mezzanino degli Occhi'. In the Meridiana wing of the palace is the Galleria del Costume.

The Courtyard

The central door in the façade leads through the atrium by Pasquale Poccianti (c. 1850) into the splendid courtyard (1560–70) by Ammannati, which serves as a garden façade to the palace. It is a masterpiece of Florentine Mannerist architecture, with bold rustication in three orders. Nocturnal spectacles were held here from the 16th to the 18th centuries, and it is still sometimes used for summer concerts. The lower fourth side is formed by a terrace with the Fontana del Carciofo (so named since it was once crowned by an artichoke), beyond which extend the Boboli Gardens (*described on p. 139*).

The **Grotto of Moses**, beneath the terrace, was designed in 1635–42 around a porphyry statue of Moses (the torso of which is an antique Roman work). In the other four niches and in the water are 17th-century statues. On either side of the entrance to the grotto are two Roman statues (copies of Hellenistic originals) above little fountains. At the end of the left colonnade is a restored Roman statue of Hercules, and, beneath, a

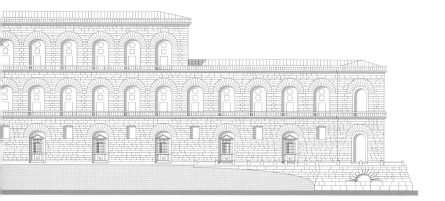

charming 16th-century bas-relief commemorating a mule who worked particularly hard during the construction of the courtyard. At the end of the right colonnade is another Roman statue of Hercules. On the right side of the courtyard is the entrance to the Cappella Palatina (*only open on special occasions*) which dates from 1776.

Galleria Palatina
Open 8.30–6.50. Closed Mon. T: 055 238 8611. Plan on p. 115.

Off the courtyard is the staircase which leads up to the entrance to the celebrated Galleria di Palazzo Pitti or Galleria Palatina, a splendid collection of paintings acquired by the Medici and Lorraine grand dukes, including numerous famous works by Raphael, Titian and Rubens. The gallery maintains the character of a private, princely collection of the 17th–18th centuries. The aesthetic arrangement of the pictures which decorate the walls produces a remarkable effect of magnificence. The elaborately carved and gilded frames, many of them original, and especially representative of the Mannerist, Baroque and Neoclassical styles, are particularly fine. The Grand Staircase by Ammannati ascends past antique sculpture and late 17th-century busts and (third landing) a bronze 16th-century statue of a young boy known as the *Genio mediceo*, to the gallery entrance. Only a selection of the paintings (all of which are labelled) is described. Particularly important works are given in bold.

History of the Palatina collection

The collection owes its origins to the 17th-century Medici grand dukes, and in particular to Cardinal Leopoldo, brother of Ferdinando II, and to Cosimo III and his eldest son the Crown Prince Ferdinando (d. 1713), who added Flemish paintings, works of the Bolognese and Veneto schools, and altarpieces from Tuscan churches. Under the Lorraine grand dukes, in 1771, the paintings were installed for the first time in the present rooms, which had been decorated by Pietro da Cortona in the 1640s for Ferdinando II (*see p. 122*). The gallery was first opened regularly to the public in 1833, and in 1911 it was acquired by the state. Unfortunately, many of the paintings which formed the nucleus of the collection were removed to the Uffizi in the 20th century (including Rembrandt's *Self-portrait* and Raphael's *Portrait of Leo X*). The present arrangement of the pictures follows, as far as possible, the arrangement of 1833.

The Entrance Rooms

(1) Anticamera degli Staffieri: Tickets are shown here. Decorated in the 18th century, it contains 16th-century sculptures by Pietro Francavilla (*Mercury*) and earlier works by Baccio Bandinelli (*Bacchus* and a bronze bust of Cosimo I). Bandinelli was the courtier artist par excellence, versatile to a degree which enabled him to rise always to the ducal command, be it architectural, sculptural or pictorial in nature. He was a virtuoso sculptor—a great performer, but not a true composer. His obsession with the colossal masks a want of true sensitivity to subject or material.

From the window there is a splendid view of the courtyard and gardens (with the Forte di Belvedere on the skyline).

(2) Galleria delle Statue: Decorated with antique sculptures from the Villa Medici in Rome.

(3) Sala del Castagnoli: The room takes its name from Giuseppe Castagnoli, the artist (b. 1754) who decorated it. It contains a magnificent circular table in *pietre dure* with *Apollo and the Muses* (the bronze pedestal with the *Four Seasons* is by Giovanni Dupré). This was the last important work in *pietre dure* made in 1837–50 in the grand-ducal workshop of the Opificio delle Pietre Dure (*see p. 164*). Some of the Opificio's best products (including table-tops and cabinets) are preserved in various rooms of Palazzo Pitti.

The 'Minor' Rooms

(4) Sala delle Allegorie: The allegories in question are Volterrano's frescoes on the richly decorated stucco-work ceiling, which date from around 1658 and show the influence of Pietro da Cortona, who had been at work in Palazzo Pitti earlier in the century (*see p. 122*). The frescoes celebrate the grand duchess Vittoria della Rovere, with allegories of her virtues. This whole wing of Palazzo Pitti is always known as the 'Volterrano' from

these frescoes. It is now thought that Volterrano may also have worked with his master Giovanni da San Giovanni on the frescoed rooms on the ground floor of the palace.

Volterrano painted numerous other frescoes in Florence during the 17th century, including those in the dome of the tribune of Santissima Annunziata and in the Niccolini Chapel in Santa Croce. Other paintings by him in this room

PALAZZO PITTI
(FIRST FLOOR)

GALLERIA PALATINA
& APPARTAMENTI REALI

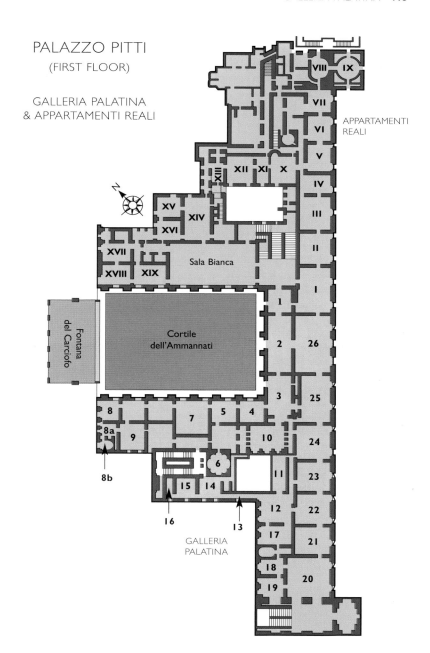

APPARTAMENTI
REALI

N

VIII **IX**

VII

VI

V

XII **XI** **X**

XIII **IV**

XV **III**

XIV

XVI **II**

XVII **XIX** Sala Bianca

XVIII

I

Fontana del Carciofo

Cortile dell'Ammannati

1

2 26

3 25

8 7 5 4

8a

9 10 24

8b 6 11 23

15 14 12 22

16 13 17 21

GALLERIA
PALATINA 18

19 20

include (on the entrance wall) *The Parson's Jest*, showing a jovial group enjoying the pranks of the Pievano Arlotto, a country chaplain who had a living near Fiesole, and who was famous for his burlesques. After his death in 1484 his witticisms were recorded in print, and Volterrano portrayed him in this well-known genre painting, which was owned by the Crown Prince Ferdinando and provides an interesting glimpse of Florentine life of the time.

There are also works here by Giovanni da San Giovanni and his contemporaries Suttermans and Artemisia Gentileschi.

(5) Sala delle Belle Arti: Paintings by Carlo Dolci and Cigoli (d. 1613), one of the finest Florentine exponents of the transition from Mannerism to the Baroque.

(6) Chapel: The early 17th-century oval chapel was built for Maria Maddalena d'Austria, wife of Cosimo II. The Corridoio delle Miniature, beyond the chapel, has tiny Dutch paintings acquired by Cosimo III in Holland in 1667, and a charming collection of paintings of fruit and vegetables by Giovanna Garzoni (1600–57), painted for Vittoria della Rovere.

(7) Salone d'Ercole: Frescoed with scenes from the *Life of Hercules* by Pietro Benvenuti (1828). The huge Sèvres vase dates from the early 19th century and there are two battle scenes by Bergognone.

(8) Sala di Psiche: Fine works by Salvatore Rosa. Rosa was a Neapolitan artist who worked mostly in Rome but was invited to Florence as court painter by Cardinal Gian Carlo de' Medici, brother of Ferdinando II. He stayed here until 1649. A character of great verve and self-confidence, Rosa (1615–73) is best known for his landscape paintings of rugged and romantic scenery that did much to inform the notion of the Picturesque in England—and also coloured his reputation, adding greatly to his popularity. Rumours began to circulate that he himself was a brigand. The vestibule and bathroom (8a and 8b) of Empress Marie Louise (the second wife of Napoleon, who stayed here in the early 19th century when the grand duchy was conferred on Elisa Baciocchi, Napoleon's sister) were designed in Neoclassical style c. 1803.

(9) Sala della Fama: Flemish works.

From the Sala del Castagnoli (*see above*) is the entrance to a series of rooms decorated in the Neoclassical style in the Napoleonic period when Elisa Baciocchi was in residence. They contain the smaller works in the collection.

(10) Sala della Musica: This Neoclassical room designed by Cacialli dates from 1811–21 and has frescoes by Luigi Ademollo, drum-shaped commodes, and a gilt-bronze and malachite table by Pierre-Philippe Thomire, who at the height of his fame was court engraver to Napoleon Bonaparte.

(11) Galleria del Poccetti: Its name comes from the traditional attribution of the frescoes in the vault to Bernardino

Poccetti, although these are now thought to be by Matteo Rosselli and his pupils (c. 1625). The beautiful table inlaid in *pietre dure* (1716) is attributed to Giovanni Battista Foggini (sculptor to the grand dukes from 1687). On either side of the door are a remarkable portrait in profile of Francesco da Castiglione by Pontormo (also attributed to Rosso Fiorentino), and a portrait of the Duke of Buckingham by Rubens. It was Buckingham who negotiated the betrothal of Henrietta Maria, grand-daughter of Francesco I, to the future Charles I of England. At the other end of the room, beside the far door, is Rubens' portrait of the Duchess of Buckingham, and, above, a portrait of Cromwell by Peter Lely. On the other side of the door is hung a *Portrait of an Artist* by Niccolò Cassana. On the wall opposite the windows are landscapes by Gaspare Dughet (Poussin's brother-in-law) and *Hylas and the Nymphs*, the masterpiece of Francesco Furini.

(12) Sala di Prometeo: Here are the earliest paintings in the Pitti including some good portraits and a number of fine *tondi* of the Madonna, the largest and most beautiful of which is the tondo of the *Madonna and Child*, a charming composition with scenes from the life of the Virgin in the background. This is one of Filippo Lippi's best works, and had an important influence on his contemporaries. Above is a delightful painting of the *Young Bacchus* by Guido Reni (the fine frame dates from the end of the 17th century). Also on this wall is a delicately painted *Epiphany* by an unknown painter of the 15th-century Umbrian school. On the left wall is a

tondo of the *Holy Family*, by Luca Signorelli, in a lovely frame, and above it a tondo of the *Madonna and Child with Angels* by the school of Botticelli. Displayed one above the other are two interesting portraits: the damaged *Portrait of a Man*, in a typical Florentine headdress, is by Botticelli, and the *Portrait of a Lady* in profile (called the *Bella Simonetta*) is attributed by some scholars only to his *bottega*, and by others considered a 19th-century work— the identity of both the sitter and the painter have been much debated. The unusual *Portrait of a Woman* in profile in a white veil (once thought to be Caterina Sforza) is now attributed to Piero di Cosimo. Above is a tondo by Beccafumi. The *Eleven Thousand Martyrs* is by Pontormo. Above the fine painting of *Mary Magdalen* by Il Bachiacca is a tondo by Mariotto Albertinelli.

On the entrance wall is a *Portrait of a Man* by Francesco Salviati and, on the other side of the door, an unusual *Adoration of the Magi* by Pontormo. On the window wall: *Dance of Apollo with the Muses*, by Baldassarre Peruzzi (beneath is a table in *scagliola* with a copy of the painting) and *Madonna and Child with the Young St John*, attributed to Botticelli. Above the door into the Sala di Ulisse (Room 17) is another tondo by Francesco Botticini. In the centre of the room is a huge Sèvres vase made in 1844.

(13) Corridoio delle Colonne: Hung with small Flemish paintings by Cornelis van Poelenburgh, Paul Brill, Frans Franken, Jan Brueghel (*Orpheus*), David Ryckaert (*Temptations of St Anthony*) and others.

(14) Sala della Giustizia: The superb *Portrait of a Man* here, thought to be Vincenzo or Tommaso Mosti, is one of Titian's first portraits. He also probably painted the other *Portrait of a Gentleman* opposite the windows, and the *Redeemer*, another early work. If the curtain is open there is a good view of the tower of Palazzo Vecchio and the hill of Fiesole behind.

(15) Sala di Flora: Contains (on the wall opposite the windows) a small half-length figure of Mary Magdalen by Perugino, similar to his self-portraits.

(16) Sala dei Putti: Has exquisite still-lifes by Rachele Ruysch, the *Girl with a Candle* by Godfried Schalken, and other 17th–18th-century Dutch works by Willem van Aelst and Ludolf Backhuysen. Also here is a fine small painting in monochrome of the *Three Graces* by Rubens.

(17) Sala di Ulisse: This lies beyond the Sala di Prometeo (*see above*). Opposite the entrance there is a good *Portrait of a Man* in a hat by the 16th-century Florentine school and an *Ecce Homo* by Cigoli. Beyond the door and on the next wall are some fine works by the great portraitist Moroni. The beautiful small painting, once part of a *cassone* (dower chest), of the *Death of Lucrezia* is by Filippino Lippi (showing the influence of Botticelli). On the last wall is Raphael's *Madonna dell'Impannata* (so named from the window covered with cloth instead of glass in the background), a mature composition, perhaps with the collaboration of his workshop.

(18) Sala dell'Educazione di Giove: This lies beyond a splendid Empire bathroom by Cacialli. It contains one of the most famous Florentine works of the 17th century, *Judith with the Head of Holofernes* by Cristofano Allori (the artist is said to have portrayed himself as Holofernes, his mistress Mazzafirra as the haughty, insouciant Judith, and her mother as the anxious-looking maidservant). On the opposite wall is another well-known painting, a *Sleeping Cupid*, by Caravaggio, painted in Malta in 1608 (in its beautiful original frame). Beyond the door is a small portrait of Claude of Lorraine by Jean Clouet. On the last wall the *Portrait of a Man* formerly attributed to Anthony van Dyck is now generally considered to be the work of van Ravesteyn.

(19) Sala della Stufa: The beautiful frescoes by Pietro da Cortona show the *Four Ages of the World*. This was Cortona's first work in Palazzo Pitti (1637), and the elaborate allegories include references to his patrons, Grand Duke Ferdinando II and his wife Vittoria della Rovere: the oak tree symbolizes the name Rovere ('oak' in Italian) and the lion refers to the *Marzocco* (the heraldic lion) of Florence. This part of the palace was formerly a loggia and the vault fresco is by Matteo Rosselli (1622). Cortona's frescoes recreate the effect of an open terrace. The room was called *della stufa* (meaning 'of the stove') when heating was installed in this wing. The majolica pavement with the *Triumph of Bacchus* dates from 1640.

The Main Rooms

(20) Sala dell'Iliade: The ceiling (1819) is by Luigi Sabatelli, one of the most important Tuscan painters of the early 19th century, and illustrates Homer's *Iliad*. Two large paintings of the *Assumption* by Andrea del Sarto are hung here: that on the right wall is one of his most important late works. The other large painting on the third wall, the *Pala di San Marco* is by Fra' Bartolomeo. Also on this wall are two full-length standing male portraits, both by Titian, one of them a portrait of Philip II of Spain. Above this is *Mary Magdalen*, by one of the few women artists represented in the gallery, Artemisia Gentileschi. Talented and independent spirited, Gentileschi trained under her father, Orazio, who in turn owed much to Caravaggio. Dramatic Caraveggesque chiaroscuro certainly suited Artemisia's choice of subject matter. She had a particular affinity for the story of Judith and Holofernes (the *Judith* on the adjoining wall is hers, though her most famous treatment of the subject is in the Uffizi). Legend relates this to the fact that Artemisia was raped as a young woman, and that her assailant was never brought to justice.

On the other side of the door, the small *Portrait of a Man* (thought to be a goldsmith) is by Ridolfo del Ghirlandaio and shows the influence of Raphael. He also painted the fine *Portrait of a Lady* on the next wall, hung beside Andrea del Sarto's altarpiece, on the other side of which is another beautiful *Portrait of a Lady*, known as *La Gravida* as she is expecting a child, painted c. 1506 by Raphael. Above is a *Portrait of a Man*, attributed to Joos van Cleve. On the

window wall is an unexpected 16th-century portrait of Elizabeth I of England by an English artist. On the last wall is a small equestrian portrait of Philip IV of Spain by Velázquez, and, on the other side of the door, a portrait of Count Valdemar Christian of Denmark by Justus Suttermans (who also painted Prince Mattias de' Medici on the opposite wall). This Flemish painter was appointed to the Medici court in 1619 and remained in its service until his death in 1681. It is through his numerous portraits that we know today what the most influential figures in 17th century Florence looked like.

Above is hung Eleonora de' Medici by Frans Pourbus the Younger, who was Suttermans' master. Above the door is the *Baptism of Christ* by Veronese. In the centre of the room is a fine early-19th-century marble group representing *Charity* by Lorenzo Bartolini. The 17th–18th-century gilded bronze decoration of the four vases displayed here is by Massimiliano Soldani.

(21) Sala di Saturno: The ceiling was completed by Pietro da Cortona's able pupil Ciro Ferri in 1665. Here are displayed some famous masterpieces by Raphael. His *Madonna della Seggiola* (named after the chair, *seggiola*), a beautifully composed tondo, is one of his most mature works (c. 1514–15). It was purchased by the Medici shortly after the artist's death, and became one of the most popular paintings of the Madonna. The frame is by Giovanni Battista Foggini. On the opposite wall is Raphael's *Madonna del Granduca*—named after Grand Duke Ferdinand III of Lorraine, who purchased it in 1800, while in exile during the Napoleonic period. It is probably an early work (c. 1504–05) and is painted in a very different style, showing the influence of Leonardo. Also on this wall is Raphael's portrait of Cardinal Bernardo Dovizi da Bibbiena. On the last wall are four more works by Raphael: the portraits of Agnolo Doni and Maddalena Strozzi (in the pose of Leonardo's *Mona Lisa*) were painted probably as a diptych about two years after their marriage in 1504. Both have splendid landscapes in the background, and monochrome scenes on the back illustrating Ovid's account of the Flood by another hand. (Michelangelo's *Tondo Doni*, now in the Uffizi, was also painted for this young couple.) The tiny *Vision of Ezekiel* is hung next to a large altarpiece known as the *Madonna del Baldacchino*, commissioned in 1507 by the Dei family for their chapel in Santo Spirito. It was left unfinished in 1508 and enlarged at the top by Niccolò Cassana after Prince Ferdinando purchased it in 1697.

Also in this room is a very fine *Deposition* painted in 1495 by Perugino; the *Head of a Man* by Annibale Carracci; a *Disputation on the Trinity* by Andrea del Sarto; and the *Martyrdom of St Agatha* by Sebastiano del Piombo.

(22) Sala di Giove: This was the throne-room of the Medici and contains Pietro da Cortona's most refined decoration of the entire suite of rooms (*see p. 122*). Beautifully restored in 1999, it shows the young prince Ferdinando in glory, surrounded by the virtues. By the far door is Raphael's, *Portrait of a Lady* (*La Velata*

or 'Lady with a Veil'), one of his most beautiful paintings. The grace and dignity of the sitter pervade the work, rendered with a skill which anticipates the hand of Titian. It was purchased by Cosimo II de' Medici. On the other side of the door is the beautiful Venetian painting known as the *Three Ages of Man* (though in fact it probably represents a concert); this has had various attributions, the most convincing of which seems to be Giorgione. On the wall opposite the window, the *Head of St Jerome*, an exquisite small work painted on paper, in an elaborate 19th-century frame, once attributed to Pollaiolo, is now thought to be by Verrocchio. Above it is *Jacobina Vogekort* by the 16th-century Flemish school. The *Annunciation* is an early work by Andrea del Sarto. On the next wall is *Guidobaldo della Rovere* in armour, by Bronzino, and the *Fates* by Francesco Salviati. The *Deposition* is Fra' Bartolomeo's last work and one of his best. During its restoration in 1983–88, the two figures of Saints Peter and Paul were revealed in the background: this proves that it is a fragment. Above it hangs a picture of nymphs and satyrs in a fine landscape by Rubens and next to the door, the *Young St John the Baptist* by Andrea del Sarto (1523), which is one of the best-known representations of the Baptist. The picture was owned by Cosimo I and formerly hung in the Tribuna of the Uffizi. On the other side of the door is the *Madonna in Adoration* by Perugino, and, at the top of the wall, the *Madonna of the House-martin*, a delightful work by Guercino. The marble statue in the centre of the room representing *Victory* is by Vincenzo Consani.

Raphael: *La Velata* (c. 1516).

THE BAROQUE CEILING DECORATIONS

The ceilings of the Sala di Saturno, Sala di Giove, Sala di Marte, Sala di Apollo and Sala di Venere were beautifully decorated in the 1640s for Ferdinando II by Pietro da Cortona, founder of the Roman Baroque school of painting. Numerous works in Rome by this famous artist attest to his ability to combine vivid colours in spectacular compositions based on complicated perspective devices and theatrical decorative schemes. The decoration in these five reception rooms, which includes fine gilded and white stuccoes by both Roman and Florentine craftsmen, illustrates the virtues of the young Medici prince and exalts the grand-ducal family by means of extravagant allegories (Ferdinando is represented by the figure of Hercules). The frescoes also celebrate Galileo and the discoveries he had made earlier in the century through numerous illustrations of the constellations and planets, after which the rooms are named. The decorative programme was designed by the librarian Francesco Rondinelli, and had a great influence in the decoration of royal apartments all over Europe, including Versailles. However, this new style of painting found little following amongst Cortona's Florentine contemporaries after he left the city in 1647, and it was only through his very able pupil Ciro Ferri that the frescoes were finally completed some twenty years later. This type of decoration is absent from other Florentine palaces of the period, and indeed it was only in the early 1960s that Cortona's work here was first studied with careful appreciation.

(23) **Sala di Marte:** The largest painting in the room is the *Consequences of War*, one of Rubens' most important works. It is an allegory showing Venus trying to prevent Mars going to war, while both figures are surrounded by its destructive and tragic consequences. It was painted in 1638 and sent by the artist to his friend and fellow countryman at the Medici court, Suttermans. Below are two beautiful small works by Andrea del Sarto with scenes from the life of St Joseph. On the right hangs Titian's superb portrait of Cardinal Ippolito de' Medici, in Hungarian costume. The Cardinal was the illegitimate son of the Duke of Nemours, and Lorenzo the Magnificent's grandson. He was nominated cardinal against his wishes by Clement VII when he was twelve years old. He commissioned this portrait from Titian to celebrate his return from Hungary, where he had been successful in a battle against the Turks. On the other side is another splendid *Portrait of a Man* in fur robes, this one by Veronese; the sitter was once identified as Daniele Barbaro. On the next wall, two paintings of the *Madonna and Child* by the Spanish painter Murillo flank Rubens' delightful portrait group known as *The Four Philosophers* (from left to right: Rubens, his brother Filippo, Justus Lipsius and Jan van Wouwer). Rubens' brother and van Wouwer were both pupils of the great Flemish humanist Lipsius, famous for his studies of Seneca, whose bust is shown in the painting. To the left of the

door into the next room is Tintoretto's supposed portrait of Luigi Cornaro, and a fine official portrait of Cardinal Guido Bentivoglio by Anthony van Dyck.

(24) Sala di Apollo: To the right of the entrance door is one of Titian's masterpieces, his *Portrait of a Gentleman*, probably dating from 1540–45 or perhaps much earlier. Recent research has suggested that the sitter might be the Genoese nobleman Gian Luigi Fieschi. The painting was acquired by Crown Prince Ferdinando, son of Cosimo III, in 1698, but its provenance is unknown. It was restored (probably for the first time) in 1999. On the other side of the door is Titian's *Mary Magdalen*, another beautifully painted work, which was frequently copied. Also on this wall is Andrea del Sarto's *Deposition* (1523). Rosso Fiorentino's *Madonna Enthroned with Saints* has been removed from the wall opposite for restoration. It is a typical Florentine Mannerist work painted in 1522 for the church of Santo Spirito; when Crown Prince Ferdinando acquired it in 1691, he had it enlarged to fit its new frame. The *Portrait of Vittoria della Rovere*, dressed as a Roman vestal, is by Suttermans. On the next wall are hung a *Holy Family* by Andrea del Sarto, *Cleopatra* by Guido Reni and, beyond the door, *Isabella Clara Eugenia* (governor of the Netherlands), dressed in the habit of a nun, by Rubens, and a double portrait of Charles I and Henrietta Maria by Anthony van Dyck.

(25) Sala di Venere: With the earliest ceiling (1641–42) by Pietro da Cortona, this room is named after the *Venus Italica* sculpted by Canova. This was presented to Florence by Napoleon in 1812, in exchange for the *Medici Venus* which he had stolen from the Tribuna in the Uffizi and transported to Paris (*see p. 98*). It is one of the masterpieces of Neoclassical art in Florence. By the door is Titian's *Portrait of a Lady* (*La Bella*), commissioned by the Duke of Urbino in 1536, apparently an idealised portrait similar to the *Venus of Urbino* in the Uffizi gallery. This superb work came to Florence as part of the dowry of Vittoria della Rovere in 1631, on her marriage to Ferdinando II. Also on this wall is Titian's exquisitely painted portrait of Pietro Aretino, one of his most forceful works. Aretino was disappointed with the painting, and after a quarrel with the artist he presented it to Cosimo I in 1545 (and it was the first of the eleven portraits by Titian here to be hung in Palazzo Pitti). Above is a large seascape (one of a pair; the second picture is on the opposite wall), painted for Cardinal Gian Carlo de' Medici, one of Ferdinando II's brothers, by Salvatore Rosa. On the wall opposite the windows are two lovely landscapes by Rubens: *Return from the Hayfields*, with a delightful joyful scene, and its companion *Ulysses in the Phaeacian Isle*. On the last wall the portrait of Pope Julius II is a copy by Titian of Raphael's painting which survives in two versions (one in the National Gallery, London, and one in the Uffizi). The famous *Concert* is a superb painting of c. 1510–12, the attribution of which has been much discussed. Some scholars believe it is by Titian, but it appears that more than one hand was involved, and Giorgione may have been responsible for the figure on the left. The portrait of Baccio Valori is by Sebastiano del Piombo.

Appartamenti Reali

Open as Galleria Palatina, but usually closed for maintenance work in January. Plan on p. 115. These lavishly decorated rooms were used as state apartments from the 17th century onwards by the Medici and Lorraine grand dukes and later by the royal house of Savoy. They have been restored (as far as possible) to their appearance in 1880–1911 when they were first occupied by the House of Savoy. The contents reflect the eclectic taste of the Savoy rulers, as well as the neo-Baroque period of the 19th-century Lorraine grand dukes, and include splendid silks and furnishings made in Florence and France during the last period of the Lorraine grand dukes; sumptuous gilded chandeliers, Neoclassical mirrors and candelabra; well preserved early 19th-century carpets from Tournai; huge oriental vases; furniture decorated with *pietre dure*; and paintings and sculptures.

(26) Sala delle Nicchie: Neoclassical room redesigned by Giuseppe Maria Terreni and Giuseppe Castagnoli in the late 18th century. The original room by Ammannati (1561–62) had been built to house Cosimo I's collection of antique sculpture which was then transferred to the Uffizi: only six uncatalogued Roman statues remain here in the niches.

(I) Sala Verde: The green silk drapes and wall hangings were made by the Florentine firm of Francesco Frullini in 1854–55. The ceiling has monochrome frescoes by Giuseppe Castagnoli with a small painting of the *Allegory of Peace between Florence and Fiesole* by Luca Giordano at its centre. On the wall opposite the window are delightful portraits of the daughters of Louis XV by Jean Marc Nattier: Marie Henriette is portrayed as Flora and Maria Adelaide as Diana. On the end wall is a portrait of a Knight of Malta, generally considered to be the work of Caravaggio. On the window wall is a very fine ebony cabinet made for Vittoria della Rovere in 1677, decorated with *pietre dure*.

(II) Sala del Trono: The red damask curtains and wall hangings, made in France in 1853–54, are typical of the Napoleonic period. The Japanese vases date from the Edo period (c. 1700), and the Chinese vases from the 19th century. The carpet was made in Tournai in 1854, and the Italian chandelier and mirrors are of the same period.

(III) Salotto Celeste: The 18th-century ceiling dates from the time of Peter Leopold. The round table (1826) has a fine top in *pietre dure*, and the chandelier was made by the Dutch carver Vittorio Crosten in 1697. The room also contains ten Medici portraits by Suttermans.

(IV) Chapel: Formerly the *alcova* (official bedroom) of Crown Prince Ferdinando (son of Cosimo III de' Medici). Here are portraits of Cosimo I and Piero il Gottoso by Cristofano dell'Altissimo and a sketch of a lady by Anthony van Dyck. The *Madonna and Child* by Carlo Dolci is in a rich frame of ebony and *pietre dure* (1697), probably designed by Giovanni Battista Foggini.

(V) Sala dei Pappagalli: This room has three doors and a large decorative wood-burning stove. By the entrance is a portrait of Giulia Varano della Rovere,

Duchess of Urbino, by the *bottega* of Titian, and (by the stove) a small portrait, thought to be the work of Andrea del Sarto (perhaps depicting his wife, who, according to Vasari, was domineering and difficult), but also attributed to Pontormo. Volterrano painted the portrait of Cardinal Giancarlo de' Medici. The table, with a top in *pietre dure*, dates from 1790–1831. The bronze clock-case is by Pierre-Philippe Thomire (c. 1812).

(VI–IX) Queen Margherita's Apartments: These rooms (*not always open*) form part of the suite of Queen Margherita of Savoy (1851–1926), wife of Umberto I (*see below*). Her Salotto (VI) is decorated with yellow silk made in France c. 1805–10. The paintings date from the 19th century, except for the delightful studio scene (based on Rubens' house in Antwerp), painted in the 17th century by Cornelis de Baellieur. Beside it is an ebony cabinet decorated with ivory, alabaster and gilded bronze, which was produced in the grand-ducal workshop by Giovanni Battista Foggini and others in 1704.

The Camera della Regina (VII) has a pretty bed decorated in 1885 and a prie-dieu in ebony and *pietre dure* made in 1687. The Gabinetto Ovale (VIII) and Gabinetto Rotondo (IX) were created by Gaspare Maria Paoletti (1765) for Grand Duchess Maria Lodovica, infanta of Spain and wife of Peter Leopold. The beautiful silk chinoiserie furnishings were made in Florence in 1780–83.

The Gabinetto Rotondo has 18th-century furniture and mirrors around the walls, and 19th-century upholstered chairs in the centre of the room.

(X–XIII) King Umberto's Apartments: There is sometimes access to these rooms, formerly the apartments of King Umberto I, who became King of Italy in 1878, and was assassinated by the Anarchist Gaetano Bresci in 1900. The yellow Camera del Re (X), decorated at the end of the 18th century, has a fine Empire-style table by Giuseppe Colzi (1822) in its centre. Off this room can be seen the Toilette del Re. The small Studio del Re (XI), with yellow silk furnishings dating from 1770, has a portrait of Claudia de' Medici, daughter of Ferdinando I, by Suttermans. The last two rooms, the Salone Rosso (XII) and the Anticamera del Re (XIII), have 19th-century paintings and furniture.

The apartments are usually left through the Sala di Bona (XIV), entirely covered with attractive frescoes by Bernardino Poccetti in 1608 celebrating Cosimo I. Poccetti was a prolific painter who left numerous frescoes in churches and cloisters all over Florence in the latter half of the 16th century.

(XV–XIX) Appartamento degli Arazzi: Ceiling decorations by Bernardino Poccetti, Passignano, Ludovico Cigoli, and Cristofano Allori and a loggia (enclosed in the 19th century) with earlier frescoes (1588) of charming domestic scenes by Alessandro Allori (father of Cristofano). Many of the tapestries were made in the Gobelin factory (some to designs by Charles Le Brun); others are Florentine. The furniture dates mostly from the early 18th–19th centuries. The 18th-century Sala Bianca is a magnificent ballroom designed by Paoletti.

MEDICI GRAND DUKES AT PALAZZO PITTI

Ferdinando I (grand duke 1587–1609)

When Ferdinando became a cardinal he bought the Villa Medici in Rome (in 1576) and turned it into one of the grandest residences in the city, with a famous collection of ancient Roman sculpture. But just ten years later, on the death of his brother (Francesco I), he had to renounce his cardinal's hat and move back to Florence to succeed him, taking Christine of Lorraine as his wife. His marriage celebrations at Palazzo Pitti were incredibly spectacular and included a naval battle in the courtyard, covered over and flooded for the occasion. It was Ferdinando who transferred the grand-ducal residence permanently to the Pitti (up until now used by the Medici only for ceremonial occasions). He arranged two other important marriages in the family which were also public spectacles: that of his niece Maria to Henri IV in 1600, and his heir Cosimo to Maria Maddalena of Austria. He carried out important agricultural reforms and land reclamation schemes in Tuscany, and proclaimed Livorno a free port with religious liberty. He had Buontalenti build the villas of the Petraia and Artimino close to Florence, where he would enjoy the country air.

Cosimo II (grand duke 1609–21)

Although Cosimo suffered from ill health and died of tuberculosis at the age of 30, he oversaw the work to enlarge Palazzo Pitti by adding the two side wings, and he arranged a small gallery on the piano nobile where he hung Raphael's painting known as La Velata (pictured on p. 121).

Ferdinando II (grand duke 1621–70)

Ferdinando was only eleven when his father (Cosimo II) died and so his mother Maria Maddalena and his grandmother Christine acted as regents. His two cardinal brothers also had an important influence on him. Cardinal Leopoldo, who acted as his minister of foreign affairs in Tuscany, had a great interest in science and was a passionate collector with a particular interest in Venetian paintings, in drawings, and in self-portraits. In 1654 he purchased The Concert attributed at the time to Giorgione, but now thought to be an early work by Titian and still one of the masterpieces of the Galleria Palatina. Ferdinando's other Cardinal brother, Gian Carlo, had a special interest in music and theatre, and kept Ferdinando informed on the artistic activities in Rome under Pope Urban VIII. Another brother, Mattias, who commanded the Tuscan army, put together the remarkable collection of ivories still to be seen in the Museo degli Argenti (see p. 137).

During Ferdinando's long reign, the Pitti reached its maximum splendour: as well as his family and brothers, some 160 members of his court lived here. The grand duke spent the winter on the piano nobile of the palace and the summer in the cooler ground-floor apartments. He married Vittoria della Rovere, daughter of the Duke of Urbino, and inherited as part of her dowry some masterpieces by Raphael and Titian. Ferdinando commissioned the frescoes by Pietro da Cortona for the palace, marking the transition from the late Renaissance to the splendours of the Baroque period.

Cosimo III (grand duke 1670–1723)

Cosimo III held the office of grand duke for longer than all the other Medici but he proved a totally inept ruler, ignoring the interests of Tuscany. In addition his marriage to Marguerite Louise d'Orléans was a disaster. An atmosphere of decadence took hold, although recent research has revealed that Cosimo, venerating the memory of his uncle Cardinal Leopoldo, did take special care of the works of art in Palazzo Pitti and began collecting together the paintings which in the following centuries formed the Galleria Palatina. Indeed the most popular of all the pictures in the gallery, Raphael's *Madonna della Seggiola,* was moved here by him from the Tribuna of the Uffizi, and given its sumptuous frame.

Crown Prince Ferdinando (died 1713)

Destined to succeed his father Cosimo III, Ferdinando predeceased him in 1713. Nevertheless, he is remembered for his passionate interest in art and music, and he made some important acquisitions for the Medici collections, including Parmigianino's *Madonna dal collo lungo*, Andrea del Sarto's *Madonna of the Harpies*, and Titian's *Portrait of a Gentleman*. He was also interested in little-known contemporary painters such as Livio Mehus and Magnasco. Though he had a habit of removing paintings he particularly liked from churches in Florence and Tuscany, he did replace them with copies.

Gian Gastone (grand duke 1723–37)

The second son of Cosimo III, Gian Gastone succeeded his father since his elder brother had died without heirs. He was an introvert interested in scientific studies but totally ignorant of affairs of state, and his rule was marked, like that of his father, with an increasing air of decadence. He became an alcoholic and led a dissipated life in his bedroom, refusing to appear in public for the last eight years of his rule. His sister Anna Maria Luisa, widow of the Elector Palatine, is fondly remembered in Florence for the 'Family Pact' she made in 1716 when living in Palazzo Pitti. This left the Medici artistic heritage (including their collections of paintings and sculpture, scientific instruments, and libraries) to the Lorraine grand dukes for 'the ornament of the State, the utility of the public, and in order to attract the attention of foreigners'—and only on the condition that not a single work would ever leave Florence or Tuscany.

Galleria d'Arte Moderna

Open 8.30–1.50; closed on second and fourth Sun, and first, third and fifth Mon of the month. T: 055 238 8616. Plan opposite.

On the floor above the Galleria Palatina is the Galleria d'Arte Moderna, opened here in 1924. The collection was formed around 1784 by the Lorraine grand duke Peter Leopold when it was part of the Accademia di Belle Arti. Later acquisitions were made by the Savoy rulers and by the Comune of Florence. Since 1914 it has been administered jointly by the Comune and the state, and the collection continues to be augmented. The works currently on show, arranged chronologically and by schools, cover the period from the mid-18th century up to the First World War. Tuscan art of the 19th century is particularly well represented, notably the Macchiaioli School, which was active in Tuscany before 1864. These artists took their inspiration directly from nature, and their paintings are characterised by *macchie* or spots of colour. The most important Macchiaioli painters, who could be termed Tuscan Impressionists, are Giovanni Fattori, Silvestro Lega and Telemaco Signorini.

(Room 1) Neoclassicism. On the entrance wall hangs *Hercules at the Crossroads* by Pompeo Batoni (1742), which was purchased for Palazzo Pitti by Ferdinand III in 1818. The charming seated statue of *Psyche*, by the window, is by Pietro Tenerani (1816–17). It was commissioned by Carlotta Lenzoni Medici, who held a salon in Florence attended by the famous literary figures of her day including Byron, Leopardi, Alfieri, Rossini and Manzoni. The charming view of the Boboli Gardens beyond the Fontana del Carciofo in the courtyard takes in the amphitheatre and the steps rising to the fountain of Neptune and the colossal statue of *Abundance* at the top of the gardens. On the skyline can be seen the Forte di Belvedere. Also in this room are two small landscapes by Philipp Hackert, a German artist who was court painter to Ferdinand IV of Naples.

(Room 2) French Influence: This room illustrates the influence the French had when they occupied Florence in the first decade of the 19th century. The most famous artist who worked for the French court was Antonio Canova, whose signed bust of the muse Calliope (1812) is displayed here. It is a very fine work which retains its original patina (numerous other Neoclassical marble works were later polished). It is probably an idealised portrait of Elisa Baciocchi, Napoleon's sister, whom Napoleon appointed Grand Duchess of Tuscany in 1809; she is also shown here with her daughter in the Boboli Gardens, in a painting by Giuseppe Bezzuoli. The huge painting of *Napoleon with his Troops* is by Pietro Benvenuti, whom Elisa appointed director of the Accademia di Belle Arti. It was commissioned for Versailles but was returned to Florence when Benvenuti was sent to Paris after the Congress of Vienna by the Grand Duke Ferdinand III, to reclaim the Tuscan works of art which had been requisitioned by the French during their occupation of Tuscany. The fine portrait of the engraver Antonio Santarelli is by François-Xavier Fabre.

PALAZZO PITTI
(SECOND FLOOR)

GALLERIA D'ARTE MODERNA

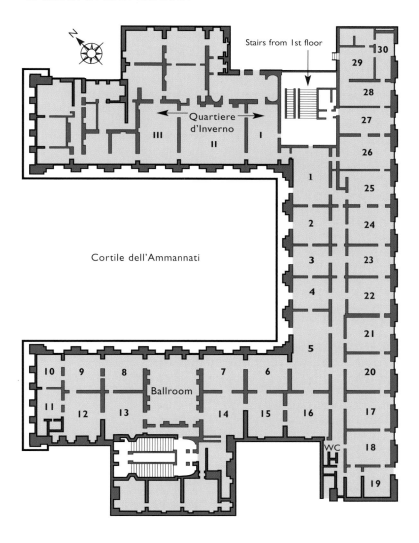

(Room 3) Florence before Italian Unification: The portraits here include one (on the left wall) of Maria Luisa of Bourbon-Parma (with two red roses in her hair) by François-Xavier Fabre. Maria Luisa was 'queen of Etruria' in 1801, wife of Lodovico. When she was widowed in 1803, she became regent for their son, but in 1807 left for Portugal with the 11-year-old boy and her place was taken by Napoleon's sister Elisa Baciocchi, whom Napoleon instated as the new Grand Duchess of Tuscany. The sumptuous lapis lazuli centrepiece, decorated with mosaics and pearls, was made for Napoleon, and the huge Sèvres vase has a bronze mount by Pierre-Philippe Thomire.

(Room 4) The Demidoff Room: The Demidoff were a wealthy Russian family who lived in Florence from 1820 onwards. Displayed here is the model for the monument on the Lungarno commissioned from Lorenzo Bartolini by Anatolio and Paolo Demidoff to commemorate their father Nicola. The portrait (in a very elaborate frame) of Anatolio's wife Matilde was painted in 1844 by the Dutch painter Ary Scheffer (1795–1858).

(Room 5) Romantic historical paintings: Included here is a huge painting of *Charles VIII Entering Florence through Porta San Frediano* by Giuseppe Bezzuoli (1829). Girolamo Savonarola, Pier Capponi and Niccolò Machiavelli are present in the crowd. The French king entered Florence in 1494, after Lorenzo the Magnificent's son Piero was ousted by the Signoria. Savonarola claimed Charles's arrival as a fulfilment of every-thing he has prophesied, and as retribution on Florence for her sinful, luxurious ways. Derived from 17th-century historical canvases, this work had a fundamental influence on the 19th-century Tuscan school of historical painters. Works by Francesco Hayez include a Venetian scene. The small *Deposition* by Francesco Coghetti (1848) is painted in the style of Caravaggio in patriotic tones of white, red and green. The two bronze statues of Cain and Abel are by Giovanni Dupré.

(Room 6) Later 19th century: The paintings here include the exquisite tiny *Cloister* (1860) by Giuseppe Abbati, which shows a new interest in light and volume: concerns which were to dominate the art of the Macchiaioli group of painters. There are also scenes of medieval Florence by Odoardo Borrani and Vincenzo Cabianca, four still-lifes by Giovacchino Toma, and a portrait of Linda Ussi by Stefano Ussi.

Room 7: This is the first of a suite of rooms known as the Quartiere Nuovo Palatino, with early 19th-century painted ceilings. It displays works by the famous portrait painter of the second half of the 19th century Antonio Ciseri, including one of Giovanni Dupré (1885). The striking portrait of another sculptor, Emilio Zocchi, is by his friend Raffaello Sorbi (1868), and there is self-portrait by Luigi Mussini.

The Ballroom: Begun c. 1825 by Pasquale Poccianti, this displays early 19th-century statues, including two of the young Bacchus by Giovanni Dupré, and works by Aristodemo Costoli and Pio Fedi.

Room 8: The ceiling is by Nicola Monti. Amongst the portraits is one, in the centre of the left wall, showing a *Noblewoman from the Morrocchi Family* by Antonio Puccinelli (1855–60). Next to it is displayed a self-portrait by Giovanni Fattori dating from 1854, who also painted the *Portrait of a Man* (c. 1865) and the oval portrait of Signora Biliotti (1870) exhibited here. The portrait of Giulia Tempestini Kennedy Lawrie is by Giovanni Boldini (an early work).

(Room 9) 19th-century landscapes: Mid-19th-century landscapes showing the influence of the Barbizon school of French painters, including works by Serafino de Tivoli (a pastoral scene of two cows), and a large painting by Antonio Fontanesi entitled *After the Rain* (c. 1861). The ceiling is by Gaspero Martinelli.

(Room 10) Cristiano Banti Collection: This room overlooks the Amphitheatre in the Boboli Gardens and the panels of its ceiling were painted by Luigi Catani. The Cristiano Banti collection was left to the gallery in 1955. Banti (1824–1904) was a painter from Tuscany; he was also a well-known collector and a great friend of the artist Giovanni Boldini. His collection includes late 19th-century works by Banti himself, and a portrait of him by Giovanni Boldini, as well as numerous charming portraits of Banti's daughter Alaide as a child at various ages (many of them by Boldini, who fell in love with her) and (by Michele Giordano) as a grown woman. The *Portrait of a Lady* in profile (to the right of the window) is by Francesco Saverio Altamura.

(Room 11) Diego Martelli Collection: This room is decorated with another ceiling by Catani. The collection was bequeathed to the Comune of Florence in 1897 with the intention of founding a modern art gallery. Martelli (1839–96) was a collector interested in both the Macchiaioli painters and the French Impressionists. He gave hospitality to some of the best known Macchiaioli painters including Fattori and Lega at his home in Castiglioncello on the Tuscan coast. On the window wall are two delightful portraits of Martelli by Federico Zandomeneghi.

The collection has some notable works by the Macchiaioli School, which Martelli encouraged, and (on the far wall) two landscapes by Camille Pissarro, acquired when the Impressionists were out of fashion. Also on this wall are two more remarkable paintings by Federico Zandomeneghi—who lived in Paris and was clearly influenced by contemporary French painters—entitled *In Bed* and *Honeymoon*. The rest of the collection consists of small works by protagonists of the Macchiaioli School including Giovanni Fattori, Silvestro Lega (the charming *Walk in the Garden*, on the wall opposite the window, and *Portrait of a Peasant Girl*), and Giuseppe Abbati who stayed with Martelli at Castiglioncello. The bust of Garibaldi is by Ettore Ximenes.

Room 12: Above the fireplace is *Singing a Stornello* (a traditional Tuscan folk song) another masterpiece by Silvestro Lega, a conversation piece showing a scene in a villa in the environs of Florence, pervaded with a delightfully evocative atmosphere. Beside it has been hung Adriano Cecioni's portrait of his wife: Cecioni is also represented in the room with a number of plaster sculptures. There are also historical and genre scenes here.

(Room 13) Military painting: This features a large historical canvas by Giovanni Fattori showing the desolate Italian camp after the Battle of Magenta in 1859, when the French and Italians (the Piedmontese) beat the Austrian troops in the second War of Independence. There are other military scenes here by Silvestro Lega, Vincenzo Cabianca, Telemaco Signorini, and Alessandro Lanfredini.

(Room 14) Historical works: Antonio Ciseri and Gabriele Castagnola. The green dome of the synagogue and the top of the tower of Palazzo Vecchio can be seen from the window.

(Room 15) Historical works: More works by Stefano Ussi are displayed here, including the large *Expulsion of the Duke of Athens* and a group of very small pieces.

Room 16: This room contains a bust of Giuseppe Verdi, commissioned by him from the Neapolitan sculptor Vincenzo Gemito. Here are more battle scenes by Giovanni Fattori and Carlo Ademollo, and a stand made in the late 19th century for the Crown of Italy.

(Room 17) Late 19th-century portraits: There is a fine view from this room which overlooks Piazza Pitti: straight ahead is the small dome and campanile of Santo Spirito with the domed San Frediano in Cestello beyond. To the left rises the church of the Carmine, and further left is the green hill of Bellosguardo, and the neo-Gothic tower in the garden of Palazzo Torrigiani, on the extreme left. The top of the façade of Santa Maria Novella next to its campanile can be seen to the right, and further right the dome of the Cappella dei Principi. On the extreme right is the Campanile and Duomo. On the walls are displayed portraits of the bourgeoisie dating from the 1870s and 1880s, including several by Vittorio Corcos (the one of the *Lady with a Dog and Umbrella* in particular shows the influence of elegant Parisian life). The statue of Victor Hugo is by Gaetano Trentanove.

(Room 18) Masterpieces of the Macchiaioli School: This room has some very important works painted in the last two decades of the 19th century and purchased by the Comune of Florence. On the wall opposite the windows are three fine works by Giovanni Fattori: *Ritratto della figliastra*, a portrait of the artist's step-daughter; and two late works, the dramatic *Staffato* showing a horse bolting and dragging its rider to death (his foot having been caught in the stirrup), and a solitary white horse (*Cavallo Bianco*), both of which express Fattori's sad last years when he was unjustly ostracised by his contemporaries. Next to them is displayed Telemaco Signorini's *Bagno penale di Portoferraio*, showing a prison scene. On the wall opposite the entrance are landscapes of the Maremma (in southwest Tuscany) by Fattori, and another famous work (in two versions) by him: the *Libecciata*, representing a windy day at the coast with a stormy sea behind a windblown tamarisk tree—an allegory of life, devoid of human figures. In the table case is Fattori's well-known *Rotonda di Palmieri*, a charming beach scene at Livorno (1866), and other delightful small works by Signorini.

(Room 19) Ambron Collection: More works by the Macchiaioli. Leone Ambron, who died in Florence in 1979, left his important private collection to the gallery. It consists mainly of Macchiaioli and post-Macchiaioli works. On the wall opposite the entrance Giovanni Fattori's small early portrait of *La cugina Argia* is displayed next to Telemaco Signorini's *Leith*, a grey street scene painted during a visit to Scotland in 1881. There are also numerous other works by Fattori, Signorini, Silvestro Lega and Antonio Mancini, as well as more sculptures by Adriano Cecioni.

Room 20: On the far wall are two charming paintings by Telemaco Signorini (*September in Settignano* and a *Hot August day in Pietramala*) flanked by two Maremma scenes by Fattori. On the opposite wall are idyllic country scenes by Egisto Ferroni, typical of the paintings favoured by Florentine bourgeois society in the 1880s.

Room 21: Continues the display of country scenes with works by Enrico Banti and Adolfo Tommasi.

Room 22: Hanging on the wall opposite the entrance are a *Cemetery Scene in Constantinople* by the important Neapolitan painter Domenico Morelli and a fine landscape (*On the Banks of the Olfanto*) by Giuseppe de Nittis.

(Room 23) Late 19th-century Tuscan works: This features works influenced by contemporary European painting. It includes a portrait of the frivolous Bruna Pagliano, dressed in black, by Edoardo Gelli, and works by European artists who came to live in Florence at the end of the 19th century. The female nude is by Adolfo de Carolis, a painter much admired by the eccentric poet Gabriele d'Annunzio.

(Room 24) Divisionism and Symbolism: This illustrates the beginning of these two art movements in the first years of the 20th century. There are some early works by Plinio Nomellini showing his experiments in Divisionism and Symbolism, and sculptures by Medardo Rosso.

(Room 25) Emilio Gagliardini Collection: Macchiaioli paintings including works by Giovanni Fattori, Telemaco Signorini, Silvestro Lega and Giuseppe Abbati.

(Room 26) Portraits by Elisabeth Chaplin: Chaplin (1890–1982) lived in Florence and donated most of her works to the gallery in 1974.

(Room 27) Early 20th-century works: Armando Spadini (1883–1925) and Oscar Ghiglia (1876–1945). Spadini's work contains elements of Symbolism, but he was also much influenced by Renoir.

(Room 28) Works influenced by European artists: Works include a *Self-*

portrait by Lorenzo Viani and a scene of the Carrara marble mines (*La Mina*) by Giuseppe Viner (1876–1925).

Room 29: Works by Giovanni Costetti (1874–1949), whose paintings were left to the gallery by his widow.

Room 30: Displays works acquired at an exhibition in Florence in 1922 by Galileo Chini, Francesco Franchetti and others.

The Mezzanino degli Occhi
Usually only open by appointment; T: 055 294 883.
The works dating from 1922–45 are exhibited in 13 rooms on the floor above, known as the Mezzanino degli Occhi, because it has round windows. These are by the best-known artists of the period including Arturo Tosi, Mario Sironi, Giovanni Colacicchi, Felice Casorati, Ardengo Soffici, Filippo de Pisis, Carlo Carrà, Gino Severini and Giorgio de Chirico.

The Quartiere d'Inverno
The Quartiere d'Inverno (I–XV) can also be seen by appointment (T: 055 294 883).
These apartments were used by the Medici grand dukes, but are named after their last occupants the Duchessa d'Aosta and Prince Luigi of the royal house of Savoy. Luigi, eldest son of Umberto I, became King Vittorio Emanuele III on Umberto's assassination, though for most of his reign he was overshadowed by Mussolini. These rooms were his home until his abdication in 1946, when Italy voted to become a republic. He died in exile the following year. The rooms are interesting for their 18th- and 19th-century decorations and furniture. The first three rooms are usually open with the rest of the Galleria d'Arte Moderna for exhibitions, or to display important works from rooms temporarily closed. The Anticamera (I) has 19th-century tempera decoration on the walls and ceiling. The Salone da Ballo (II) was designed in 1815–30 by Pasquale Poccianti and has Neoclassical stuccoes by Luigi Catani. The Sala da Pranzo (III; formerly called the Sala della Musica) was designed c. 1795 by Gaspare Maria Paoletti with painted decoration by Giuseppe Maria Terreni.

Galleria del Costume
Entrance from Galleria d'Arte Moderna. Open at the same times.
The Galleria del Costume was founded in 1983 on the ground floor of the Palazzina della Meridiana. It is the only museum of the history of fashion in Italy.

This wing of Palazzo Pitti, which faces the Boboli Gardens, was begun for the Lorraine grand dukes in 1776 by Gaspare Maria Paoletti and was finished in 1832 by Pasquale Poccianti. The decoration of the rooms dates mostly from the 1860s. The delightful collection is made up largely from private donations—which continue all the time—and illustrates the history of costume from the 18th to the mid-20th centuries. The beautiful displays of clothes are changed about every two years and frequent exhibitions are held. There are also some clothes dating from the 16th century, including those worn by Eleonora di Toledo, wife of Cosimo I de' Medici, and her son Don Garzia. The precious 18th-century collection includes some rare men's apparel. The Umberto Tirelli (1928–90) collection of costumes used in theatrical and cinematographic productions has been donated to the museum. Other donations include those of the Sicilian noblewoman Donna Franca Florio, and (in 2000) the Italian fashion designer Gianfranco Ferrè. Decorating the rooms are contemporary paintings and sculpture from the Galleria d'Arte Moderna.

Museo degli Argenti

Open 8.30–dusk, closed on first and last Mon of the month; T: 055 238 8709. Entrance from the left side of the courtyard.
The Museo degli Argenti is arranged in the summer apartments of the grand dukes, some of which were used as state rooms. They now contain the eclectic collection formed by the Medici and Lorraine grand dukes of precious objects in silver, ivory, amber and *pietre dure*, including antique pieces, jewellery, and some exotic curiosities. The silver was first exhibited here in the middle of the 19th century (hence the name of the museum) and in the 20th century all that remained of the grand-ducal treasury (formerly kept in the Uffizi) was collected here and opened to the public.

Ground Floor

Sala di Luca Pitti: This is named after the first owner of the palace Luca Pitti, who is commemorated here in a delightful polychrome terracotta bust made in the 15th century. The series of terracotta busts of the seven Medici grand dukes from Alessandro to Gian Gastone are by the workshop of Giovanni Battista Foggini (they are on pretty early-18th-century brackets). The two Medici portraits are by Suttermans, and their genealogical tree dates from 1669. The two serpentine marble vases were decorated in gilded bronze by Massimiliano Soldani Benzi.

Sala di Giovanni da San Giovanni: Exuberant and colourful frescoes by Giovanni da San Giovanni completely cover the walls and ceiling of this room. They were begun after the marriage of Ferdinando II and Vittoria della Rovere in 1634 (an allegory of which is represented on the ceiling). The apotheosis of the Medici family is illustrated through the life of Lorenzo the Magnificent. The sequence begins at the far end of the entrance wall which has two scenes symbolising the *Destruction of Culture* including the *Muses fleeing from Mount Parnassus*. The particularly successful third scene (around the entrance door) shows the *Muses and Poets Finding Refuge in Tuscany* (represented by an allegorical female figure). The two scenes on the adjacent short wall by San Giovanni's pupil Cecco Bravo show *Lorenzo the Magnificent Receiving the Muses* and *Prudence Instructing Lorenzo* (as a consequence Peace, represented by a woman on the lower part of the wall, takes off her armour, while high above War, in the form of the chariot of Mars, gallops away). The scenes on the window wall are by Ottavio Vannini: the central one shows *Lorenzo Seated in the Sculpture Garden of San Marco* while the young Michelangelo presents him with his sculpture of the head of a faun. On the last wall, two scenes by Francesco Furini show *Lorenzo at his Villa of Careggi Surrounded by Members of the Platonic Academy* and an elaborate allegory of his death. On the painted pilasters are trompe l'œil decorations imitating bas-reliefs of classical myths and the seasons.

Sala Buia: The central case in this room displays the magnificent collection of 16 *pietre dure* vases which belonged to Lorenzo the Magnificent, and which bear his monogram 'LA V.R.MED'. Although it is very difficult to date many of them and their provenance is usually unknown, they include late Imperial Roman works, as well as Byzantine and medieval Venetian works. Others come from Persia and Egypt. The collection was begun by Piero il Gottoso and enlarged by Lorenzo. Many of the vases were formerly used as reliquaries and were mounted in silver-gilt in the 15th century or later in the grand-ducal workshops. Lorenzo the Magnificent's death mask and portrait by Luigi Fiammingo are also displayed here.

Four more cases display exquisite smaller works, including Roman cups and dishes in *pietre dure*, and some Byzantine works (most of them with later mounts). Also exhibited here are late 15th-century church vestments made for the Medici.

The Grotticina: This lies beyond the Sala Buia and contains a small fountain and a frescoed ceiling with birds by Florentine artists (1623–34), and a lovely pavement in *pietre dure* and soft stone. The exquisitely carved limewood relief by Grinling Gibbons was presented to Cosimo III in 1682 by Charles II of England. The table in *pietre dure* was made in Prague in the early 17th century. There is a display of 17th- and 18th-century frames, including four by the Dutch craftsman Vittorio Crosten (who also carved the base of the table).

Cappella: This lies to the right of the Sala di Giovanni da San Giovanni and was decorated by local craftsmen in 1623–34.

Reception Rooms: The three rooms beyond the cappella are decorated with delightful trompe l'œil frescoes by the Bolognese painters Angelo Michele Colonna and Agostino Mitelli (1635–41), who worked as partners for over 20 years. The frescoes—which are in exceptionally good condition—cover the wall surfaces with architectural perspectives, animated by the occasional human figure. The first room was a public audience chamber and has an elaborate cabinet made in Augsburg and brought to Florence in 1628, and a 17th-century prie-dieu in ebony and *pietre dure*. In the next room are five tables in *pietre dure* (16th–17th centuries) and the partial reconstruction of the unfinished ciborium designed for the altar for the Cappella dei Principi (*see p. 186*). Commissioned by Don Giovanni de' Medici, it was designed by Matteo Nigetti: the eight rock crystal columns are by Buontalenti and the statuettes in *pietre dure* by Orazio Mochi.

The last room contains a cabinet commissioned from Giovanni Battista Foggini in 1709 by Cosimo III as a present for his favourite child Anna Maria Luisa, when she married the Elector Palatine. When in 1719 she returned as a widow to Florence she was careful to bring this beautiful piece of Florentine craftsmanship back with her from Düsseldorf. It is the most famous of the many cabinets and table tops designed in *pietre dure* by Foggini for the Medici. Foggini was a particularly versatile artist who also worked as a painter and architect as well as producing small bronzes and reliquaries, and even perhaps the frame commissioned by Cosimo III for Raphael's famous tondo of the *Madonna della Seggiola*. Also in the room are a table with an antique Roman porphyry top and a 16th-century base; and two tables decorated with agate tops made in the 17th century. On the window wall is a table designed by Giorgio Vasari and made by Dionigi Nigetti, which belonged to Cosimo I.

The rooms towards the Boboli Gardens were the living quarters of the grand dukes. It is here, and on the mezzanine floor, that their eclectic collection of personal keepsakes is displayed— these include gifts presented by other ruling families and objets d'art made specially for them.

Camera da letto del Granduca Gian Gastone:

This was the bedchamber of Gian Gastone, who made his last public appearance in 1729, and then spent the rest of his life here, where he held his levée at noon. The room contains three splendid gilded-wood display cabinets displaying 16th–17th-century amber and ivories. On an 18th-century table there is an amber centrepiece in the form of a fountain dating from c. 1610. The framed terracotta models of the *Four Seasons* are by Soldani Benzi.

Rock Crystal Collection:

The room to the right displays exquisitely made vessels in rock crystal and *pietre dure* including, in the case to the right of the entrance, a lapis lazuli vase (1583) designed by Buontalenti with a gold mount by Jacques Bylivelt, a rock-crystal vase in the form of a bird (with a gold enamelled mount, c. 1589), and a lapis lazuli shell, with the handle in enamelled gold in the form of a snake. The next case contains a goblet in rock crystal, with an intricately decorated enamelled gold lid, which is thought to have been made for Henri II of France. Displayed on its own is a reliquary casket in rock crystal and gilded silver by Valerio Belli dated 1532. In the centre of the room is a splendid antique marble table with Kufic inscriptions.

Ivories Collection:

The rooms to the left contain one of the most important collections in the world of 17th-century ivories, many of them made for Cardinal Leopoldo by the German artists Balthasar Permoser, Balthasar Stockamer, and Christoph Daniel Schenck (including a *Madonna* signed and dated 1680). Particularly remarkable pieces from a technical point of view are the seated long-haired dog, given to Maria Maddalena d'Austria by her husband Cosimo II, the horse in a spherical cage, the series of turned vases (1618–31) and an elaborate composition of Curtius riding his horse into the abyss.

Mezzanine Floor

A pretty little staircase leads up to the mezzanine floor where the grand-ducal collection of jewellery has always been kept.

Jewellery Collections: In the room at the top of the stairs on the right, a central display case contains a relief of Cosimo I and his family in *pietre dure* by Giovanni Antonio de' Rossi (1557–62; it used to contain a medallion with the personification of Florence); an oval in *pietre dure* by Bernardo Gaffurri of the equestrian statue of Cosimo I in the Piazza Signoria (1598); a Roman head of Hercules; and seven bas-reliefs in gold set on precious stones made for the Studiolo of Francesco I (in Palazzo Vecchio) by Giambologna.

The adjoining room has a magnificent display of the jewellery collection of the last of the Medici, the electress Anna Maria Luisa, including numerous charming pieces made with huge Baroque pearls, rings with cameos and intaglio, and an ex-voto in precious stones of Cosimo II at prayer, made in the grand-ducal workshops in 1617–24.

The rooms at the top of the stairs on the left contain gold and silversmiths' work from the Treasury of Ferdinand III brought to Florence in 1814 (mainly from Salzburg), including elaborate nautilus shells, a double chalice made from an ostrich egg mounted in silver gilt (c.

1370–80) and two ornamental cups made from buffalo horns with silver-gilt mounts (14th century). The series of silver-gilt dishes from Salzburg were made by Paul Hübner, c. 1590.

Off the early 17th-century painted loggia with four 17th-century Mexican vases, is access to the tiny *tesoretto* (*not always open*). This has a frescoed barrel vault and a charming display of miniature vases and objects in *pietre dure* made in the 16th century.

The frescoed room beyond the loggia, which overlooks the courtyard, contains exotic and rare objects from all over the world. These include an Islamic powder horn, nautilus shells, 17th-century shell figurines, and a mitre with scenes of the Passion depicted in gold thread and birds' feathers (Mexican, c. 1545).

The last four rooms have a display of 18th-century Chinese porcelain; Japanese porcelain and lacquer work; 18th- and 19th-century watches, silverware and jewellery; and plaster casts of the silver plates belonging to the last Medici grand dukes which were melted down in 1799, and 18th-century church silver.

Museo delle Carrozze

Closed at the time of writing; T: 055 238 8614.

The Museo delle Carrozze is in the south wing of Palazzo Pitti. It contains seven carriages and two sedan chairs dating from the period of the Lorraine grand dukes and the royal house of Savoy, including the gilded silver carriage of Ferdinand III made in 1818, and decorated by Antonio Marini. There are other berlins (carriages), decorated with charming paintings, and a coupé of 1730.

BOBOLI GARDENS

Open 8.30–dusk, closed on first and last Mon of month; T: 055 265 1838. There are at present three entrances (with ticket offices): one from the courtyard of Palazzo Pitti, one at the Annalena gate on Via Romana (see plan), and one at the gate at Porta Romana. The gate at the top of the hill which leads into Forte di Belvedere is at present closed but can sometimes be used as an exit from the gardens when exhibitions are in progress at the Forte di Belvedere. The Grotticina di Madama and the Grotta Grande can be visited by appointment (T: 055 265 1838).

On the hillside behind Palazzo Pitti lie the magnificent Boboli Gardens, among the most beautiful and best-preserved gardens in Italy. Laid out for Cosimo I on the slope of the hill stretching up from behind Palazzo Pitti to Forte di Belvedere, they were designed by Tribolo. Known as the 'father of the Italian formal garden', Tribolo was also a talented hydraulic engineer, and he made creative use of fountains and cascades. The gardens were continued after his death in 1550 by his son-in-law Davide Fortini, as well as by Vasari and Ammannati. After 1574, Francesco I employed Bernardo Buontalenti to direct the works. The gardens were extended downhill to the west in the early 17th century, between the 14th-century walls and Via Romana as far as Porta Romana, by Giulio Parigi and his son Alfonso. The Parigi were especially known for their talents as set designers and architects. Alfonso the Elder (c. 1535–90) was called in by Ammannati to help with work at the Pitti, but his son Giulio (1571–1635) became more famous especially for his work for the grand dukes as a stage designer and civil engineer (it was he who produced the spectacular celebrations for the wedding of Cosimo II and Maria Maddalena d'Austria).

The gardens were opened to the public for the first time in 1766. The origin of the name Boboli is unknown, but may be derived from the name of the former proprietors of the hillside (Borbolini). This is the biggest park in the centre of Florence, and the gardens are beautifully maintained. They are always cool even on the hottest days in summer. Laid out on two main axes, the gardens are divided into two distinct areas: the lower gardens around the Viottolone and the Isolotto, which are the most attractive, tend to be visited mostly by Florentines with their children, while tourist groups often only visit the upper part of the gardens.

The plants are predominantly evergreen, and a special feature of the gardens has always been the tall double hedges (5m–8m high) formed by a variety of shrubs and bushes in different shades of green—such as laurel, laurustinus, viburnum, box, myrtle and prunus—below a higher hedge of ilex. About half the area of the gardens is covered with ilex woods: these thickets were used up to 1772 for netting small birds. The first deciduous trees were planted in 1812. The botanical sections of the gardens, introduced by the Medici, where mulberries, potatoes and pineapples were once grown, no longer survive. However, there is a splendid collection of citrus fruits (including a rare type of orange) and flowers, cultivated in pots (although many of these were severely damaged in the great freeze of 1985).

There are plans to restore the complicated 17th-century hydraulic system created by Buontalenti and the Parigi to irrigate the gardens and feed the fountains: at present only two fountains work. There are pebble mosaics in some areas of the gardens, and there used to be hidden jets of water to take visitors unawares. The appearance of the gardens was drastically altered in 1833, when Leopold II created the long carriage road which crosses them from west to east.

About 170 statues decorate the walks, a typical feature of many Renaissance gardens derived from ancient Roman villas. Many of them are restored Roman works, while others still remain unidentified; some came to Florence in the 18th century from the Medici collection in Rome, and others in the 18th and early 19th centuries from the Villa di Pratolino outside Florence. Two worn statues in the gardens were recognized as works by Cellini (1500–71) only just before the last war (they are now in the Bargello museum). Other statues were added in the 16th and 17th centuries by Giambologna and others. Since 1984, some of the statues have been restored *in situ*; others have been removed for restoration and may not be returned to the gardens (unless they can be safeguarded against deterioration). For conservation reasons, casts of some of the marble statues have replaced the originals, though it has not yet been decided whether casts in synthetic materials or copies in marble or stone will be made of the restored works in future. Restored statues which cannot be returned to the open air are eventually to be exhibited in a museum here.

A Walk through the Gardens

The entrance at the back of the courtyard of Palazzo Pitti emerges onto the terrace behind the palace, overlooking the courtyard and the splendid Baroque **Fontana del Carciofo Ⓐ**, by Francesco Susini (1641), named after a bronze artichoke on top, which has been lost. It has 12 little statues of cupids on the basin. It replaced a fine 16th-century fountain by Ammannati (now reassembled in the Bargello). There is a magnificent view of the Duomo and Campanile behind Orsanmichele from the terrace.

The **Amphitheatre Ⓑ** was laid out as a garden (probably with ilexes and olive trees) by Ammannati in 1599, in imitation of a Roman circus. The open-air theatre was constructed in 1630–35 by Giulio and Alfonso Parigi for the spectacles held here by the Medici. These elaborate theatrical performances were designed to exalt the prestige of the Medici and offer the public entertainment on a grand scale—sometimes there were elephants or horses combined with fantastic scenery and dramatic lighting. The most stunning event were the 20-day festivities for the marriage of Cosimo, son of Ferdinando II, to Marguerite Louise of Orléans in 1661.

The obelisk of Rameses II, taken from Heliopolis by the Romans in 30 BC, found its way to the Villa Medici in Rome in the 17th century. It was set up here in 1789. The huge granite basin, from the Baths of Caracalla, was installed in 1840. The restored statues in the niches include some classical works (restored in later centuries), notably the young

The amphitheatre in the Boboli Gardens, adorned with the obelisk of Rameses II and a granite basin from the Baths of Caracalla in Rome.

BOBOLI GARDENS

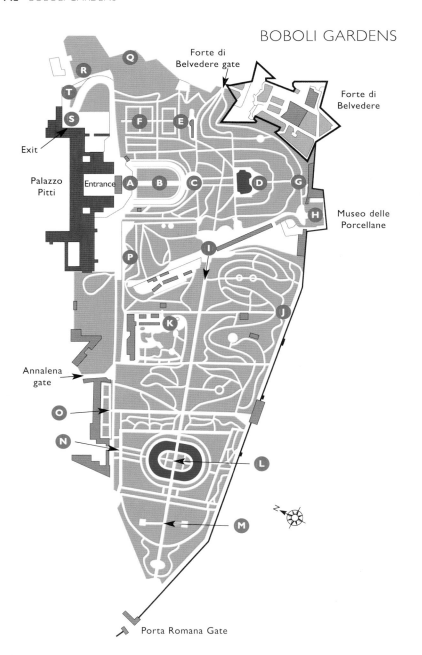

Forte di Belvedere gate

Forte di Belvedere

Museo delle Porcellane

Exit

Palazzo Pitti

Entrance

Annalena gate

Porta Romana Gate

athlete in the fifth niche on the right side, as well as 16th- and 17th-century works.

A series of terraces rise above the amphitheatre. On the **first terrace** Ⓒ are three Roman statues, standing on funerary altars, including a fine *Ceres*, and there are hedged walks with pretty vistas on either side. On the upper level is a large **fishpond** Ⓓ with a very fine statue of Neptune by Stoldo Lorenzi (1571), an allegory of Cosimo I as Prince of the Seas. Lorenzi was a very skilled Mannerist sculptor in bronze. This 16th-century masterpiece shows the influence of both Giambologna and Tribolo. The pond was surrounded by terraces in the 17th century and planted with plane trees in the Napoleonic era. The Forte di Belvedere can be seen above on the hilltop.

A short detour to the left leads through romantic winding alleys overshadowed by ilexes and a cypress grove, to the Rococo **Kaffeehaus** Ⓔ (*closed at the time of writing*), built in 1775 by Zanobi del Rosso, as a pavilion for Peter Leopold to while away lazy afternoons. Del Rosso also designed the Orangery and Casino del Cavaliere in the gardens for the Lorraine grand duke, and in the same period was at work on the Niobe room in the Uffizi. In the garden in front of the Kaffeehaus, which has a good view of Florence and Fiesole, there is a cast of the **Ganymede Fountain** Ⓕ. The 16th-century original is attributed to Stoldo Lorenzi. Behind the Kaffeehaus there is a gate which sometimes provides a secondary exit from the gardens if you wish to visit the Forte di Belvedere (*see p. 281*) when exhibitions are in progress there.

From the Neptune Fountain steps continue to the top of the garden and a colossal **statue of *Abundance*** Ⓖ, in a niche of bay and ilex. Begun by Giambologna as a portrait of Joanna of Austria, first wife of Francesco I, it was originally intended for a column in Piazza San Marco. Instead it was finished—and transformed into an allegory of Abundance—by Pietro Tacca, pupil of Giambologna and successor to him as sculptor to the Medici grand dukes. It was placed here in 1636 by order of Joanna's daughter, Maria de' Medici. Pietro's talented son Ferdinando took over from him as court sculptor to Ferdinando II and designed scenery for spectacles held by his brother Cardinal Gian Carlo dei Medici and he also built a permanent theatre, called the Pergola, which opened in Florence in 1658 (and its successor survives to this day). The view from here embraces the whole city, beyond the Pitti and the tower of Santo Spirito.

A short double flight of steps to the right, designed in 1792, continues to the **Giardino del Cavaliere** Ⓗ, a delightful secluded walled garden with box hedges laid out at the time of Cosimo III on a bastion constructed by Michelangelo in 1529. The fountain has a putto attributed to Pierino da Vinci or Stoldo Lorenzi (originally there were three bronze monkeys attributed to Pietro Tacca, though these have not been returned since their restoration). The view from the terrace is one of the most charming in Florence, embracing the rural outskirts of the city. The fields and olive groves are dotted with beautiful old villas. To the right is the residential area of Bobolino beside a splendid stretch of the city walls.

Museo delle Porcellane

Open as the gardens; closed on second and fourth Sun and first, third and fifth Mon of the month; T: 055 238 8605. Combined ticket with the Museo degli Argenti and Giardino di Boboli.

The Museo delle Porcellane is housed in the 17th-century Casino del Cavaliere. The building may have been used by Cardinal Leopoldo for meetings of the Accademia del Cimento (*see p. 108*). It was rebuilt in the 18th century for the Lorraine grand dukes by Zanobi del Rosso.

The museum contains a well-displayed collection of 18th–19th-century Italian, German and French porcelain from the Medici and Lorraine grand-ducal collections. The last Medici grand duke, Gian Gastone, whose wife was from Saxony, had a special interest in porcelain, which was much in vogue in the early 18th century. Room 1 displays 18th-century French porcelain (Tournai, Chantilly, Vincennes, Sèvres, including the delicate *alzata da ostriche*, used for serving oysters). In the centre, beneath a Venetian chandelier, are two Sèvres dinner services which belonged to Elisa Baciocchi (grand duchess of Tuscany), and a plaque with a portrait of her brother Napoleon in Sèvres porcelain, after François Gérard (1809–10). Examples from the Doccia Ginori factory include works made in 1736 for the Lorraine family, and a 19th-century service with views of Florence. In the second room are works in biscuit ware made in Vienna, and in the last room chinoiserie ware from Meissen.

At the foot of the double stairs, a flight of steps leads down between two fine Roman seated statues of the Muses in white marble to the Prato dell'Uccelare, with a grove of cedars of Lebanon, at the end of a range of garden houses.

The Lower Gardens

The magnificent long **Viottolone** ❶ descends steeply through the second part of the gardens, laid out on an east–west axis, which extends as far as Porta Romana. This majestic cypress avenue was planted in 1612 by Giulio Parigi, but some of the trees have recently been attacked by disease. It is lined with statues, many of them restored Roman works from the Villa Medici in Rome (and others carved in the 16th and 17th centuries); some of these have been removed for restoration. The 17th-century arboured walks beneath trellises over which ilex branches are trained, and little gardens to the right and left, with delightful vistas, are amongst the most beautiful spots in the gardens. The paths are laid out between box hedges and laurel avenues; these were originally symmetrically designed around three labyrinths, destroyed in 1833 when the curving paths were introduced.

There are two fine Roman statues (replaced by casts) known as *Gladiators* at the top of the avenue: the one with a beard was freely restored by Romolo Ferrucci del Tadda. On the right is a little garden where citrus fruit trees are cultivated. On either side of the avenue are two more Roman statues, one of a divinity (restored c. 1610–20) and one of a Roman matron with a veil. They were given to Cosimo I on a visit to Rome in 1560. At the first crossing are four statues of the Four Seasons—*Spring* and *Winter* by Giovanni Battista Caccini (c. 1608; replaced by copies), and *Summer* and *Autumn* by Pietro Francavilla. A path to the left ends at a colossal **bust of Jupiter** ❶ by Giambologna or his school. An unusual path, lined with a water 'staircase' composed of late 16th-century fountains with grotesque heads, follows a stretch of the 13th-century city walls.

On the other side of the Viottolone an ilex tunnel dating from the 17th century leads to remains of the **Botanical Gardens** Ⓚ, known as the Giardino degli Ananas when pineapples were cultivated there. The Sicilian botanist Filippo Parlatore was director of the gardens between 1842 and 1872, and he designed the circular pools for aquatic plants. The larger of the two unheated greenhouses was built by Giuseppe Cacialli. Ammannati's statues for a fountain in Palazzo Vecchio were kept here up until 1920, when they were removed to the courtyard of the Bargello. The garden was abandoned after 1966, though restoration has been under way since 1989.

At the next crossing, lower down the Viottolone and beyond two more restored Roman statues, are three more statues (again restored Roman works). The main avenue continues downhill past a 16th-century statue to end at a short 19th-century avenue of plane trees which runs across it at right-angles (the orangery described below can be seen at the right end). Of the four statues here, two are restored Roman works: *Aesculapius* has an antique torso and a head restored by Gian Simone Cioli in the early 17th century. The statue of Venus, usually considered an allegory of Secrecy, also has an antique torso (it was restored by Giovanni Francesco Susini). The statue of Andromeda dates from the 17th century. Beyond, in niches in the hedges, are two groups of statues depicting folk games; the one on the left is by Orazio Mochi and Romolo Ferrucci del Tadda (17th century), and the one on the right was added c. 1770 by Giovanni Battista Capezzuoli.

The **Isolotto** Ⓛ, or Vasca dell'Isola, was laid out by Giulio Parigi in 1612, when it had some 200 fountains. The island recalls the design of the so-called Naval Theatre, Hadrian's retreat at his villa near Tivoli. A circular moat with fine sculptural decorations surrounds an island and the huge *Fountain of Oceanus* designed by Tribolo for Cosimo II. Three statues of the rivers Nile, Ganges and Euphrates surround the central figure of Neptune, which is a copy (c. 1910) by Raffaello Romanelli of the original by Giambologna, which is now in the Bargello museum. These stand above a huge granite basin quarried by Tribolo in Elba—the design included another large basin, but it cracked during transportation. Some 200 terracotta pots, some still with the Medici crest, filled with citrus trees, are put out here in the rose garden from the end of April for the summer, and the island is usually open at this time.

Four marble statues of cupids (one of which has been removed) by Domenico Pieratti, Cosimo Salvestrini and Giovanni Francesco Susini (with Giovanni Battista Pieratti) were placed to the north and south of the island in 1623–24. On the other two sides, by the gates with capricorns (the emblems of Cosimo II) on the gateposts, are grotesque harpies by the school of Giambologna to a design by Giulio Parigi (these are copies of the originals, made in marble by Innocenzo Spinazzi in 1776). In the water are *Perseus on Horseback*, restored by Giovanni Battista Pieratti, and *Andromeda*, also attributed to Pieratti. A high ilex hedge surrounds the water with niches cut into it, which contain delightful restored 17th-century statues in *pietra serena* (some of them in very poor condition and propped up by scaffolding) of peasants and hunters by Giovanni Battista and Domenico Pieratti. Other statues include *Two Men Fighting*, a *Hunter with Two Dogs* and a *Moorish Hunter* (removed and restored) by Gian Simone and

Valerio Cioli, Bartolomeo Rossi and Francesco Generini. The dogs are by Romolo Ferrucci del Tadda.

Beyond two small 17th-century obelisks made in Carrara marble is the **Hemicycle** (M), an English-style green surrounded by plane trees, which provides a cool playground for children in summer. The two Roman columns in Egyptian granite surmounted by Neoclassical vases were purchased from Lord Cowper by Grand Duke Peter Leopold. On the central path are a statue of Vulcan by Chiarissimo Fancelli, and a 16th-century seated female statue. Some of the colossal busts in the laurel hedge which surrounds the lawn are Roman (including the fine *Head of Zeus*, although the bust is modern). The path continues past (right) a Roman restored statue of Bacchus and (left) a female statue known as *Flora* (in need of restoration). This has the body of an ancient Roman statue of Venus (derived from a Hellenistic original), but the head and arms were added by Giovanni Battista Caccini. The statuary group of peasants is an 18th-century copy by Giovanni Battista Capezzuoli of a 17th-century work; the three grotesque figures in *pietra serena* dancing in silly attitudes, opposite, once thought to be by Romolo Ferrucci del Tadda, have recently been attributed to Tribolo or Caccini (they have been restored). Beyond two other 17th- and 18th-century statues, at the end of the garden, on top of a Roman sarcophagus of the 3rd century AD, is a marble fountain of a peasant with a barrel by Giovanni Fancelli, bought here in 1773 from the Villa di Pratolino.

At the Porta Romana gate is a statue of Perseus by Vincenzo Danti. The very fine Roman sarcophagus, with the *Labours of Hercules* (2nd century AD), has been removed for conservation reasons. Both the sarcophagus and statue were made for the Villa of Pratolino and moved here in the 18th century.

A path leads back through the gardens following the left wall along Via Romana. Beyond a statue of a peasant at work by Valerio and Simone Cioli is the **Fontana della Vedemmia** (N) (1599–1608), also by the Cioli (showing a grape harvest), beside two terracotta dogs by Romolo Ferrucci del Tadda.

Entered through a fine gate dating from 1818 is the handsome **Orangery** (O), built by Zanobi del Rosso (1777–78) and painted in its original green and white colour. The pots of citrus fruit trees are kept here in winter. The 18th-century gardens in front are planted with antique roses and camellias and four Roman statues adorn the walls. This was on the site of a small zoo for exotic animals. Near the Annalena gate, an entrance to the garden on Via Romana, is a small grotto with statues of Adam and Eve by Michele Naccherino. A path continues past more greenhouses to emerge beside the charming 18th-century Meridiana wing of Palazzo Pitti, which houses the Galleria del Costume (*see above*). The hillside was used probably since Roman times as a quarry for *pietra forte*, and much of the palace was built with the stone quarried here. It was covered over in the 18th century, and is now surrounded by cedar trees. This is the setting for a huge Roman granite basin and a Roman **statue of Pegasus** (P). Wheels were installed beneath the statue and a metal track laid so that it could 'fly' during opera performances given here in the 1960s. The other statues are mostly restored Roman works.

The path continues past the Fontana del Carciofo (*described above*), below which on the extreme left can be seen a secret hanging-garden; this is the Giardino delle Camelie, which is open for three weeks in late March and early April when the camellias are in flower (*Tues, Thurs and Sat; 10–12; for information, contact the Amici dei Musei, T: 055 286 465*). In the 17th century, this was a small private water-garden with two grottoes, one in the form of an arch, beside an exit from the apartment of Prince Mattias, brother of Grand Duke Ferdinando II. Camellias, first introduced into Italy around 1780, were planted here in the early 19th century, and all 42 different species were replanted in the 1990s, although the taller ones survive from the first garden.

On the other side of the Fontana del Carciofo, a wide gravel carriage-way descends past two pine trees (right) at the entrance to a narrow path lined with box hedges, which leads through a pretty little garden of parterres with peonies and roses (planted with dwarf fruit trees in the time of Cosimo I) to the **Grotticina di Madama** (admission *by appointment*). This was the first grotto to be built in the gardens, which later became famous for them. It was commissioned by Eleonora di Toledo in 1553–55, and is the work of Davide Fortini and Marco del Tasso. The sculptures are by Baccio Bandinelli and Giovanni Fancelli. It contains stalactites and bizarre goats. The frescoes are attributed to Bachiacca, and the fine terracotta pavement was designed by Santi Buglioni. The gravel road continues to wind down past a rose-garden and a **colossal seated figure** by Baccio Bandinelli.

Representing *God the Father*, it was made for the high altar of the Duomo, but was moved in 1824 to Boboli, where it has been known ever since as *Jupiter*. The ancient square bell-tower of Santa Felicita is visible nearby. The beginning of the carriage-way is flanked by two colossal porphyry and marble Roman statues (2nd century AD) of Dacian prisoners (brought here from the Villa Medici in Rome), with bas-reliefs of the late 3rd century on their pedestals.

On the right is a cast of the so-called **Fontana del Bacco**, really an amusing statue of Pietro Barbino, the pot-bellied dwarf of Cosimo I (*see p. 225*), seated on a turtle, by Valerio Cioli (1560).

The Fontana del Bacco, representing Cosimo I's court dwarf Pietro Barbino.

The last stretch of the Corridoio Vasariano connecting the Pitti Palace to the Uffizi (*see p. 105*), with remains of graffiti decoration, can be seen from here.

A new flight of steps descends to the **Grotta Grande** 🅣 (*admission by appointment*). Begun in 1557 by Vasari, the upper part was finished by Ammannati and Buontalenti (1583–93). The two statues of Apollo (or *David*) and Ceres (or *Cleopatra*) in the niches on the façade (probably by Vasari) are by Baccio Bandinelli, and the decoration above was added by Giovanni del Tadda. The original 16th-century paving with pebble mosaic in front of the entrance was discovered during recent restoration work. The interior completely preserves its intimate 16th-century atmosphere. The walls of the first chamber are covered with fantastic figures and animals carved in the limestone by Piero di Tommaso Mati (on a design by Buontalenti). Francesco I installed Michelangelo's unfinished *Slaves* in the four corners in 1585 (replaced by casts when the originals were removed to the Accademia in 1908). The charming painted vault is by Bernardino Poccetti. Beyond is a sculptural group of *Paris Abducting Helen* by Vincenzo de' Rossi (a gift from the sculptor to Cosimo I). The innermost grotto contains a very beautiful statue of *Venus Emerging From her Bath* (c. 1570) by Giambologna, designed to be seen from every point of view, above an antique fountain, and more pretty murals by Poccetti.

Piazza Pitti

The (signposted) exit from the gardens is nearby, through an archway of Palazzo Pitti, which emerges in the Cortile dell'Ammannati. In Piazza Pitti, in the pretty row of houses facing the palace, no. 16 was the home of Paolo dal Pozzo Toscanelli (1397–1482), mathematician and cosmographer, and one of the most celebrated scientists of his day. It is said that before setting out on his journey to the Americas, Columbus sought Toscanelli's advice. Toscanelli's most famous memorial in Florence is the gnomon in the Duomo (*see p. 44*). Dostoyevsky wrote *The Idiot* while staying at no. 21 in 1868.

SAN MARCO,
GALLERIA DELL'ACCADEMIA
& SANTISSIMA ANNUNZIATA

THE CONVENT OF SAN MARCO
Map p. 399, D1

The Church

The church of San Marco, founded in 1299, and rebuilt with the convent next door in 1442, assumed its present form in 1588 on a plan by Giambologna, who also designed a number of altars and chapels inside the church decorated by his contemporaries. The present façade dates from 1778.

The Interior

Numbering refers to the plan on p. 151.

On the south side there is a devotional figure of Christ **(1)** dating from 1654. Brightly lit and honoured by numerous candles, it is untypical of 'shrines' of this kind, being particularly well carved. The *Madonna and Six Saints* **(2)** (1509) by Bartolomeo della Porta, who was a friar in the convent (also known as Fra' Bartolomeo), shows how strongly this painter was influenced by Raphael. The Byzantine mosaic of the *Madonna in Prayer* **(3)**, which, as can be seen, had to be cut into two pieces for its journey from Constantinople, is a remarkable work thought to date from the 8th century, and thus the earliest of the few mosaics to be seen in Florence. It is surrounded by frescoes of saints in imitation of mosaic, added in the 17th century. At the east end of the church the tribune was added in 1678 by Pier Francesco Silvani; and the dome was frescoed by Alessandro Gherardini in 1717.

The Sacristy, designed by Michelozzo, contains a black marble sarcophagus with the bronze figure of the prior of the convent, St Antoninus, attributed to Giambologna. The saint's body is buried in the Chapel of St Antoninus **(4)**, also designed by Giambologna. On the north side are the tomb-slabs **(5)** of Pico della Mirandola (1463–94) and his friend Poliziano (1454–94). Pico was a great humanist scholar and Neoplatonic philosopher, and Poliziano a poet in the vernacular famous for his eloquence, considered the most original genius among writers of his period. Born Angelo Ambrogini, he adopted the Latin name, 'Politian', Italianised as Poliziano, of his Tuscan birthplace Montepulciano. Both men were members of the Platonic Academy in Florence, a body which saw the birth of the humanist movement of the Renaissance.

Fragments of 14th–15th-century frescoes have come to light on this wall and in a niche is a charming little crèche; the *Christ Child* in terracotta is a 15th-century work. On the west wall, there is a striking *Transfiguration*, a painting of 1596 by the little-known painter Giovanni Battista Paggi.

The Museo di San Marco

Open 8.30–1.50; Sat–Sun 8.30–7; closed first, third and fifth Sun and second and fourth Mon of the month; T: 055 2388608.
The Dominican convent of San Marco contains the Museo di San Marco, chiefly famed for its paintings and frescoes by Fra' Angelico, who was a friar here. Peaceful and beautifully maintained, this is one of the most delightful museums in Florence.

History of the convent and museum

Originally a medieval convent of the Silvestrine Order, the house was transferred to the Dominicans of San Domenico di Fiesole by Cosimo il Vecchio, who ordered Michelozzo to enlarge the buildings (1437–52). Cosimo founded a public library here, the first of its kind in Europe. The founding prior, the Dominican reformer Antonino Pierozzi (1389–1459), was made Archbishop of Florence in 1446, and was canonized in 1523 as St Antoninus. But its most famous prior was Savonarola (*see p. 73*), who dominated the religious and political scene in Florence in the last decade of the 15th century—terrorizing his congregations through his fiery sermons. He remains one of the most interesting and controversial figures in Florentine history to this day. The painter Fra' Bartolomeo (who painted Savonarola's portrait) was a friar here. The museum was founded at the convent in 1869, and in 1921 nearly all Fra' Angelico's panel paintings were collected here from churches and convents in the environs of Florence and from other museums. In 1898 the Museo di Firenze Antica was opened to house architectural fragments saved during demolitions in the centre of Florence. In the early 1980s Fra' Angelico's frescoes, which are very well preserved, were exquisitely restored.

Ground Floor

A Cloister of St Antoninus: With its broad arches and delicate Ionic capitals, this attractive cloister was built by Michelozzo. A venerable cedar of Lebanon stands at its centre. The lunettes are decorated with early 17th-century frescoes showing scenes from the *Life of St Antoninus*, begun by Bernardino Poccetti and finished by Matteo Rosselli and others. In the corners are smaller frescoes by Fra' Angelico: *St Thomas Aquinas* (**6**) (very worn); *St Dominic at the Foot of the Cross* and *St Peter Martyr*, the first Dominican to die for his faith (**7**); a restored *Pietà* (**8**); and *Christ as a Pilgrim welcomed by two Dominicans* (**9**).

B Pilgrims' Hospice: The Hospice was built by Michelozzo. Its walls are now hung with superb paintings by Fra' Angelico, collected here from churches and convents in Florence and its environs. Some are large altarpieces, while others are tiny works, exquisitely painted as if they were miniatures for illuminated manuscripts. All repay the closest examination and exude a joyous spirit, with superb colouring and decoration in gold leaf, and numerous delightful botanical details. Most date from the 1430s and are very well preserved. The *Deposition*, one of Angelico's most beautiful paintings, was commissioned by Palla Strozzi for the church of Santa Trinita, c.

MUSEO DI SAN MARCO
CHURCH & CONVENT

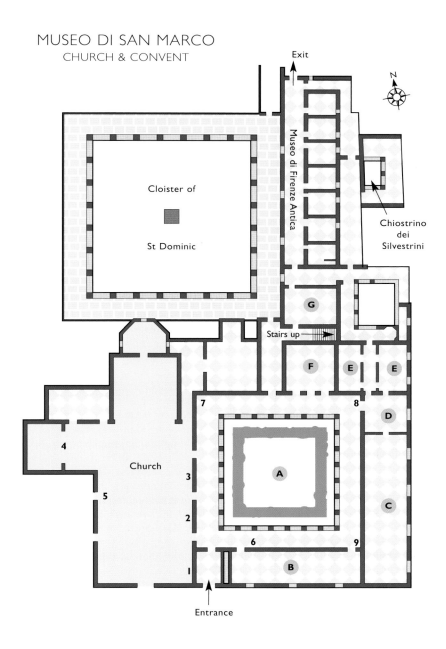

Exit

Museo di Firenze Antica

Cloister of
St Dominic

Chiostrino
dei
Silvestrini

G

Stairs up

F   E   E

7   8

D

4

Church   A

3

2   C

5

6   9

1   B

Entrance

1435–40. The earlier cusps are the work of Lorenzo Monaco, a monk at the nearby convent of Santa Maria degli Angeli, who was also a famous painter. The *Last Judgement* (1431), from Santa Maria degli Angeli, is painted with extraordinary skill and numerous charming details, including the dance of the blessed with angels in Paradise, which is separated from the vivid scenes of the dammed in Hell by a stark representation of the empty tombs of the dead. The 35 beautifully painted small panels which served as cupboard doors in Santissima Annunziata illustrate scenes from the life of Christ. The *Madonna della Stella* is a charming little reliquary tabernacle from Santa Maria Novella. Beyond is another *Deposition* painted for the Compagnia del Tempio (the lower part was damaged when the Arno flooded in 1966).

At the end of the room is the large *Tabernacle of the Linaiuoli*, with the *Madonna Enthroned with Saints*, commissioned by the Flax-workers Guild for their headquarters in 1433 (removed for restoration). The beautiful marble frame was designed by Lorenzo Ghiberti, whose work evidently influenced Angelico. On the last wall, there are three more altarpieces of the *Madonna and Child with Saints*: one, a late work, painted for Bosco ai Frati (c. 1450); one for the high altar of the church of San Marco (c. 1438–40; in poor condition), with two scenes from the predella of the patron saints of doctors, Saints Cosmas and Damian (one showing a leg transplant), displayed on either side; and the last one painted for the convent of the Annalena (which preserves most of its predella). There are also two more exquisite small reliquary tabernacles from

Santa Maria Novella, one with the *Coronation of the Virgin*, and the other, even more beautiful, with a bright gold ground showing the *Annunciation* and *Adoration of the Magi*.

C Great Refectory: On the end wall is a fresco of *St Dominic and his Brethren fed by Angels* by Giovanni Antonio Sogliani (1536). Also displayed are 16th- and 17th-century paintings.

D Lavatorium: Here is a seated *Madonna and Child* in polychrome terracotta attributed to Luca della Robbia.

E Room with works by Fra' Bartolomeo, including a *Portrait of Savonarola* in profile (Savonarola's preachings had convinced Bartolomeo to take the Dominican habit in 1500). He also began the large *Madonna with St Anne and Other Saints* in monochrome, commissioned in 1510 by Piero Soderini, the last *gonfaloniere* of the Florentine Republic (*see p. 83*), for the Salone dei Cinquecento in Palazzo Vecchio, but never finished since the Medici returned in 1512. However, when the Republican government was restored in 1529, it was installed in the room for a few years. The room on the left has 15th-century paintings and frescoes including a processional standard with a Crucifix and *St Antoninus* by Alesso Baldovinetti (in a beautiful 15th-century frame, but in very bad condition), and, above a door, a very damaged detached fresco lunette of the *Madonna and Child* recognised in the middle of the last century as by the hand of Paolo Uccello. There is access from the corridor here to a little cloister.

Chapter House: *The Crucifixion and Saints* by Fra' Angelico and assistants (1441–42).

F Chapter House: A large fresco of the *Crucifixion and Saints* by Fra' Angelico and assistants (1441–42) covers one wall. The figure of Mary Magdalen supporting the grieving Madonna is particularly striking. The convent bell, with a frieze of putti, was commissioned by Cosimo il Vecchio and is attributed to Donatello and Michelozzo. It was rung in defence of Savonarola before his arrest here, and after he was burnt at the stake it was seized and taken to San Miniato al Monte. In 1501 the monks of San Marco succeeded in having Pope Julius II order its return to them.

G Small Refectory: Here is a charming *Last Supper* frescoed by Domenico Ghirlandaio and his workshop. This is one of four similar frescoes of this subject painted by Ghirlandaio in Florence between 1476 and 1480.

First Floor

The convent dormitory upstairs consists of 44 small monastic cells beneath a huge wooden roof, each with its own vault and adorned with a fresco for each monk's private devotion by Fra' Angelico and his assistants. It is still uncertain how many of the frescoes are by the hand of the master alone, and how many are by artists (whose names are unknown) employed in his studio. Others are attributed to Zanobi Strozzi and Benozzo Gozzoli. The old wooden shutters and doors have been preserved, and the cells retain their intimate atmosphere. At the head of the staircase is Fra' Angelico's *Annunciation*, justly one of his most famous works, the scene set in a delightful loggia overlooking a garden.

FRA' ANGELICO

Guido di Piero, born in the Mugello just north of Florence, became a Dominican friar around 1418 at the convent of San Domenico below Fiesole (where he took the name of Giovanni) and then moved to this convent. Because of the deeply religious sentiments in his paintings he came to be known as *angelico* and *beato* (blessed) since he seemed to be divinely inspired. At the time he was at work on the frescoes in the chapter house and monastic cells at San Marco he was one of the most famous artists of his day. He painted numerous altarpieces for churches in and around Florence and also worked for Pope Eugenius IV in Rome and in the cathedral of Orvieto. His works have a universal appeal since they combine a deeply religious sentiment with a sense of serenity and joy, and seem to encourage meditation. At the same time they have a highly intellectual content, and carefully worked out perspective and numerous complicated compositional elements. Angelico's use of colour is also remarkable and he was a master of the technique of fresco as well as that of panel painting and illumination.

Left Corridor

Fra' Angelico's frescoes in the cells are as follows (*see plan on p. 156*):

(**1**) *Noli me tangere.*

(**3**) *Annunciation* (with a particularly beautiful angel).

(**5**) *Nativity* (perhaps with the help of an assistant).

(**6**) *Transfiguration.*

(**7**) *Mocking of Christ in the Presence of the Madonna and St Dominic* (perhaps with the help of an assistant).

(**8**) *The Marys at the Sepulchre.*

(**9**) *Coronation of the Virgin.*

(**10**) *Presentation in the Temple.*

(**11**) *Madonna and Child with Saints* (probably by an assistant).

(**22**) A glass panel in the floor shows the remains of the previous convent here with two late 14th-century fresco fragments of a monk, a *Pietà* and geometric decoration.

(**23–29**) Frescoed by assistants of Fra' Angelico, while on the wall outside in the corridor is a *Madonna Enthroned with Saints*, attributed to the master himself.

Fra' Angelico: *Noli me Tangere.*

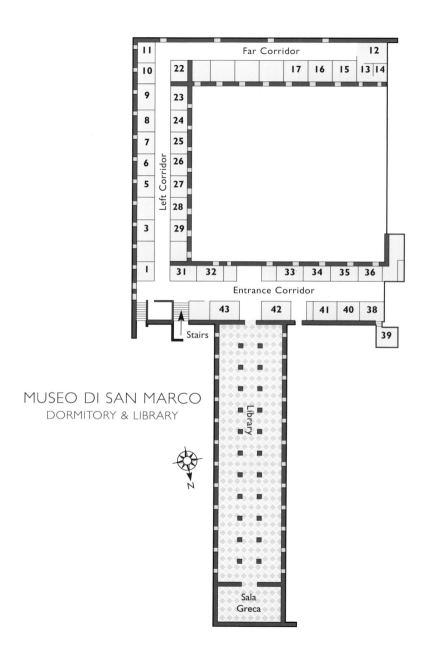

Far Corridor

Left Corridor

Entrance Corridor

Stairs

MUSEO DI SAN MARCO
DORMITORY & LIBRARY

N

Library

Sala
Greca

Far Corridor
The frescoes of *Christ on the Cross* in the cells here are by followers of Fra' Angelico. At first glance they look identical, but each is slightly different. The contents of the cells is described below.

(17) Important medieval fresco fragments (c. 1290–1310, among the earliest known in Florence), can be seen beneath the floor. They are thought to depict the founder of the Silvestrine convent, Silvestro Gozzolini, and St Anthony Abbot.

(16) The standard here belonged to Savonarola.

(15) Here is displayed Savonarola's cloak, carefully preserved over the centuries by a series of (documented) proprietors. The pieces missing were cut out as relics of the great churchman. Also here is a small polychrome wooden Crucifix attributed to Baccio da Montelupo or Benedetto da Maiano, which used to be in Savonarola's cell.

(12–14) These three little rooms were occupied by Savonarola when he was prior in 1482–87 and 1490–98. Above the door is an oval detached fresco of the *Glory of St Catherine* by Alessandro Gherardini (1701). In the former chapel **(12)** is a monument to Savonarola, with a bronze bust and marble relief, by Giovanni Dupré (1873). Also here are detached frescoes by Fra' Bartolomeo, Savonarola's supporter and fellow friar, and a portrait of him (with the attributes of St Peter Martyr, c. 1497). A panel dating from c. 1498 shows the *Burning of Savonarola in Piazza della Signoria*, and there is also a book of his preachings and sermons. In the adjoining cell **(13)**, arranged as a little study, is a 19th-century desk, and a chair traditionally supposed to have been used by the prelate. In the last cell **(14)** are some more Savonarola relics, fragments of Dominican habits, and another late 15th-century painting of the *Burning of Savonarola in Piazza della Signoria*.

Entrance Corridor

(31) The cell of St Antoninus, with *Christ in Limbo* by an assistant of Angelico, who probably also painted the scenes in the next four cells.

(32–35) Frescoes show the *Sermon on the Mount*, *Arrest of Christ*, *Agony in the Garden* and the *Institution of the Eucharist*.

(36) Has an unusual scene of *Christ Being Nailed to the Cross*.

(38–39) These cells were occupied as a retreat by Cosimo il Vecchio; the *Adoration of the Magi*, painted by Benozzo Gozzoli in collaboration with Fra' Angelico, was restored in the 19th century.

(40–43) The worn frescoes of the *Crucifixion* are by Angelico's workshop.

The Library

This light and delicate hall by Michelozzo (1441), is one of the most pleasing architectural works of the Florentine Renaissance. During restoration work in 2000 the original emerald green colour of the frescoed *intonaco* on the walls and vaults was discovered under four layers of plaster (and this can now be seen in several places). It is known that the colour green was symbolic of contemplation and repose and was used on the walls of other Renaissance libraries and studies. Before this discovery art historians had praised the clear lines of this hall where the grey *pietra serena* stands out against the white walls and vaults as representing a typical Renaissance interior.

The library of San Marco was famous for its collection of Greek and Roman authors and was augmented by donations from the Florentine humanists. However, dispersal of the books had already begun by the early 16th century, and in 1571 many of them went to the Biblioteca Laurenziana (and in the 19th century to the Biblioteca Nazionale). Some that remain are usually exhibited here, together with illuminated choirbooks and psalters (mostly 15th–16th century, including a missal illuminated by Fra' Angelico as a young man), and a small display illustrates the fascinating technique of manuscript illumination. Over the two doors are frescoes (1671) of the Blessed Albertus Magnus and his pupil St Thomas Aquinas. Above the two blocked doors on the left wall are small paintings of the two saints teaching attributed to Zanobi Strozzi. At the end of the room is the **Sala Greca**, added in 1457, which preserves its painted ceiling from that time. The cupboards, dating from 1741, now contain vases made in Montelupo in 1570 for the pharmacy of San Marco.

Just outside the main entrance to the library is a plaque commemorating the arrest of Savonarola, which took place on this spot on the night of 8 April, 1498.

Museo di Firenze Antica

To the right at the bottom of the stairs is the Museo di Firenze Antica, arranged in the cells of the *foresteria*. These were guest-quarters of the convent and some of them have a lunette over the door by Fra' Bartolomeo. The material salvaged from the demolition of the Mercato Vecchio and part of the Ghetto at the end of the 19th century (the central part of this area of the city is now occupied by Piazza della Repubblica; *see p. 61*) was collected here. This includes numerous architectural fragments dating from the medieval and early Renaissance periods. The arrangement of 1904 has been preserved. From the windows can be seen the Cloister of St Dominic (not open to the public since it is still used by the Dominican friars), also by Michelozzo (1437–43), with frescoes of the life of St Dominic (1697–1701) by Cosimo Ulivelli and others. In the centre of the cloisters, with palm trees and box, is a statue of St Dominic (1700).

One of the rooms displays the pavement tomb of Luigi Tornabuoni (1515), with its fine marble effigy in relief and another, with a 15th-century painted wooden ceiling, contains 14th–16th-century fragments of painted wall decoration and a wooden model of the church of San Giuseppe by Baccio d'Agnolo. Material from the Sepolcreto di San Pancrazio has been arranged in the Chiostrino dei Silvestrini, usually only open in summer. The exit at the end of the corridor is through a little garden.

Giardino dei Semplici

Open Mon–Fri 9–1; closed Sat and Sun, except first Sun of the month; T: 055 2757402. Entrance at no. 3 Via Micheli.

Across Via Giorgio La Pira are the railings of the Botanical Garden, the Giardino dei Semplici. This is on the site of a garden laid out in 1545–46 by Tribolo for Cosimo I, the third oldest botanical garden in the world. The garden contains medicinal plants, Tuscan flora, azaleas, irises, water plants, coniferous trees, yews and cork trees. In the greenhouses (the two largest of which date from the end of the 19th century) are tropical plants, palms, ferns, orchids and citrus fruits.

PIAZZA SAN MARCO & SANT'APOLLONIA
Map p. 399, D1

This is one of the liveliest squares in the city and, with several cafés, is a meeting-place for students from the University and Academy of Art, both of which have their headquarters here. The statue in the centre is of general Manfredo Fanti, an important military and political figure in the movement for Italian Unity. He died in Florence in 1865.

On the west side of the square is the Casina di Livia, built by Grand Duke Peter Leopold in 1775 for his mistress Livia Raimondi (now an officers' club). A plaque on the garden wall beside five tall cypresses records the **site of the Giardino di San Marco**. We know from Vasari that this garden contained collections of antique sculpture put together by Cosimo il Vecchio and his grandson Lorenzo the Magnificent. Here it was that Lorenzo's great friend the expert bronze caster Bertoldo di Giovanni, who had been a pupil of Donatello's, restored antique sculpture, as well as instructing young sculptors. The painter Francesco Granacci took Michelangelo as a child to see the school and pointed him out to Lorenzo, who soon recognized his exceptional talents and obtained Michelangelo's father's permission for him to come and live in the Medici household.

Via degli Arazzieri (once the site of the Florentine tapestry workshops) leads into Via XXVII Aprile. Here on the left is the inconspicuous door into the former **convent of Sant'Apollonia**, founded in 1339 and enlarged in 1445 (*open 8.30–1.50; closed first, third and fifth Sun and second and fourth Mon of the month; T: 055 238 8607*). The vestibule contains works by Neri di Bicci and Paolo Schiavo, Andrea del Castagno's master. In the Refectory is a *Last Supper*, the masterpiece of Andrea del Castagno (c. 1450), set in an unusual painted marble loggia. This is the first of the great Renaissance frescoes of the *Last Supper* in Florence (and one of the most beautiful), thought to date from around 1447. Its particularly peaceful setting is usually little disturbed by visitors. It is extraordinarily innovative in the use of perspective to create the illusion of space, and a superb example of how Castagno, an unsentimental painter (his figures often appear more like sculptures placed against a severe, abstract backdrop), produces work of enormous power. This scene portrays the moment when Christ consecrates the Bread and reveals the name of the person who will betray Him—the drama is expressed through the apostle's hands as well as their faces: John is shown resting on the left of Christ while Judas is on the viewer's side of the table. The work is undocumented and not mentioned by Vasari, but it must have been known to Castagno's contemporaries including Piero della Francesca. It was only discovered in 1808 since it had, up until then, been inside the convent of a closed order.

The equally fine frescoes of the *Crucifixion*, *Deposition* and *Resurrection* above are also by Castagno (very damaged, but recently restored). Also displayed are lunettes with the *Crucifixion between the Madonna and Saints* and a *Pietà with Two Angels*. The detached fresco fragments on the end wall with panels of painted marble are all that remains of the important frescoes of stories from the life of the Virgin in Sant'Egidio by Domenico Veneziano, Piero della Francesca, Andrea del Castagno and Alesso Baldovinetti.

On the east side of Piazza San Marco is the Loggia dell'Ospedale di San Matteo, one of the oldest porticoes in Florence (1384). The seven arches may have inspired Brunelleschi's Loggia degli Innocenti (*see p. 166*). This is now the seat of the Accademia di Belle Arti, an art school opened in 1784 by Grand Duke Peter Leopold, but formerly part of the Accademia delle Arti del Disegno, the first of all art academies founded in 1563 by members of the Compagnia di San Luca which already existed by 1339. The founders included Vasari, Bronzino, Francesco di Giuliano da Sangallo and Ammannati; Cosimo I and Michelangelo were elected the first Academicians. (The present seat of this academy is near Orsanmichele, *see p. 65*.)

Over the three doors there are fine della Robbian lunettes: those showing the *Madonna of the Cintola* and the *Resurrection* are by Andrea della Robbia. The Mannerist courtyard has unusual columns. A little chapel can sometimes be seen on request (entrance at no. 11 Via Cesare Battisti) with a 17th-century fresco of the *Rest on the Flight into Egypt*, one of Giovanni da San Giovanni's best works. The charming scene shows the Madonna stepping off a mule onto a stool, while above a woman with a child holding a cat look down. It was moved here in 1788 by Peter Leopold.

GALLERIA DELL'ACCADEMIA

Map p. 399, D1

Entrance at no. 58 Via Ricasoli. Open 8.30–6.50, closed Mon; summer: Thurs, Fri and Sat also 8.30–11.30; T: 055 238 8609. The gallery can be very crowded with tour groups and there is often a long queue: it is therefore always best to book a visit (T: 055 294 883; booking charge). The least crowded time is late afternoon. The works are all labelled in English.

History of the Gallery

The gallery was founded for study purposes in 1784, with a group of paintings given to the Accademia di Belle Arti by Grand Duke Peter Leopold. After 1786 paintings from convents and churches suppressed by Peter Leopold's brother, Emperor Joseph II, as part of his reform of the Church, were transferred here. Some of these were subsequently moved to the Uffizi. In 1873, a huge tribune was constructed to exhibit

Michelangelo's *David*, when it was decided to remove it from its original location in Piazza della Signoria. In 1882 a museum dedicated to Michelangelo was inaugurated here, consisting exclusively of casts of his sculptures, with the *David*, the only original piece of work at that time, as centrepiece. In 1909 most of these casts were replaced by five originals by Michelangelo (his four *Slaves* and *St Matthew*), and the last casts were removed in 1938 to the Gipsoteca at Porta Romana (*see p. 325*).

Ground Floor

The Galleria: Here are **five great sculptures by Michelangelo**. The four *Slaves* or *Prisoners* (variously dated 1521–23 or around 1530) were begun for the tomb of Pope Julius II in St Peter's, Rome, which was never finished—other sculptures which were to form part of it are in San Pietro in Vincoli in Rome.

The *Slaves* were presented to the Medici in 1564 by Michelangelo's nephew, Leonardo. In 1585, they were placed in the Grotta del Buontalenti (Grotta Grande) in the Boboli Gardens (*see p. 148*), and they were brought here in 1909. In the centre of the right side is the *St Matthew* (1504–08), one of the twelve apostles commissioned from the sculptor by the Opera del Duomo for the cathedral, and the only one he ever began. It was left abandoned in the courtyard of the Opera del Duomo until 1831, and moved here in 1909. These five sculptures are magnificent examples of Michelangelo's unfinished works, some of them barely blocked out, the famous *non-finito*, much discussed by scholars. They evoke Michelangelo's unique concept expressed in his poetry, that the sculpture already exists within the block of stone, and it is the sculptor's job merely to take away what is superfluous. The way in which Michelangelo confronted his task, as Cellini noted, was to begin from a frontal viewpoint, as if

carving a high relief, and thus the statue gradually emerged from the marble.

The Tribune: This was specially built in 1882 by Emilio de Fabris to exhibit Michelangelo's ***David*** (*see overleaf*) when it was removed from Piazza della Signoria. On the walls are hung paintings by Michelangelo's Florentine contemporaries, well restored in 2003.

Salone: At the end of the hall to the left of the *David* is a huge light room. This was formerly the ward of the hospital of San Matteo, which was founded in the 14th century; a small detached monochrome fresco by Pontormo of the interior of the hospital is displayed here. It is now filled with a splendid display of plaster models by Lorenzo Bartolini (1777–1850), considered the most important sculptor in Italy during his lifetime, arranged more or less as they were in his studio in Borgo San Frediano in Florence. They include the original models for his best known works, including public monuments (the allegorical figures from the Demidoff monument on Lungarno Serristori are in the centre of the room), as well as numerous tombs and portrait busts. There are also some other 19th-century sculptures and paintings by members of the Accademia di Belle Arti.

MICHELANGELO'S DAVID

This is perhaps the most famous single work of art in Western civilization, and has become something of a cult image, all too familiar through endless reproductions, although it is not the work by which Michelangelo is best judged. It was commissioned by the city of Florence to stand outside Palazzo Vecchio, where its huge scale fits its setting. Here it seems out of place in its cold, heroic niche. The colossal block of marble, over 5m high, quarried in 1464 for the Opera del Duomo, had been left abandoned in the cathedral workshop. The marble was offered to several other artists, including Andrea Sansovino and Leonardo da Vinci, before it was finally assigned to Michelangelo. The figure of David, uncharacteristic of Michelangelo's works, stands in a classical pose suited to the shallow marble block. The hero, a young colossus, is shown in the moment before his victory over Goliath. A celebration of the nude, the statue established Michelangelo as the foremost sculptor of his time, at the age of 29. The statue was cleaned and restored *in situ* in 2004.

Early Florentine Paintings: Off the hall to the left of the *David* are three rooms which display the earliest Florentine paintings in the gallery. A room dedicated to works dating from the 13th- and early 14th centuries contains a Crucifix by a Florentine painter close to Cimabue, and *Mary Magdalen with Stories from her Life* by an unknown artist now known as the Maestro della Maddalena after this work. Another room displays works by Andrea Orcagna and his brothers Jacopo di Cione and Nardo di Cione. The last room contains works by followers of Giotto, including Taddeo Gaddi and Bernardo Daddi.

15th-century Paintings: Off the Galleria with Michelangelo's *Slaves* are three more rooms of Florentine paintings. The panel known as the *Cassone Adimari*, showing a busy wedding scene with elegant guests in period dress in front of a Romanesque building, is by Lo Scheggia (1440–45), Masaccio's brother. The *Nativity*, which comes from the Villa Medici di Castello, is by an unknown artist known after this work as the Master of the Castello Nativity. The altarpiece of *Saints Stephen, James and Peter* (the figure of St Stephen is particularly striking) is by Domenico Ghirlandaio. The *Annunciation* is an early work by Filippino Lippi, a copy of a painting by his father, Fra' Filippo Lippi.

In a small room are displayed *Scenes from Monastic Life* (or *The Thebaids*), thought to be by Paolo Uccello, and a *Pietà*, a very fine work attributed to Jacopo del Sellaio.

The third room displays the *Madonna and Child with the Young St John and Two Angels*, a beautiful early work by Botticelli, who probably also painted the enchanting small *Virgin of the Sea* (which has a seascape in the background). Also here are *St John the Baptist and St Mary Magdalen* by Filippino Lippi, and a *Resurrection*, probably the best work of Raffaellino del Garbo.

The Sala del Colosso: This room is named after the huge plaster model for the *Rape of the Sabines* (in the Loggia della Signoria, *see p. 72*) by Giambologna (1582). The paintings here date from the first two decades of the 16th century. The *Descent from the Cross* was painted for the high altar of Santissima Annunziata: Filippino Lippi carried out only the upper part before his death in 1504, and it was completed by Perugino, who also painted the *Assumption and Saints* (signed and dated 1500). Ridolfo del Ghirlandaio painted the two *scenes of St Zenobius*, which include remarkable contemporary portraits among the crowds as well as views of Florence.

Museum of Musical Instruments

Florence has held a special place in the history of music since the change of style between Jacopo Peri's musical drama *Dafne*, performed in Palazzo Corsi in 1597, and his *Euridice*, composed in 1600 to honour the marriage in Florence of Maria de' Medici (daughter of Francesco I) to Henri IV of France. First performed in Palazzo Pitti, it is generally held to mark the beginning of opera. The pianoforte was invented in Florence in 1711 by Bartolomeo Cristofori (1655–1731). The composer Jean-Baptiste Lully (1632–87) was born in the city.

Part of the museum of musical instruments is displayed in two rooms reached from the Sala del Colosso. It belongs to the conservatory of music next door, named after the composer Luigi Cherubini (1760–1842), Florentine by birth though he spent most of his career in Paris.

This collection, begun by the last of the Medici and the Lorraine grand dukes, is one of the most interesting in Italy. There are 17th-century 'cellos including one by Nicolò Amati (c. 1650), a late-17th-century dulcimer, and the famous *Viola Medicea* built by Antonio Stradivari in 1690. A double bass is attributed to Bartolomeo Cristofori (1715). The violins include one by Antonio Stradivari (1716). In the second room are a harpsichord and an oval spinet by Bartolomeo Cristofori (1690), and an upright piano made in 1739 by his assistant Domenico del Mela.

First Floor

14th- and early 15th-century Paintings: Four rooms on the first floor contain a fine collection of Florentine paintings dating from the end of the 14th and early 15th centuries, including numerous polyptychs. The first room is named after Giovanni da Milano, one of the most interesting painters to succeed Giotto, represented here by a splendid *Pietà* (1365). Room 2 contains many more works by late 14th-century painters. Also here is an exquisitely embroidered altar frontal from Santa Maria Novella made by Florentine craftsmen, and signed and dated 1336 by a certain Jacopo Cambi.

In the centre is the *Coronation of the Virgin between Angels and Saints* and on the border are scenes from the life of the Virgin and numerous birds. In Room 3 are nine beautiful works by Lorenzo Monaco, including *Prayer in the Garden*, an early work painted around 1400 for the convent of Santa Maria degli Angeli where Lorenzo was a monk. The wall cases contain a display of 16th–18th-century Russian icons which entered the Lorraine grand-ducal collections in 1771–78. The last room displays works in the International Gothic style, including a *Madonna and Child with Saints John the Baptist and Nicholas and Angels* by Gherardo Starnina.

MUSEO DEL OPIFICIO DELLE PIETRE DURE
Map p. 399, D1–D2

Entrance at no. 78 Via degli Alfani. Open daily 9–2 except Sun and holidays; T: 055 265 111.

The Opificio was founded in 1588 by the Medici grand duke Ferdinando I, to produce mosaics in hard or semi-precious stones. His brother Francesco I, who had died the previous year, invented the idea of making mosaics out of *pietre dure*, in imitation of classical works in marble intarsia. This refined craft, perfected in Florence (also known as *mosaico fiorentino*), is remarkable for its durability. Exquisite pieces were made in the workshops (which moved here from the Uffizi in 1798) to decorate such objects as cabinets and table-tops. Many of the best examples are preserved in Palazzo Pitti. The grand dukes were fond of using them as gifts, often to foreign rulers. The most characteristic products are decorated with flowers, fruit and birds, against a black background. The museum, founded here at the end of the 19th century, has newly arranged galleries which provide a superb account of the workshop's history.

The headquarters of the Opificio delle Pietre Dure is also housed in this building. Since 1975, the Institute has been the seat of a restoration and conservation laboratory dedicated to the restoration of stone, marble, bronze, terracotta and *pietre dure*. A restoration school was set up here in 1978, and there is also a restoration archive and library. Another branch of the restoration laboratory, largely concerned with paintings and frescoes, operates in the Fortezza da Basso (*see p. 329*).

Piles of *pietre dure* left over from the deposits amassed by the grand dukes can be seen in the courtyard. Highlights of the displays are Francesco Ferrucci del Tadda's portrait of Cosimo I, as well as works made for the Cappella dei Principi in San Lorenzo (*see p. 186*), an ambitious project begun by Ferdinando I which, if completed, would have been one of the most remarkable decorative schemes ever produced. These include 17th–19th-century panels executed for the altar, and panels intended for the decoration of the chapel walls which were begun some ten years before building commenced. There are also 17th-century works made for the Medici, including some by Giovanni Battista Foggini. When going up the stairs, note the *pietre dure* risers. The mezzanine floor has 18th- and 19th-century work benches and instruments once used by the craftsmen. The 18th-century painted designs by Antonio Cioci, with shells and compositions with antique or porcelain vases, were used for the exquisite tables in *pietre dure* now in Palazzo Pitti.

On the ground floor are 18th-century examples of *scagliola* works, many of them from Carpi in the province of Modena, which was particularly famous for its *scagliola* craftsmanship. Imitating marble and *pietre dure*, this material made from selenite was incised with a metal point. The *pietre dure* exhibits continue up until the early years of the 20th century, with 19th-century works by Niccolò Betti and Art Nouveau designs by Edouard Marchionni, who was in charge of the Opificio in 1873–1923.

PIAZZA SANTISSIMA ANNUNZIATA
Map p. 399, E1

Piazza Santissima Annunziata was designed by Brunelleschi. Surrounded on three sides by porticoes, it is the most beautiful square in Florence. The Spedale degli Innocenti has a portico by Brunelleschi with its famous della Robbia medallions, and the colonnade opposite, modelled on Brunelleschi's work, was designed over one hundred years later by Antonio da Sangallo and Baccio d'Agnolo (1516–25). The church of the Annunziata also has a portico and the convent of the Servite order has remains of five Gothic windows. Via dei Servi was used by Brunelleschi in his Renaissance design of the piazza to provide a magnificent view of the cupola of the Duomo. This street, on the line of an ancient thoroughfare documented as early as the 12th century leading north from the city, is now lined by a number of handsome 16th-century palaces.

In the middle of the square is an equestrian statue of Grand Duke Ferdinando I, Giambologna's last work. It was cast by his talented pupil Pietro Tacca in 1608, who also designed the base and the two small symmetrical bronze fountains with bizarre monsters and marine decorations, which are delightful Mannerist works. Fairs with market stalls are held in the piazza on certain days, including the festival of the Annunziata (25 March), 7 September (and the weekend before), and 8 December.

In the corner of the piazza opposite the church is Palazzo Grifoni Budini Gattai. It is thought to have been begun in 1557 by Ammannati for the Grifoni, probably to a design by Giuliano di Baccio d'Agnolo, then finished by Buontalenti and Giambologna. It has two ornate brick façades (one on the piazza and one on Via dei Servi) with decorative friezes and a delightful garden. Browning's poem *The Statue and the Bust* is set here:

> There's a palace in Florence, the world knows well,
> And a statue watches it from the square...

The story goes that as duke Ferdinando I rode by in the square below, he met the glance of a young bride at a window of this palace and they fell in love. Neither had the courage to consummate their love, and many years later each decided to order their portraits to be put up here to perpetuate that moment: Ferdinando's on horse-back in the square (Giambologna's fine statue, and the first public monument to a Medici ruler in his own lifetime) and the lady's a della Robbia bust set at the upper window (today pointed out as the one with the shutter always half open).

SPEDALE DEGLI INNOCENTI

The Spedale degli Innocenti (its correct name is Ospedale degli Innocenti) was opened in 1445 as a foundling hospital, the first institution of its kind in Europe. It operated as an orphanage up until 2000, and is still an institute dedicated to the education and care of children, and since 1988 has been a research centre of the United Nations Children's Fund (UNICEF). The Arte della Seta (silk-makers guild) commissioned Brunelleschi (who, as a goldsmith, was a member of the guild) to begin work on the building in 1419.

History of the Spedale degli Innocenti

Vincenzo Borghini, who had an important influence on Cosimo I's intellectual tastes, was prior here from 1552–80. At that time the Institute was already able to care for some 2,000 babies (by the 19th century this figure had increased to 3,000). The first school of obstetrics in Italy was founded here, and pioneering studies into nutrition and vaccination were carried out in the hospital (cows and goats were kept in the garden). Some of the 2,000 precious volumes dating from the 16th–19th centuries which formed part of the library of the Società Filoiatrica Fiorentina, a learned society of doctors founded by Giuseppe Bertini in 1812 for the study of medicine, are preserved here, including some rare medical tracts, as well as surgical instruments and models used for study purposes.

The Exterior

The colonnade (1419–26) of nine arches is one of the first masterpieces of Renaissance architecture by Brunelleschi, inspired by classical antiquity as well as local Romanesque buildings. The last bays on the right and left were added in the 19th century. In the spandrels are delightful medallions, perhaps the best-known work of Andrea della Robbia (1487), each with a baby in swaddling-clothes against a bright blue background (the two end ones on each side are excellent copies made in 1842–43). Beneath the portico at the left end is the *rota* (turning-box or wheel) constructed in 1660 to receive abandoned babies. Before that time, orphan babies used to be left between the figures of Mary and Joseph in a terracotta crib by Matteo Civitali, which is still kept in the hospital. The *rota* was only walled up in 1875. The church of the Innocenti (*open in the early morning only*) was remodelled in Neoclassical style in 1786 by Bernardo Fallani.

Medallion by Andrea della Robbia (1487) on the Spedale degli Innocenti.

Interior of the Convent

Open 8.30–2 except Wed; T: 055 249 1708.

The convent houses the Museo dello Spedale degli Innocenti. The main Chiostro degli Uomini (1422–45, reserved for the men who worked in the Institute) was decorated in 1596 with a clock-tower, and graffiti (drawn with lime) showing the emblems of the Arte della Seta and the other two hospital foundations (San Gallo and Santa Maria alla Scala), which were united here in the 15th century. Over the side door into the church is a pretty lunette of the *Annunciation* by Andrea della Robbia.

A door on the right leads out of the far side of the courtyard to the oblong Chiostro delle Donne (1438), another beautiful work by Brunelleschi, with 24 slender Ionic columns beneath a low loggia. The charming perspective of the colonnades is reminiscent of the background which appears in some Renaissance paintings. This part of the convent was reserved for the women who worked in the Institute. There is now a collection of games and toys in rooms off the cloister, which is open to children (who can borrow them, as in a lending library). Exhibitions are also held in this part of the convent. The archives, housed in an 18th-century room with handsome 19th-century bookcases, are preserved intact, including the first register of 1445.

The Pinacoteca

On the left of the Chiostro degli Uomini, stairs lead up to a long gallery (formerly the day nursery), which has been arranged as a Pinacoteca, with paintings dating from the 15th and 16th centuries. On the left of the ticket desk, the *Coronation of the Virgin* is considered the masterpiece of the unknown artist called the Master of the Madonna Straus. The *Madonna and Child with an Angel* is an interesting early work by Botticelli, copied from his master Filippo Lippi. Also here are works by Giovanni del Biondo and Neri di Bicci.

Beyond the archway is a little room dominated by the splendid *Adoration of the Magi* by Domenico Ghirlandaio. The brightly coloured work includes a scene of the *Massacre of the Innocents* with two child saints in the foreground. The predella is by Bartolomeo di Giovanni (1488), one of the few documented and dated works by this artist. The altarpiece was commissioned for the high altar of the convent church by the prior, Francesco Tesori (d. 1497), whose tomb-slab has been placed in the floor here. The *Madonna and Child* in glazed terracotta by Luca della Robbia (c. 1445–50) is one of his most beautiful works. The painting of the *Madonna Enthroned* is by Piero di Cosimo.

On the right side of the ticket desk the paintings include Madonnas protecting the *innocenti* attributed to Pontormo and Jacopino del Conte. At the far end of the room are illuminated choir books and a case which displays a touching series of identification tags left by destitute mothers with their babies in the 19th century, in the hope that one day they would be able to be reunited with them.

Work is under way to expand the museum and open other parts of the convent to the public.

SANTISSIMA ANNUNZIATA

Open 9–12 & 4–5, daily except Weds.

The church of the Santissima Annunziata was founded by the seven original Florentine members of the Servite Order in 1250, and rebuilt, along with the cloister and atrium, by Michelozzo and others in 1444–81. Housing a famous painting of the *Annunciation*—held to be miraculous—it was one of the most important sanctuaries dedicated to the Madonna in Europe. The central arch of the portico is ascribed to Antonio da Sangallo, the rest is by Giovanni Battista Caccini (1600).

It was in this church, in 1817, that Leopold, last Grand Duke of Tuscany, married Maria Anna Carolina of Saxony. Leopold lost the Grand Duchy in 1859, leaving the city quietly in the early evening of 27 April, after an efficient—and bloodless—revolution.

The Chiostrino dei Voti

The series of Mannerist frescoes on the walls is particularly interesting since most of them were painted in the second decade of the 16th century by the leading artists of the time. Right to left they are as follows (*see plan overleaf*):

(1) Rosso Fiorentino: *Assumption*, a very early work.

(2) Pontormo: *Visitation*, showing the influence of Andrea del Sarto.

(3) Franciabigio: *Marriage of theVirgin*—the head of the Virgin was damaged by the painter himself in a fit of anger. Beyond, the marble bas-relief of the *Madonna and Child* is by an unknown sculptor (sometimes attributed to Michelozzo).

(4) Andrea del Sarto: *Birth of the Virgin.*

(5) Andrea del Sarto: *Coming of the*

Magi, containing Andrea's self-portrait in the right-hand corner. Two bronze stoups by Antonio Susini (1615) stand in front of the west door.

(6) Alesso Baldovinetti: *Nativity* (1460–62), the colours have faded because they were badly prepared by the artist. The landscape is particularly beautiful.

(7) Cosimo Rosselli: *Vocation and Investiture of San Filippo Benizzi*, (1476).

(8–12) Andrea del Sarto: More scenes of San Filippo, interesting (but damaged; 1509–10).

The Interior

The dark interior was heavily decorated in the late 17th century, with a rich ceiling on a design by Volterrano, who also carried out the huge fresco of the *Coronation of the Virgin* in the dome at the east end.

(A) Near the entrance to the church the pews are turned towards the west end since services usually take place at the shrine of the Madonna, still highly venerated by Florentines, and bedecked with ex-votos, hanging lamps and can-

dles. The huge tabernacle (almost hidden by the devotional images), commissioned by Piero il Gottoso, was designed by Michelozzo and executed by Pagno di Lapo Portigiani (1448–61) to protect the miraculous painting of

SANTISSIMA ANNUNZIATA

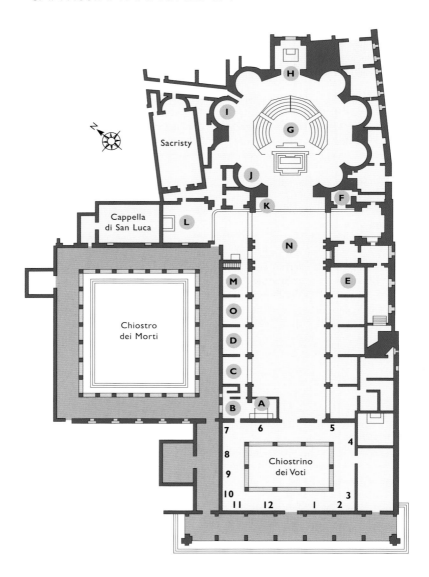

Sacristy

Cappella di San Luca

Chiostro dei Morti

Chiostrino dei Voti

the *Annunciation*. It has a bronze grille by Maso di Bartolomeo and an incongruous 17th-century canopy. The highly venerated painting of the *Annunciation* (also difficult to see) was traditionally thought to have been painted by a friar who was miraculously assisted by an angel.

B This was formerly a private oratory for the Medici. Although it is also covered with ex-votos, there are five beautiful panels inlaid in *pietre dure* dating from 1671 with the symbols of the Virgin (the rose, lily, moon, sun and star), and an exquisite small painting of the *Redeemer* (1515) by Andrea del Sarto, who is buried in the church.

C The elaborate Cappella Feroni is a fine Baroque work by Giovanni Battista Foggini (1692). Behind the altarpiece (shown on request) there is a fresco by Andrea del Castagno of *St Julian and the Saviour*.

D This chapel has another fresco by Andrea del Castagno, the *Holy Trinity with St Jerome*.

E Monument to Orlando de' Medici, a delicate work by Bernardo Rossellino (1456). Orlando, a cousin of Cosimo il Vecchio, was employed in his bank, and paid for some work in the church.

F The sculpture of the *Dead Christ Supported by Nicodemus* is by Baccio Bandinelli. It is the burial place of the artist, and the head of Nicodemus is a self-portrait. On the back of the monument there are two small reliefs with the portraits of the artist and his wife.

G The Tribune. Although begun by Michelozzo, this was completed by the great Renaissance architect Leon Battista Alberti in 1477 and paid for by his patron in Mantua, Ludovico Gonzaga. It has a very unusual design: a rotonda preceded by a triumphal arch, derived from ancient Roman architecture, but is today one of Alberti's lesser-known works, difficult to appreciate beneath the later decorations.

The high altar, with a frontal by Giovanni Battista Foggini (1682), bears a silver ciborium. Behind (difficult to see) are the choir stalls and two lecterns of English workmanship (15th century).

H The east chapel was reconstructed by Giambologna as his own tomb, and contains fine bronze reliefs and a bronze Crucifix by him, and statues by his pupils. His closest follower, Pietro Tacca, is also buried here. The *Madonna and Child* is attributed to Bernardo Daddi.

I *Madonna and Saints* by Perugino, and *Resurrection* by Bronzino.

J Alessandro Allori's *Birth of the Virgin*, and a painting by his son, Cristofano.

K On the left of the great arch is the tomb of Bishop Angelo Marzi Medici, signed by Francesco da Sangallo (1546) and with an expressive effigy of the bishop, charged with the fervour of the Counter Reformation.

L The chapel in the north transept is the work of Michelozzo (1445–47), and contains a terracotta statue of the

Baptist by him. The walls are covered in mid-18th-century trompe l'œil frescoes. A door leads from here to the cloisters.

M *Assumption* by Perugino.

O The *Last Judgement* by Alessandro Allori is a copy of various figures in Michelangelo's fresco in the Sistine Chapel.

N The Nave. The stucco and painted decoration by Cosimo Ulivelli, Francesco Silvani and Pier Dandini dates from around 1703. The splendid organ (1509–21) by Domenico di Lorenzo da Lucca and Matteo da Prato is the oldest in the city, and the second oldest in Italy. It is the only organ by Domenico di Lorenzo to have survived virtually intact. It can be heard when concerts are given in the church (usually around Christmas time).

The Cloisters and Cappella di San Luca

The Chiostro dei Morti (Cloister of the Dead), so named from its memorial slabs, is entered from the door in the north transept of the church or from outside the church by the door on the left of the portico, although it is now often kept locked. Over the door into the church is Andrea del Sarto's *Madonna del Sacco* (which gets its name from the sack that St Joseph is leaning on), an original portrayal of the *Rest on the Flight into Egypt* and one of the artist's best works. The other colourful frescoed lunettes in the cloister are by Bernardino Poccetti, Matteo Rosselli and others: they are interesting documents of 17th-century Florence, illustrating the origins of the Servite Order.

The Cappella di San Luca has belonged to the Accademia delle Arti del Disegno since 1565 and a special Mass for artists is held on St Luke's Day (18 October; Luke is the patron saint of artists, deriving from the tradition that he himself was a painter and made an icon of the Virgin). In the vault below are buried Cellini, Pontormo, Franciabigio, Montorsoli, Bartolini, and many other artists. The chapel altarpiece of *St Luke Painting the Madonna* is an interesting self-portrait by Vasari, a founder member of the Academy. The walls and ceiling were decorated by Pontormo, Alessandro Allori, Santi di Tito, and Luca Giordano. The clay statues which lean dramatically out of their niches are the work of various Academicians, including Montorsoli (who was also a member of the Servite Order). The small organ dates from 1702.

The cloister of the former Compagnia della Santissima Annunziata (or di San Pierino) is entered at no. 4 Via Capponi, just out of Piazza Santissima Annunziata. Above the entrance, there is a lunette in glazed terracotta; this shows the *Annunciation* with two members of the confraternity in white hooded robes and is the work of Santi Buglioni. The delightful little cloister has frescoes (c. 1585–90) by Bernardino Poccetti and others. The lunettes, representing the *Martyrdom of the Apostles*, are separated by monochrome figures of the Christian Virtues, and, above the doors, the *Resurrection* and *Pietà*.

MUSEO ARCHEOLOGICO
Map p. 399, E2

Open Mon 2–7; Tues and Thurs 8.30–7; Wed, Fri, Sat, Sun 8.30–2; in summer also Sat 9–midnight; T: 055 23575.
Via della Colonna leads out of Piazza Santissima Annunziata beneath an archway and skirts Palazzo della Crocetta, with its garden. This palace was built for Grand Duchess Maria Maddalena, wife of Cosimo II, in 1620, probably by Giulio Parigi. Since 1879 it has been the home of the Museo Archeologico, and houses one of the most important collections of Etruscan antiquities in existence (though most of the section devoted to Etruscan sites in Tuscany is at present closed).

History of the Museum
The Etruscan Museum was founded in 1870 and many of its most precious artefacts came from the Medici collections. The Etruscan Topographical Museum was inaugurated in 1897 by Luigi Adriano Milani. The Egyptian Museum was founded by Leopold II after the expedition to Egypt in 1828–29 organised by the Egyptologist Ippolito Rosellini (who published *The Monuments of Egypt and Nubia* in 1832–44) and François Champollion, the French archaeologist and founder of modern Egyptology. In 1845, Leopold II also acquired the famous François Vase (*see p. 175*).

Egyptian Museum
The Egyptian Museum is on the first floor (entrance at the top of the stairs on the left). The decoration of the rooms, in Egyptian style, was carried out in 1881–94. After the Egyptian Museum in Turin and the Vatican collection, this is considered the most important museum of its kind in Italy. Of the very earliest exhibits, two of the finest are the two polychrome statuettes (restored) of a maidservant preparing yeast for beer and a maidservant kneading dough (c. 2480–2180 BC). The portrait of a young woman from the Fayum necropolis dates from the Roman period (1st–2nd centuries AD). The very rare Hittite chariot made of wood and bone, which was found in a Theban tomb, dates from the 14th century BC (it was probably used by the man with whom it was buried). There are also finds from Thebes (1552–1186 BC), including sarcophagi, vases and stele. Around the walls are exhibited papyri of the *Book of the Dead*. Room VII contains finds from Saqqara (1552–1186 BC). Room VIII preserves its delightful decorations in the Egyptian style and old-fashioned show-cases. It contains mummies and mummy-cases, canopic vases, basket work, furniture, objects of daily use and musical instruments. The museum also has a remarkable collection of Coptic fabrics, including clothing.

The Etruscan, Greek and Roman Collections
The long gallery contains the famous bronze *Chimera*, which was found outside Arezzo in 1553 and acquired by Cosimo I. The work was incorrectly restored in 1785, and gives the mythical animal the body and head of a lion, the head of a goat on its

back, and a serpent's tail. The myth relates that the chimera was killed by Bellerophon, and it is here shown wounded. It is an Etruscan ex-voto probably dating from the end of the 5th or beginning of the 4th century BC, and it was made in southern Etruria (Chiusi, Arezzo or the Val di Chiana). Another monumental bronze is the *Minerva* (removed for restoration), which was found in 1541 in Arezzo and acquired by Cosimo I in 1552. In the 16th century, the lower part of the statue was assembled in plaster, and in the 18th century the right arm was wrongly restored. It is thought to be a Roman or Etruscan copy of an original by Praxiteles. The *Arringatore*, a third celebrated bronze, shows the orator Aule Meteli (son of Vel). Found at Pila near Perugia and acquired by Cosimo I in 1566, it is a votive statue made in seven parts, dating from the late Republican era.

Two rooms entered from the right of the gallery are devoted to Etruscan funerary sculpture and contain some of the prize exhibits in the collection. These include the the famous *Mater Matuta*, a canopic vase in the form of a woman (a portrait of the deceased) on a throne holding a baby. Made out of volcanic tufa, it was found in 1846–47 and dates from c. 440. The tomb of the noblewoman Larthia Seianti (wife of Sevnia) shows her reclining effigy adorned with jewels. Her name is incised on the border of the sarcophagus. It was found in 1877 and is dated 150 BC. The cinerary urn (no. 73577) with a man (the head is not original) and a woman (late 5th or early 4th century) is the earliest known large polychrome alabaster urn. The other urn bears a realistic portrait of the dead with the goddess Vanth. It is made out of stone similar to volcanic tufa and dates from the beginning of the 4th century BC. At the end of the long gallery is a room with a fine display of Etruscan inscribed mirrors in bronze, and Etruscan bronze armour.

Corridoio delle Gemme

(Unlocked on request for a maximum of 10 people about every hour.)

This long covered passageway was built in the 15th century to connect the monastery to the church of Santissima Annunziata. It was restored in 1996 to exhibit the Medici and Lorraine grand-ducal collection of precious stones, gems, cameos and jewellery. They are beautifully arranged by subject matter, with classical pieces displayed beside those dating from the 15th–18th centuries. They are labelled in Italian: AC, or *avanti Cristo*, means before Christ, and DC, or *dopo Cristo*, means after Christ. In the first case is a cameo restored in gold by Benvenuto Cellini, and a gem bearing the initials of Lorenzo the Magnificent. At the far end of the corridor a passageway leads to a balcony overlooking the inside the church of Santissima Annunziata. This was built for Maria Maddalena, wife of Cosimo II, who was an invalid, so that she could be present when Mass was held in the church.

On the balcony there is also usually a fine display of jewellery found in Italy, which comes mostly from 18th- and 19th-century collections, much of it from that of Grand Duke Peter Leopold. This includes goldsmiths' work from the 8th to the 3rd centuries BC, Hellenistic pieces, and late antique jewellery (7th century AD). The antique gold jewellery from the collection of Sir William Currie, which he donated to the museum in 1863, consists of Etruscan gold ornaments from Southern Etruria. The gold fibula from Populonia, acquired in 1911, is now usually recognised as a fake.

The Attic Vases

This outstanding collection is displayed in 11 rooms on the second floor. All the exhibits are well labelled and they make an extremely interesting study of the development of black-figure and red-figure vases in the 6th and 5th centuries BC. They are decorated with numerous representations of the Greek myths as well as scenes of everyday life. The nucleus of the collection goes back to the time of the Medici, but it was considerably augmented by finds from excavations in Tuscany ordered by the Lorraine grand dukes and in particular in the early 19th century. Some of the works come from the important collection of Augusto Campana.

THE FRANÇOIS VASE

This unique work is displayed on its own. It is a huge and magnificent Attic krater—beautifully proportioned despite its vast dimensions—which bears the signatures of the potter Ergotimos and the painter Cleitias. One of the earliest black-figure Attic vases known, it was made in Athens c. 570 BC. It was discovered by Alessandro François in an Etruscan tomb at Fonte Rotella, Chiusi, in 1844 and was restored in 1845—and twice more, in 1900–02 (after it had been broken) and in 1973. It was used for mixing wine with water at banquets. The decoration comprises six rows of more than 200 exquisite black-figure paintings of mythological scenes, identified by inscriptions.

The largest and widest band shows the arrival of the gods after the wedding of Peleus and Thetis. In the band below, we can see the pursuit of Troilus by Achilles, and the return of Hephaistos to Olympus. In the lowest band are six decorative groups of symbolic animals, while on the foot of the vase there is an exquisite little frieze showing the battle between the pygmies and cranes. Around the rim of the krater is the Calydonian boar hunt, and a dance of the youths and maidens liberated by the killing of the Minotaur by Theseus (who is shown playing the lyre, opposite Ariadne). In the band below, the chariot race at the funeral games of Patroclus is depicted, and the battle between Centaurs and Lapiths. On the handles are the winged figure of Artemis as queen of wild beasts, and Ajax carrying the dead body of Achilles (slain by Paris).

Greek and Roman Bronzes

Highlights of this collection include a bronze torso of an athlete, found in the sea off Livorno, and now thought to be a Greek original of c. 480–470 BC. Owned by Cosimo I, it is the earliest known example of a Greek bronze statue cast with the lost-wax technique. The horse's head probably came from a Greek quadriga group of the

2nd–1st century BC. Owned by Lorenzo the Magnificent, it is thought that both Verrocchio and Donatello saw it in the garden of the Palazzo Medici-Riccardi (where it was used as a fountain) before they began work on their own equestrian statues (Verrocchio's *Colleoni Monument* in Venice, and Donatello's *Gattamelata* in Padua). The display includes a bronze head of Antinous, which belonged to the Medici and has recently been identified as an original (it is the only bronze head of Antinous to survive). The last room contains four bronze heads, known as the *Philosophers of Melonia*, which were found in the sea near Livorno in 1722. Long considered rare Roman replicas of Greek originals, they are now believed to date from the 17th century. The Roman bronze model of the branch of a tree with a serpent emerging from the trunk (1st century AD), found in the sea near the island of Gorgona in 1873, was used as a candelabrum for oil lamps.

Greek and Roman Sculpture

Sculptures, some Greek originals and some Roman copies of Greek works, are displayed in a corridor beyond the bronzes rooms. Among them are two fine Archaic Greek kouroi. The date of the larger one, known as *Apollo*, is usually placed c. 530 BC. The *Apollino* is slightly later (520–510 BC). At the end of the corridor is the most famous work in the collection, the *Idolino*. This is a remarkable bronze statue of a young man, thought to have been used as a lampstand at banquets. There is still uncertainty about its date and attribution: the torso appears to date from the 1st century BC and the head is in the style of Polyclitus. It is now usually considered a Roman copy of a Greek original. It was found at Pesaro in 1530 and donated to Francesco Maria della Rovere, Duke of Urbino. It passed to the Medici when Ferdinando II married Vittoria della Rovere. The pedestal (c. 1543–50) is attributed to Girolamo Lombardo.

The Garden

(*Admission by appointment; enquire at the ticket office.*)
Laid out in 1903, it includes reconstructions (using the original stones) of Etruscan tombs at Casale Marittimo, Vetulonia, Populonia and the Tomba Inghirami in Volterra. Plants include pines and cedars of Lebanon, and tubs of azaleas in spring.

VIA DEGLI ALFANI
Map p. 399 D1–E2

On Via degli Alfani you pass the so-called **Rotonda di Santa Maria degli Angeli**. This octagonal building was begun by Brunelleschi in 1434 as a memorial to the soldier Filippo degli Scolari (d. 1424), who served the King of Hungary in a number of battles against the Turks, and was nicknamed 'Pippo Spano'—probably after he was made the king's chief officer (*ispán* in Hungarian). For a period he was in charge of military campaigns in the Veneto, and in 1414 he was put in charge of the antipope

John XXIII after he had been deposed at the Council of Constance. Filippo was also a cultivated man and a patron of the arts (it is thought that he himself commissioned the project for the Rotonda of Santa Maria degli Angeli just before his death), and apparently it was he who called the painter Masolino to Hungary in 1426, where he worked for an Italian patron. The Rotonda was left unfinished in 1437. Modelled on the Temple of Minerva Medica in Rome, it was one of the first centralised buildings of the Renaissance. After a period of use as a church, it was then completed as a lecture-hall in 1959, and is now used as a language laboratory for Florence University (perhaps not altogether inappropriate for a building built to honour a Florentine who spoke German, Hungarian, Wallachian, Bohemian and Polish). In the square behind is the Faculty of Letters.

Palazzo Giugni, at no. 48 Via Alfani, is a beautiful Florentine palace, the courtyard of which can usually be seen through the open door. It is a characteristic work by Ammannati (1571) with a small garden (with orange trees and a grotto). The interesting garden façade, with a loggia, bears a copy of the family coat of arms (the original can be seen in the courtyard). The international Lyceum Club for ladies has occupied rooms on the first floor of the palace since 1953, and it maintains a tradition of high-quality concerts, exhibitions and lectures to which the public are welcomed. Founded in 1908 by Constance Smedley (who had founded the first such club in London in 1904), the first exhibition of the Impressionists in Italy was held here in 1910. The well-kept rooms are delightfully furnished, and include a library and a 17th-century *galleria* which preserves its decorations intact, including paintings by Alessandro Gherardini.

ANGLO-AMERICANS IN FLORENCE

There were numerous Anglo-American residents in Florence in the 19th century. Attracted initially as visitors by its art and architecture, they found themselves seduced by its climate and its atmosphere, bought themselves houses, and never returned home. Mementoes of their stay and the legacies they left can be seen in the Brownings' Casa Guidi in the Oltrarno (*see p. 279*), and the museums founded by Herbert Percy Horne near the church of Santa Croce (*see p. 245*) and by Frederick Stibbert on the outskirts of the city (*see p. 313*). The distinguished art historian Bernard Berenson lived at the Villa I Tatti, where he created a very fine art collection, library and garden. More recently, one of the best-known English residents was the historian and aesthete Sir Harold Acton, who inherited the art collection and lovely garden at Villa La Pietra. Both these villas are now owned by American universities. Many illustrious foreigners are buried in the English Cemetery (*see overleaf*).

WALK TWO

TOWARDS THE ENGLISH CEMETERY

This walk visits the palace occupied by Bonnie Prince Charlie during his sojourn in Florence, as well as the last resting-place of many illustrious members of the city's foreign community.

From Piazza Santissima Annunziata, Via Gino Capponi leads to **Palazzo Capponi** (no. 26), the grandiose home of the statesman and historian after whom the street is named. The palazzo was built in 1698–1713 by Carlo Fontana, and has a fine garden. The poet Giuseppe Giusti died here suddenly in 1850. **Palazzo di San Clemente** on the corner of Via Michele is an interesting building by Gherardo Silvani, one of the most prolific Florentine architects of the 17th century. In the entrance hall is the British royal coat of arms. The palace was bought by Charles Stuart, the Young Pretender, in 1777. The Young Pretender—Bonnie Prince Charlie—was born in Rome in 1720. After his defeat by the English at Culloden in 1746, he spent some years in France, where he assumed the title Charles III of Great Britain, but where his habitual drunkenness cost him many of his supporters. He retired to Florence, where he also stayed at the Palazzo Corsini and Palazzo Guadagni. In 1772 he married Louisa, Countess of Albany, though the marriage was a disaster and she fled from here to the nearby Convento delle Bianchette in 1780, before beginning a liaison with the dramatist Vittorio Alfieri. The Young Pretender spent the last three years of his life in Rome, where he died in 1788. He was buried in the Vatican grottoes, and has a monument in St Peter's by Canova.

From here **Via Giuseppe Giusti** takes you past a bizarre little house (no. 43), built by the painter Federico Zuccari (who collaborated with Vasari on the frescoes on the cupola of the Duomo) as his studio. It is connected by a garden to a larger house, also owned by Zuccari, which had been built by the painter Andrea del Sarto in 1520 on his return from France (and this was where he died ten years later). In 1988 the property was acquired by the German Institute.

At the junction with Borgo Pinti, a lovely old road (*see pp. 252–53*), turn left. The street ends in Piazzale Donatello, very busy with traffic as it lies on the wide avenues (the Viali) which were laid out in 1865–69 by Giuseppe Poggi after he had demolished the last circle of medieval walls. The architect left some of the ancient gates as isolated monuments in the course of this ring-road. On an island in the centre of Piazzale Donatello is the Protestant cemetery (*open Mon 9–12, Tues–Fri 2–5; ring at the main gate*), which has always been known as the Cimitero degli Inglesi, or **English Cemetery**. It was opened in 1828, and many distinguished British, Swiss,

North American, Italian and Russian non-Catholics are buried here. The cemetery was closed in 1878 when the new Cimitero degli Allori on the Via Senese was opened, but in 1996 the Russian ballet dancer Evgenij Poljakov was allowed to be buried here. The little gatehouse dates from 1860.

To the left of the central path Elizabeth Barrett Browning (1809–61) is buried. The tomb, raised on six little columns, was designed by Robert Browning and sculpted by Lord Leighton (finished by Luigi Giovannozzi). Behind it is the Pre-Raphaelite sarcophagus of Holman Hunt's wife Fanny, who died in Fiesole at the age of 33. Also buried here are the poet Walter Savage Landor (1775–1864); Swiss bibliophile Gian Pietro Vieusseux (1779–1863; see p. 210); the writer Fanny Trollope (1780–1863); the American sculptor Hiram Powers (1805–73); the Boston reformer Theodore Parker of Lexington (1810–60); Isa Blagden (1818–73; see p. 306), and Robert Davidsohn (1853–1937), the German historian of Florence.

SAN LORENZO
& PALAZZO MEDICI-RICCARDI

SAN LORENZO
Map p. 397, A1–B1

Open 10–5.30 except Sun and holidays; T: 055 272 8487.

The church of San Lorenzo was intimately connected with the Medici after they commissioned Brunelleschi to rebuild it in 1425–46. It is the burial place of all the principal members of the family from Cosimo il Vecchio to Cosimo III. A basilica on this site, outside the old town walls, was consecrated by St Ambrose of Milan in 393, and is thought to be the earliest church in Florence. As the church of St Zenobius, the most famous Bishop of Florence, this served as cathedral of the city before the bishop's seat was transferred, probably in the late 7th century, to Santa Reparata (on the site of the present cathedral). On 14 July 1564, a solemn memorial service was held here in honour of the 'divine' Michelangelo, organized by the Accademia del Disegno.

The Exterior

The church, with the large dome of the Cappella dei Principi and the smaller cupola of the Sagrestia Nuova (the gilded bronze sphere on the lantern was designed by Michelangelo), rises above the market stalls of Piazza San Lorenzo. The west front remains in rough-hewn brick, as it has been since 1480. Leo X held a competition for a façade, and the participants included Raphael, Giuliano and Antonio da Sangallo, Jacopo Sansovino and Baccio d'Agnolo, but in 1516 Michelangelo was given the commission. He spent much time designing a grandiose façade (his model survives in the Casa Buonarroti, *see p. 249*), but only the interior façade was ever built. The campanile dates from 1740.

The Interior

The grey cruciform interior, built with *pietra serena*, with pulvins above the Corinthian columns in *pietra forte*, is one of the earliest and most harmonious architectural works of the Renaissance. It was completed to Brunelleschi's design by Antonio Ciacheri Manetti (1447–60) and Pagno di Lapo Portigiani (1463). The fine wood ceiling has been restored. On the inner façade, above the west door, and supported by two columns in *pietra serena*, is a little balcony built by Michelangelo (1530) for Clement VII, for the exhibition of the Holy Relics (kept in a treasury behind the three doors).

(A) The *Marriage of the Virgin* (1523) by Rosso Fiorentino (*see p. 258*) and the Gothic tomb-slab (1398) of Francesco Landini. Landini (also known as Landino) was born in 1325 and, having been blinded as a child, he found great solace in music. He worked as organist at San Lorenzo for many years and was one of the most important composers of his time—his secular music is typical of the Florentine 'Ars Nova' style, and many of his beautiful madrigals survive (the term *madrigale* was coined at this period).

(B) Tabernacle by Desiderio da Settignano, of extremely fine workmanship (perhaps intended for the high altar of the church).

(C) – (D) Bronze pulpits: These are the last works of Donatello, made up of sculptured panels (c. 1460), and were finished by his pupils Bertoldo and Bartolomeo Bellano. The exquisitely carved panels (unfortunately very difficult to see, as they are raised on Ionic marble columns of c. 1560), which may have been intended for the former high altar of the church, have a border of Classical motifs around the top. Many of the scenes are crowded and grim and present a unique iconography. The pulpit on the north side shows the *Agony in the Garden*, *St John the Evangelist* and the *Flagellation* (these last two both 17th-century imitations in wood); *Christ Before Pilate* and *Christ Before Caiaphas*; the *Crucifixion* and *Lamentation over the Dead Christ*; and the *Entombment*. The pulpit on the south side shows the *Marys at the Sepulchre*; *Christ in Limbo*; the *Resurrection*; *Christ Appearing to the Apostles*; *Pentecost*; the *Martyrdom of St Lawrence*, *St Luke* and the *Mocking of*

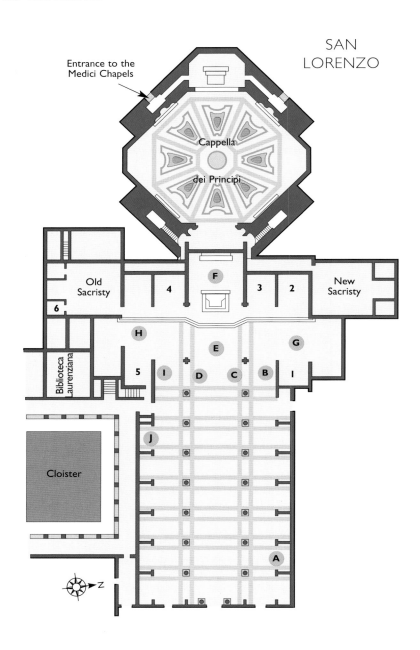

SAN
LORENZO

Entrance to the
Medici Chapels

Cappella
dei Principi

Old
Sacristy

New
Sacristy

Biblioteca
Laurenziana

Cloister

Christ (the last two both 17th-century imitations in wood).

E Tomb of Cosimo il Vecchio: Beneath the dome frescoed by Vincenzo Meucci (1742), three grilles in the pavement and a simple inscription with the Medici arms mark the grave of Cosimo il Vecchio (d. 1464), named *Pater Patriae* by the Signoria.

F High altar: In *pietre dure*, to a design by one of Grand Duke Peter Leopold's most favoured architects, Gaspare Maria Paoletti, this was consecrated in 1787; it incorporates a panel of the *Fall of Manna* designed by Bernardino Poccetti. Above is a Crucifix by Baccio da Montelupo, one of many made for churches in Tuscany by this local artist.

G South transept: (*This area of the church is reserved for prayer.*) The architecture here, with splendid Corinthian columns, is particularly beautiful and was certainly carried out by Brunelleschi himself. The first chapel (**1**) contains a Roman sarcophagus and a Crucifix made of cork by Antonio Pollaiolo. In another chapel (**2**) are two funerary monuments by Leopoldo Costoli (1871), one to the goldsmith Bernardo Cennini, who printed the first book in Florence in 1471, and one to

the painter Pietro Benvenuti. In the chapel to the right of the high altar (**3**) is a charming triptych of the *Annunciation* by Puccio di Simone.

H North transept: In the first chapel (**4**) is a fine statue of the *Madonna and Child* in polychrome wood by an unknown sculptor working in the mid 14th century. Another chapel (**5**) contains a monument to Donatello (d. 1466; buried in the vault below) erected in neo-Renaissance style in 1896. The marble sarcophagus opposite of Niccolò and Fioretta Martelli (c. 1464) in the form of a wicker basket is probably by Donatello. The painting of the *Annunciation* is one of the most beautiful early works of Filippo Lippi.

I The *Martyrdom of St Lawrence*: This huge fresco is the work of Bronzino.

J *Christ in the Carpenter's Workshop* by Pietro Annigoni, a skilled Florentine painter, who died in 1988. Annigoni became well known in Britain when he painted a portrait of Queen Elizabeth II. This is one of the very few 20th-century works which have been hung in a church in the centre of Florence, although Annigoni painted other religious subjects, which hang in modern churches in Tuscany.

Old Sacristy

Inlaid doors in the north transept provide access to the Old Sacristy or Sagrestia Vecchia (1422–28). This was the first part of the church to be rebuilt. One of the earliest and purest monuments of the Renaissance by Brunelleschi, it was erected at the expense of Giovanni di Bicci de' Medici, who is buried here. The vault is particularly beautiful and the chapel has been painstakingly restored. The decorative details are mainly by Donatello: above the frieze of cherubs' heads, the *tondi* in the pendentives and lunettes depict the four Evangelists and scenes from the life of St John the

Detail from Bronzino's *Martyrdom of St Lawrence*. The saint is said to have been roasted alive on an iron griddle. Here wood to fuel the flames is being collected.

Evangelist. Modelled in terracotta and plaster, they are remarkable for their composition. Over the two little doors are large reliefs of Saints Cosmas and Damian and Saints Lawrence and Stephen (the former may have been designed by Michelozzo).

The remarkable dark blue fresco in the small dome over the altar depicts the zodiacal sky as it was on 6 July 1439 (the date of the conclusion of the Council of Florence between the Greek and Roman Catholic churches). The bronze doors have figures of the Apostles and Martyrs in animated discussion (usually considered the work of Donatello, but now also attributed by some scholars to Michelozzo). The terracotta bust of St Lawrence (or St Leonard) has been attributed to Donatello or Desiderio da Settignano. The raised seats and presses are decorated with exquisite inlay. In the centre is the sarcophagus of the founder of the Medici dynasty, Giovanni di Bicci de' Medici (d. 1429), and his wife Piccarda Bueri, the parents of Cosimo il Vecchio, by Buggiano (c. 1433). Set into the wall is the magnificent porphyry and bronze sarcophagus of Giovanni and Piero de' Medici, the sons of Cosimo il Vecchio. This was commissioned from Verrocchio in 1472 by Lorenzo the Magnificent and his brother Giuliano. In the little chapel **(6)** is an exquisitely carved lavabo with fantastic creatures, commissioned by Piero de' Medici c. 1467, by an unknown master (variously attributed to Verrocchio, Antonio Rossellino, Desiderio da Settignano, and Donatello).

The Cloister

The cloister was designed by Manetti (1457–62), and is entered from the north aisle or from the left of the façade. It has graceful arcades with Ionic capitals and an orange tree is planted at its centre. From the cloister there is an entrance (*sometimes open for exhibitions*) to the crypt of San Lorenzo and the vaults with the simple classical tomb of Cosimo il Vecchio by Verrocchio. Nearby is the tomb of Ferdinand III, surrounded by commemorative inscriptions to the other Lorraine grand dukes, arranged here in 1874 by Emilio de Fabris. Donatello is also buried here.

BIBLIOTECA LAURENZIANA

Open 9–1 except Sun and holidays; T: 055 210 760. Exhibitions of the libraries' holdings are usually held here about twice a year.

A staircase near a statue of the historian Paolo Giovio, by Francesco da Sangallo (1560), ascends to the Biblioteca Laurenziana (or Laurentian Library). It was begun by Michelangelo c. 1524 at the order of Clement VII (Giulio de' Medici) to house the collection of manuscripts made by Cosimo il Vecchio and Lorenzo the Magnificent. It is a remarkable monument of Mannerist architecture.

The solemn **vestibule**, filled with an elaborate free-standing staircase, was constructed by Vasari and Ammannati from Michelangelo's design in 1559–71. This highly idiosyncratic work (*see also p. 18*) has been interpreted by scholars in numerous ways, but whatever their conclusions, it clearly shows Michelangelo's sculptural conception of architecture. In the tall room there is a pronounced use of *pietra serena* in the blind windows and empty niches, columns and volutes, and to stand in this strange space cannot fail to affect you. All the elements combine to provide a vertical emphasis, and the columns and volutes are set into the wall, producing strange shadow effects. The decoration of the architectural elements is kept to a minimum, with subtle, classically-inspired carvings. As Vasari observed, this room did much to encourage Michelangelo's successors to explore new designs, and the subversion of architectural rules meant that later architects no longer felt obliged to conform to established styles in their work.

The peaceful **reading room**, a long hall, provides an unexpected contrast. Here the angle at which the architectural decoration can be seen has been carefully calculated, and the carved desks, also by Michelangelo, form an intricate part of the design. It is interesting to note that the heavily decorated vestibule is invisible from the aisle (only a blank wall is framed in the doorway). The very fine wood ceiling and beautiful terracotta floor are by Santi Buglioni to a design by Tribolo, and the stained glass is original.

Exhibitions from the collection are held every year in the adjoining rooms (the circular tribune was added in 1841). The library is famous above all for its Greek and Latin manuscripts; it has been augmented over the centuries and now includes 11,000 manuscripts and 4,000 incunabula. The oldest codex is a famous 5th-century Virgil. Other works owned by the library include Syrian gospels of the 6th century; the oldest manuscript of Justinian's *Pandects* (6th–7th centuries); the *Codex Amiatinus* (from Monte Amiata) written in the monastery of Jarrow in England in the 8th century; a choir book illuminated by Lorenzo Monaco and Attavante; a *Book of Hours* which belonged to Lorenzo the Magnificent; the *Città di Vita* of Matteo Palmieri, with illuminations in the style of Pollaiolo and Botticelli; a *Treatise on Architecture* with manuscript notes by Leonardo da Vinci; the manuscript of Cellini's *Autobiography*; and a parchment of the Union of Greek and Roman churches recording the abortive effort of the Council of Florence to reunite the Churches in 1439.

MEDICI CHAPELS

Open 8.30–4.30; closed second and fourth Sun of month and first, third and fifth Mon of month; T: 055 282 984. Entrance in Piazza Madonna degli Aldobrandini.
The Medici Chapels, or Cappelle Medicee, are approached from outside the east end of San Lorenzo, where a 20th-century statue by Raffaello Salimbeni of Anna Maria Luisa, the Electress Palatine—the last descendent of the Medici family, who settled her inheritance on the city of Florence—was placed behind a railing in 1995.

The crypt of the Cappella dei Principi was designed by Buontalenti and contains the tomb slabs of numerous members of the Medici family. A selection of the most precious objects from the church treasury is exhibited here: reliquaries by Massimiliano Soldani Benzi, and two early 15th-century Venetian reliquaries. The mitre, made in Rome in the 16th century and decorated with numerous Baroque pearls, was donated to the basilica by Leo X, and the pastoral stave with St Lawrence is also a 16th-century Roman work.

Cappella dei Principi

A staircase leads up from the crypt to the Cappella dei Principi, the opulent—if gloomy—mausoleum of the Medici grand dukes, begun by Matteo Nigetti (1604) to a plan by Don Giovanni de' Medici, illegitimate son of Cosimo I. It is a high octagon, 28m in diameter, entirely lined with dark-coloured marbles and semi-precious stones, a tour de force of craftsmanship in *pietre dure*. The lowest part of the walls is adorned with particularly fine mosaic coats of arms (1589–1609), belonging to the 16 towns which were bishoprics of Tuscany. Between them are 32 inlaid vases in red and green jasper (early 17th century). In the sarcophagi around the walls, from right to left, are buried Ferdinando II, Cosimo II, Ferdinando I, Cosimo I, Francesco I and Cosimo III. The second and third sarcophagi are surmounted by colossal statues in gilded bronze, by Pietro and Ferdinando Tacca (1626–42). Work continued until 1836 when the decoration on the drum of the cupola was completed (but not to the original design, which envisaged a covering in *pietre dure*). The vault frescoes were painted at this time by Pietro Benvenuti. The pavement was executed in 1882–1962.

The altar is a model in wood, hastily set up in 1938, which bears *pietre dure* panels of various dates, including the *Supper at Emmaus* (1853–61) and four fine panels with liturgical emblems against a deep blue ground (1821–53).

New Sacristy

A passage to the left leads past two trophies attributed to Silvio Cosini, intended to decorate a tomb in the Sagrestia Nuova. This so-called New Sacristy may have been begun by Giuliano da Sangallo c. 1491. Work was continued by Michelangelo in 1520–24 and 1530–33, but was left unfinished when he finally left Florence for Rome in 1534, in anger at the political climate in the city. It balances Brunelleschi's Old Sacristy (*see pp. 183–84 above*) and drew inspiration from it, but was used from its inception as a funerary chapel for the Medici family. It is built in dark *pietra serena* and white marble in a severe style, which produces a strange, cold atmosphere, in part due to the diffusion of light exclusively from above, and the odd perspective devices on

Michelangelo: tomb of Lorenzo, Duke of Urbino.

the upper parts of the walls. Vasari is known to have worked on the chapel in 1550–56.

The tombs were commissioned by the Medici pope Clement VII in an attempt to re-establish the glory of the dynasty when the position of the Medici in Florence was at a particularly low ebb. Michelangelo executed only two of the famous Medici tombs, out of the three or more originally projected. To the left of the entrance is the tomb of Lorenzo, Duke of Urbino (1492–1519), grandson of Lorenzo the Magnificent. He was an unpopular ruler, who governed by force rather than by consensus. Machiavelli dedicated *The Prince* to him after he conquered Urbino in 1516–17. The statue of the duke shows nothing of this, portraying him seated, absorbed in meditation, and on the sarcophagus below are the reclining figures of *Dawn* and *Dusk*.

Opposite is the tomb of the third son of Lorenzo the Magnificent, Giuliano, Duke of Nemours (1479–1516; he received his title from the king of France). Well-liked for the brief year that he ruled in Florence, he famously exonerated Machiavelli from charges of having taken part in a plot against him. But Giuliano was more interested in a life of ease than of politics. He counted Castiglione a personal friend (and is in fact one of the characters in *The Courtier*). On his sarcophagus are the figures of *Day* and *Night*, the last, with the symbols of darkness (the moon, the owl, and a mask), is considered to be among the finest of all Michelangelo's sculptures. The head of the male figure (*Day*) is hardly worked on at all and the marks of the sculptor's toothed chisel (or *gradina*) can clearly be seen here (and they recall the 'hatching' made by Michelangelo's pen in his drawings). This massive nude seems to have been influenced by the ancient Torso del Belvedere in the Vatican in Rome. The entrance wall was intended to contain an architectural monument to Lorenzo the Magnificent and his brother Giuliano (murdered in the Pazzi Conspiracy); the only part carried out by Michelangelo is the *Madonna and Child*. It is his last statue of a Madonna and one of his most beautiful. The figures on either side are St Cosmas and St Damian, the medical saints who were the patrons of the Medici, and are by Montorsoli and Raffaello da Montelupo. Lorenzo the Magnificent's coffin was transferred here from the Old Sacristy in 1559.

The austere altar bears two candelabra designed by Michelangelo (the one on the left, with the more delicate carving, is the work of Silvio Cosini and that on the right was made in 1741). On the walls behind the altar are architectural graffiti, some of them attributed to Michelangelo, and others to his pupils, including Tribolo. The door to the left of the altar gives access to a little room where **charcoal drawings** of great interest were discovered on the walls in 1975. Small groups of visitors are usually shown the room every 30–60 minutes or so (*by appointment at the ticket office, 9–12*). The drawings have aroused much discussion among art historians, most of whom recognize them as works by Michelangelo. It is thought that he hid here for a time under the protection of his friend, the prior of San Lorenzo, after the return of the Medici in 1530. Michelangelo had supported the Republican government (in fact his *David* had had its left arm broken in a pro-Republican revolt in 1527); when the Medici returned the Florentine governors issued an order calling for his execution. Michelangelo went into hiding until later in the year when Pope Clement requested that he be treated with clemency. The drawings clearly refer to works by Michelangelo, such as his statue of Giuliano in the adjoining chapel. The large figure study for a *Resurrection of Christ* on the entrance wall is particularly remarkable.

PIAZZA SAN LORENZO

Piazza San Lorenzo is filled with a busy street market open all day (except Sun and Mon in winter); the stalls sell leather-goods, clothing and jewellery (usually good value). The seated statue of Giovanni delle Bande Nere (father of Cosimo I) is by Baccio Bandinelli (1540). On the corner is the back of Palazzo Medici-Riccardi. The long façade (14th–15th centuries) of Palazzo della Stufa (no. 4) overlooks the piazza.

The animated Via dell'Ariento (*map p. 398, C2–C1*), also lined with numerous market stalls, passes the huge **Mercato Centrale**, or Mercato di San Lorenzo (*open Mon–Sat 7–1; also 4.30–7.30 on Sat except in July and Aug*). Until a few years ago this was the principal food market in town but many of the stalls have closed down in recent years and others now appear to cater mainly for tourists. The magnificent cast-iron building (1874) by Giuseppe Mengoni—best known for the Galleria Vittorio Emanuele II in Milan—was restored in 1980 when a mezzanine floor was constructed for the sale of fruit and vegetables, and a car park opened in the basement. In Via Panicale (locally known as Shanghai) are more market stalls selling cheap clothes.

PALAZZO MEDICI-RICCARDI
Map p. 397, B1

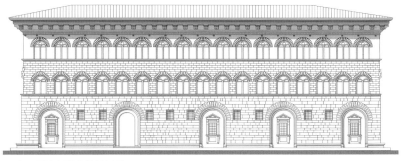

PALAZZO MEDICI-RICCARDI

Chapel and gallery open 9–7 except Wed. To book a visit, T: 055 276 0340.

Palazzo Medici-Riccardi was built for Cosimo il Vecchio by Michelozzo after 1444 as a town mansion on Via Larga (renamed Via Cavour in the 19th century). Michelozzo was Cosimo's favourite architect, and Cosimo also used him to design the convent of San Marco and his villas on the outskirts of Florence. He was also a very fine sculptor, and worked with Donatello. This palace remained the residence of the Medici family until 1540, when Cosimo I moved into Palazzo Vecchio. The rusticated façade served as a model for other famous Florentine palaces, including those built by the Strozzi and Pitti. Charles VIII of France stayed here in 1494 and the Emperor Charles V in 1536. It was bought by the Riccardi in 1659 and before the end of the century was extended towards Via de' Ginori; the façade on Via Cavour was lengthened by seven bays. It is now the seat of the Prefect, the provincial representative of central government, and of the Province of Florence, and it is used for exhibitions. The only parts open permanently to the public are the courtyard, the famous little chapel (the Cappella dei Magi) frescoed by Benozzo Gozzoli and the *galleria* frescoed by Luca Giordano.

Cortile d'Onore

The dignified main courtyard has composite colonnades dating from the 15th century and twelve *tondi* in relief (copies of ancient sculptures inspired by antique gems in the

THE MEDICI

The Medici first came to Florence from the fertile valley of the Mugello. They are recorded during the 13th century as money changers, and as bankers in the 14th. The family emblem, the *palle*, red balls on a gold background, probably represents the coins of their earliest profession, although they have also been linked somewhat romantically in family legend to the dents on the shield received by a Medici knight in an encounter with a giant.

Giovanni di Bicci de' Medici (1360–1429), the founder of the family's great fortune and political respectability, started life humbly. He was in Florence by 1378, and worked his way up the family business, until he was undisputed head of the bank. By 1401 he was well respected enough to be on the committee judging the competition for the Baptistery doors. But Giovanni never forgot that he was an outsider, and he carefully but quietly sided with popular feeling. It is said that he advised his son Cosimo (il Vecchio) never to go near the Piazza della Signoria unless summoned there, and never to make a show before the people or go against their will. Cosimo, already forty when his father died in 1429, followed the advice.

It was Cosimo who set in hand the building of a family palace. Up to now the family had lived in a palazzo taken over from the Bardi family, but by the 1440s Cosimo felt secure enough in the city to build his own. However, he still needed to act prudently, and the story goes that the model produced by Brunelleschi was turned down by Cosimo as too ostentatious. Those attuned to Cosimo's ways have argued that the affair was set up to allow him to present the more modest palace built to the design of Michelozzo as a sign of his restraint. Visitors to the completed building would be greeted by Donatello's *David* and its Latin inscription exhorting the citizens to stand up against tyranny.

It seems clear that the palace was used for formal city business after 1458. It was also here that the bags which contained the names of citizens eligible for office were made up (they were drawn out at random), and there is no doubt that Cosimo controlled the *accoppiatori*, the scrutineers of the appointments. Nevertheless, the Medici were never truly secure in their position. Even at the height of Lorenzo's power in the 1480s there were those who talked of Medici tyranny, and their rule collapsed quickly in 1494, with the inept behaviour of Lorenzo's son Piero. The Medici palace was sacked in an outburst of popular fury. Yet the family had an uncanny ability to reinvent itself. Few would have predicted that it would once again be a Medici, Cosimo I (1519–74), who would dominate the city after the siege of 1530, and this time to a greater extent than any of his predecessors. The glorification of the dynasty began with Cosimo's symbolic move out of the family residence into the seat of government, Palazzo della Signoria. The Medici palace was sold to the Riccardi family—though luckily its finest Medici treasure, the frescoes of the *Procession of the Magi*, remains intact. c.f.

Medici collections) and the Medici arms. These were carried out c. 1450 by Donatello's circle (usually ascribed to Bertoldo) and are united by graffiti festoons by Maso di Bartolomeo. When the Medici lived here, Donatello's statue of *Judith and Holofernes* was in the garden, and his bronze *David* adorned the courtyard until 1495. After 1715, Francesco Riccardi arranged the courtyard as a museum of ancient sculpture, setting up numerous reliefs and inscriptions inside decorative frames. The statue of *Orpheus and Cerberus*, under the arch towards the garden, is by Baccio Bandinelli. In the pretty second court are more statues, some of them Roman works, and pots of lemon trees.

Chapel

The main staircase off the Cortile d'Onore leads up to the dark little chapel (only 15 people are admitted at one time), the only unaltered part of Michelozzo's work. It is one of the oldest chapels in Florence to have survived in a private palace. It has a lovely carved wood ceiling and a splendid inlaid floor in red porphyry and green serpentine marble. The finely carved wooden choir stalls are to a design by Giuliano da Sangallo. The walls are entirely covered with decorative frescoes that are Benozzo Gozzoli's masterpiece.

Benozzo Gozzoli's fresco cycle

The *Procession of the Magi to Bethlehem* (begun in 1459 and finished before 1463), is one of the most pleasing, even if not one of the most important, fresco cycles of the Renaissance. It was probably commissioned by Cosimo il Vecchio, but it is known that his son Piero di Cosimo (il Gottoso; the Gouty) also took an active interest in the work. The procession was probably intended partly as an evocation of the festival held by the Compagnia dei Magi of San Marco at Epiphany, in which the Medici usually took part. The decorative cavalcade is shown in a charming landscape with hunting scenes, which seems to be inspired by Flemish tapestries. Some members of the Medici family are depicted wearing their emblem of the three ostrich feathers, but discussion continues about the identification of the various figures, some of which are vivid portrait studies.

The frescoes were designed around an altarpiece (commissioned c. 1444–56) of the *Adoration of the Child* by Filippo Lippi, which was already on the altar of the chapel.

The procession is seen approaching along the distant hills on the right wall. The two men mounted on the extreme left are usually identified as Sigismondo Pandolfo Malatesta and Galeazzo Maria Sforza. In the crowd behind (just above their heads) the two boys in red hats may have been intended to portray Lorenzo and Giuliano, sons of Piero il Gottoso, then around ten and six years old. Above them, the man looking out of the fresco is a self-portrait of Benozzo with his signature in gold lettering on his red hat. In front, the man in a red beret on a mule is often taken as a portrait of Cosimo il Vecchio; the man just in front of him, dressed in green and gold brocade, on a grey horse with the Medici emblems on its bridle, may be his son, Piero il Gottoso. The man on foot beside the horses' heads could be Piero's brother Carlo or Giovanni. The young king on this wall, on a splendid grey charger, is usually considered to be an idealized portrait of Lorenzo the Magnificent.

Face in the crowd: Benozzo Gozzoli (with his name on his hat) in the Medici-magi procession.

On the wall opposite the altar, the three girls on horseback with the Medici feathers in their hair may be Piero il Gottoso's daughters. The second king is dressed in splendid Oriental dress, with green and gold brocade. On the last wall, the older grey-bearded king on a grey mule was cut in two when the wall was moved to accommodate the staircase in the 17th century. In front of him the huntsman in blue with a cheetah sitting on his horse is sometimes taken to be an idealized portrait of Giuliano, son of Piero il Gottoso and later Duke of Nemours (*see pp. 187–88*). The head of the man just in front of his horse, with a blue and white turban, may be a second self-portrait by Benozzo. The procession, with camels and horses, winds on uphill towards Bethlehem.

On the walls on either side of the altar are beautiful landscapes with angels, recalling those of the painter's master, Fra' Angelico. The altarpiece of the *Adoration of the Child* is a copy by the *bottega* of Filippo Lippi (late 15th century) of the original altarpiece by Filippo Lippi which was here until 1494 when it was taken to Palazzo Vecchio, and after 1814 found its way to Berlin. The copy was put here in 1929.

Second Floor
Here is a room with a beautiful painting of the *Madonna and Child* by Filippo Lippi (with the sketch of a head on the back) and the hall where the Provincial Council meets, decorated with tapestries of the Four Seasons made before 1643 in Florence from cartoons by Jacopo Vignali. The gallery, an example of Baroque decoration unique in Florence (1670–88), is covered by a fresco of the *Apotheosis of the Second Medici Dynasty* by Luca Giordano (1683). The stucco decoration was designed by Giovanni Battista Foggini. The four painted mirrors are by Antonio Domenico Gabbiani and Bartolomeo Bimbi.

SANTA MARIA NOVELLA
& OGNISSANTI

SANTA MARIA NOVELLA
Map p. 398 B2–C2

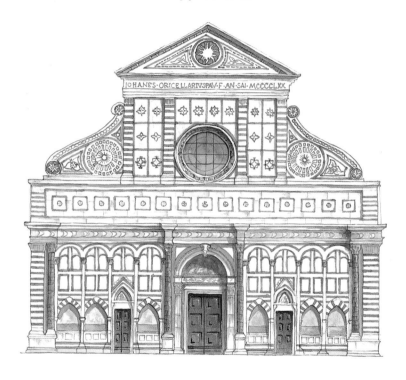

Open 9.30–5; Fri, Sun, and holidays 1–5; T: 055 215918.

Santa Maria Novella is the most important Gothic church in Tuscany. The first church (the foundations of which have been found), called Santa Maria delle Vigne, was built in 1094 on the site of a chapel (probably 9th century). The Dominicans were given the property in 1221, and building began in 1246 at the east end of the present church. The Dominican friars Sisto and Ristoro are thought to have been the architects of the impressive nave, begun in 1279. The church was completed under the direction of another friar, Jacopo Talenti, in the mid-14th century, when the great Dominican preacher Jacopo Passavanti was prior. A small group of Dominican friars still lives in the convent.

The Façade

The lower part of the splendid marble façade above the Gothic arcaded recesses (the *avelli* or family vaults of Florentine nobles) is typically Tuscan Romanesque in style and is also attributed to Fra' Jacopo Talenti. Its geometrical design in white and dark green marble was inspired by the exteriors of the Baptistery and San Miniato al Monte. The upper part of the façade was completed together with the main doorway in 1456–70, and its classical lines are in perfect harmony with the earlier work. It was commissioned by Giovanni Rucellai, from the famous Renaissance architect Leon Battista Alberti, and exquisite inlaid friezes bear the emblems of the Rucellai (a billowing ship's sail) and of the Medici (a ring with ostrich feathers), since in 1461 Giovanni's son Bernardo married Nannina, sister of his close friend Lorenzo the Magnificent. Below the tympanum, an inscription in handsome classical lettering records the name of the benefactor and the date 1470. Alberti also built Giovanni's town house, the Palazzo Rucellai (*see p. 211*). The architect's ingenious use of scrolls to connect the nave roof with the lower aisle roofs was an innovation which was frequently copied in church façades of later centuries (however he only built the left scroll and that on the right—a perfect replica—was finally added in 1920).

The two astronomical instruments (a quadrant with eight sundials and an equinoctial armilla) were made by another friar, Egnazio Danti, in 1572–75. The campanile, also attributed to Fra' Jacopo Talenti, was grafted onto an ancient watchtower. The Gothic arcades are continued to the right of the façade, extending round the old cemetery.

The Interior

Entering the church from the cemetery through the south door, your eye is immediately drawn to Masaccio's *Trinity* and Giotto's Crucifix (*see below*). The spacious nave has remarkably bold stone vaulting, its arches given prominence by bands of dark grey *pietra serena*. Frescoes of saints dating from the 14th century have been exposed on the intrados of the arches. The composite pillars between nave and aisles have classical capitals. The bays decrease in width as they approach the three fine stained glass lancet windows at the east end. The interior was altered by Vasari in 1565, when the roodscreen (which formerly divided the church at the steps in the fourth bay) and the friars' choir were demolished, and side altars were set up in the nave (replaced by the present neo-Gothic ones in the 19th century).

A Masaccio's *Trinity*: This famous fresco dates from 1427. It shows God the Father supporting the Cross, with the Virgin and St John the Evangelist and donors beneath it. On the sarcophagus at the bottom is a skeleton representing Adam's grave. The symbol of Death is thus shown beneath the symbol of the Resurrection. This fresco is one of the earliest works to use accurately the system of linear perspective developed by Brunelleschi; indeed, it may be that the architect himself intervened in the design of the shadowy niche. The prefect composition gives it an almost metaphysical quality. The fresco was detached in the 16th century and was later moved several times to other places in the church.

Masaccio: detail of the *Trinity* (1427).

B In the nave hangs a huge Crucifix by Giotto, an early work (c. 1290) which probably once adorned the rood-screen. It is one of at least three monumental Crucifixes by Giotto to be seen in Florentine churches. Although paint- ed well over a hundred years before Masaccio's fresco, it is interesting to confront these two great masters here at close range and see how both contributed in such a fundamental way to the development of Italian painting.

C West wall: The stained glass in the rose window dates from around 1365. Over the door is a frescoed lunette of the *Nativity* attributed as an early work to Botticelli. The artist's famous *Adoration of the Magi*, now in the Uffizi (*see pp. 94–95*), was commissioned for a small altar here by a money dealer called della Lama. On the left of the door is a painting of the *Annunciation* by Santi di Tito.

D The monument to the Blessed Villana delle Botti (1332–61) is by Bernardo Rossellino (1451). Born into a wealthy merchant family, Villana renounced her riches and her husband, and became a lay Dominican here.

E Monument to Giovanni da Salerno: This 16th-century imitation of the Botti monument by Vincenzo Danti commemorates the founder of the convent. There are a number of altarpieces in this aisle by the 16th-century painter Giovanni Battista Naldini.

F Cappella della Pura, or Purità: This 15th-century chapel (*sometimes closed*) has a sculpted Crucifix dating from c. 1340. The paintings on the Cross itself are a rare example of English workmanship of the late 13th century.

G South transept: Here there are Gothic tombs and the monument to Joseph, Patriarch of Constantinople, who attended the Council of Florence in 1439 (aimed unsuccessfully at reuniting the Eastern and Western Churches) and died in the convent in the following year (the fresco is a contemporary portrait).

H Cappella Rucellai: Preceded by the simple, classical sarcophagus of Paolo Rucellai, this chapel (no admission) housed Duccio's famous painting of the *Madonna Enthroned* (the *Maestà*) in the 18th century (so that when the work was removed to the Uffizi in 1948, it became known as the *Rucellai Madonna*). It now contains a marble statue of the Madonna and Child signed by Nino Pisano, almost the only work in Florence by this Pisan sculptor, although his father Andrea was well-known for the masterpieces of sculpture he made for the Baptistery and Campanile. The bronze tomb-slab of the Dominican general Lionardo Dati is by the great bronze sculptor Lorenzo Ghiberti (1425). It was formerly in the nave in front of the high altar, but is now easy to overlook since it is so difficult to see. The walls have traces of 14th-century frescoes. The large painting of the *Martyrdom of St Catherine* is an early 16th-century work by Giuliano Bugiardini.

I Cappella dei Bardi: This chapel (*at present covered for restoration*) was formerly used by the Laudesi brotherhood, which was founded c. 1245 by the first Dominican saint Peter Martyr. They commissioned the *Maestà* from Duccio for this chapel (later moved to the Cappella Rucellai) in 1285. The bas-relief of *Riccardo di Ricco Bardi Kneeling Before St Gregory* dates from the year after his death, 1335, when his heirs took possession of the chapel. Frescoes of the late 14th century partially cover earlier fresco fragments. The damaged lunettes above (with the *Madonna Enthroned*), contemporary with Duccio's

SANTA MARIA NOVELLA

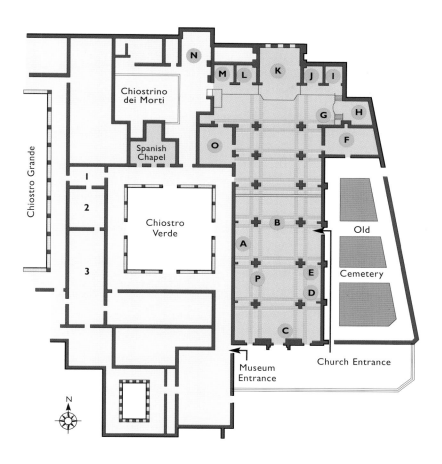

Maestà, are of great interest since they have recently been attributed to Cimabue—if confirmed as such they would be the only frescoes known in Florence by this master, considered the founder of the Florentine school of painting (*see p. 11*). The altarpiece of

the *Madonna of the Rosary* is by Giorgio Vasari.

J Cappella di Filippo Strozzi: This Gothic chapel, decorated with splendid exuberant frescoes by Filippino Lippi, was acquired in 1486 by the great

Florentine banker Filippo Strozzi, who built Palazzo Strozzi (*see p. 209*) and was agent for the Medici in Naples. He commissioned the frescoes from Filippino as soon as the latter had finished work on the Brancacci Chapel in the church of the Carmine (*see p. 273*), and the contract for the work survives (and makes copious mention of the necessity to add lapis lazuli to the surface of the fresco after it had dried, *a secco*). The artist interrupted work here when he was called to Rome to fresco the Carafa chapel in Santa Maria sopra Minerva, and only finished it after his return to Florence in 1502. Full of allusions to antiquity and including grotesques, this is quite different from other Florentine fresco cycles of this period. It shows that Filippino was a superb draughtsman (the preparatory drawings for the frescoes survive in the Uffizi). On the right wall is the *Crucifixion of St Philip the Apostle*, and his *Miracle Before the Temple of Mars* (on the extreme right is a portrait of Filippino's black servant). On the left wall is the *Martyrdom of St John the Evangelist* and the *Raising of Drusiana*. In the vault are *Adam*, *Noah*, *Abraham* and *Jacob*. Filippino also designed the beautiful stained glass window and the splendid classical trompe l'œil frescoes in grisaille on the altar wall. Strozzi ordered that his tomb, exquisitely carved by Benedetto da Maiano, should be given pride of place on the altar wall itself (although an altar was subsequently placed in front of it). The *Four Patriarchs* in the vault were the first part of the chapel to be painted. In the *Decameron*, Boccaccio uses this part of the church as the meeting-place of a group of young people determined to enjoy life during the plague year of 1348.

K Sanctuary: The main altar has a bronze Crucifix by Giambologna. The sanctuary is decorated with delightful frescoes by Domenico Ghirlandaio, who was buried in the church after his death (aged 45) from the plague. They were commissioned in 1485 by Giovanni Tornabuoni, whose sister Lucrezia married Piero il Gottoso. Giovanni was for years manager of the Rome branch of the Medici bank. The frescoes are Ghirlandaio's masterpiece, and he was assisted by his brother Davide, his brother-in-law, Sebastiano Mainardi, and his pupils, including perhaps the young Michelangelo. They replaced a fresco cycle by Orcagna (fragments of which, with heads of prophets, have been detached from the vault), and follow a similar iconographical design. Many of the figures are portraits of the artist's contemporaries, including members of the Tornabuoni family, and the whole cycle mirrors Florentine life in the late 15th century.

On the right wall are scenes from the life of St John the Baptist, including (lower register) the *Angel Appearing to St Zacharias in the Temple* (with portraits of the Tornabuoni and famous humanist scholars), the *Visitation*, and (above) *Birth of St John the Baptist*.

On the left wall, there are scenes from the life of the Virgin, including (lower register) the *Expulsion of St Joachim from the Temple* (with members of the Tornabuoni family, and, in the group on the right, the self-portraits of the artists), and the *Birth of the Virgin* (with portraits of the Tornabuoni ladies).

On the end wall, there are a *Coronation of the Virgin*, *Miracle of St Dominic*, *Death of St Peter Martyr*, *Annunciation*, *St John the Baptist in the Desert*, and the two kneeling figures of the donors, Giovanni Tornabuoni and his wife Francesca Pitti. In the vault, the four Evangelists are shown. The stained glass windows (c. 1491) were also designed by Ghirlandaio. The stalls are attributed to Baccio d'Agnolo.

L Cappella Gondi: The handsome marble decoration is by Giuliano da Sangallo. There is also a Crucifix by Brunelleschi, his only sculpture to survive in wood (obviously made to wear a loin cloth but this has since been removed). Vasari recounts the story that Brunelleschi carved this work after he had criticized Donatello for representing a mere 'peasant' on the Cross in his Crucifix (now in Santa Croce, *see p. 239*). When finished he invited Donatello to his house to show him how he thought the crucified Saviour was supposed to look. Donatello was so amazed by what he saw that he promptly dropped the food, including eggs, he had been carrying in his overalls for their lunch. When Brunelleschi remonstrated with him about the loss of their meal, Donatello declared that he had had his fill for that day, and that evidently Brunelleschi had been made to carve figures of Christ and Donatello figures of peasants. The damaged vault frescoes of the Evangelists may date from the late 13th century.

M Cappella Gaddi: Designed by Giovanni Antonio Dosio, this retains its 16th-century decorations by Alessandro Allori, Bronzino, and Giovanni Bandini.

N Cappella Strozzi: A remarkably well-preserved example of a mid-14th-century Tuscan chapel. It contains celebrated frescoes (c. 1357) by Nardo di Cione; they are his most famous work and are carefully designed to cover the entire chapel. They represent (in the vault), *St Thomas Aquinas* and the *Virtues*; on the end wall, the *Last Judgement*; on the left wall, *Paradise*, a huge crowded composition; and on the right wall, *Inferno*, a pictorial commentary on Dante's *Inferno*. The splendid frescoed decoration is completed on the intrados of the entrance arch with a frieze of saints. The stained-glass window was also designed by Nardo and his brother Andrea di Cione (better known as Orcagna), who painted the fine altarpiece of the *Redeemer Giving the Keys to St Peter and the Book of Wisdom to St Thomas Aquinas* (1357), remarkable for its unusual iconography.

O Sacristy: The cross-vault is another work by Fra' Jacopo Talenti (c. 1350). The stained glass windows date from 1386. On the left of the door is a lavabo in terracotta with a charming landscape—the first documented work by Giovanni della Robbia (1498); the upper part may be by his father Andrea. The huge cupboard on the opposite wall was designed by Buontalenti (1593). On the walls are 16th-century paintings, including a *Crucifixion* by Vasari.

P North Aisle: The pulpit was designed by Brunelleschi and executed by his adopted son Buggiano. The 16th-century altarpieces in this aisle are by Alessandro Allori, Vasari and Santi di Tito.

Museo di Santa Maria Novella

Open 9–5; Sun and holidays 9–2; closed Fri; T: 055 282 187.
To the left of the church is the entrance to the Museo di Santa Maria Novella, arranged in part of the Convent of Santa Maria Novella. The cloisters remain an oasis of calm in this busy part of the city. The convent was one of the richest and largest in Florence, and Eugenius IV transferred the entire Papal court here in 1434–43 during sessions of the Council of Florence (1439) which attempted to heal the Eastern schism.

Chiostro Verde

The Romanesque Chiostro Verde (c. 1330–50) takes its name from the green colour of its famous decoration (in the vaults are roundels of Dominican saints). The damaged frescoes by Paolo Uccello and assistants (including Dello Delli) are painted in *terraverde*. They illustrate stories from Genesis (the biblical references are given below each scene), and the cycle begins at the far end of the east (entrance) walk beside the door into the church. The numerous frescoes with animals are particularly charming. The following scenes are usually considered to be mostly by Paolo Uccello himself: the *Creation of Adam and the Animals*, the *Creation and Temptation of Eve* (c. 1425), and the *Flood*, and the *Recession of the Flood* (with Noah's ark), and the *Sacrifice and Drunkenness of Noah* (c. 1446). Although much damaged, they are most remarkable for their figure studies and perspective effects; the Flood and Noah scenes are among the most mysterious and disturbing paintings of the Florentine Renaissance.

At the beginning of the north walk is a lunette of the *Madonna and Child* dating from around 1330, possibly by the great Sienese painter Lippo Memmi.

At the centre of this peaceful cloister stand four cypresses around a raised well, and there is a good view of the side of the church, the exterior of the sacristy with its stained glass windows, and of the campanile.

Spanish Chapel

Off the cloister opens the Spanish Chapel, or Cappellone degli Spagnuoli. It received its name in the 16th century when it was assigned by Duchess Eleonora di Toledo (wife of Cosimo I) to the Spanish members of her retinue. It was originally the chapter house, also built by Fra' Jacopo Talenti in the mid-14th century, with a splendid cross-vault and two fine Gothic windows. The walls and vault are entirely covered with colourful frescoes by Andrea di Bonaiuto (sometimes called Andrea da Firenze) and assistants (c. 1365), the most important work by this otherwise little-known artist, who was influenced by the Sienese school of painting.

The pictorial decoration, on a monumental scale, is carefully designed to fit the wall space. In the vault are the *Resurrection*, the *Ascension*, and *Pentecost*. The *Navicella* is particularly beautiful and thought to have been painted before the other scenes by a master close to Giotto. On the altar wall are the *Via Dolorosa*, *Crucifixion*, and *Descent into Limbo*. On the right wall are various scenes illustrating the *Mission, Works and Triumph of the Dominican Order*. In front of the elaborate church, the artist's vision of the completed Duomo, is the *Church Militant with the Pope and Emperor and Church*

Dignitaries. In the foreground (right), behind a group of kneeling pilgrims, are the presumed portraits of Cimabue, Giotto, Boccaccio, Petrarch and Dante. The scene on the bottom right shows *St Dominic Sending Forth the Hounds of the Lord* (*domini canes*), with St Peter Martyr and St Thomas Aquinas. Above, four seated figures symbolizing the Vices are surrounded by representations of dancing Virtues. *A Dominican Friar Taking Confession* shows the way to salvation, and those absolved are sent on towards the Gate of Paradise guarded by St Peter. On the other side of the gate, the Blessed look up towards Christ in Judgement surrounded by angels.

The opposite wall shows the *Triumph of Catholic Doctrine*, personified by St Thomas Aquinas, shown enthroned beneath the winged Virtues. On his right and left are Doctors of the Church. In the Gothic choir stalls below are 14 female figures symbolizing the Arts and Sciences, with, at their feet, historical personages representing these disciplines. On the entrance wall is the *Life of St Peter Martyr* (damaged). The polyptych by Bernardo Daddi painted for the chapter house in 1344 has been removed for restoration. The apse chapel was decorated in 1592 by Bernardino Poccetti and Alessandro Allori.

Cappella degli Ubriachi and Refectory
From the cloister, there is a passage **(1)**, which displays the *sinopie* of the frescoes of Paradise by Nardo di Cione that are in the Cappella Strozzi (inside the church). The passage leads towards the imposing Chiostro Grande (no admission as it is part of a police barracks), which can be seen through a glass door. The frescoes were carried out in the early 1580s by Bernardino Poccetti and others and are the first example in Florence of religious painting inspired by the Counter Reformation.

The 14th-century Cappella degli Ubriachi **(2)** was also built by Fra' Jacopo Talenti and it preserves the tomb-slab of the Ubriachi family and traces of wall decoration showing their emblem. Here also are displayed detached frescoes of prophets by Andrea Orcagna and his school, from the vault of the main chapel in the church, and the *sinopie* of the first frescoes by Paolo Uccello from the east walk of the Chiostro Verde. In the showcases are charming reliquary busts (Sienese school, late 14th century), and a frontal made for the high altar of the church, beautifully embroidered with scenes from the life of the Virgin (Florentine, c. 1460–66).

The large refectory **(3)** has superb cross-vaulting in three bays also by Talenti. On the entrance wall there is a large fresco of the *Manna in the Desert* by Alessandro Allori which surrounds a good fresco attributed to a follower of Agnolo Gaddi, contemporary with the building, and probably part of a larger composition which covered the entire wall. It shows the *Madonna Enthroned Between St Thomas Aquinas, St Dominic, St John the Baptist and St Peter Martyr* (the tiny figure of the Prior of the convent, Fra' Jacopo Passavanti, is shown at the feet of St Dominic). On the left wall there is a *Last Supper* by Alessandro Allori (1583). The showcases display 16th- and 17th-century reliquaries, church silver and vestments belonging to the convent.

Other parts of the convent have been closed for restoration for some years. They include the oldest part, the Chiostrino dei Morti (c. 1270), and chapels adjoining it, with mid-14th-century frescoes. Additional parts of the convent off the Chiostro Grande only open on special occasions include the remarkable vaulted dormitory and (upstairs) the Cappella dei Papi built in 1515 for Leo X, with frescoes by Pontormo of the story of Veronica and of putti on the barrel vault.

PIAZZA SANTA MARIA NOVELLA
Map p. 398, B2–C2

Piazza Santa Maria Novella, with its irregular shape, was created by the Dominicans at the end of the 13th century. The two obelisks were set up in 1608 (resting on bronze tortoises by Giambologna) as turning posts in the course of the annual chariot race (*Palio dei Cocchi*) which was first held here in 1563. The **Loggia di San Paolo** was erected on the southwest side of the square in 1489–96. It is a free copy of Brunelleschi's Loggia degli Innocenti, with polychrome terracotta roundels of Franciscan saints by Andrea della Robbia, who also produced the beautiful lunette beneath the arcade (right) of the *Meeting of St Francis and St Dominic*. There are plans by Alinari (*see p. 328*) to reopen their museum dedicated to the history of photography here.

The large tabernacle on the corner of Via della Scala contains an early 15th-century fresco by a little-known artist called Francesco d'Antonio. It marks the house where Henry James began writing his first novel *Roderick Hudson* in 1874 during the second of many trips to Europe in the next two decades. Earlier in the century both Henry Wadsworth Longfellow and Ralph Waldo Emerson had travelled from America to visit Florence and they also stayed in this piazza at the Hotel Minerva. In Via della Scala (no. 16) is the **Farmacia di Santa Maria Novella** (*open 9–1 & 3.30–7.30 except Sat afternoon and Mon morning*). The pharmacy attached to the convent of Santa Maria Novella had become important as a chemist's shop by the mid-16th century, and it is still famous as such in Florence, producing its own luxury perfumes and soap. The present shop is in the 14th-century ex-chapel of San Niccolò decorated in a delightful neo-Gothic style in 1848. It has Art Nouveau lamps and frescoes representing the four continents. The other rooms are shown on request: one overlooking the former physic garden has late 18th-century furnishings and pharmacy jars (including Montelupo ware). The charming old chemist's shop, off the Great Cloister (*see above*), has 17th-century vases including *albarelli* (pharmacy jars) and mortars. The sacristy of San Niccolò has early 15th-century frescoes of the *Passion* thought to be by Mariotto di Nardo.

Just off the east side of Piazza Santa Maria Novella, along the winding Via delle Belle Donne, is the **Croce del Trebbio**, a granite column reconsecrated in 1338 with a Gothic capital bearing symbols of the Evangelists. Above this, protected by a quaint little wooden roof, is a Cross of the Pisan school. It is traditionally thought to commemorate a massacre of heretics which took place here in 1244. Its name comes from the Latin, *trivium*, because it is at the meeting of three streets.

Florence's main railway station, the **Stazione Centrale di Santa Maria Novella** (*map p. 398, B1*), is a Functionalist building designed in 1935 by a group of Tuscan

Santa Maria Novella railway station (1935).

architects, including Giovanni Michelucci, Piero Berardi and Italo Gamberini. In the café inside there are two paintings by Ottone Rosai. The handsome subsidiary pedestrian entrance (near the Fortezza da Basso) was designed in 1990 by Gae Aulenti.

OGNISSANTI
Map p. 398, B2

Open 7.45–12 & 5–6.30; Sun and holidays 8.45–1 & 5–7.30.
The church was founded in 1256 by the Umiliati, a Benedictine Order particularly skilled in manufacturing wool. This area of the city became one of the main centres of the woollen cloth industry, on which medieval Florence based her economy. Mills on the Arno were used for washing, fulling and dying the cloth. In 1561 the church was taken over by the Franciscans and it was rebuilt in the 17th century. The original *pietra serena* façade by Matteo Nigetti (1637) was replaced by one in travertine in 1872. When in 2000 the Franciscan friars of the Osservanza left the abbey after over four centuries, a Benedictine community was re-established here, but they, too, have now decided to move away from the church. Above the portal is a lunette of the *Coronation of the Virgin* ascribed to Benedetto Buglioni, virtually the only artist after the della Robbia workshop halted production in the early 16th century who still knew how to produce fine works in glazed terracotta. The campanile dates from 1258.

The Interior

The trompe l'œil ceiling frescoes date from 1770. The fine large pavement tomb of Antonio di Vitale de' Medici, a philosopher and doctor who paid for the façade of the church and died in 1656, bears the Medici arms in marble intarsia.

The frescoes of the *Pietà* and the *Madonna della Misericordia* on the south side, early works by Domenico Ghirlandaio, are interesting as the Madonna is shown protecting members of the Vespucci family (Amerigo is supposed to be the young boy whose head appears between the Madonna and the man in the dark cloak). The family tombstone (1471) is in the pavement left of the altar. The Vespucci, who lived in Borgo Ognissanti, were merchants involved in the manufacture of silk. As supporters of the Medici, they held political office in the 15th century. Amerigo (1454–1512), a Medici agent in Seville, gave his name to the continent of America, having made two voyages in 1499 and 1501–02 following the route charted by his Italian contemporary Columbus. Their neighbours in Borgo Ognissanti were the Filipepi, the most famous of whom was Sandro who became known as Botticelli, probably because he was apprenticed to a jeweller as a boy (*battigello* means silversmith), and who is also buried in the church. The Vespucci, who commissioned some works from Botticelli, also paid for his fresco of the philosopher and father of the Church St Augustine (between the third and fourth altars), which is the artist's most important work in Florence to survive in the church for which it was made (1480). It is also one of the few frescoes in the city by Botticelli, and shows his skill in this technique. St Augustine is shown deep in thought in his study with a clock and an armillary sphere. Together with the pendant of St Jerome opposite (by Domenico Ghirlandaio), it used to be in the choir of the church, but was carefully (and successfully) detached and moved here when the church was altered in 1564. Ghirlandaio's work is dated (on the desk) 1480, and the exquisite detail of the objects on the desk and shelf, including the saint's spectacles, recall contemporary Flemish works.

The transepts and east end of the church are kept cordoned off, but visitors can usually visit this area on request. The frescoes and stuccoes in the Baroque chapels in the south transept date from c. 1717–27 (by Matteo Bonechi and Vincenzo Meucci). The simple round tombstone in the pavement marks the burial place of Sandro Filipepi (Botticelli). There are also altarpieces by Vincenzo Dandini (1667) and Matteo Rosselli. The handsome pavement tomb of Lorenzo Lenzi (d. 1442), with a coat of arms bearing a bronze relief of the head of a bull, is a little-studied work which has sometimes been attributed to the great bronze sculptor Lorenzo Ghiberti. The choir chapel is decorated with precious marbles and has frescoes in the dome (1616–17) by Giovanni da San Giovanni. The beautiful high altar (1593–1605), probably by Jacopo Ligozzi, has a frontal of exquisite workmanship, in polychrome marble intarsia and mother-of-pearl, and three mosaic panels in *commesso fiorentino*, with a tabernacle above in *pietre dure*.

The church also owns a small portable organ by Giovanni Francesco Cacioli of Lucca and Tronci of Pistoia (1741), and a full size one by Onofrio Zeffirini (1565).

Cenacolo di Ognissanti

On the left of the church, beneath a fine polychrome terracotta della Robbian coat of arms of Alessandro de' Medici, who, with his brother Antonio paid for the façade of the church, is the entrance (no. 42) to the convent (*open Mon, Tues and Sat 9–12*). In the vestibule are early 17th-century frescoes of the *Life of Mary*. The 15th-century cloister, with reused Ionic capitals, in the style of Michelozzo, was altered in the 16th century. It incorporates octagonal pilasters which support part of the Gothic church. The 13th-century campanile can also be seen here.

The frescoes of the life of St Francis were executed in the first decades of the 17th century under the direction of Jacopo Ligozzi. We know that in 1752 Sir Joshua Reynolds came here to copy them.

The pretty vaulted refectory, with its lavabos and pulpit in *pietra serena*, contains a *Last Supper* by Domenico Ghirlandaio (1480), the most beautiful of his several frescoes of this subject in Florence. The delightful background includes plants and birds which are Christian symbols. Its sinopia is displayed on another wall. The fresco of the *Annunciation* dates from 1369.

The sacristy, also off the cloister, has decorative wall-paintings of the early 14th century. The large painted Crucifix (being restored), for long attributed to a close follower of Giotto, is now thought by most scholars to be by the master himself. A small museum (*closed indefinitely*), on the other side of the cloister, has a charming 15th-century *Madonna and Child* in polychrome terracotta by Nanni di Bartolo, as well as choir books, altar frontals, church silver and reliquaries.

SANTA TRÌNITA
& VIA TORNABUONI

SANTA TRÌNITA
Map p. 398, C3

Open 9–12 & 4–6. The church is unusually dark (the best light is in the morning), though each chapel has a light: the switches are inconspicuously placed to the left.

The Latin pronunciation of the name of the church of Santa Trìnita (as opposed to Santa Trinità) betrays its ancient foundation. A church of the Vallombrosan Order (*see opposite*) existed on this site at least by 1077. Probably rebuilt in 1250–60, its present Gothic form dates from the end of the 14th century and is attributed to Neri di Fioravante. The façade was added by Buontalenti in 1593–94. The relief of the Trinity is by Giovanni Caccini, who also carved the statue of St Alexius in the niche. The campanile (1396–97) can just be seen behind to the left.

The Interior

The fine interior has the austerity characteristic of all Cistercian churches. On the entrance wall, the interior façade of the Romanesque building survives. High up on the outside arches of many of the chapels are remains of 14th–15th-century frescoes; the most interesting are those by Giovanni dal Ponte outside the choir chapels.

In the first chapel of the **south aisle** there is a highly venerated wooden Crucifix which may date from the 14th century, and the fourth chapel (covered for restoration) has damaged but beautiful frescoes (including the entrance arch) by Lorenzo Monaco (1422) of the life of the Virgin. These are the most important frescoes, still Gothic in spirit, by this elegant painter, who was a monk in Florence. The altarpiece of the *Annunciation*, with a lovely predella, is also by him. The organ by Onofrio Zefferini (1571) was reconstructed in 1763 by the Tronci brothers.

The **sacristy** (opened on request) was formerly a Strozzi chapel, begun by Onofrio and completed by his son Palla Strozzi, who was known for his learning as well as his wealth, and who died in exile as an opponent of the Medici. Onofrio's tomb here has had various attributions, but most recently it has been assigned to Lorenzo Ghiberti. The painted decoration on the arch is by Gentile da Fabriano, who also painted his famous *Adoration of the Magi* (now in the Uffizi) for this chapel.

Of the chapels in the choir the **Sassetti Chapel** is one of the best preserved Renaissance chapels in Florence. Its delightful frescoes by Domenico Ghirlandaio (coin-operated light in chapel) of the life of St Francis, were commissioned in 1483 by Francesco Sassetti, a merchant, manager of the Medici bank, and typical figure of Renaissance Florence. The scene in the lunette above the altar (*St Francis Receiving the Rule of the Order from Pope Honorius*) takes place in Piazza della Signoria, and those present include (in the foreground, right) Lorenzo the Magnificent with Sassetti and his son, and, to his right, Antonio Pucci. On the stairs are Angelo Poliziano with

Lorenzo's sons, Piero, Giovanni and Giuliano. In the *Miracle of the Boy Brought Back to Life* (beneath) is Piazza Santa Trìnita (with the Romanesque façade of the church and the old Ponte Santa Trìnita). The altarpiece shows the *Adoration of the Shepherds* (1485) and is also by Ghirlandaio. It is flanked by the kneeling figures of the donors, Francesco Sassetti and Nera Corsi, his wife. Their tombs, with black porphyry sarcophagi, are attributed to Giuliano da Sangallo. The decoration of the chapel includes numerous references to classical antiquity illustrating the influence of the new spirit of the Renaissance (the sibyl announcing the coming of Christ to Augustus on the outside arch; the four sibyls on the vault; the Roman sarcophagus used as a manger in the *Adoration of the Shepherds*; and the carved details on the tombs).

In the **sanctuary** there is a 15th-century classical altar above which is a triptych with the *Trinity and Saints* by Mariotto di Nardo (1424). The fine figures in the vault of David, Abraham, Noah and Moses are almost all that remains of the fresco decoration of the sanctuary by Alesso Baldovinetti (the Bishop Saint in a niche in the north aisle has also recently been attributed to him).

The first chapel left of the altar was redecorated in 1635 and the bronze altar frontal of the *Martyrdom of St Lawrence* is by Tiziano Aspetti. In the second chapel left of the altar is the **tomb of Benozzo Federighi**, Bishop of Fiesole (d. 1450), by Luca della Robbia (1454–57). This was moved here in 1896 from a deconsecrated church and is only part of the original monument, which was formerly in a raised position. However, the fact it is now at eye level means we have been given a rare opportunity to study the splendid workmanship with ease. The beautiful marble effigy is surrounded by an exquisite frame of enamelled terracotta mosaic on a gold ground.

In the fifth chapel of the **north aisle** is a fine wooden statue of Mary Magdalen by Desiderio da Settignano, finished by Benedetto da Maiano: both were extremely skilled sculptors better known for their reliefs and portrait busts, and this is one of the few life-size statues they made (and a rare instance of collaboration between the two artists). The next chapel has frescoes illustrating the life of St John Gualberto by Bicci di Lorenzo and his son Neri di Bicci. This family of three generations of painters called Lorenzo, Bicci and Neri, are each confusingly known by their father's name—hence Lorenzo di Bicci, Bicci di Lorenzo and Neri di Bicci. They were prolific artists, producing numerous similar altarpieces and frescoes for churches in Florence and all over Tuscany from the late 14th century until the end of the 15th: competent engaging works still in the Gothic decorative tradition and little affected by the major new developments that took place in art during the Renaissance. St John Gualberto was a Florentine nobleman who changed his way of life after he saw a Crucifix in the church of San Miniato al Monte bow approvingly to him when he pardoned his brother's assassin. He founded the Vallombrosan Order in 1040 in the hills of Vallombrosa just outside Florence. Santa Trìnita was one of the first churches founded after his death in 1073 (he was canonized in the following century). A little chapel in the **north transept**, decorated in 1574 by Domenico Cresti, called Passignano after his birthplace, where St John Gualberto is buried, contains a reliquary of the saint.

The tomb of Giuliano Davanzati (1444, attributed to Bernardo Rossellino) was adapted from an early Christian sarcophagus with a relief of the Good Shepherd. *The Annunciation* and *St Jerome*, in the second chapel are good works by Ridolfo del Ghirlandaio, one of Domenico's nine children. The vault of the first chapel has early-17th-century works by Bernardino Poccetti, Giovanni Caccini, and Empoli.

The 11th-century crypt (*often closed*) which survives from the earlier church, contains a head of the Saviour in painted terracotta attributed to Pietro Torrigiano (c. 1519).

WALK THREE

VIA TORNABUONI

Via Tornabuoni, which runs from Piazza Santa Trìnita away from the river, has been the most elegant street in Florence since the 19th century. It is lined with numerous palaces, including Palazzo Strozzi, a Renaissance masterpiece. The celebrated Palazzo Rucellai is also included on this walk.

In the little Piazza Santa Trìnita stands the **Column of Justice**, a huge granite monolith transported all the way from the Baths of Caracalla in Rome—on rollers as far as Civitavecchia, and then by sea from there. It was presented by Pius IV to Cosimo I in 1560, and set up here in 1563 to commemorate his victory at Montemurlo in 1537. The porphyry figure of Justice, by Tadda (1581), has a bronze cloak added subsequently. Palazzo Buondelmonti (no. 2) has a façade of c. 1530 attributed to Baccio d'Agnolo, but probably Baccio's best work is **Palazzo Bartolini-Salimbeni** (no. 1), across Via delle Terme, dating from 1520–23. Various types of stone were used in the fine façade, and the unusual courtyard has good graffiti decoration, and a delightful loggia on the first floor. The Hôtel du Nord was opened here in 1839, and the American writers Ralph Waldo Emerson, James Russell Lowell and Herman Melville all stayed here.

In the 19th century and for much of the 20th, **Via Tornabuoni** was an elegant commercial thoroughfare. In the last few decades, however, its historic shops and cafés have been replaced by the boutiques of international fashion houses. Here until 1986, for example, was the famous Café Doney, frequently mentioned in descriptions of the city and a meeting place for foreigners in Florence, including Edmond and Jules Goncourt, 'Ouida', D.H. Lawrence, Norman Douglas and the Sitwells. Another café, Giacosa's, founded here in 1815, closed down in 2001. In the same year the 'English and American Chemists' which had opened in the street in 1843 (at no. 97) and had been replaced by a perfumery in 1974, also disappeared, although the international shoe shop which took over its premises was obliged to preserve its splendid old wooden showcases and furnishings. The Florentine firm of Gucci, once renowned for its leathergoods and shoes, also had its shop here for many years, but the family was bought out by a large fashion group in 1992, retaining only its name. The only old shop to survive today is Procacci, which retains its Art Nouveau décor: it is a tiny luxury-quality grocers famous for its truffle sandwiches.

At the river end of Via Tornabuoni stands the splendid battlemented **Palazzo Spini-Feroni**, one of the best-preserved and largest private medieval palaces in the city. It was built for Geri degli Spini in 1289, possibly by Lapo Tedesco, master of Arnolfo di Cambio, and was restored in the 19th century. The palace was bought by the Comune in 1846 and was the seat of the town council in 1860–70. In 1938 it was purchased by Salvatore Ferragamo, a shoe designer who set up his famous shoe manufactory here. The shop is still on the ground floor, and on the second floor is the **Museo Salvatore Ferragamo**, a private museum illustrating the history of the firm (*open Mon–Fri 9–1 & 2–6; closed Aug; prior appointment advisable; T: 055 336 0456*). It contains a collection of some 10,000 shoes made out of the most diverse materials; these are beautifully exhibited in rotation every two years, taking a particular theme or period. Ferragamo, who was born into a poor family in southern Italy in 1898, emigrated to America in 1914 and set up a shoe shop in Hollywood. He returned to Italy in 1927 and became world famous for his skill as a fashion shoe designer (his clients included Greta Garbo, Audrey Hepburn and Marilyn Monroe) before his death in 1960.

Among the other fine town mansions which line Via Tornabuoni are Palazzo Minerbetti (no. 3) dating from the 14th–15th centuries, Palazzo Strozzi del Poeta (no. 5) reconstructed by Gherardo Silvani in 1626, and Palazzo del Circolo dell'Unione (no. 7) which may have been designed by Vasari and has a pretty doorway surmounted by a bust of Francesco I by Giambologna.

By far the most impressive palace on Via Tornabuoni is the huge **Palazzo Strozzi**, the last and grandest of the magnificent Renaissance palaces in Florence, built for Filippo Strozzi (d. 1491). It is a typical 15th-century town mansion—half-fortress, half-palace—with all three storeys of equal emphasis, constructed with large rough blocks of stone but left unfinished. The most complete side faces Piazza Strozzi. It is thought that Strozzi himself took an active part in the design of the building, but it is uncertain who drew up the project. It was begun in 1489 and Cronaca is known to have been involved at a certain stage: he was responsible for the great projecting cornice, suggested by ancient classical examples, which was left half-finished when money ran out after the death of Filippo Strozzi. Cronaca also built the courtyard (finished in 1503). Giuliano da Sangallo executed a model (now in the Bargello museum), but he is no longer thought to have been involved in the building work. The wrought-iron torch-holders and fantastic lanterns

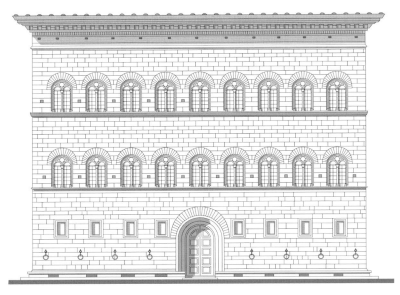

PALAZZO STROZZI

were designed by Benedetto da Maiano and executed by Caparra. The palace now belongs to the Italian state. It is the seat of various institutes (including the Gabinetto Vieusseux) and is also used for exhibitions.

The **Gabinetto Scientifico Letterario G.P. Vieusseux** has an excellent lending library (*open Mon–Fri 9–1 & 3–6; Sat 9–1*). It has some 300,000 volumes, dating mostly from the 19th and 20th centuries, and covering literature, history, the arts and sciences, travel and biography. Sadly, 90 per cent of the library's holdings were severely damaged in the Arno flood in 1966. The scientific and literary association from which the library takes its name was founded nearby in Palazzo Buondelmonti, on Via Tornabuoni, in 1819 by the Swiss scholar Gian Pietro

Vieusseux. It ran a circulating library with reading rooms and was directed as a commercial enterprise throughout the 19th century by a member of the Vieusseux family. It stayed open every day until 11pm, membership was available to all (there were even daily subscriptions), and both reading rooms (where foreign periodicals were also available), and conversation rooms (where chess and other board games could be played) were provided, as well as a café. It has been housed in Palazzo Strozzi since 1940.

In Piazza Strozzi, **Palazzo dello Strozzino**, also built for the Strozzi, has a façade by Michelozzo, completed by Giuliano da Maiano. The language school of the British Institute (*see p. 325*) has its headquarters here. Nearby the Odeon, which dates from 1922 and retains its Art Nouveau decorations, is one of the few cinemas in Florence which shows films in English.

The crossroads in Via Tornabuoni with Via Strozzi, Via della Vigna Nuova and Via della Spada, marks the centre of the Roman colony, and subsequently the west gate of the Roman city. The palace fitting the awkward site between Via della Vigna Nuova and Via della Spada was from 1614 the home of Sir Robert Dudley (1574–1649), Duke of Northumberland, son of the more famous Sir Robert Dudley, Earl of Leicester, who was Elizabeth I's favourite. Dudley was a navigator and mapmaker, but in 1605, when he failed to prove he was the Earl of Leicester's legitimate son, he moved to Italy and took up a successful career as naval engineer, administering the port of Livorno for the Medici grand dukes and supervising the draining of the marshes between Livorno and Pisa. The plaque was placed in Via della Vigna Nuova in the 19th century by his biographer John Temple Leader (*see p. 300*). In the corner house (left) George Eliot stayed while gathering material for *Romola*, her great historical novel set in 15th-century Florence, published in 1863.

On Via della Vigna Nuova, named the street of the 'new vineyard' since it was on the site of a huge orchard, is **Palazzo Rucellai**, the town house of Giovanni Rucellai (1403–81), one of the most respected intellectual figures of Renaissance Florence (author of the *Zibaldone*, his memoirs), as well as one of the wealthiest businessmen in Europe (his bank was the second largest in Florence in the mid-15th century). Scholars now agree that the palace must have been designed by Leon Battista Alberti, although it was actually built by Bernardo Rossellino (c. 1446–51). Alberti is famous not only as an architect but also as a theorist of the Italian Renaissance, and his writings are of fundamental importance to the understanding of the new spirit of humanism which pervaded the country in the 15th century. Although he worked on major buildings in other parts of Italy—the Tempio Malatestiano in Rimini and several churches in Mantua—Florence was the place where he worked the most under the generous patronage of Rucellai, apparently a close friend. There are no fewer than three other architectural works by Alberti within a few metres of this palace, described below. Although his family had lived in Florence since the 13th century, they were exiled in 1387, and Alberti first came to the city in 1432 at the age of 28.

The dignified façade of the palace, with incised decoration, is in striking contrast to the heavy rustication of Palazzo Strozzi and the other Florentine palaces of the period. The three storeys, with classical pilasters and capitals of the three orders, are divided by delicately carved friezes bearing the Rucellai and Medici emblems. The five bays of the front were later increased on the right to seven bays. The design of the façade had a lasting influence on Italian architecture. Although the Rucellai family still live on the top floor, the piano nobile of the palace has been occupied since 2001 by a United States university programme and can be visited by appointment (*T: 055 2645 910; entrance at no. 4 Via de' Palchetti*).

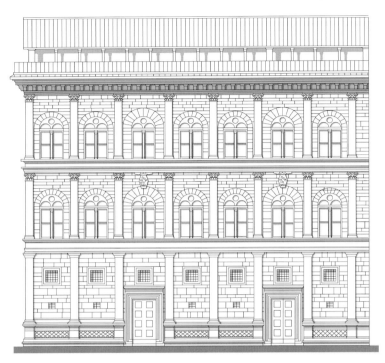

PALAZZO RUCELLAI

The **Loggia dei Rucellai**, also the work of Alberti, has three beautiful high arches and a graffiti frieze repeating the Rucellai emblems. After many vicissitudes, this charming decorative piece of architecture, built to enhance the tiny piazza in front of the Rucellai palace, is now used by a fashion boutique and the arches of the loggia have been glassed in so that many hurried visitors probably fail even to notice it.

The former **church of San Pancrazio**, one of the oldest in the city, founded before 1000, was deconsecrated in 1809, and later used as a tobacco factory, and then a military store. The beautiful classical porch is by Alberti. Again, this is easy to miss, since the building has been entirely modernised and converted into the **Museo Marino Marini** (*open 10–5; closed Tues, Sun and holidays and the whole of Aug; T: 055 219 432*), which displays works left to the city by the sculptor Marino Marini (1901–80). Exhibitions are held in the 15th-century crypt.

In Via della Spada (no. 18) is the entrance (*usually open only on Sat at 5.30, but closed July–Sept*) to the remarkable **Cappella del Santo Sepolcro**, built by Alberti in 1467, also for Giovanni Rucellai. In the middle of the lovely barrel-vaulted oratory, there is a perfectly preserved chapel by Alberti in inlaid marble with exquisite carving, the proportions of which recall the famous sanctuary of the Holy Sepulchre in Jerusalem.

Returning to Via Tornabuoni and continuing away from the river, you pass Palazzo Larderel (no. 19), a model of High Renaissance architecture begun in 1580, attributed to Giovanni Antonio Dosio, and Palazzo Corsi, which was built in the mid-15th century for the Tornabuoni by Michelozzo (its court-yard is preserved although it was recon-structed in 1862 and has been the headquarters of a bank since 1924).

Preceded by a wide flight of steps, **San Gaetano** (correctly called Santi Michele e Gaetano) is the most impor-tant 17th-century church in Florence (*usually open 9–12 & 3.30–6*). The fine façade (1648–83) was designed by Pier Francesco Silvani. There was a Romanesque church on this site, men-tioned in 1055. The dark grey interior (best appreciated in the morning) in *pietra serena* was built in 1604–49 by Matteo Nigetti (possibly influenced by a design of Bernardo Buontalenti) and (after 1630) by Gherardo Silvani. The sombre decoration in various precious marbles and dark wood survives almost totally intact, and nearly all the frescoes and altarpieces were painted in the 1630s and 1640s by the most impor-tant artists of the day including Ottaviano Vannini, Jacopo Vignali, Angelo Michele Colonna, Matteo Rosselli, Fabrizio Boschi, Giovanni Biliverti, Lorenzo Lippi, and Jacopo da Empoli. The colossal white marble stat-ues (with bas-reliefs below) of the

Apostles and Evangelists (1640–90) are by Giovanni Battista Foggini (Saints Peter and Paul on the triumphal arch), Antonio Novelli and others. Splendid hangings in silk, gold thread and velvet from Lyon were made in Florence in 1728–50 to adorn the church on festivals; they still survive and are sometimes displayed.

In the first chapel on the south side there is a *Madonna* in glazed terracotta by Andrea della Robbia (1465–70). In the choir chapel the bronze Crucifix is by Giovanni Francesco Susini and is his most important work (1634–35). The third chapel on the north side contains an altarpiece of the *Death of St Andrea Avellina*, signed and dated by the English painter Ignazio Hugford (1738), who lived in Tuscany. In the next chapel there is another scene of a martyrdom (of St Lawrence) by Pietro da Cortona (c. 1653).

Palazzo Antinori (no. 3) has been owned by the Antinori since 1506 and is one of the most beautiful smaller Renaissance palaces in Florence. Built in 1461–69, with a splendid courtyard, it is attributed to Giuliano da Maiano. The Antinori are an old-established Florentine family, now well-known for the wine they produce on their estates in Tuscany.

At the end of Via Tornabuoni, the road curves round to the right to become Via Rondinelli. Turning right at the end of it into Via Cerretani brings you to the church of **Santa Maria Maggiore** (*open 7–12 & 3.30–5.30*), which has a rough exterior in *pietra forte*. It is of ancient foundation (first mentioned in 1021), and was rebuilt in its present Gothic Cistercian form at the end of the 13th century. At the corner of the façade is the Romanesque campanile, and high up on the corner of Via Cerretani, there is a half-bust of a woman in marble embedded in the masonry (left of the two windows), fondly known to Florentines over the centuries as 'Berta'. It is almost certainly an ancient Roman carving. In the dark interior on the pilasters and on the west wall are 13th–14th-century frescoes, some by Mariotto di Nardo. The inner façade was designed in the late 16th century by Ludovico Cigoli, who also painted the altarpiece to the right of the door. On the north side are two 17th-century altarpieces, the first by Matteo Rosselli. The middle altarpiece on the south side of *Santa Rita* is a mid-20th-century work by Primo Conti, and the third altarpiece of *St Francis Receiving the Stigmata* is by Pier Dandini (flanked by two statues by Giovanni Battista Caccini). In the chapel to the left of the choir is a *Madonna Enthroned*, a remark-able relief in painted wood, the date of which has been much discussed by art historians, some of whom considered it a Byzantine work of the 12th century. But since its recent restoration it is thought to be a very late work by the first great Florentine painter Coppo di Marcovaldo. The column survives from the tomb here of Brunetto Latini (1220–94), who was Chancellor of the Republic and an erudite writer remembered with great affection by Dante (who devotes Canto XV of his *Inferno* to him and refers to him as his 'maestro'). The tomb of Bruno Beccuti bears an effigy attributed to Tino da Camaino, but the earlier sarcophagus, which belonged to the Lupicini family and is decorated with their coat of arms and two pelicans, is dated 1272. The two frescoes (in very poor condition) in the sanctuary, which has a neo-Gothic stained glass window (1901), are attributed to a contemporary of Spinello Aretino.

THE BARGELLO &
ITS MEDIEVAL DISTRICT

THE BARGELLO
Map p. 397, C3

The massive crenellated Palazzo del Bargello dominates Piazza San Firenze. Built in 1255 as the Palazzo del Popolo, it is the oldest seat of government that survives in the city.

History of the palace

The Bargello was begun, according to Vasari, to a design by a certain Lapo, the master of Arnolfo di Cambio. Building continued until 1330–50. The ancient tower is 57m high. Well restored in 1857–65, the building, constructed in *pietra forte*, still preserves its 14th-century appearance.

At first it was the seat of the Capitano del Popolo, who, during his one-year term of office, held supreme authority in the government of the city. From the end of the 13th century until 1502, the palace was the official residence of the Podestà, the governing magistrate of the city, who was traditionally a foreigner. In the 16th century, the building became known as the Bargello, when the police headquarters were moved here and prisons were installed (in use until 1858–59, when Tuscany joined the Kingdom of Italy). In 1786, when the enlightened grand duke Peter Leopold abolished the death sentence, instruments of torture were burnt in the courtyard. This was only a short time after Cesare Beccaria (1735–94) had made his famous denunciation of capital punishment and torture, and published his far-sighted theories on crime prevention. On the exterior of the building (corner of Via dell'Acqua and Via Ghibellina) a neo-Gothic tabernacle (1859) protects a fresco by Fabrizio Boschi (1588). This commemorates the feast day of St Bonaventura, when the prison was opened to various confraternities of the city and charitable companies, who were allowed to visit the prisoners and bring them food and clothing.

Museo Nazionale del Bargello

Open 8.30–1.50; closed first, third and fifth Sun and second and fourth Mon of month; T: 055 238 8606. Entrance in Via del Proconsolo.

Contained within the Bargello, this is one of the most important museums in Florence, and all the more appealing for hardly ever being overcrowded. This is perhaps the best place in the city to understand the significance of the Florentine Renaissance. It is famous for its superb collection of Florentine Renaissance sculpture, including numerous works by Donatello and the della Robbia family. Florentine sculpture from the 16th century is also well represented, with pieces by Michelangelo, Cellini and Giambologna, among others, and an exquisite collection of small Mannerist bronzes. The building also houses a notable collection of decorative arts.

The museum came into being in 1859 when the collection of sculpture and applied arts formerly in the Uffizi was transferred here, and it was first opened to the public in 1865. In 1888, the important Carrand collection was left to the museum, and later acquisitions included the Ressmann collection of armour and Franchetti collection of fabrics.

Ground Floor
NB: Letters assigned to the rooms correspond to the plan available at the museum.

(A) The Courtyard: The Gothic courtyard, the finest part of the palace, is adorned with a large number of coats of arms of the former *Podestà*. Under the north colonnade (on the left as you enter) is an unusual large high relief of the *Coronation of Ferdinand of Aragon*, with six boy musicians, by Benedetto da Maiano, and a seated statue of Alfonso of Aragon attributed to Francesco Laurana. The cannon, cast by Cosimo Cenni in 1620, shows the planet Jupiter with its four satellites discovered by Galileo in 1610. The extraordinary lamp on the wall dates from the 16th century.

Under the east colonnade are six fine statues (including *Juno*) by Ammannati (1556–63) from an allegorical fountain which was intended for the south end of the Salone dei Cinquecento in Palazzo Vecchio. Instead it was first set up for eight years in the Villa di Pratolino, and then, in 1588, moved to the terrace above the courtyard of Palazzo Pitti (where it is now replaced by the Fontana del Carciofo). The statues were then dispersed in the Boboli Gardens and were only finally reassembled here in the 1970s. The *Fisherboy* (1877) is by the Neapolitan sculptor Vincenzo Gemito.

Under the south colonnade is Giambologna's colossal statue of *Oceanus* from the Boboli Gardens and the *Cannon of St Paul*, a wonderful piece of casting by Cenni (1638) which was commissioned by Grand Duke Ferdinando II for Livorno Castle.

Off the courtyard is the Sala del Trecento (or Medieval Sculpture Room, *closed for restoration*) with 14th-century sculpture, including colossal statues of the *Madonna and Child* and *Saints Peter and Paul* from the Porta Romana, by Paolo di Giovanni, a pedestal with three *Acolytes* by Arnolfo di Cambio, and a high relief of the *Madonna and Child* by Tino da Camaino.

(B) The Michelangelo Room: This fine hall contains 16th-century **sculpture by Michelangelo** and his Florentine contemporaries. The four superb works by Michelangelo represent different stages in the great sculptor's highly successful career. The *Bacchus Drunk* is his first important sculpture, and shows the influence of classical works. It was made on his first visit to Rome c. 1497 for the banker Jacopo Galli, who kept it in his garden for over 50 years. Galli was an important patron for Michelangelo when he was in Rome, and he also commissioned his famous *Pietà*, now in the Vatican. The *Bacchus Drunk* was later purchased by the Medici and brought to Florence. The tondo of the *Madonna and Child with the Infant St John* was made for Bartolommeo Pitti c. 1503–05. It is a charming work, and a fine example of the sculptor's *schiacciato* (very low relief) technique. The bust of *Brutus* is a much later work (probably dating from the 1540s), derived from Imperial Roman portrait busts, and is the only bust Michelangelo ever sculpted. It was made for Michelangelo's friend Cardinal Niccolò Ridolfi after the murder of Duke Alessandro de' Medici by his cousin Lorenzaccio, and is an exaltation of Republicanism—more idealistic than strictly appropriate to the circumstances. Alessandro was certainly a tyrant, but his cousin Lorenzaccio, who murdered him, was not much more wholesome. His bid to glorify himself as a tyrannicide led merely to the election of his kinsman Cosimo, son of Giovanni delle Bande Nere, as duke, ushering in the second period of hereditary Medici rule. The *Brutus* was left unfinished, and Michelangelo's pupil Tiberio Calcagni added the drapery. The small figure called *Apollo*, who is apparently extracting an arrow from his back, is another beautiful unfinished work by Michelangelo with a *contrapposto* (serpentine) pose. Also known as *David*, it formed part of the Medici collection, and was set up in the Boboli Gardens before being displayed in the Uffizi corridor, with the antique sculpture collection.

Also in this part of the room are works which show Michelangelo's influence on other artists, such as Giovanni Francesco Rustici and Andrea Sansovino and his pupil Jacopo, whose own *Bacchus* takes its inspiration from Michelangelo's statue close by. The statuettes, models and replicas (in cases against the wall) by followers of Michelangelo include works by Pietro Francavilla, Tribolo, Giambologna, Bartolommeo Ammannati and Vincenzo Danti. The marble figure of *Leda* by Ammannati (c. 1540–50) is one of the best works inspired by a famous painting by Michelangelo commissioned by Alfonso d'Este and later destroyed. The *Allegory of Fiesole* by Tribolo, in the delicate stone known as *pietra serena*, was one of a series of statues (the others now lost) representing allegories of the cities and mountains of Tuscany, made for the garden of the Medici Villa di Castello.

The marble bust of Cosimo I is a fine work by Baccio Bandinelli, who became the Medici's favourite sculptor after Michelangelo. He left for Rome in 1534, having overstepped the mark by carving the two colossal nude statues of Adam and Eve for the Duomo, which were thought unsuitable for a church. Out of jealousy, Bandinelli saw to it that the two statues by Ammannati (also displayed here), intended for a tomb in the church of Santissima Annunziata, were never set up there. The *Dying Adonis* is by Bandinelli's pupil Vincenzo de' Rossi.

There follow a group of works by Bandinelli's famous rival **Benvenuto Cellini**, who was one of the greatest sculptors of the age, with a style all his own, less influenced than his contemporaries by the art of Michelangelo. His works often have echoes of Hellenistic sculpture. The *Narcissus*, carved from a worn block of grey Greek marble with two holes (hence the position of the arms), was damaged in Cellini's studio during a flood of the Arno. There are charming naturalistic details on the pedestal showing classical influence. Together with the *Apollo and Hyacinth*, also displayed here, it was given to Francesco I, who sent them to the park of Pratolino. They later found their way to the Boboli Gardens, and the two statues were only re-identified and brought under cover just before the Second World War. The figure of Apollo was never finished as the marble was defective (since this had been ordered specially for him by Bandinelli it seems this was a deliberate plot to discredit him). The *Ganymede* (a Trojan prince carried to Olympus by an eagle to be cup-bearer to the gods) consists of an antique marble torso, to which Cellini added the beautiful head and arms, the eagle and the naturalistic details on the base. We know that Cosimo I kept this piece in his bedroom, together with the statue of *Bacchus* by Andrea Sansovino (*see above*) and another statue of *Bacchus* by Baccio Bandinelli (now in Palazzo Pitti). The splendid bronzes exhibited here include a scale model of Cellini's famous statue of *Perseus* (*see p. 72*), and the relief (*Perseus Releasing Andromeda*) and statuettes (*Danae and Perseus, Mercury, Minerva and Jove*) displayed on the original pedestal of this statue (which has

been replaced *in situ* by a copy). A small wax model for the *Perseus* is also preserved here. Vincenzo Danti's statue representing *Honour Overcoming Deceit* (his first work in marble, which was placed in the Boboli Gardens in 1775), is exhibited near Giambologna's colossal *Virtue Repressing Vice* (or *Florence Victorious over Pisa*). The bronze *Mercury* is Giambologna's most successful and influential statue: it seems almost on the point of flying away. It was a fountain in front of the garden façade of the Villa Medici in Rome and was brought from there to Florence by the Lorraine grand dukes. The cupboard door made for Cosimo I, and the relief of *Moses and the Serpent*, are both bronzes by Vincenzo Danti. The colossal bust of Cosimo I was Cellini's first work cast in bronze (1545–48). His talent as a goldsmith can be seen in the delicate carved details of the armour. The portrait bust of Michelangelo is by Daniele da Volterra.

First Floor

(G) The Loggia: This provides a charming setting for **works by Giambologna**, born in Flanders, and perhaps the greatest Mannerist sculptor who worked in Florence, exerting a wide influence on his contemporaries. The life-like group of bronze birds was made for the grotto at Villa di Castello, and are masterpieces of casting. The turkey, 'fluffed up' in anger, is particularly fine (turkeys were first introduced from America into Italy in the 16th century). The female statue in marble represents *Architecture*. The statue of *Jason* is by Pietro Francavilla (1589), and the stemma of the Amico

della Torre on the wall nearby is probably an early work by Luca della Robbia.

(H) The Donatello Room: This splendid Gothic hall, known as the Salone del Consiglio Generale, was vaulted by Neri di Fioravante and Benci di Cione in 1345. The neo-Gothic painted decorations were carried out in 1857–65. Works by Donatello and his contemporaries are displayed here.

In the middle of the room is Donatello's *Marzocco*, the Florentine heraldic lion, in *pietra serena*. On the end wall is the reconstructed tabernacle from

Orsanmichele which contains *St George*, as the young champion of Christendom, made for the guild of armourers c. 1416. By endowing this remarkably well-composed statue with a sense of movement, Donatello's work represents a new departure from traditional Gothic sculpture where the static figure was confined to its niche. The bas-relief of *St George and the Dragon* is a remarkable work in low relief, using the new *schiacciato* technique and showing a fresh interest in linear perspective and pictorial space. Other works by Donatello include his bronze *David with the Head of Goliath*. One of the earliest and most beautiful free-standing male statues of the Renaissance, it was probably made between 1430 and 1440 for the courtyard of the Medici palace. In 1495, a year after Lorenzo the Magnificent's son Piero was expelled from Florence (for ceding a part of Florentine territory to France), it was moved to Palazzo della Signoria. Donatello's portrayal of David nude follows the story in the Book of Samuel, where he is described as shedding his armour before his famous fight, so most statues of David, including Michelangelo's, portray the hero naked. The statue was designed to stand on a column and to be seen from below. Here Donatello invented a new concept in sculpture where the silhouette produced by the dark bronze is its most important feature.

DONATELLO

Donatello (c. 1386–1466) was the most important sculptor of the Quattrocento and of fundamental importance to the development of Renaissance art; indeed, he is often considered the greatest sculptor of all time. He was born in Florence around 1386 of humble parentage (his father was a wool-carder who had taken part in the famous Ciompi revolt of 1378, when workers in the woollen industry—the name *ciompi* comes from the clogs they wore—rose up in protest at starvation wages), and he probably had little idea how to read and write. Donatello first worked as assistant to Lorenzo Ghiberti, the bronze sculptor, and as a young man visited Rome with his friend Brunelleschi to study antique sculpture. He worked almost exclusively throughout his long life (he died in his eighties) in Florence, except for an important period in Padua. He produced superb sculptures in all media, whether bronze, marble or terracotta. Cosimo il Vecchio recognized his exceptional talent and protected him and ordered that he be buried beside him in the Medici vaults below San Lorenzo (the great ruler died just two years before the sculptor). In this room in the Bargello are some of his most famous works in bronze, marble, terracotta and *pietra serena* (the attribution of some of them is still under discussion; indeed the attribution of many undocumented works to Donatello remains a great art historical issue to this day). Other splendid works by him in Florence can be seen in San Lorenzo, the Museo dell'Opera del Duomo, Palazzo Vecchio, Santa Croce and the Baptistery.

The other *David*, in marble (in the centre between the windows), is an early work by Donatello. It was commissioned by the Opera del Duomo, but placed in Palazzo della Signoria in 1416.

The two statues of St John the Baptist are of uncertain attribution: the one of him as an older man is ascribed to the school of Donatello (Michelozzo?), and the *Young St John* (owned by the Martelli) is attributed to Desiderio da Settignano.

Also in the centre of the room are two fine busts of a young woman and a boy, excellent works by Desiderio da Settignano, and a bust in coloured terra-cotta (c. 1430), full of character, traditionally thought to be a portrait of Niccolò da Uzzano, and now usually considered to be by Donatello. The humorous bronze putto known as *Atys-Amorino* (removed for restoration), also by Donatello, represents a mythological subject of uncertain significance and dates from 1430–40. The statuette of a cupid in bronze is by Bonacolsi.

At the end of the entrance wall are a reliquary urn (1428) by Lorenzo Ghiberti and fine works by Bertoldo di Giovanni, Donatello's pupil, including a battle scene (a relief based on a Roman sarcophagus at Pisa), an unfinished statuette of Apollo (or Orpheus), and reliefs of the *Pietà*, *Triumph of Bacchus* and the *Crucifixion*.

On the next wall are displayed the trial reliefs by Ghiberti and Brunelleschi for the second bronze doors of the Baptistery (*see box opposite*). The *Bust of a Youth* (with a medallion at his neck) is usually attributed to Desiderio da Settignano (or possibly Bertoldo). One of the fine painted marriage-chests below, which shows the procession of San Giovanni (with a view of the Baptistery), is by Giovanni Toscani (c. 1428–29). The gilded relief of the *Crucifixion* is now attributed to Donatello, and the profile relief of the *Young St John* is by Desiderio da Settignano.

On the next wall can be seen a bronze head of a sea god attributed to Donatello, and (above) coat of arms of the Martelli (*see p. 332*), almost certainly by Donatello (acquired by the Italian state in 1998; repainted in the 19th century). The exquisite marble relief of the *Madonna and Child with Angels* in a *pietra serena* tabernacle is a masterpiece by Agostino di Duccio, who was born in Florence but worked mostly in other regions of Italy. The *Madonna and Child* (from Palazzo Panciatichi) is a beautiful work in very low relief by Desiderio da Settignano. The other two reliefs—of the same subject—one in marble and one in terracotta are by Michelozzo, the architect and sculptor who worked with Donatello on some projects. There follow a number of charming glazed enamelled Madonnas by Luca della Robbia. Luca invented a special technique of enamelled terracotta sculpture, which was a jealously guarded secret of his workshop for most of the 15th century and was handed down through three generations of his family. His colourful, luminous half-length Madonna reliefs became popular for private devotion. He is recognised as one of the most important early Renaissance sculptors, also highly skilled in marble, and was clearly influenced by classical art. The *Madonna and Child in a Rose Garden* is by Luca; the tondo of the *Madonna and Child with Two Angels* is thought to be an early work by his nephew Andrea. Below, there is a bronze

COMPETITION RELIEFS FOR THE BAPTISTERY DOORS

These two trial reliefs of the *Sacrifice of Isaac* were executed by Brunelleschi (*pictured left*) and Lorenzo Ghiberti (*pictured below*) in competition for the second bronze doors of the Baptistery (*see p. 49*). Ghiberti was given the commission, in 1403, a decision reached by a narrow majority. It is remarkable that the reliefs have survived from this famous contest—the first of its kind and usually regarded as the point at which Renaissance art was born. The subject chosen presented each contestant with a series of difficulties. These included fitting the narrative into an awkward space (the quatrefoil frames copied from the first set of doors by Andrea Pisano) and the need to depict both the nude figure of Isaac as well as the clothed figures of Abraham and his servants, and also animals and the rural setting of the event. The greater technical skill of Ghiberti is not perceptible; nevertheless his composition conveys more of the drama of the scene, as contrasted to Brunelleschi's artful assemblage of the component elements. Ghiberti's victory meant that he went on to carve the superb east door of the Baptistery, considered one of the greatest masterpieces of sculpture ever produced in Western art. Brunelleschi was left free to concentrate his energies on the construction of the huge dome of the Duomo.

effigy of Mariano Sozzino, which for a long time was attributed to the Sienese artist Vecchietta, but is now thought to be the work of Francesco di Giorgio Martini. The fine wooden model of Palazzo Strozzi is by Giuliano da Sangallo. The *Bust of a Lady*, probably a female saint, is attributed to Luca della Robbia or his nephew Andrea.

On the last wall, there are two marble reliefs of the *Deliverance and Crucifixion of St Peter* made for an altar in the Duomo and left unfinished in 1439 by Luca della Robbia, who also made the *Madonna of the Apple* (c. 1460), which was owned by the Medici.

The next three rooms are dedicated to the decorative arts and display the Carrand collection. This includes pieces from all over Europe, dating from earliest times up until the 17th century, which were assembled by Louis Carrand, a wealthy Lyon art-collector who bequeathed his collection to the museum in 1888.

(I) The Islamic Room: This room (Sala della Torre) has a fine collection of Islamic art including 15th-century armour, 16th- and 17th-century brocade, damascened dishes, works in brass and ivory, a case of ceramics (including Persian tiles), and carpets.

(L) The Carrand Room: Amongst the many exquisite works here are the *Money-changer and his Wife* by Marinus van Reymerswale (1540); Limoges enamels; 11th–12th-century ivories; French and Italian cutlery (15th–16th centuries); European clocks; ecclesiastical ornaments, many of them enamelled, including reliquary caskets, pastoral staves, processional crosses and ewers; 15th–16th-century metalwork from France; a 15th-century Venetian astrolabe in gilt bronze; a painted diptych of the *Annunciation and the Presentation in the Temple* (with monochrome figures on the reverse), a 15th-century Flemish work attributed to the Master of the St Catherine Legend, a close follower of Rogier van der Weyden; and Venetian and Bohemian glass (16th–17th centuries). At the end of the room, flat cases

contain a beautiful collection of jewellery and goldsmiths' work from the Roman period to the 17th century, and tiny Flemish and Italian paintings are displayed together here including a *Madonna and Child* by Dirk Bouts.

(M) The Chapel of Mary Magdalen: This chapel dates from the early 14th century. A sensation was caused in 1840 when the frescoes were discovered on the walls by Richard Henry Wilde, an American writer and lawyer and former member of Congress, and an elderly English painter Seymour Kirkup, who carried out studies here following Vasari's reference to works by Giotto in this chapel. On the altar wall, the scene of *Paradise* includes a portrait of Dante as a young man (in the group to the right, dressed in maroon), and the whole cycle was immediately attributed to Giotto. As a consequence this little room became one of the sites in the city most visited by Anglo-American travellers. It is now considered much less interesting as the frescoes are usually attributed only to the school of Giotto and dated 1340. The triptych of the *Madonna and Saints* by

Giovanni di Francesco, the lectern and stalls all date from the 15th century. In the small adjoining room (the former sacristy) cases contain two paxes decorated with *niello* by Maso Finiguerra, a bronze dove by Luca della Robbia, goldsmiths' work, chalices, processional crosses and reliquaries.

(D) The Ivories Room: A fine collection of ivories from the Etruscan period onwards, including Persian, Arabic, German and Sicilian ivories, and Carolingian reliefs (9th century). There is also one valve of a diptych which belonged to the Roman Consul Basilio (6th century); part of a Byzantine diptych with the Empress Arianna (8th century); an early Christian diptych (5th century) showing *Adam in Earthly Paradise* and scenes from the life of St Peter in Malta. The case on the entrance wall contains a fragment of an Anglo-Saxon coffer (8th century) in whalebone (the rest is in the British Museum). The chessboard with intarsia ornament and bas-reliefs is a 15th-century Burgundian work.

Displayed around the walls are wooden sculptures including an unusual seated female statue (sometimes interpreted as a *Madonna Annunciate* or a sibyl) by Mariano d'Angelo Romanelli (c. 1390), and early 15th-century gold-ground panel paintings.

(E) The Bruzzichelli Room: Currently being rearranged, this room displays the collection of furniture donated to the museum in 1983 by the Florentine antiquarian Giovanni Bruzzichelli. Also usually exhibited here is a a large relief in papier mâché of the *Madonna and Child* by Jacopo Sansovino.

(F) The Majolica Room: Part of the Medici collection of Italian majolica (mostly 15th and 16th century) is shown in this room, including works from the Deruta, Montelupo, Faenza and Urbino potteries, and part of a service which belonged to Guidobaldo II della Rovere, Duke of Urbino. The beautiful garland, on the end wall, with the Bartolini-Salimbeni and Medici emblems, is by Giovanni della Robbia.

Second Floor

(N) The Giovanni della Robbia Room: Colourful and elaborate enamelled terracottas are displayed in this room, many of them by Giovanni della Robbia, son of Andrea, who used more colours than either his father or great-uncle Luca. These include a fine tondo of the *Madonna and Child and Young St John*, partly unglazed. The large relief in white terracotta (*Noli me tangere*) is by Francesco Rustici. Works by Benedetto

Buglioni include a polychrome terracotta statue of the *Madonna and Child* and a relief of the *Noli me tangere*. The four-figure group of the *Lamentation* is an unglazed terracotta work by Andrea della Robbia.

There is a superb collection of bronze plaquettes and medals arranged by artists and schools from the early 15th to the 18th centuries. Most of them were collected by the Medici grand dukes, but some come from the Carrand collection. Italian masters represented include L'Antico (Jacopo Alari Bonacolsi), Caradosso, Cellini, Filarete, Giambologna, Leone Leoni, Moderno, Riccio (Andrea Briosco) and Giovanni Francesco Rustici. There are also examples from France and Germany.

(O) The Andrea della Robbia Room:
Arranged in this room are beautiful works in enamelled terracotta by Andrea della Robbia. His charming *Bust of a Boy* is displayed next to a *Portrait of a Lady* (a circular high relief), now usually attributed to Andrea's uncle, Luca. The tabernacles include the *Madonna of the Cushion* and *Madonna of the Stonemasons* (1475). A collection of seals and coins is also displayed here.

(Q) The Verrocchio Room: Here there is a superb display of Renaissance portrait busts and some very fine works by Verrocchio. In the centre is Verrocchio's bronze *David* made for the Medici in 1469, and then acquired by the Signoria in 1476. Beautifully restored in 2003, it owes much to Donatello's earlier statue of the same subject (*see p. 219*). Also in the centre is a wooden Crucifix, attributed to Verrocchio since its recent restoration. To the right of the door are charming marble works by Mino da Fiesole: busts of Cosimo il Vecchio's two sons, Giovanni and Piero il Gottoso (1453; the first dated portrait bust of the Renaissance) on either side of a portrait of Rinaldo della Luna.

The works exhibited along the window wall include *Pietro Mellini*, signed and dated 1474 by Benedetto da Maiano, a remarkable portrait of this rich Florentine merchant as an old man; a 15th-century bust of Giuliano de' Medici, murdered in the Pazzi Conspiracy (*see p. 241*), of unknown attribution; an exquisite little tabernacle by Desiderio da Settignano, and a statue of the *Young St John* by Michelozzo (from the Casa dell'Opera di San Giovanni).

On the end wall, the works by Antonio Rossellino include a bust of Francesco Sassetti (the general manager of the Medici bank under Lorenzo the Magnificent, and who commissioned the Sassetti Chapel in Santa Trinita), also attributed to Verrocchio; busts of a young boy and of the *Young St John the Baptist*; and the portrait bust of Matteo Palmieri, Renaissance statesman and scholar (1468). This was on the façade of his Florentine palace until the 19th century, which accounts for its weathered surface.

On the wall opposite the windows can be seen *Young Cavalier* by Antonio Pollaiolo, a bust thought to be a portrait of a member of the Medici family (in painted terracotta, c. 1470); and works by Verrocchio, including a portrait bust of Piero di Lorenzo de' Medici (in terracotta; sometimes attributed to Piero Pollaiolo); and the *Bust of a Lady Holding Flowers*. Formerly part of the Medici collection, this is one of the loveliest of all Renaissance portrait busts, and was once attributed to Verrocchio's pupil Leonardo da Vinci. It is particularly interesting as it is the first instance in a 15th-century portrait bust in which the hands are depicted. There follow another marble portrait bust of a man by Antonio Pollaiolo, the *Death of Francesca Tornabuoni-Pitti*, a tomb relief by Verrocchio, and two reliefs (*Faith* and the *Portrait of a Lady*) by Matteo Civitali. The remarkable marble bust of Battista Sforza, duchess of Urbino, is by Francesco Laurana, a Dalmatian artist who worked at the Court of Urbino.

(R) The Baroque Sculpture and Medals Rooms: These rooms contain part of a huge collection of Italian medals started by Lorenzo the Magnificent. The first room has works by L'Antico, Pisanello, and Matteo de' Pasti. In the centre of the room is Bernini's bust of his mistress Costanza Bonarelli. The next room has an allegorical female statue and a marble bust of Virginia Pucci Ridolfi, both by Domenico Poggini; a bas-relief of *Christ in Glory* in a tabernacle by Jacopo Sansovino; a marble *Bust of Christ* by Tullio Lombardo, and a bust of Cardinal Paolo Emilio Zacchia Rondanini by Alessandro Algardi. Here the chronological display of medals is continued with works by Francesco di Giorgio Martini, Francesco da Sangallo, Gasparo Mola, Leone Leoni, and Massimiliano Soldani Benzi.

(P) The Small Bronzes Room: This superb display of small Renaissance bronzes constitutes the most important collection in Italy. The fashion of collecting small bronzes was begun by Lorenzo the Magnificent following a Roman tradition. The statuettes, which include animals, bizarre figures and candelabra, were often copies of antique works, or small replicas of Renaissance statues. In the wall cases on the right, there are splendid bronzes by Giambologna including several statuettes: *Venus, Architecture* and *Hercules and the Calydonian Boar*; as well as Benvenuto Cellini's relief of a dog. There are works by Danese Cattaneo (including *Fortune*), Tribolo and a fine group of statuettes by Baccio Bandinelli. The splendid chimneypiece is the work of Benedetto da Rovezzano, and the firedogs are by Niccolò Roccatagliata. The *Ganymede* is attributed to Cellini or Tribolo.

The wall cases on the opposite wall contain an *Anatomical Figure*, a famous work made in wax by Lodovico Cigoli (1598–1600) and fused in bronze by Giovanni Battista Foggini after 1678. Beyond are charming animals by 15th- and 16th-century artists from the Veneto and Padua; including fantastical works by Il Riccio. The *Frightened Man* or *Pugilist* is a very unusual work attributed by most scholars to Donatello (c. 1435–40).

The central cases contain copies from works by Giambologna, as well as the *Dwarf Morgante Riding a Monster* by Giambologna himself. Morgante is thought to have been Pietro Barbino, Cosimo I's favourite dwarf, who can also be seen in a statue in the Boboli Gardens; works by Giovanni Francesco Susini; *Satyr* by Massimiliano Soldani Benzi; and 16th–18th-century bronzes from the Veneto. In the centre of the room, there is a *Hercules and Antaeus* by Antonio Pollaiolo, a beautiful small bronze group—he also made a painting of this subject, now in the Uffizi.

(S) The Armoury: The magnificent display of arms and armour is from the Medici, Carrand and Ressmann collections. It includes saddles decorated with gold, silver and ivory, a shield by Gasparo Mola (17th century), and numerous sporting guns, dress armour and oriental arms. There is also a fine bust in marble by Francesco da Sangallo, which is an idealized portrait of Giovanni delle Bande Nere (father of Cosimo I). The bronze bust of Ferdinando I is by Pietro Tacca.

THE BADIA FIORENTINA

Open all day for prayer. Cloister open Mon 3–6. Entrance on Via Dante Alighieri.
The Badia Fiorentina is the church of an ancient Benedictine abbey founded and rich-ly endowed in 978 by Willa, the widow of Uberto, Margrave of Tuscia, in memory of her husband. At this time Tuscia (Tuscany) was a province of the Frankish empire with its capital at Lucca. Willa and Uberto's son, Count Ugo of Brandenburg, also a benefactor of the abbey, was buried in the church when he died in 1001. Since he pre-ferred Florence to Lucca he is praised by Dante as the '*gran barone*' in his *Paradiso* (Canto XVI, 127) and the poet mentions that he is remembered every year on the feast-day of St Thomas the Apostle (a Mass is still said here on 21 December to hon-our his memory). One of the first hospitals in the city was established in the abbey in 1031. The tolling of the bell at the beginning and end of the working day, also men-tioned by Dante (*Paradiso*, Canto XV, 97–98), regulated life in the medieval city. At one time, the Consiglio del Popolo met here. The church was rebuilt on a Latin cross plan in 1284–1310, probably by Arnolfo di Cambio, but was radically altered in 1627–31. Since 1998 the church has been used by a monastic institution known as the Communion of Jerusalem, founded in Paris in 1975.

Tour of the church

The vestibule, with a Corinthian portico, is by Benedetto da Rovezzano. From here there is a good view of the graceful campanile, the bottom portion of which is Romanesque (1307) and the top Gothic (after 1330). At the main entrance (kept closed) on Via del Proconsolo is a portal by Benedetto da Rovezzano (1495), with a Madonna in enamelled terracotta by Benedetto Buglioni.

The 17th-century interior preserves fragments of frescoes from the old church on the west wall. The carved wooden ceiling dates from 1629. On the left, the painting of the *Madonna Appearing to St Bernard* (c. 1485) is a large panel of great charm by Filippino Lippi. The church contains three important sculptural works by Mino da Fiesole: an altarpiece of the *Madonna and Saints* (1464–69), the tomb of Bernardo Giugni, a Florentine statesman (1396–1466), with a good effigy and statue of *Justice*, and (in the left transept) the monument to Ugo, Margrave of Tuscia (*see above*), an exquisite work dating from 1469–81. Above is a good painting of the *Assumption and two Saints* by Vasari. A Baroque chapel has vault frescoes by Vincenzo Meucci and an altarpiece by Onorio Marinari (1663). The fine organ (1558; well restored) by Onofrio Zeffirini is decorated with paintings by Francesco Furini and Baccio del Bianco.

In another chapel four damaged frescoes are displayed (detached from a wall of the church) which illustrate the *Passion of Christ* (including the suicide of Judas) and are attributed to Nardo di Cione. In the choir, interesting but very damaged fragments of 14th-century frescoes showing the *Life of the Virgin* (by Giotto and his *bottega*) were detached in 1959 with their sinopie.

On the right of the choir (with stalls of 1501), a door opens onto a flight of stairs which lead to the upper loggia of the Chiostro degli Aranci, a peaceful cloister where orange trees were once cultivated. It was built in 1432–38 to designs by Bernardo Rossellino. The interesting and well-preserved fresco cycle illustrates scenes from the life of St Benedict. The frescoes are by an unknown master (usually called the Master of the Chiostro degli Aranci), working in the decade after the death of Masaccio. They have been attributed to Giovanni di Consalvo, a Portuguese artist and follower of Fra' Angelico. In a lunette in the north walk is an early fresco by Bronzino. Part of the large convent building (with another fine courtyard) is now occupied by law courts.

WALK FOUR

THE MEDIEVAL DISTRICT
ASSOCIATED WITH DANTE

Via Dante Alighieri (*map p. 397, C2*) is probably near the site of the birthplace of the greatest Italian poet, Dante Alighieri (1265–1321). His famous *Divina Commedia* established Tuscan as the literary vernacular of Italy. As a young man he fought in the huge battle of Campaldino in the Casentino (1289) on the winning (Guelph) side against the Ghibellines of Arezzo. In 1295 Dante entered Florentine politics and in 1300 served a two-month term as one of the six priors of the city. At this time the Guelph party split into two factions, the Bianchi and the Neri (*see p. 22*). Dante was sent to Rome as part of an official delegation to dissuade Pope Boniface VIII from his support of the Neri in Florence, but during his absence the Neri were able to take control of the government of Florence and there followed a period of vindictive repression of the Bianchi. Dante was accused of corruption and when he failed to return in 1302 to defend himself he was sentenced to death and so went into exile. Although at first he kept in touch with the other Bianchi, he soon became totally disillusioned with politics and was bitterly disappointed with his Florentine contemporaries who became dominated by the factious rivalry between the

White Guelphs (the Bianchi) and the Blacks (the Neri). He never returned to Florence, and died in 1321 in Ravenna. His love for Beatrice inspired much of his work: Boccaccio, his biographer, identified her as the daughter of Folco Portinari, although Dante married Gemma Donati. We know that he was a friend of Giotto.

The so-called **Casa di Dante**—where the poet is said to have been born—is one of a group of 13th-century-style houses that were restored in 1911. It contains a museum on three floors with material (little of it original) relating to Dante (*closed at the time of writing; T: 055 219 416*).

The little church of **Santa Margherita de' Cerchi**, of 12th-century foundation, is where Dante is supposed to have married Gemma Donati. The 14th-century porch bears the arms of the Cerchi, Adimari and Donati, who lived in the parish. In the interior there is a lovely altarpiece of the *Madonna Enthroned with Four Female Saints* by Neri di Bicci.

The 13th century Palazzo Cerchi is in nearby Via Condotta (no. 52 red). This was the residence of the leaders of the Bianchi faction in the Guelph party, supported by wealthy landowners as well as the populace, and opposed to papal interference. The building also bears a plaque to Dante, one of several set up in this district in 1907.

An archway leads out onto the Corso, a Roman road. Here is **Palazzo Salviati** (now the head office of the Banca Toscana; Dante plaque), built in 1470–80 by the Portinari family. This was the family of Dante's beloved celestial muse, Beatrice. In 1546 the palace was bought and enlarged by Jacopo Salviati, nephew of Maria Salviati, wife of Giovanni delle Bande Nere and mother of Cosimo I. In the banking hall there is a 14th-century fresco of the *Madonna and Child*.

Going west along the Corso brings you to the church of **Santa Margherita** (1508), preceded by a portico by Gherardo Silvani (1611). The interior was reconstructed by Zanobi del Rosso in 1769, and contains paintings by Giovanni Camillo Sagrestani (1707). Nearly opposite is the 13th century **Torre dei Donati** which belonged to the family who headed the Neri faction supported by the merchants of Florence, and who were responsible for Dante's exile. Even earlier towers can be seen on the corner of Via Sant'Elisabetta. Towers were first built in the 12th century by wealthy Florentines next to their houses, for defensive reasons, as refuges in times of trouble, as well as status symbols. It is estimated that there were as many as 100 towers in the medieval city, many of them over 50 metres high. They were connected to the family residence well above ground level by means of scaffolding supported by beams inserted into holes in the masonry (many of which can still be seen) and this is why today some of the 'doors' appear suspended in mid-air. After 1250 the regime of the *primo popolo* ordered that the towers be lowered, and later in the 14th century many of them were adapted as houses.

The narrow medieval streets in this district are well worth exploring. Turn left down **Via dei Cerchi** (named after the famous leaders of the Guelph party; Dante plaque)—a local shopping street—noting the pretty iron lamp brackets and the medieval Palazzo Giugni (reconstructed). Turn left again into Via dei Cimatori—with another Cerchi family tower which was erected just at the time when Dante first became interested in Florentine politics. At the end of the street go left again. On the corner of Via Dante Alighieri is the charming little **Oratory of San Martino del Vescovo** or San Martino dei Buonomini (*open 10–12 & 3–5, except Sun and holidays and some Fri afternoons*). This stands near the site of the 10th-century parish church of the Alighieri and Donati families. On the exterior there is a 17th-century tabernacle by Cosimo Ulivelli showing *St Martin Distributing Alms*. The chapel was rebuilt in 1479 when it became the seat of the Compagnia dei Buonomini di San Martino, a charitable institution of 'good men' founded in 1442 by St Antoninus for Florentine citizens (often merchants) who had fallen into penury, sometimes for political reasons, and were too proud to beg for charity. It was administered by 12 men who each held the office of *proposto* for one month of the year, and the charter stipulated that alms should be distributed as soon as they were collected. When their resources ran out, the Compagnia would light a candle (*lumicino*) over the doorway to alert the populace to their need for funds (a Florentine expression '*essere al lumicino*' survives to this day, indicating that someone is in dire straits). The 12 members of the confraternity, with their assistants, still meet in a hall behind the oratory every Friday afternoon to deliberate: they receive written requests for financial help and then decide how to distribute the donations they receive (visitors are kindly asked to make a contribution).

Inside, the lunettes are decorated with charming 15th-century frescoes by the workshop of Domenico Ghirlandaio. They are of great interest for their portrayal of contemporary Florentine life. They illustrate the seven works of mercy carried out by the Buonomini: (over the entrance) the *Distribution of Clothing*, *Giving Food and Drink to the Hungry and Thirsty*, and (on the left wall): *Visiting the Sick*, *Visiting Prisoners* (the painting of the grey-haired official in a red cloak shows the influence of Filippino Lippi), *Giving Lodging to Travellers* and *Burying the Dead*. On the altar wall are two scenes from the life of St Martin: *St Martin Dividing his Cloak with the Beggar*, and *Christ Appearing to St Martin in a Dream Wearing his Cloak* (the angels are reminiscent of the hand of Botticelli). On the right wall are two scenes of the Buonomini at work: *Compiling an Inventory of Possessions Left to Them in a Will* and *Providing a Poor Girl with a Dowry in a Marriage Settlement*. Also here are two beautiful paintings of the Madonna, one of them Byzantine (11th century) and the other very close to the style of Perugino, but attributed to his near contemporary the little-known painter Nicolò Soggi. On the altar is a bust of St Antoninus attributed to Verrocchio. Two terracotta angels by the school of Verrocchio are kept in the meeting hall.

The splendid 13th-century **Torre della Castagna** stands in this little piazza; it is one of the best-preserved medieval towers in the city and was the residence of the Priors in 1282, before they moved to Palazzo Vecchio.

THE DISTRICT OF SANTA CROCE

PIAZZA SANTA CROCE
Map p. 399, E3

Piazza Santa Croce is in the centre of a distinctive district of the city, with numerous narrow old streets of small houses above artisans' workshops. In medieval Florence, this area was a centre of the wool industry. Corso dei Tintori, which runs out of the piazza, takes it name from the dyers' workshops which are documented here as early as 1313.

One of the most attractive and spacious squares in the city, it has been used since the 14th century for tournaments, festivals and public spectacles, and the traditional football game celebrating St John's Day (24 June, *see p. 363*) has been held here for many centuries. One side of the piazza is lined with houses whose projecting upper storeys rest on brackets; these are known as *sporti* and were a familiar architectural feature of the medieval city. The wooden brackets were replaced in the 15th and 16th centuries by stone supports.

THE CHURCH OF SANTA CROCE

Open 9.30–5.30; Sun 1–5.30. Entrance fee which includes the Pazzi Chapel and Museo dell'Opera di Santa Croce.

Santa Croce is the Franciscan church of Florence. It was rebuilt in 1294, possibly by Arnolfo di Cambio. The nave was still unfinished in 1375 and it was not consecrated until 1442. The campanile was added in 1842 by Gaetano Baccani. The bare stone front was covered with its neo-Gothic marble façade in 1857–63 by Niccolò Matas; it was paid for by an English benefactor, Francis Sloane. Although the overall design is lacking in style, it is a tour de force of local craftsmanship. The lunette above the main door of the *Triumph of the Cross* is by Giovanni Dupré. Along the left flank of the church a picturesque 14th-century arcade survives, and at 5 Via San Giuseppe there is access to the exterior of the Gothic apse.

The Interior

The huge wide interior has an open timber roof. The vista is closed by the polygonal sanctuary and the 14th-century stained glass in the east windows. The Gothic church was rearranged by Vasari in 1560 when the choir and rood-screen were demolished and the side altars added, with tabernacles by Francesco da Sangallo. Some of the painted altarpieces are by Vasari himself and others are by his contemporaries, including Alessandro Fei (also called del Barbiere), Andrea del Minga, Stradano, Bronzino, Santi di Tito and Giovanni Battista Naldini *(marked A–H on the plan on pp. 234–35)*. The church also contains very fine sculptures, since for 500 years it has been the custom to erect monuments to notable citizens of Florence here; it is the burial place of the great artists Lorenzo Ghiberti and Michelangelo, the statesman Machiavelli and the scientist Galileo. But the church is above all famous for its frescoes by Giotto and his school in the chapels at the east end.

The Peruzzi and Bardi Chapels

1 The Peruzzi Chapel: The mural paintings (not true frescoes) by Giotto are damaged and in extremely poor condition. They were painted in the artist's maturity, probably after his return to Florence from Padua. The architectural settings contain references to classical antiquity. In the archivolt, there are eight heads of prophets; in the vault, symbols of the Evangelists; on the right wall, scenes from the life of St John the Evangelist (*Vision at Patmos, Raising of Drusiana, Ascent into Heaven*);

and on the left wall, scenes from the life of St John the Baptist (*Zacharias and the Angel, Birth of St John, Herod's Feast*). A drawing by Michelangelo survives (now in the Louvre) of the two male figures on the left in the *Ascension of St John the Evangelist*. The altarpiece of the *Madonna and Saints* is by Giotto's pupil Taddeo Gaddi.

2 The Bardi Chapel: The frescoes by Giotto were certainly designed by him, although it is possible that some parts were executed by his pupils. They illustrate scenes from the life of St Francis. Giotto received commissions for other Franciscan fresco cycles in Rimini and Padua, both now lost, but his most famous works on this subject are in the upper church of San Francesco in Assisi. On the entrance arch here is the *Saint Receiving the Stigmata*; in the vault, *Poverty*, *Chastity*, *Obedience* and the *Triumph of St Francis*. On the end wall, Franciscan saints, including St Catherine. Left wall: the *Saint Stripping off his Garments*; the *Saint Appearing to St Anthony at Arles;* and the *Death of St Francis*. Right wall: the *Saint Giving the Rule of the Order*; the *Saint Being Tried by Fire Before the Sultan* (a particularly fine work); and the *Saint Appearing to Brother Augustine and Bishop Guido of Assisi*. On the altar is a panel painting of *St Francis with Twenty Scenes from his Life* by a Florentine artist of the 13th century, now generally attributed by scholars to Coppo di Marcovaldo, the most important artist then at work in the city.

GIOTTO'S FRESCOES IN SANTA CROCE

Giotto di Bondone (1266/7–1337) was born in the Mugello just north of Florence. A pupil of Cimabue and friend of Dante, his painting had a new monumentality and sense of volume which had never been achieved in medieval painting. His remarkable figures are given an intensely human significance, which the art historian Bernard Berenson defined as 'tactile values'. Giotto carried out his most famous frescoes in the Cappella degli Scrovegni in Padua in 1303–05 (the only cycle of his which survives intact). In Florence, he was appointed *capomaestro* of the cathedral works and was the architect of the Campanile (1334). Paintings by him which are still in Florence can be seen at the Uffizi, Museo Horne and Museo Diocesano dell'Arte Sacra, and in the churches of Santa Maria Novella, Ognissanti and San Felice there are painted Crucifixes by his hand.

However, it is in the Peruzzi and Bardi chapels in Santa Croce (*described above*) that his greatest Florentine works survive. These frescoes probably date from the 1320s and were commissioned by the Peruzzi and Bardi, two of the richest merchant families in the city, and had a fundamental influence on Florentine painting. The Giottesque school continued to flourish in the city throughout the 14th century. Michelangelo was later to make careful studies of these frescoes. When they were rediscovered in 1841–52, the lower scenes in the Bardi Chapel had been irreparably damaged by funerary monuments. They were restored by Gaetano Bianchi and others and the missing parts skilfully repainted, but in another restoration in 1957–61 the controversial decision was taken to remove the repainting so that the unsightly plasterwork now disturbs the overall effect of the scenes. (Bianchi's 'integrations' were preserved and can still be seen in a room near the Sacristy.)

Other Giottesque works in Santa Croce

A group of Giotto's followers also carried out remarkable fresco cycles in Santa Croce, which is the best place in Florence to examine their work.

3 Baroncelli Chapel: This chapel has frescoes of the *Life of the Virgin* by Taddeo Gaddi, who worked with Giotto for many years and was his most faithful pupil. These are considered among his best works, executed in 1332–38, and reveal his talent as an innovator within the Giottesque school (they include one of the earliest known night scenes in fresco painting). On either side of the entrance arch are prophets and the tomb (right) of a member of the Baroncelli family (1327) with a *Madonna and Child* in the lunette, also by Gaddi. The altarpiece of the *Coronation of the Virgin* (restored) is by Giotto, perhaps with the intervention of his workshop (including possibly Taddeo. Taddeo also designed the stained glass in this chapel. His skill as a fresco painter can also be seen elsewhere in this church: in the Sacristy **(19)** where he painted a *Crucifixion*, and in the Refectory (*see p. 242*) which is decorated with his important *Last Supper* and *Tree of the Cross*. Some of his panel paintings are still to be seen in Florence (including Santa Felicita and San Martino a Mensola) and he may even have been responsible for the design of Ponte Vecchio.

On the back wall of the chapel is a large 15th-century fresco of the *Madonna of the Girdle* by Bastiano Mainardi and a 16th-century statue of the *Madonna and Child*, a good work by Vincenzo Danti.

4 Castellani Chapel: Taddeo's son Agnolo Gaddi produced decorative frescoes for this chapel. They depict (right) the histories of St Nicholas of Bari and St John the Baptist, and (left) St Anthony Abbot and St John the Evangelist. He was given the even more important commission around 1380 to decorate the Sanctuary of the church (*see below*). Like his father, Agnolo was also known as a designer of stained glass, and he was responsible for the fine lancet windows in this chapel (his skills meant that he was also asked to design some of the stained glass for the Duomo). He apparently also worked as a sculptor, since some of the decoration on the Loggia della Signoria is attributed to him, and he worked outside Florence, notably in the Duomo of Prato.

The chapel also contains two white terracotta statues of saints by the della Robbia workshop. The memorial to Louisa, Countess of Albany, who married Charles Stuart the Young Pretender (*see p 178*), and later Vittorio Alfieri, is by Emilio Santarelli.

5 Sanctuary and High Altar: The polygonal vaulted space is entirely covered with Agnolo Gaddi's frescoes of *Christ*, the *Evangelists*, *St Francis*, and the *Legend of the Cross*.

Above the altar is a large polyptych made up in 1869 from panels by various hands when it was given its neo-Gothic frame (probably designed by

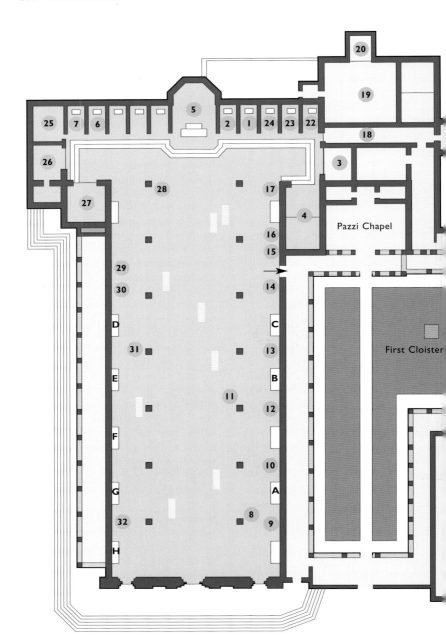

SANTA CROCE

CHURCH & CLOISTERS

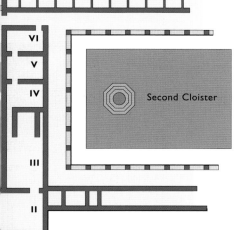

VI

V

IV

Second Cloister

III

II

ALTARPIECES

A   Giorgio Vasari: *The Way to Calvary*
B   Alessandro Fei: *The Flagellation*
C   Andrea del Minga: *Agony in the Garden*
D   Giovanni Stradano: *Ascension*
E   Giorgio Vasari: *Incredulity of St Thomas*
F   Santi di Tito: *Supper at Emmaus*
G   Santi di Tito: *Resurrection*
H   Giovanni Battista Naldini: *Deposition*

Niccolò Matas). This was a fairly usual practice at this time and of course has resulted in decades of discussion about attributions from art historians. They now seem to agree that the most important (and original) sections, all dating from the late 14th century, are the central *Madonna and Saints* (by Niccolò di Pietro Gerini and Lorenzo di Niccolò), the four seated *Fathers of the Church* (by Giovanni del Biondo), and the central panel of the predella which is a very fine work by Lorenzo Monaco. Above hangs a beautiful Crucifix by the Master of Figline who was at work in the first half of the 14th century. The *Assumption of the Virgin* frescoed above the chapel to the left of the Sanctuary is also attributed to this unknown master.

6 Bardi di Libertà Chapel: Another Giottesque painter was Bernardo Daddi, who decorated this chapel with frescoes of the *Life of St Lawrence* and the *Life of St Stephen*. He is better known for his charming panel paintings, many of

which can be seen in the galleries and churches of Florence. The chapel has an altarpiece by Giovanni della Robbia.

7 Bardi di Vernio Chapel: Perhaps the most original of all the followers of Giotto was Maso di Banco whose colourful frescoes of the *Life of St Sylvester and the Emperor Constantine*, carried out after 1367, can be seen here. The first Gothic tomb contains a fresco, also attributed to Maso, of the kneeling figure of the patron of the chapel Bettino de' Bardi with Christ in the sky above receiving his soul into heaven (c. 1367); in the second niche, the *Deposition*, is attributed to Maso's contemporary Taddeo Gaddi. The stained glass is also by Maso (only the two lower figures are modern replacements), who it seems also worked for the Opera del Duomo as a sculptor but who remains a rather mysterious figure and very few works are attributed to him with certainty.

Tour of the rest of the church

8 *Madonna del Latte*: A relief carved by Antonio Rossellino in 1478, above the tomb of Francesco Nori, who was killed in the Pazzi Conspiracy (*see p. 241*).

9 Tomb of Michelangelo: This rather disappointing monument was designed by Giorgio Vasari, who knew the great artist well and who described his life in his famous *Vite* (Michelangelo being the only living and fully active artist included in that book). The paintings and sculptures, none of them of particular

distinction, are the work of artists of the Michelangelesque school (Battista Lorenzi, Valerio Cioli, Giovanni dell'Opera, and Giovanni Battista Naldini). Michelangelo died in 1564 in Rome, where he had lived for the last 30 years of his life. Nevertheless, he always considered himself a Florentine, and his heir and nephew, Leonardo, saw to it that his body returned to Florence for an elaborate funeral service in San Lorenzo before his burial here.

10 Dante's Cenotaph: A Neoclassical work by Stefano Ricci (1829). Dante, exiled in 1302 as an opponent of the Guelph faction in the government, never returned to his native city (*see pp.* 227–28). He died and was buried in Ravenna in 1321.

11 Pulpit: This is perhaps the masterpiece of Benedetto da Maiano (1472–76), a beautifully composed work decorated with delicately carved *Scenes from the Life of St Francis* and *Five Virtues*.

12 Monument to Vittorio Alfieri: A very fine work by Canova. The central theme in the works of this tragic poet (1749–1803) is that of the liberty of the individual in opposition to tyranny, and in many ways he anticipated the spirit of Romanticism. After 1787 he lived in Florence with the Countess of Albany (*see p. 262*), and when he died here she commissioned Canova to erect this monument to him, in which the female figure of Italy is shown weeping at his tomb.

13 Tomb of Machiavelli: The monument to the great statesman is by Innocenzo Spinazzi (1787), the best work of this refined classical sculptor.

14 Cavalcanti Tabernacle: An unusual monument with a beautiful high relief of the *Annunciation* in gilded limestone by Donatello. It was commissioned by Niccolò Cavalcanti for his chapel which used to be beside the choir screen of the church (its present unhappy position is not its original one). There is a remarkable spiritual bond between the figures of Mary and the Angel Gabriel, which makes this one of Donatello's most moving works. The architecture of the tabernacle and the background are intriguing and show the influence of Leon Battista Alberti. The six terracotta putti standing on top of the tabernacle who are playing with the garland are delightful works, also by Donatello. As Vasari says, they look as if they are holding on tight to each other so that they don't tumble to the ground: their spirit is in deliberate contrast to the dramatic scene below.

15 Tomb of Leonardo Bruni: By Bernardo Rossellino (c. 1446–47), this is one of the most harmonious and influential sepulchral monuments of the Renaissance. The architectural setting takes its inspiration from Brunelleschi. Bruni, who died in 1444, was an eminent Florentine humanist and a Greek scholar who translated Aristotle and Plato into Latin. Also an historian, he wrote a history 'in praise of the City of Florence', and he was the biographer of both Petrarch and Dante. He was papal secretary in 1405–15 and then Chancellor of the Republic in 1427, and was greatly admired by his contemporaries for his diplomatic ability and skill in public speaking. He was given an official public funeral in this church and on his tomb here he is shown crowned with a laurel wreath in a serene effigy. The touching epitaph was composed by Carlo Marsuppini, his successor as Chancellor, who is buried opposite (*see below*). In translation, the epitaph reads: 'After Leonardo departed this life, history is in mourning and eloquence is dumb, and it is said that the Muses, Greek and Latin alike, cannot restrain their tears'.

16 Tomb of Rossini: This memorial to the composer (1792–1868), by Giuseppe Cassioli, is a sad imitation of the Bruni tomb, and placed too close to it.

17 Memorial to Foscolo: The sepulchral statue of Ugo Foscolo is by the Florentine sculptor Antonio Berti (1939). Foscolo (1778–1827), a well-known Italian poet, whose most famous poem is *I Sepolcri,* died in London in 1814; he was re-interred here in 1871.

18 Michelozzo Corridor: This passage, by Cosimo il Vecchio's favourite architect, contains a large *Deposition* by Alessandro Allori (1560), and a monument to Lorenzo Bartolini (d. 1850). Bartolini was the most important Italian sculptor of the early 19th century. He carved a number of sepulchral monuments in this church *(see 24, 27 and 28 below)* and is commemorated here with a monument by his pupil Pasquale Romanelli.

19 Sacristy: Bust of the *Redeemer* by Giovanni della Robbia, late-14th-century frescoes by Spinello Aretino and Niccolò di Pietro Gerini, and antiphonals displayed in fine inlaid cupboards.

20 Rinuccini Chapel: Giovanni da Milano was a Lombard artist who worked for a short time in Florence, and was one of the best and most sophisticated followers of Giotto, although his pictorial output was very limited. His frescoes entirely cover this chapel, with scenes from the life of the Virgin and St Mary Magdalen (c. 1365). This little chapel has survived intact from that time, still protected by its original Gothic grille, and with the polyptych commissioned from Giovanni del Biondo still on the altar.

21 Medici Chapel: This chapel by Michelozzo (1434) contains a *Madonna with Saints* by Paolo Schiavo and *St John the Baptist* by Spinello Aretino, both dating from the early 15th century. The terracotta altarpiece of the *Madonna and Child with Angels* is by Andrea della Robbia (c. 1480; the saints were probably added by an assistant).

22 Velluti Chapel: Here are some of the earliest frescoes in the church, damaged works by a follower of Cimabue (possibly Jacopo del Casentino, who lived in the first half of the 14th century), illustrating the life of St Michael Archangel. The polyptych on the altar by Giovanni del Biondo dates from the latter part of the same century.

23 Calderini Chapel: This dates from the first decades of the 17th century, the work of Gherardo Silvani; it preserves its decorations intact with a painted vault by Giovanni da San Giovanni, and an altarpiece by Giovanni Biliverti.

24 Giugni Chapel: Contains the tomb of Charlotte Bonaparte (d. 1839) by Lorenzo Bartolini. She was the daughter of Napoleon's brother, Joseph, who became King of Naples in 1806 and then King of Spain in 1808.

25 Niccolini Chapel: The design is by Giovanni Antonio Dosio c. 1580, using a profusion of rare marbles. The dome has good frescoes by Volterrano (1652–64). The statues are by Pietro Francavilla and the paintings by Alessandro Allori.

26 Donatello's Crucifix: Although one of the most famous works in the church, it is easy to miss as it is poorly displayed in a dark chapel (one of four chapels here patronised by the Bardi family). This is the Crucifix which Donatello's friend Brunelleschi called a mere 'peasant on the Cross' (*for the full story, as recounted by Vasari, see p. 199*).

27 Salviati Chapel: This contains the tomb of Sofia Zamoyska Czartoryska, with a beautiful Romantic effigy by Lorenzo Bartolini. Zofia z Czartoryskich Zamoyska (1778–1837) was a singer and composer, and was the daughter of the Polish Prince Adam Kazimierz. When in 1833 all her property was seized by the Russian Czar and she was forced to leave Poland, she came to live in Florence.

One of the most recent pavement tombs in the church is that of the philosopher Giovanni Gentile, killed by a group of partisans at his villa in Florence in 1944 for having supported Mussolini and having accepted a post as minister in the Fascist regime, one of the most disturbing events which took place in the bitter vindictive atmosphere in Italy during the aftermath of the last war.

28 Monument to Leon Battista Alberti by Lorenzo Bartolini.

29 Monument to Carlo Marsuppini: Marsuppini was a humanist scholar and Chancellor of the Republic (d. 1453). The monument is by Desiderio da Settignano. It takes its inspiration from the Bruni monument opposite, and incorporates some exquisite carving. The fine classical sarcophagus may possibly be the work of Verrocchio.

30 Monument to Fossombroni: Vittorio Fossombroni (1754–1844) was a Tuscan hydraulic engineer who served under the Lorraine grand dukes as foreign minister to Ferdinand III, and then, after a period in Paris where he had been summoned by Napoleon, as prime minister of the Grand Duchy of Tuscany from 1815 until his death.

31 Tomb of Ghiberti: A handsome tomb-slab with *niello* decoration and the emblem of an eagle marks the burial place of the famous sculptor Lorenzo Ghiberti and his son Vittorio, also a sculptor.

32 Monument to Galileo: The great scientist (1564–1642) spent the latter part of his life in Florence. The monument was set up in 1737, to a design by Giovanni Battista Foggini, when Galileo's remains were finally allowed a Christian burial here (*see p. 109*). Foggini carved the bust, and the statue of *Geometry* (on the right) is by Girolamo Ticciati. In the pavement in the centre of the nave, in front of the west door, is the tomb-slab with a relief of the scientist's ancestor and namesake Galileo Galilei, a well-known physician in 15th-century Florence.

The Cloisters and Pazzi Chapel

Open at the same time and with the same ticket as the church. Entrance from inside the church (marked with an arrow on p. 234).

The **first cloister** dates from the 14th century, and beneath the arcade, along the bare Gothic flank of the church, is a gallery with a fine series of 19th-century monuments (including works by Aristodemo Costoli and Ulisse Cambi) from the Romantic Chiostro dei Morti (sadly demolished in 1969). On the lawn is a group of cypresses with acanthus plants (and two incongruous statues: the seated figure of *God the Father* by Baccio Bandinelli, made for the choir of the Duomo and now serving as a war memorial, and the statue of a *Warrior*, donated to the city by Henry Moore).

PAZZI CHAPEL

Pazzi Chapel

The Pazzi Chapel (Cappella dei Pazzi) is one of the most famous works by Brunelleschi. It was commissioned as a chapter house by Andrea de' Pazzi in 1429 or 1430. Most of the work was carried out by Brunelleschi from 1442 until his death in 1446, but it was not finished until the 1470s.

The portico may have been designed by Giuliano da Maiano. The terracotta frieze of cherubs' heads is attributed to the della Robbia workshop. In the centre of the barrel vault is a shallow cupola lined with delightful polychrome enamelled terracottas by Luca della Robbia, with a garland of fruit surrounding the Pazzi arms. Over the door is a medallion with St Andrew, also by Luca (c. 1461). The carved wooden door is by the Maiano brothers.

The serene interior is one of the masterpieces of the early Renaissance. Delicately carved *pietra serena* is used to articulate the architectural features against a plain white ground. The illumination in the chapel is increased by little oculi in the rib-vaulted dome. The 12 roundels in enamelled terracotta of the seated Apostles (c. 1442–52) are by Luca della Robbia. In the pendentives of the cupola are four polychrome roundels of the Evangelists, thought to have been added c. 1460. These may have been designed by Donatello and glazed by the della Robbia (although some scholars attribute them to Brunelleschi). In the sanctuary are decorations by the school of Donatello and a stained glass window attributed to Alesso Baldovinetti.

On the left of the chapel, nearly 6 metres above ground-level, is a plaque marking the water level of the Arno in the terrible flood of 1966. In a room here there is an exhibition of woodcuts by Pietro Parigi.

The **second cloister** is reached through a doorway by Michelozzo. This is another beautiful work by Brunelleschi, finished in 1453 after his death. It is one of the most peaceful spots in the city.

THE PAZZI CONSPIRACY

In 1478 Francesco de' Pazzi came close to bringing Medici power in Florence to a bloody end. Though the Pazzi had little influence in Florentine affairs, they were an old-established banking family who had recently won business from the papacy under Sixtus IV, who distrusted Lorenzo the Magnificent and was suspicious of his alliance with Milan. Supported by Rome, Francesco and his fellow conspirators planned to assassinate Lorenzo and his brother Giuliano, at a moment when their attention was distracted by some kind of public spectacle. The event chosen was Mass in the Duomo. Giuliano's killers dealt him a mortal stab wound in the neck when he bowed his head in prayer. Lorenzo's assailants were less deft: Lorenzo parried the blow, and vaulted to safety over the Communion rail, taking refuge in the north sacristy.

Soon the hue and cry was raised all over town. The conspirators were apprehended, and vengeance was terrible. All those complicit in the plot—and, in the ensuing confusion, many who were not—were hounded out and killed. The ringleaders had ropes fastened to their necks and were tossed from the high windows of Palazzo della Signoria, to dangle to their deaths.

The Museo dell'Opera di Santa Croce

The refectory: This is a fine Gothic hall with large windows. Cimabue's great Crucifix is displayed here. It was the most important work of art destroyed in the 1966 Arno flood: a skilled restoration has recuperated the little original paint that survived. The end wall of the refectory is decorated with a huge fresco by Taddeo Gaddi (detached in one piece and restored) of the *Last Supper* below the *Tree of the Cross* and four scenes showing St Louis of Toulouse, St Francis, St Benedict and *Mary Magdalen Anointing the Feet of Christ in the House of Simon the Pharisee*. On the two long walls (below roundels of saints) are detached fragments of a large fresco by Orcagna showing the *Triumph of Death* and *Inferno*, which used to decorate the nave of the church before Vasari's side altars were set up.

The detached 14th-century fresco (attributed to Giovanni del Biondo) has one of the earliest views of the city (with the Baptistery and Duomo). In a reconstructed tabernacle (a cast) is Donatello's colossal gilded bronze *St Louis of Toulouse*, commissioned by the Parte Guelfa for a niche in Orsanmichele (but replaced there by the *Incredulity of St Thomas* by Verrocchio). On the entrance wall, there are two detached frescoes by Andrea di Giusto of *Christ Carrying the Cross* and the *Crucifixion*. Above the door into the next room is a fragment of a *Coronation of the Virgin* by Maso di Banco and, to the right, *St John the Baptist and St Francis* by Domenico Veneziano.

Room II: Here are displayed stained glass fragments, including a tondo of a prophet and two martyred saints, formerly part of a large window at the end of the south aisle of the church, which have recently been attributed to Giotto. The large fresco of *St Francis Distributing Bread to Friars* is by Jacopo Ligozzi. Also here are two smaller detached frescoes, one of the *Madonna and Child* by the 15th-century Florentine school, attributed by some scholars to Paolo Uccello (and by others to a 14th-century artist), and the other an unusual scene showing *St Anne and the Madonna as a Girl Sewing*, a charming work attributed to the Master of the Bambino Vispo.

Room III: This former chapel contains traces of late 13th-century painted decorations. Enamelled terracottas by Andrea della Robbia and his workshop, and frescoes by Niccolò di Pietro Gerini are on display here. The silver reliquary bust of the blessed Umiliana de' Cerchi is a Florentine work of c. 1380. The painted 14th-century Crucifix is by Filippo Benivieni. In the corridor is a fine fresco from the 15th-century tomb of a cardinal.

Room IV: The three large sketches exhibited here were detached from the walls of the Pazzi Chapel during restoration work in 1966. These interesting studies include a colossal head of St John the Baptist and an architectural study, which have been attributed by some scholars to Donatello; and another colossal head (with a halo) attributed to Desiderio da Settignano. Also here are 14th–15th-century detached frescoes, including a fragment of the Virgin attrib-

Detail of Taddeo Gaddi's *Last Supper*.

uted to Giotto, and a sinopia of the *Madonna Enthroned* by the Master of the Madonna Straus.

Room V: This room contains sculptural fragments including the reconstructed tomb of Gastone della Torre (1318/19), and a *Madonna Annunciate*, both by Tino da Camaino; and a relief of *St Martin Dividing his Cloak with a Beggar* in *pietra serena*, from a demolished rood-screen chapel in the church (15th century).

Room VI: 17th-century works including ceiling paintings of two angels by Matteo Rosselli.

Beneath the colonnade beside the exit from the first cloister is a memorial to Florence Nightingale, named after the city where she was born in 1820, and famous for her devotion to reform in medical care and the nursing profession.

WALK FIVE

MUSEO HORNE & ITS DISTRICT

Palazzo Corsi (no. 6 Via de'Benci) is an attractive small palace (1495–1502, now generally attributed to Cronaca) housing the **Museo Horne** (*open 9–1 except Sun and holidays; T: 055 244 661*). The English art historian and architect Herbert Percy Horne (1864–1916) presented the palace to the Italian nation, along with his collection of 14th–16th-century paintings, sculpture and decorative arts (notably furniture and majolica). Horne first came to Florence in 1904 and purchased Palazzo Corsi in 1911. He carefully restored every detail (including the doors and shutters) to its late-15th-century appearance. He lived on the top floor for the last few months of his life. The works (unlabelled) are numbered to correspond to a catalogue lent to visitors.

The lovely courtyard has interesting capitals. On the ground floor is kept a copy of Horne's book on Botticelli, published in 1908; and a selection of the 929 very fine drawings by Renaissance and 16th- and early 17th-century artists, which he collected from 1890 onwards, is to be displayed here. A ramp (originally for beasts of burden) leads down to the cellars where small exhibitions are held.

Room I on the first floor has works by Correggio, Dosso Dossi (*Allegory of Music*, c. 1530), Pietro Lorenzetti, Bernardo Daddi, and Piero di Cosimo. In a wall case is a fascinating tiny work

by Masaccio: *Scenes from the Legend of St Julian*. On the left the saint is shown returning from the hunt with his dog (superbly drawn from behind) and being told by the devil (in the guise of a man) that his wife is in bed with a lover (in fact the bed is occupied by Julian's long-lost parents); the central scene shows the couple in bed; and the scene on the right shows Julian with his wife in despair after Julian has unknowingly killed his parents in rage. These two figures anticipate Masaccio's famous portrayal of Adam and Eve expelled from Paradise in the Brancacci Chapel. Unfortunately this exquisite work, which was once part of a triptych painted together with Masolino for the church of Santa Maria Maggiore in Florence, has been damaged by scratches and is in very poor condition. On the table are small sculptures (*bozzetti*) by Ammannati, Giambologna, and Gianfrancesco Rustici. The *Deposition*, a crowded composition by Benozzo Gozzoli, was left unfinished at the death of the painter (the colours have darkened with time).

Room II contains the most precious piece in the collection, Giotto's *St Stephen*, one of the most important paintings known by the master. The gentle face is full of expression, as only Giotto was able to portray at this time, and the quality of the paint is exceptional with the deacon's robes exquisite-

St Stephen by Giotto, the most precious piece in the Museo Horne collection.

ly decorated. Stephen was one of the first seven deacons of the church and here he is shown with his attribute of stones (on his head), recording his famous martyrdom when he was stoned to death (Stephen was the first Christian martyr). Horne purchased the work in London in 1904, having recognized it as the work of this great master, and his attribution is now generally accepted by art historians, some of whom believe it to have been part of a polyptych (the central panel of which is in the National Gallery of Washington). It may have been painted around the same time as Giotto's frescoes in the Peruzzi Chapel in Santa Croce nearby.

Room III has a very fine tondo of the *Holy Family* by Beccafumi, in a beautiful contemporary frame.

Room I on the second floor contains several fine pieces of 15th-century furniture. Here are displayed a portable diptych attributed to Simone Martini, a *Pietà* (a pax) by Filippo Lippi, a panel from a marriage chest by Filippino Lippi (*Queen Vashti leaving the Palace of Susa*, derived from a drawing by Botticelli), and a contemporary copy of Leonardo's lost fresco of the *Battle of Anghiari* in Palazzo Vecchio. The *Madonna and Saints* is attributed to the Master of the Horne Triptych, a 14th-century Florentine artist named from this panel. On the window wall of Room II is the *Archangel Raphael, Tobias and St Jerome* by Neri di Bicci, and on the far wall *The Drunkenness of Noah* (in a tondo surrounded by putti), attributed to Beccafumi. The old kitchen, also on this floor, has a collection of cutlery and utensils.

Museo Horne stands on **Via de' Benci**. From the 13th century onwards the Alberti, an influential merchant family who were patrons of the church of Santa Croce, but who were exiled in 1387 for political reasons, owned numerous properties on this street, some of them distinguished still by the old rustication on their ground floors. The splendid polygonal 13th-century Torre degli Alberti, with a 15th-century loggia below, is well sited on the corner of Borgo Santa Croce. Adjoining it is the most important of the Alberti palaces to survive, still called **Palazzo Alberti**, where the great architect Leon Battista (who had been born while the family were in exile in Genoa) also lived for a time. It is trapezoidal in plan with a good courtyard. On the other side of Via de' Benci, Palazzo Malenchini (no. 1) was reconstructed in the 19th century on the site of a 14th-century residence of the Alberti, as a plaque here records.

The **Palazzo Bardi alle Grazie** (Serzelli no. 5) is an early Renaissance palace attributed to Brunelleschi (c. 1430) with a fine courtyard. Here the famous Camerata Fiorentina di Casa Bardi introduced operatic melodrama in 1598. Via de' Benci is closed to the north by a distant view of the tower of the Duomo of Fiesole, and to the south, across the river, the green hills of the Oltrarno provide a background to the medieval buildings in Piazza dei Mozzi.

Via dei Neri was named after the confraternity who comforted criminals on their way from the Bargello to execution. In Via delle Brache the medieval houses preserve their *sporti*. On Via de' Rustici, Palazzo Rustici (Neri) dates from the end of the 14th century. The road bends at its junction with Via

Mosca following the shape of the Roman port on the river. Here, at no. 23, is the 14th-century Palazzo Soldani.

A road with plaques showing the water levels of the Arno in the floods of 1333 and 1966, leads to the church of **San Remigio** (*open 9–11 & 4–6.30 except Sun*) founded in the 11th century, with an exterior in *pietra forte*. The interior, a fine Gothic hall, contains fresco fragments by the school of Giotto and worn roundels of saints in the vaults (14th century). The beautiful panel painting of the *Madonna and Child* in the chapel to the right of the sanctuary has in the past been attributed to both Duccio and Cimabue, but is now usually considered to be by a follower of Cimabue known from this work as the Master of San Remigio. The portrayal of the Christ Child, shown reaching up to hug His mother, is particularly delightful in this lovely painting dating from around 1290. In the chapel to the left of the sanctuary is a fine painting of the *Immaculate Conception* by Empoli, which dates from 1591. In a room below the campanile (*admission on request*), there are monochrome frescoes with hunting scenes, and in the refectory of the former convent upstairs are more very worn monochrome frescoes of scenes from the Last Supper and the Passion.

Piazza Peruzzi is named after the famous Florentine family of bankers who reached their greatest prosperity at the end of the 13th century, and their (reconstructed) palace survives here amongst the other medieval buildings.

Via dei Bentaccordi follows the curved shape of the Roman amphitheatre (2nd–3rd century AD) which used to be on this site. It is estimated that it was big enough to hold about 15,000 spectators. In a little piazza stands the church of **San Simone** (*open for services only*), founded in 1192–93. The fine doorway is in the style of Benedetto da Rovezzano. The sombre interior is by Gherardo Silvani (1630), with a carved 17th-century wooden ceiling. The lovely painting of *St Peter Enthroned* (first altar on the right) was painted by the Master of Santa Cecilia in 1307. *Christ Showing his Wounds to St Bernard* (1623) by Jacopo Vignali hangs over the last altar on the south side. At the end of the north side, there is a charming Gothic tabernacle (1363) with a 15th-century bust of a lady surrounded by enamelled terracotta decoration by the della Robbia.

Opposite is **Vivoli**, the best-known ice-cream shop in the city.

On Via delle Stinche, named after a prison on this site since the early 14th century, is **Palazzo da Cintoia** (Salviati), one of the most interesting medieval palaces to survive in the city. It dates from the 14th century, and its façade in *pietra forte* has picturesque *sporti*. In Via della Vigna Vecchia is the 14th-century Palazzo Covoni (no. 9).

CASA BUONARROTI & SANT'AMBROGIO

CASA BUONARROTI

Map p. 399, E3

Open 9.30–1.30 except Tues; T. 055 241 752.

At no. 70 Via Ghibellina is the Casa Buonarroti, a delightful little museum dedicated to Michelangelo. Three houses on this site were purchased in 1508 by the great artist who left the property to his only descendant, his nephew Leonardo, who joined the houses together following a plan already drawn up by Michelangelo. In turn, his son, called Michelangelo Buonarroti the Younger (1568–1647), an art collector and man of letters, made part of the house into a gallery in 1612 as a memorial to his great-uncle. His small collection of Etruscan and Roman works was continued by the archaeologist Filippo Buonarroti (1661–1733). The last member of this branch of the Buonarroti family founded the present museum in 1858 (when the bust of Michelangelo was made for the façade), and it is still run by a foundation. In the charming little rooms of the house on the first floor are preserved three of Michelangelo's sculptures and some of his drawings and *bozzetti*.

Ground Floor: the Buonarroti family collections

Here is displayed the eclectic collection of works of art made by Michelangelo's descendants. The archaeological collection of Etruscan and Roman works include two stelae from Fiesole in *pietra serena* dating from the 6th century BC, which are among the best preserved Etruscan carvings of this period. The two Roman statues of magistrates (1st century AD), found in Florence in 1627, were restored for Michelangelo Buonarroti the Younger by Antonio Novelli.

The next room contains paintings and sculptures based on works by Michelangelo, many by unknown 16th-century artists. The small *Crucifixion* was copied by Marcello Venusti from a drawing made by Michelangelo for his close friend Vittoria Colonna (1490–1547), a remarkable Renaissance figure and poet. The statue of Venus and two cupids is attributed to Vincenzo Danti. The next room displays a charming portrait of *Three Young Men* from the Buonarroti family by Gregorio Pagani. The *Love Scene* (perhaps Cornelia and Pompey) is a 16th-century Venetian copy of a lost work by Titian. In the courtyard, there is a statue made up from a classical head and a medieval draped toga, a little Roman relief with two goats (1st century AD), and an ancient Ionic capital used as a model by Giuliano da Sangallo in the cloister of Santa Maria Maddalena dei Pazzi (*see p. 253*). The rooms on the other side of the courtyard are used for exhibitions.

First Floor: works by and in homage to Michelangelo

In the vestibule are 16th–19th-century portraits of Michelangelo based on a prototype (c. 1535) by Jacopino del Conte (also displayed here). The sword is thought to have belonged to Buonarroto Buonarroti, Captain of the Guelph party in 1392.

The room to the left contains two small **sculptures by Michelangelo**: the *Madonna of the Steps*, a marble bas-relief, is his earliest known work, carved at the age of 15 or 16. The low *schiacciato* relief shows the influence of Donatello. In the 17th century, it was owned by the Medici who then returned it to the Buonarroti family. It was a work intended for private devotion, possibly part of a triptych. The relief showing a battle scene is also one of his earliest works, carved just before the death of Lorenzo the Magnificent in 1492, and then worked on a few years later, but left unfinished. This is the only early work documented by his biographers Vasari and Condivi, and it demonstrates Michelangelo's prodigious skill as a sculptor. Modelled on ancient sarcophagi, it represents a mythological battle between Greeks and centaurs. It shows the influence of Bertoldo di Giovanni who carved a very fine bronze battle relief (now in the Bargello), based on a Roman sarcophagus in Pisa.

Another room (left) contains the wooden **model for the façade of San Lorenzo** designed by Michelangelo for Leo X in 1516 but never carried out. The model is by Pietro Urbano. The colossal torso by Michelangelo, a model in clay and wood for a river god, was intended for the New Sacristy in San Lorenzo. It was presented by Ammannati to the Accademia del Disegno in 1583.

In the room in front of the stairs are displayed (in rotation) five or six **drawings by Michelangelo** owned by the museum.

Beyond are four rooms decorated for Michelangelo Buonarroti the Younger c. 1613–37 as a celebration of his famous great-uncle and his family. The first room, the Galleria, painted in 1613–35, illustrates Michelangelo's life and apotheosis, with paintings by Giovanni Biliverti, Jacopo da Empoli, Artemisia Gentileschi, Francesco Furini, Giovanni da San Giovanni, Passignano and Matteo Rosselli. On the wall opposite the statue of Michelangelo by Antonio Novelli is a copy of the cartoon of the so-called *Epiphany* by Michelangelo's pupil, Ascanio Condivi. In the niches on either side are statues representing the *Active and Contemplative Life* by Domenico Pieratti.

The Stanza della Notte e del Dì, begun in 1624, is dedicated to the Buonarroti family, and off it is the tiny little study of Michelangelo the Younger. The predella with *Scenes from the Life of St Nicholas of Bari* is by Giovanni di Francesco, and the marble Cupid was begun by Valerio Cioli and finished by Andrea Ferrucci. The portrait of Michelangelo in a turban is attributed to Giuliano Bugiardini, and the painting of Michelangelo the Younger is by Cristofano Allori. The **bronze head of Michelangelo** (1564–66, commissioned by Leonardo Buonarroti and based on his death mask) is by Daniele da Volterra. The Camera degli Angeli was used as a chapel. The bust of Michelangelo the Younger is the masterpiece of Giuliano Finelli, Bernini's pupil. The library was decorated in 1633–37 with a delightful frieze of illustrious Tuscans by Cecco Bravo, with the help of Domenico Pugliani and Matteo Rosselli. Roman fragments in marble and terracotta are displayed here. In case 410, there is a beautiful terracotta head of a child attributed to the school of Verrocchio or Antonio Rossellino.

In the Stanzina dell'Apollo, an alcove, Roman sculptures are displayed, including a statuette of Apollo, and a fragment, the right arm and hand, from a good Roman copy of Myron's most famous work, his bronze *Discobolos* (Discus Thrower) which only survives in marble replicas made in ancient Rome, the best of which is in the Museo Nazionale Romano.

The room to the right of the stairs displays *bozzetti* in wax, terracotta, wood and plaster attributed to Michelangelo and his circle. In the centre, the *Two Wrestlers* in terracotta is recognised as by the hand of Michelangelo (c. 1530). The wood Crucifix and *River God* in wax are also attributed to him. The two terracottas of a female nude and a male torso may be by him, while the terracotta *Madonna and Child* is attributed to Vincenzo Danti.

Another room has two paintings of the *Noli me tangere* derived from a lost cartoon by Michelangelo, one attributed to Pontormo, and the other by Battista Franco. Beyond the Stanza dei Paesaggi decorated with early 18th-century frescoes, is a room dedicated to the cult of Michelangelo in the 19th century, with a 19th-century marble sculpture of the young Michelangelo at work by Cesare Zocchi. Documentation relating to the celebrations in Florence in 1875 for the fourth centenary of Michelangelo's birth include designs for graffiti decoration which was to have been added to the façade of the Casa Buonarroti. Beyond a narrow corridor, a few steps lead down to a little room with plaster casts of works by Michelangelo, a large eagle, once thought to be a Roman work, and a wooden model for the 'carriage' built to transport the statue of the *David* from Piazza della Signoria to the Accademia in 1873.

On the second floor, there is an important library (*open to scholars*) with material relating to Michelangelo.

SANT'AMBROGIO
Map p. 399, F3

The church of Sant'Ambrogio was rebuilt in the late 13th century and it still has an open timber roof although the façade dates from the 19th century.

The interior has pretty Renaissance side altars, and the tribune, with its side chapels, was designed in 1716 by Giovanni Battista Foggini, (with 18th-century frescoes in the sanctuary by Luigi Ademollo). No fewer than four important artists are buried here and their tomb-slabs can be seen in the pavement: the sculptor Mino da Fiesole (1484); the painter and sculptor Verrocchio (1488); Cronaca, the architect of a number of fine palaces in the city (1508); and the painter Francesco Granacci (1541). On the south side there are interesting 14th-century works: a beautiful fresco of the *Madonna Enthroned with St John the Baptist and St Bartholomew*, attributed to the school of Orcagna, and a fragment of a mural drawing of St Onophrius, attributed to the Master of Figline.

In the chapel to the left of the sanctuary (the Cappella del Miracolo) is an exquisite tabernacle by Mino da Fiesole (1481), which contains a miraculous chalice. Tradition relates how, in 1230, Uguccione, the parish priest, found blood instead of wine inside it while celebrating Mass. A large fresco here by Cosimo Rosselli shows a procession with this very chalice in front of the church. It includes portraits of many of the artist's contemporaries as well as the artist's self-portrait (to the left). The sinopia is displayed on the wall nearby.

On the north side there is an altarpiece of the *Madonna in Glory with Saints* by Cosimo Rosselli, and a wooden statuette of St Sebastian by Leonardo del Tasso, which stands in a graceful niche with a tiny painted roundel of the *Annunciation*, attributed to the workshop of Filippino Lippi. The fresco of the *Martyrdom of St Sebastian*—with the emaciated figure of the saint standing high up on a stake with his hands tied above his head—is attributed to Agnolo Gaddi. The painting on the wall is by Alesso Baldovinetti (*Angels and Saints*) and his pupil Graffione (*Nativity*).

MERCATO DI SANT' AMBROGIO
Map p. 399, F3

Open Mon–Sat mornings.

This is now probably the biggest (and certainly the busiest) produce market in Florence, perhaps because it is easier for Florentines to reach by car than the central market at San Lorenzo. The cast-iron building dates from 1873: butchers, grocers and fishmongers have their stalls inside, while fruit and vegetables, some grown locally, are sold from stalls outside. On the two short sides of the building there are stalls selling clothes, shoes, household linen, hardware, and plants, all generally good value. It is especially crowded on Saturday mornings and it is to be hoped that the new 'piazza' and underground car park under construction here will not alter its bustling character and genuine Florentine atmosphere.

Nearby there is a junk and antique market, known as the 'Mercatino', housed in sheds in **Piazza dei Ciompi**, but this is destined to be moved to new premises in the piazza of the market of Sant'Ambrogio. It used to be easy to find bargains here but in the last few years the prices have soared and business is much less good. This piazza is named after the *ciompi* (wool-carders) who in 1378 led a revolt by the Florentine clothworkers against harsh working conditions and pitiful pay. As a result they won significant concessions, including (for a time) direct representation in the government of the city and the right to form a guild. Although this proved to be only a temporary victory, the protest has always been seen as a significant moment in the history of labour unrest. A graceful loggia designed in 1568 by Vasari and once used for the sale of fish in the Mercato Vecchio was reconstructed here after the demolition of that area of the city: it looks somewhat incongruous in these humble surroundings.

A damaged inscription on a house in the piazza records the home of the sculptor Lorenzo Ghiberti, while Cimabue lived in Borgo Allegri, which—according to Vasari—was given this name after Cimabue's painting of the *Madonna in Maestà* (now in the Uffizi) left his studio in a joyous procession down the street. There is a pleasant little public garden in this street, opened and maintained by old-age pensioners who live in the district.

WALK SIX

BORGO DEGLI ALBIZI & BORGO PINTI

This walk explores the eastern districts of central Florence: the attractive Borgo degli Albizi, named after the great merchant family exiled from Florence when Cosimo il Vecchio came to power; the church of a visionary mystic saint and member of the Pazzi family; and the enormous Synagogue.

The walk begins in the small Piazza San Pier Maggiore at the top of Via Palmiere (*map p. 399, E3*), the centre of a local shopping area with a handful of market stalls, and an archway known as the Volta di San Piero. The 17th-century portico by Nigetti is all that survives of the church which gave the square its name. The little Palazzo Corbizzi (no. 1) dates from the 13th century. Next to a pretty house with a projecting upper storey rises the splendid 13th-century Torre Donati (Cocchi). Nearby is a large, incongruous building built as a post office by Giovanni Michelucci in 1959–67.

Borgo degli Albizi is one of the most handsome streets in the city, following the line of the Roman Cassia. The Borgo is named after one of the wealthiest families in Florence in the 14th and 15th centuries, who owned numerous palaces in the street, and who were rivals to the Medici for power. At no. 11, a 16th-century house bears a marble bust of Cosimo II. A medieval tower, which belonged to the Donati, rises from the top of this house. No. 10 has a bust of the poet Vincenzo Filicaia (1642–1707), who was born here. **Palazzo degli Alessandri** (no. 15) is the best-preserved palace on the street. A worn cornice divides the two storeys of its fine 14th-century façade in *pietra forte*, rusticated on the lower part. Canova had his studio here for a while.

The grandiose **Palazzo degli Albizi** (no. 12) was the principal residence of the Albizi. The 14th-century fabric survives on the left, and the nine bays on the right were reconstructed by Silvani in the 17th century. Facing a piazzetta is a narrow 14th-century house (no. 14). The huge **Palazzo Altoviti** (or dei Visacci; no. 18), which dates from the early 15th century, was enlarged in the late 16th century when the amusing marble portraits of celebrated Florentine citizens by Caccini were placed on the façade. By Volta dei Ciechi there is a house (no. 22) with medieval fragments. Palazzo Matteucci Ramirez di Montalvo (no. 26) is a severe work by Ammannati (1568). The graffiti decoration is attributed to Bernardino Poccetti. The owner set up the arms of his friend Cosimo I on the façade. On the corner of Via de' Giraldi is a 14th-century tabernacle with the *Madonna Enthroned*. Palazzo Vitali (no. 28) is a beautiful building attributed to Bartolommeo Ammannati (late 16th century), with a handsome coat of arms.

Retrace your steps to Piazza San Pier Maggiore, then into **Borgo Pinti**, a long, narrow winding old street leading out of the city, with some handsome palaces. Near no. 58 is the entrance to the **Convent of Santa Maria Maddalena dei Pazzi**, named after a Florentine Carmelite nun (1566–1607). From a patrician Florentine family, and an invalid, after she became a Carmelite nun she had mystical visions and was known for her miraculous healing powers. Her cult became popular in Italy after her death in 1607 and her canonization in 1669, together with that of her near contemporary St Teresa of Avila, also a Carmelite. A Cistercian convent, founded here in 1321, was taken over by the Carmelites from 1628 until 1888, and fathers of the Assumption of the Augustinian order (founded in Nimes in 1850) have been here since 1926 (the church serves the French community of Florence).

The cloister, really a quadriporticus, is by Giuliano da Sangallo (1492) with beautiful large Ionic capitals supporting a low architrave. Although the door of the church is kept closed it is usually unlocked (otherwise ring at no. 58). Although state-owned, a donation is requested for the lighting.

The church was begun in 1257 and the side chapels were added in 1488–1526, with pretty carved arches in *pietra serena*. The trompe l'œil ceiling painting is by Jacopo Chiavistelli and Marco Antonio Molinari (1677), and the paintings in the nave are by Cosimo Ulivelli (c. 1700).

On the south side, the first chapel contains the *Martyrdom of St Romulus* (1557), a huge painting signed and dated by Carlo Portelli. The second chapel was decorated in 1778. In the third chapel there is a *Coronation of the Virgin* by Matteo Rosselli in a fine frame of c. 1490. The fourth chapel has a *Madonna and Child with Saints*, the masterpiece of Domenico Puligo (1526; with a good frame by Baccio d'Agnolo). The fifth chapel has a stained glass window of St Francis (c. 1500), and the sixth chapel early 19th-century frescoes by Luigi Catani and a small Crucifix attributed to Bernardo Buontalenti. The well-lit main chapel, with colourful marbles, is one of the most important and complete examples of Florentine Baroque church decoration. It was designed in 1675 in honour of Santa Maria Maddalena by Ciro Ferri, who painted the high altarpiece, and by Pier Francesco Silvani. On the side walls are two paintings by Luca Giordano. The statues are by (left) Antonio Montauti (c. 1690) and (right) Innocenzo Spinazzi (1781). The cupola was frescoed in 1701 by Pier Dandini.

On the north side of the church, the Renaissance organ (restored in 1719) has a cantoria attributed to Giuliano da Sangallo. In the fourth chapel, in a pretty frame, is *St Ignatius and St Roch* by Raffaellino del Garbo, flanking a wood statue of St Sebastian. The third chapel has stained glass designed by Domenico del Ghirlandaio and on the altar is a wooden processional statue of the Madonna and Child. The painting of the *Agony in the Garden* by Santi di Tito is signed and dated 1591. The second chapel contains a *Coronation of the Virgin* by Cosimo Rosselli in another fine frame.

The **chapter house** (*entrance at the end of the south side; open 9–11.50, and for a short time between 5–6.50*) is now approached from the crypt since the second cloister was cut in two when Via della Colonna was built. It contains one of Perugino's masterpieces: his beautiful and well-preserved fresco of the *Crucifixion and Saints* (1493–96).

The domed Cappella del Giglio (or Cappella dei Neri; *for admission ask at the convent*), built c. 1505, is interesting for its frescoes by Bernardino Poccetti and assistants (1598–1600).

East of here is the huge **Synagogue**, an elaborate building in the Spanish-Moresco style with a tall green dome (*open daily except Sat 11–1 & 2–5; 15 June–15 September, 9.30–5.30*). It was built in 1874–82 by Marco Treves, Mariano Falcini and Vincenzo Michele. The Jews are first mentioned as a community in Florence in the 15th century when they were encouraged by the Republican government to operate in the city as money-lenders. In 1571, they were confined to a ghetto in the area of the present Piazza della Repubblica by Cosimo I, and this was not opened until 1848. The ghetto was demolished at the end of the 19th century.

There is a small museum on the upper floor of the synagogue (*open Sun–Thurs 10–dusk; Fri 10–2; T: 055 2346654*). The display is well labelled and includes ceremonial objects, silver and vestments, dating from the 17th–18th centuries. In the garden is a Jewish School. The Jewish cemetery in Florence is at no. 14 Viale Ariosto and is open the first Sunday of the month, 10–12.

THE ARNO

PONTE VECCHIO
Map p. 397, A4

Standing near the site of the Roman crossing (which was a little farther upstream), Ponte Vecchio was the only bridge over the Arno until 1218. The present bridge of three arches was reconstructed after a flood in 1345, probably by Taddeo Gaddi, better known as a painter of the Giottesque school (but the bridge is also attributed to the architect Neri di Fioravante). The bridge on this site has been lined by shops since the 13th century, but an edict issued by Grand Duke Ferdinando I in 1593 established that the butchers' shops and grocery shops should be replaced by those of goldsmiths and silversmiths, who remain here to this day. These excellent jewellers, whose shops with pretty fronts with wooden shutters and awnings overhang the river supported on brackets, maintain the skilled tradition of Florentine goldsmiths, whose work first became famous in the 15th century. Many of the greatest Renaissance artists trained as goldsmiths (including Ghiberti, Brunelleschi and Donatello). The most famous Florentine goldsmith was the 16th-century sculptor Benvenuto Cellini, who was aptly recorded in 1900 when his bust was set up in the middle of the bridge. The goldsmiths of present-day Florence can be seen at work in the Casa dell'Orafo, a rambling edifice in an alley beside the dark Volta dei Girolami close to the north end of the

bridge. Above the shops on one side of the bridge are the round windows of the Corridoio Vasariano, the covered way built by Vasari (*see p. 105*) to link Palazzo Vecchio and the Uffizi with the new residence of the Medici, Palazzo Pitti, on the other side of the river. It leaves the bridge on the south side, supported on elegant brackets in order not to disturb the Torre dei Mannelli, the medieval angle tower which served as a defence on the Arno (restored after the war). From the centre of the bridge there is a superb view of Ponte Santa Trìnita (*see p. 263*). On the corner of a house a sundial and worn inscription survive from 1345.

The fame of Ponte Vecchio saved it from war damage in 1944 (although numerous ancient buildings at either end were blown up instead, in order to render it impassable). Some of the old houses mined on the two approach roads to the bridge, Via Por Santa Maria and Via de' Guicciardini, and the medieval buildings destroyed on both banks of the river, were replaced in the immediate post-war years by a medley of undistinguished buildings along the lines of the old ones. Although this attempt to reconstruct this historic area failed to recapture the atmosphere of the old city, at least more drastic proposals by some of the leading architects of the day to erect modern buildings in a totally alien style were successfully avoided by an official local committee of distinguished residents appointed by the city government.

THE ARNO

From its source on the heights of Monte Falterona east of Florence, the Arno cuts a wide loop across the plain of Arezzo before flowing northwest to Florence itself, below which it continues through the centre of Pisa, reaching the sea after a course of some 240 kilometres. Once navigable all the way from the coast, it was of great importance to the economy of Florence: during the Middle Ages mills on the Arno were used in the wool industry, on which the city's economy was based from the 13th century onwards. By this time all four bridges in the centre of the city had been built: the other bridges up and down stream were only added after 1836. As much as it brought prosperity, however, the Arno also brought devastation. Since the first recorded flood in 1177, the river has overflowed its banks no fewer than 57 times (small plaques throughout the city show the level the water reached during some of these inundations). The last great flood was in 1966, when buildings, works of art and hundreds of artisans' workshops were severely damaged. Even today, a 15-year programme of flood prevention still awaits definitive approval.

The roads along the Arno embankment (recorded as early as the 13th century) are known as the Lungarni (singular, Lungarno). Lined with handsome palaces and some elegant shops, they provide magnificent views of the city on the river.

SANTA FELICITA

At the southern end of Ponte Vecchio is a fountain reconstructed here in 1958, with a bronze statue of Bacchus by Giambologna and a Roman sarcophagus. A short way along Via Guicciardini, which leads towards Piazza Pitti, is the little Piazza Santa Felicita with a granite column of 1381 marking the site of the first Christian cemetery in Florence.

The church of Santa Felicita is probably the oldest church in the city after San Lorenzo. In the 2nd century, Syrian Greek merchants came to settle here, on a site near the river and on a busy Roman consular road, and they are thought to have introduced Christianity to the city. The early Christian church, built at the end of the 4th or the beginning of the 5th century, was dedicated to the Roman martyr St Felicity (a tombstone dated 405 has been excavated here). A new church was built in the 11th century and the present church was erected in 1736–39 by Ferdinando Ruggieri, and his design of the interior takes its inspiration from late-16th-century Florentine architecture.

The church is chiefly visited for its superb **works by Pontormo**, considered among the masterpieces of 16th-century Florentine painting, in the Cappella Capponi. They were commissioned by Ludovico Capponi in 1525, after he purchased the chapel from the Barbadori. The remarkable altarpiece of the *Deposition* (*see overleaf*) is in a magnificent contemporary frame attributed to Baccio d'Agnolo. The head of St Nicodemus on the right may be Pontormo's self-portrait.

The fresco of the *Annunciation* was detached when it was restored. The *tondi* in the cupola of the Evangelists are attributed to Pontormo and Bronzino. The chapel was originally designed for the Barbadori by Brunelleschi (c. 1420–25), but was altered in the 18th century, when the cupola was lowered and some of its frescoes destroyed. The 15th-century stained-glass window is by Giullaume de Marcillat, a French artist who lived in Arezzo, famous as a designer of stained glass.

Over the fourth altar on the right is a striking painting, the *Martyrdom of the Maccabei Brothers*, by Antonio Ciseri (1863). The choir chapel was designed by Ludovico Cigoli in 1610–22. The high altarpiece of the *Adoration of the Shepherds*, traditionally attributed to Santi di Tito, is now thought to be the work of the little-known painter Francesco Brina.

On the north side, the last chapel (beneath the organ) contains a late-15th-century wooden Crucifix by Andrea Ferrucci from Fiesole, and a later funerary monument by Girolamo Ticciati. The second chapel has a painted altarpiece by Ignazio Hugford. The chapel opposite the Capponi Chapel has a fresco of the *Miracle of Santa Maria della Neve* by Bernardino Poccetti and a vault fresco by Tommaso Gherardini.

The pretty sacristy off the right transept (unlocked on request), in the style of Brunelleschi, has 14th-century works including a polyptych of the *Madonna and Child with Saints* by Taddeo Gaddi, in its original frame; a Crucifix and two detached frescoes. The lovely polychrome terracotta half-figure of the *Madonna and Child* is attributed to Luca della Robbia or his *bottega*. The chapter house (sometimes unlocked on request) has a fresco of the *Crucifixion* signed and dated 1387–88 by Niccolò di Pietro Gerini.

MANNERISM & PONTORMO'S 'DEPOSITION'

The term 'Mannerism' denotes the deliberate and cultivated stylization of human and architectural forms which characterises much of the art produced in Italy in the 16th century, and most especially in Florence. That stylization consisted in a variety of effects: the elongation of figures; the etiolation of face and flesh; a tendency to kaleidoscopic colour in drapery; the use of architectural elements to perform functions often contrary to their traditional purpose; and the construction of expressive, but often wholly artificial, poses for groups of figures. In this way Mannerism is a rejection of the restraint and naturalism of classical style: the emphasis is noticeably more on virtuosity, both formal and technical, with the artist holding our attention as performer and entertainer. The great Mannerist artists in Florence—Pontormo and Rosso Fiorentino—turned their backs on the desire to give the illusion of reality which had so dominated early and high Renaissance art, in order to create instead images and effects of formalised elegance, capable nonetheless of conveying intense feeling.

Pontormo's *Deposition* in the Capponi Chapel of Santa Felicita is a superb example of Mannerist painting. Three things may immediately be observed: the colour is no longer achieved through careful naturalism and unifying tones, but by an unreal and startling brilliance of contrasts; the mutilation and the heaviness of the dead body—so central to the pathos evoked by earlier representations of this scene—is here transformed into an airy weightlessness of great beauty but almost total unphysicality; and the figures do not seem to inhabit the three-dimensional space which would have been so painstakingly created around them by a Filippo Lippi or a Piero della Francesca, but to float instead on the surface with no immediately logical relation one to another. The breach with naturalism intensifies the scene's spirituality and the picture's theatrical effect.   N.McG.

VIA DE' BARDI

The winding Via de' Bardi (*map p. 399, D4*) is named after the palaces of the Bardi, one of the richest mercantile families in medieval Florence, though they were bankrupt by 1340. At the foot of Ponte Vecchio, the street passes beneath the Corridoio Vasariano and then, beyond the archway where the old Costa dei Magnoli runs uphill to Costa San Giorgio, it becomes a well preserved narrow medieval street of noble town houses. The Capponi family (whose chapel is in Santa Felicita) own three palaces in a row (with their gardens across the street): Palazzo Capponi delle Rovinate, Palazzo Larioni dei Bardi and Palazzo Canigiani. **Palazzo Capponi delle Rovinate** (no. 36) was built for the banker and ambassador Niccolò da Uzzano in the early 15th century, and on his death it went to his daughter's husband's family, the Capponi, who have lived here ever since. It retains its handsome rough stone façade and its original studded wooden doors. The property originally extended as far as the Arno: when Giuseppe Poggi constructed the Lungarno Torrigiani after 1872, he supplied the palace with a rear façade. The Capponi family archives and art collection survive here in rooms splendidly decorated in the 18th and and 19th centuries (*admission by appointment*). The Renaissance courtyard was altered in the 18th century when copies of the busts were made.

The family chapel has a *Madonna and Child* (1524–28; partially repainted) by Pontormo. The paintings include works by Suttermans, Pontormo (*St Jerome*), and five seascapes and landscapes by Salvatore Rosa. There is also a contemporary copy of a work by Andrea del Sarto. The sculpture includes a Roman porphyry lion (on the stairs) and a terracotta relief model of the *Stoning of St Stephen* probably by Ferdinando Tacca.

Next door is **Palazzo Larioni dei Bardi** (no. 30) which has a courtyard begun by Michelozzo and perhaps completed by Benedetto da Maiano. The third palace, **Palazzo Canigiani** (no. 28) has a Neoclassical façade. The English scholar of Florentine Renaissance sculpture John Pope Hennessy (1913–94) lived here at the end of his life. He was made an honorary citizen of Florence.

At no. 24 is the little church of **Santa Lucia dei Magnoli** (*open only for evensong*). The glazed terracotta lunette over the door is by Benedetto Buglioni. Inside on the first altar on the left is a beautiful painting of St Lucy, one of the few works in Florence by the great Sienese artist Pietro Lorenzetti (and the only one still in a Florentine church). A photographic reproduction of the famous altarpiece painted for this church by Domenico Veneziano (now in the Uffizi, *see p. 91*) has been placed on the entrance wall; the predella was divided up between various museums outside Italy.

Opposite the church, an attractive old road called the Costa Scarpuccia climbs the hill between gardens to Costa San Giorgio. Via de' Bardi ends in Piazza dei Mozzi, where, on the bend, are the fine old **Palazzi dei Mozzi**, which were built in the 13th–14th centuries and are among the most noble private houses of medieval Florence. The severe façades in *pietra forte* have arches on the ground floor. The Mozzi were one of the richest Florentine families in the 13th century but, like the Bardi, they too lost most of their wealth in the 14th century. Gregory X was their guest here in 1273, when he came to Florence to arrange a peace between the Guelphs and Ghibellines. The huge garden which stretches right up to the walls at the top of the hill was acquired by the Mozzi in the 16th century. The building, garden and Villa Bardini were left indirectly to the state in 1965 by Ugo Bardini, together with a vast collection of decorative arts, including marble architectural fragments recovered during the demolition of the old centre of the city. There are long-term plans to open a museum here, which will probably be called the Galleria di Palazzo Mozzi-Bardini and to make the garden public.

The piazza opens out onto the Arno with, at no. 1, the **Museo Bardini**. (*At the time of writing the museum was due to reopen after restoration. T: 055 234 2427.*) Ugo Bardini, antiquarian and collector, amassed an enormous, eclectic hoard of artworks from which he was able to supply museums all over the world, including the Louvre, the National Gallery of Washington and the Hermitage. He built many of the rooms in this museum especially to contain fine doorways, staircases and ceilings from demolished buildings. The rooms in turn are crowded with a miscellany of works, which include architectural fragments, sculpture, paintings, chimneypieces, carpets, furniture, inlaid stalls, bronze medals, plaques and statuettes, majolica, arms and armour and musical instruments. Highlights include a statue of *Charity* attributed to Tino da Camaino and an altarpiece of the *Madonna and Child with Angels* in enamelled terracotta, thought to be an early work by Andrea della Robbia or his *bottega*.

PONTE ALLE GRAZIE & PORTA SAN NICCOLÒ

Ponte alle Grazie was first built in 1237 and called Ponte Rubaconte (mentioned by Dante), after an illustrious *podestà* of the city. Its present name is taken from an oratory that was formerly on the bridge. After its destruction in 1944, the bridge was redesigned and the present structure is unfortunately of little distinction.

Via de' Bardi is continued on the other side of Piazza dei Mozzi by Via di San Niccolò, a narrow street of medieval houses. Palazzo Alemanni (no. 68) is decorated with a row of little demons, copies from Giambologna.

The important church of San Niccolò sopr'Arno stands here (*described on pp. 320–21*). Via San Niccolò continues past simple houses with workshops on the ground floor, to the massive **Porta San Niccolò**, with a high tower, built around 1340. From here a ramp leads up the hill towards San Miniato (*see p. 282*). A 9m-high monument to Galileo was set up here in 1997, donated to the city by the sculptor Giò Pomodoro—its size caused consternation to many.

Lungarno Serristori takes you back to Ponte alle Grazie. At no. 25 the Austrian lyric poet Rainer Maria Rilke stayed in 1898: 'At the Lungarno Serristori, not far from the Ponte alle Grazie, stands the house whose flat roof—both its closed-in part and its part wide-open to the sky—is mine' (*The Florence Diary*). It overlooks a small public garden with a pavilion and a monument to Nicola Demidoff (1773–1828), who made his fortune in Siberian mines, and moved to Florence from Paris in 1820. He took up residence here in **Palazzo Serristori** where he founded a school (the palace dates from 1515, but was given a river front in 1873). The monument was commissioned from Lorenzo Bartolini by Nicola's sons Paolo and Anatolio in 1830 and includes four allegorical figures of *Art*, *Charity*, *Truth* and *Siberia*.

WALK SEVEN

ALONG THE NORTH BANK OF THE ARNO

From the north end of Ponte Vecchio **Lungarno Acciaiuoli** follows the Arno with a good view of the bridge and its shops built out above the river. In a group of old houses overhanging the opposite bank, the little tower and river gate belonging to the church of San Jacopo sopr'Arno can be seen. Narrow alleyways connect the Lungarno with **Borgo Santi Apostoli**, a Roman road which led from outside the south gate of the city to the Via Cassia, the ancient road for Rome.

In the attractive little Piazza del Limbo, well below the level of the pavement, is the Romanesque stone façade of the parish church of **Santi Apostoli**, one of the oldest in the city (mentioned as early as 1075). According to legend (and the copy of the ancient inscription on the façade), it was founded by Charlemagne in 786, but in fact it probably dates from the 10th century, when it was built partly on the remains of a Roman building. It was restored in 1938. The east end and campanile, the upper part of which is attributed to Baccio d'Agnolo, can be seen from the piazza behind. The basilican interior (*open 10–12 & 3–5*), probably dating from the 11th century, has fine green

marble columns and capitals (the first two are from Roman baths). It contains three 16th-century funerary monuments to members of the distinguished Altoviti family, who lived in the parish and were benefactors of the church. At the end of the north aisle is the tomb of Prior Oddo Altoviti, by Benedetto da Rovezzano (with a classical sarcophagus); Benedetto probably also built the prior's palace for him which survives in the piazza outside (at no. 1), as well as the stoup in the nave and the handsome doorway of the church itself. In the apse Antonio Altoviti, archbishop of Florence, is commemorated in a monument by Giovanni Antonio Dosio, and two busts above the side doors by Giambattista Caccini show Antonio in pride of place beside Charlemagne. Over the Sacristy door the tomb of Bindo Altoviti has an allegorical figure of *Charity* by the workshop of Bartolomeo Ammannati.

The tabernacle of the Sacrament (1512) is by Andrea della Robbia (and assistants): below are two beautiful sculpted panels from the tomb of Donato Acciaioli (1333), member of another well-known family who resided in this area and were also patrons of the church. The high altarpiece is a beautiful late-14th-century Gothic polyptych of the *Madonna Enthroned with Saints and Angels*, complete with its predella. It has had various attributions but is now considered the work of Jacopo di Cione with the help of Niccolò di Pietro Gerini. Together with many works of art in this church it was severely damaged in the Arno flood of 1966, but is now restored.

In the north aisle there is a sinopia of the fresco of the *Madonna and Child*, formerly on the façade, by Paolo Schiavo (an early-15th-century fresco painter about whom little is known apart from the fact that he is traditionally supposed to have been Andrea del Castagno's master), and 16th-century altarpieces by Maso di San Friano (*Nativity*) and Giorgio Vasari (*Immaculate Conception*).

In the piazza, where an old lane leads out to the Arno, **Palazzo Rosselli del Turco** has various inscriptions and a relief of the Madonna by Benedetto da Maiano. The main façade in the Borgo is by Baccio d'Agnolo (1517) where the entrance faces a charming little garden, created in 1534. The 14th-century Palazzi Acciaioli at no. 8 preserves its tower, bearing the emblem of the Certosa del Galluzzo, which was founded by Niccolò Acciaioli (1340–65). Part of the building at no. 27 (red) Borgo Santi Apostoli dates from the 13th century, as does **Palazzo Usimbardi** (Acciaioli) at no. 19 (red), whose main 16th-century façade on the Arno was destroyed in the Second World War. In the 19th century, when it was the Grand Hotel Royal, Ruskin, Dickens, Swinburne, Longfellow and

Henry James all stayed here. The original masonry of the Buondelmonti palaces next door has been destroyed except for a 14th-century rusticated ground floor and a few stone arches; no. 6 is the oldest residence of this Florentine family to have survived; the remainder of the street was badly damaged in the war.

After Ponte Santa Trìnita (*see box*), the Lungarno continues as Lungarno Corsini. Here the **British Consulate** occupies Palazzo Masetti (Castelbarco) where Louisa, Countess of Albany, widow of Prince Charles Edward Stuart, the Young Pretender (*see p. 178*), lived from 1793 until her death in 1824. Her salon was frequented by Chateaubriand, Shelley, Byron, Foscolo and Von Platen. The dramatist Alfieri, her second husband, died here in 1803. The Countess was later joined here by François-Xavier Fabre, the French painter. She is buried in Santa Croce.

The Lungarno here is dominated by the huge **Palazzo Corsini**, in grandiose Roman Baroque style, and very different from other Florentine town houses of this period. It was begun in 1656 by Alfonso Parigi the Younger and Ferdinando Tacca, and continued (after 1685) by Antonio Ferri (perhaps to a design by Pier Francesco Silvani). It was not completed until around 1737. The façade is crowned by statues and has a terrace overlooking the river. In autumn it hosts a biennial antiques fair (odd years: 2005, 2007), one of the best-known and oldest such events in Italy, known as the Mostra Mercato Internazionale dell'Antiquariato (it has been held at this venue only since 1997).

PONTE SANTA TRÌNITA

A bridge has spanned the Arno on this site since 1252, though the present Ponte Sante Trìnita dates only from 1957. It is an exact replica of the bridge commissioned from Ammannati by Cosimo I. Ammannati worked for the Medici on Palazzo Pitti and the Boboli Gardens. This graceful bridge (1567) linking the Medici residence with the centre of the city is his masterpiece, and the finest of all the bridges across the Arno—it is probable that Ammannati submitted his project to Michelangelo for approval. The bridge was destroyed in 1944, when it was mined by the retreating German army. The replacement was financed by public subscription from a committee presided over by Bernard Berenson, and built under the careful direction of the architect Riccardo Gizdulich and engineer Emilio Brizzi in 1955–57. Most of the original decorative details and the four statues from the parapet were salvaged from the bed of the river. The high flat arches, known as catenaries (from the Latin *catena*, chain), which span the river recreate the unique curve of a chain suspended from two terminal points. The arches of Santa Trìnita are perfectly proportioned and provide a magnificent view of the city. The statues of the Four Seasons were set up on the parapet for the marriage of Cosimo II; *Spring* (on the corner of Lungarno Acciaiuoli), is the best work of Pietro Francavilla (1593; its head, for long thought to have been lost in the War, was dredged up from the Arno in 1961).

The palace contains the **Galleria Corsini**, the most important private art collection in Florence (*admission by appointment only at 11 Via del Parione; T: 055 218 994*). In the left wing is an ingenious spiral staircase by Pier Francesco Silvani. The monumental staircase in the other wing by Antonio Ferri leads up to the piano nobile and the splendid Salone del Trono designed by Ferri with statues and busts and two huge wood chandeliers made for the room. The fresco of the *Apotheosis of the Corsini Family* is by Antonio Domenico Gabbiani. The collection, formed in the 17th century by Marchese Bartolommeo Corsini and his son Filippo, is arranged in six rooms frescoed in 1692–1700 by Alessandro Gherardini and Antonio Domenico Gabbiani. The paintings are representative of the 17th-century Florentine school and are displayed in magnificent frames. Artists include Carlo Maratta (*Portrait of Filippo di Bartolomeo Corsini*); Luca Giordano (*bozzetto* for the vault fresco in the Cappella Corsini in the Carmine); Carlo Dolci; Suttermans (portrait of his friend Pietro Fevre, who was tapestry-maker to the Medici, and the first of many portraits of court officials in Florence by this Flemish painter); Domenico Fetti, and Giacinto Gimignani. Earlier works include a tondo of the *Madonna* by Luca Signorelli and his *bottega*; a Crucifix by Giovanni Bellini; *Madonna and Child with the Young St John* by Pontormo; a tondo of the *Madonna and Angels* by Botticelli (or his *bottega*); five allegorical figures, thought to be early works by Filippino Lippi; *Portrait of a Man* by Ridolfo del Ghirlandaio; and the cartoon of Raphael's *Portrait of Julius II*. The marble bust of Lorenzo Corsini, who became pope Clement XII in 1730, is by Edmé Bouchardon, who was at work in Rome at that time, and was considered the most important French sculptor of his day. The porcelain *Deposition* was made in the Doccia factory (just outside Florence) around 1752 to a design by Massimiliano Soldani Benzi.

The present residence of the Corsini family is fairly close by in **Palazzo Corsini sul Prato**. It was begun in 1591–94 by Buontalenti, and was acquired in 1621 by Filippo di Lorenzo Corsini who employed Gherardo Silvani to complete the palace and garden. The Young Pretender stayed as a guest here in 1774–77. It has a fine garden, beautifully maintained, with interesting statuary and parterres which can be seen on request (*Mon–Sat 9–1 & 2–5. Entrance at no. 58 Via il Prato*).

Ponte alla Carraia was the second bridge to be built over the Arno after Ponte Vecchio. Constructed in wood on stone piles in 1218–20, it was first called Ponte Nuovo. It was reconstructed after floods in 1269 and 1333; the 14th-century bridge may have been designed by Giotto. In 1559 it was repaired by Ammannati and then enlarged in 1867; it was replaced by a new bridge (a copy of the original) after it was blown up in 1944. From the foot of the bridge, there is a view looking southeast to the campanile of Santo Spirito, with the Forte di Belvedere and the bell-tower of San Miniato on the skyline.

THE CASCINE

The Lungarno Vespucci was opened in the 19th century: it leads downstream from Ponte alla Carraia, past the American Consulate, which has been here since 1949 (although Florence has had an American Consul since 1825). Beyond the end of the Lungarno begins the huge park of the Cascine, which lines the right bank of the river for over three kilometres. The Cascine is the largest public park in Florence (160 hectares), although only a few hundred metres wide, with fine woods. During the day it is used as a recreation ground by Florentines, old and young, and huge public concerts and festivals are held here in summer. Not as well maintained as it might be, it is unenclosed and it is not advisable to visit the park at night. A big general market (excellent value) is held here on Tuesdays and the Festa del Grillo (*see p. 364*) on Ascension Day.

The park has its origins in the lands of a dairy-farm (*cascina*) that were acquired by Duke Alessandro de' Medici; it was later enlarged by Cosimo I. It was used as a ducal chase in the 17th century, and public spectacles and festivals were held here under Grand Duke Peter Leopold in the 18th century. The grounds were planned as a huge park by Napoleon's sister Elisa Baciocchi, whom Napoleon made Grand Duchess of Tuscany in 1809, and first opened regularly to the public c. 1811. Orchards and vegetable gardens used to be cultivated on the fertile, well-watered land in the first part of the park, and, beyond the present Piazzale delle Cascine, there were woods where deer were hunted.

The broad walk along the Arno, Viale Abramo Lincoln, is the most pleasant area in the park. On Viale degli Olmi is the Narcissus Fountain, on which a plaque (1954) commemorates the composition of Shelley's *Ode to the West Wind*, which was 'conceived and chiefly written' here in 1819. In the central Piazzale delle Cascine is the Palazzina Reale (the seat of the faculty of Agriculture of Florence University since 1914) which was built in 1785. Since 1997 the 12 horses and carriages which serve as horse-cabs for tourists have had their stables near here. In Piazzale John Fitzgerald Kennedy, near the footbridge which leads over the Arno, is a plain marble stele set up in 1982 in memory of the Allied soldiers who lost their lives in Europe during the Second World War. Nearby is a monument to George Washington donated by American residents in Florence in 1932 (the marble bust is a replica of the famous portrait of the President made around 1786 by Jean-Antoine Houdon). At the extreme far end of the park a very well preserved little pavilion with good ironwork, known to Florentines as the *Monumento dell'Indiano* commemorates Rajaram Chuttraputti, the Maharajah of Kolhapur who died in Florence in 1870 at the age of 20 on his return from England to India and was cremated here at the confluence of the Arno and Mugnone rivers. At this point the view is dominated by a suspension bridge built over the Arno in 1978.

THE OLTRARNO

The south bank of the Arno is known as the Oltrarno (meaning 'beyond the Arno'), a district away from the heart of the city and so generally more peaceful. Its centre is the delightful little Piazza Santo Spirito which has a fountain and a few trees, a little daily market and some pleasant cafés. The square is surrounded with modest houses except for Palazzo Guadagni (no. 10), probably built by Cronaca c. 1505. Its pleasing, well-proportioned façade with a top-floor loggia became the model for many 16th-century Florentine mansions. Borgo Tegolaio, which leads out of one corner of the piazza, is a medieval street which takes its name from the *tegola* kilns (a *tegola* is a roofing tile) which were once here. In Via delle Caldaie the wool-dyers had their workshops. Numerous artisans' workshops—cabinet makers, restorers, gilders, frame-makers—are still to be found in the vicinity, and give this area a character all of its own.

SANTO SPIRITO
Map p. 398, B4

The modest 18th-century façade of the church of Santo Spirito fronts the square. On the left is the rough stone wall of the convent's refectory and behind rises a familiar feature of the Florence skyline, Baccio d'Agnolo's slender campanile (1503). Santo Spirito is an early Augustinian foundation, dating from 1250, just six years after Pope Innocent IV had commanded Tuscan hermits to adopt the rule of St Augustine, a rule which the Dominicans also accepted. The first church was begun in 1292, and by the end of the 14th century, the convent had become a centre of intellectual life in the city, with an extremely important library. In 1428 Brunelleschi was commissioned to design a new church, the project for which he had completed by 1434–35. However, building was not begun until 1444, just two years before the great architect's death. Construction continued for most of the 15th century, first under the direction of his collaborator Antonio Manetti. It is surprising that the names of the other artists involved are unknown considering that this is such a beautiful and important building.

The Interior

Open 10–12 & 4–6 except Weds afternoon.

The interior is a superb creation of the Renaissance, remarkable for its harmonious proportions, its solemn colour, and the perspective of the colonnades and vaulted aisles, but it also points the way forward to the more elaborate and less delicate 16th-century style of architecture. The plan is a Latin cross, with a dome over the crossing. The colonnade has 35 columns in *pietra forte* (including the four piers of the dome) with fine Corinthian capitals and imposts above. It continues around the transepts and east end to form an unbroken arcade.

The elaborate high altar (1599–1607) has a *pietre dure* ciborium and statues by Giovanni Battista Caccini (an important artist of the period) beneath a high baldacchino. It replaces a simpler altar designed by Brunelleschi, and despite being a fine Baroque work in itself, it disturbs the overall harmony of the interior. The cupola of the church was completed by Salvi d'Andrea, who also designed the handsome interior façade in the 1480s. The stained glass oculus is from a cartoon by Perugino. Some of the loveliest painted altarpieces, commissioned by various Florentine families for their chapels in the semi-circular niches around the walls, are described below.

Tour of the church

A The *Martyrdom of St Stephen* is one of Passignano's best works, dating from the early 17th century. The artist left many altarpieces and frescoes all over the region.

B The *Madonna del Soccorso* is a 15th-century painting whose author has recently been rescued from anonymity and recognised as the Master of the Johnson Nativity. The story told is that of a mother threatening her child who has been misbehaving with the devil at which, to her consternation, the devil in fact appears. The child is shown being succoured (hence, 'soccorso') by the Madonna, who is depicted towering above the mother, child and devil

SANTO SPIRITO

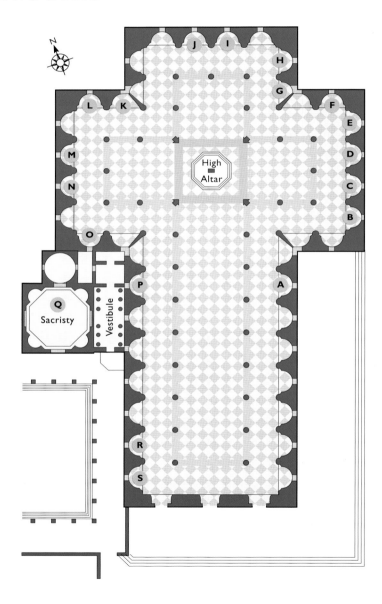

wielding a stick, but she is still a beautifully composed, elegantly-dressed figure. The scene takes place in a court with a colourful pavement and marble walls above which can be seen a row of stylized trees (typical of the backgrounds of numerous Florentine paintings and frescoes).

C The polychrome marble niche (1601) is by Bernardo Buontalenti, one of the most skilled of the Florentine Mannerist artists. It encloses a 14th-century wooden Crucifix from the earlier church.

D The altarpiece of the *Madonna and Child with the Young St John, Saints and Donors*—the donors are Tanai and Nanna (Capponi) dei Nerli—is one of the best and most mature works of Filippino Lippi, executed sometime after 1494. In the background is an interesting early view of Florence, showing Tanai in a red cloak, taking leave of his family in front of Palazzo dei Nerli near Porta San Frediano (also in the Oltrarno) before setting out on a journey. There are numerous classical elements in the altarpiece, and the 'dialogue' between the Young St John and the Christ Child is an interesting detail which was to be developed by later painters such as Leonardo da Vinci. The splendid original frame was also designed by Filippino.

E The original painting of the *Vision of St Bernard* by Perugino (now in Munich) was replaced in 1656 by a beautiful (and almost indistinguishable) copy by Felice Ficherelli. In past centuries this was often an accepted practice when a family wished to enjoy for

themselves an important painting they had commissioned, and Ficherelli was known above all as a copyist.

F The *Marriage of the Virgin* is the best work by the early 18th-century Florentine artist Giovanni Camillo Sagrestani. The sarcophagus of Neri Capponi, who was one of the early benefactors of the church and who died in 1457, is by the *bottega* of Bernardo Rossellino and it was the only tomb that was allowed inside the church.

G The *Madonna and Saints*, in a beautiful contemporary frame, is a good painting in the style of Lorenzo di Credi by an unknown artist, named after this work as the Maestro della Conversazione di Santo Spirito.

H The polyptych of the *Madonna and Child with Saints*, the earliest painting in the church (c. 1340), is by Maso di Banco, one of the most interesting followers of Giotto.

I The Pitti family chapel, which belonged to Luca Pitti from 1458, still contains the altarpiece of *Martyred Saints* commissioned by the family from the best known artist of the day, Alessandro Allori (1574). It is remarkable for its figure studies of the male nude, and incorporates a portrait of Allori's patron, Cosimo I, in the centre. The predella is especially interesting for the view of Palazzo Pitti before it was enlarged, with its owner Luca Pitti standing outside (in a red hat). The original 15th-century altar frontal with a painting of St Luke by Neri di Bicci survives, one of a number still *in situ* in the church.

J This chapel preserves its original little 15th-century stained glass tondo and altar frontal, but the splendid altarpiece of *Christ and the Adulteress* is another very fine work. Signed and dated 1577 by Alessandro Allori, it foreshadows the 17th century. The beautiful figure of the adulteress is particularly striking.

K The *Madonna Enthroned Between Saints John the Evangelist and Bartholomew* is attributed to the *bottega* of the Mazziere brothers (late 15th century). Formerly known as the Master of Santo Spirito, these artists are at present only known for their work in this church.

L Altarpiece of *St Monica*, the mother of St Augustine, with Augustinian nuns, traditionally attributed to the minor artist Francesco Botticini, is now thought by many scholars to be the work of his famous contemporary Verrocchio, whose *bottega* included the young Leonardo da Vinci. It is a very unusual and beautifully composed painting in muted tones with the striking dark habits of the nuns exquisitely painted. The two circles of nuns include intense character studies.

M The Cappella Corbinelli has a beautiful altarpiece sculpted by Andrea Sansovino, with statues of St Matthew and St James above a carved predella with reliefs of scenes from their lives and a *Last Supper*. The altar frontal has a carved *Pietà*, and above the statues are two *tondi* of the *Annunciation*, and in the lunette above, the *Coronation of the Virgin*. The Classical pilasters bear reliefs of the symbols of the Passion. After 1502, Sansovino completed the decoration of the chapel by adding the side panels in marble. This was the only chapel in the church in which a sculptured rather than painted altarpiece was allowed, since it was used for the Holy Sacrament. The balustrade dates from the 17th century.

N The particularly fine *Trinity with Saints Mary Magdalen and Catherine* is attributed to the Mazziere brothers, as is the *Trinity* in the next chapel.

O The Segni Chapel has a beautiful *Madonna Enthroned with Saints* by Raffaelino del Garbo (1505), the only one of four altarpieces commissioned from him for this church which has remained here. The altar frontal is attributed to the *bottega* of the Mazziere brothers.

P A copy by Francesco Petrucci of the *Pala Dei* by Rosso Fiorentino, which was commissioned by Crown Prince Ferdinando in 1691 when he removed the original to Palazzo Pitti. The copy is particularly interesting since it shows the original dimensions of the altarpiece (it was enlarged when it was hung in the Pitti).

Q A door beneath the organ leads into a grandiose vestibule with 12 Corinthian columns supporting an elaborately coffered barrel vault, built in *pietra serena* by Cronaca in 1491 to a design by Giuliano da Sangallo. The decoration includes the Medici coat of arms and doves, and *tondi* with mythological scenes which are copies of the antique gems owned by Lorenzo the Magnificent. The adjoining sacristy is an octagonal chamber inspired by the

architectural works of Brunelleschi; it has Corinthian pilasters with delicately carved capitals also designed by Sangallo (1489), beneath a lantern and dome. After its restoration in 2000, a Crucifix attributed to Michelangelo in painted poplar wood, found in Santo Spirito in 1963, has been displayed here. It is known that the prior of the convent allowed Michelangelo to study anatomy here in the early 1490s. Documents also confirm that Michelangelo made a Crucifix for the Augustinians for the high altar of this church, which was thought to have been lost. Many scholars believe this is that Crucifix, but others attribute it to Taddeo Curradi (mid-16th century). Exquisitely carved, it shows the slight figure of Christ in an unusual *contrapposto* position, a design subsequently much copied.

R In this chapel there is a 1579 copy of a statue of the *Risen Christ* by Michelangelo in the church of the Minerva in Rome (in the opposite chapel can be seen a free copy of the artist's more famous *Pietà* in St Peter's, made around the same time).

S The *Resurrection* is one of three works in the church by Pier Francesco di Jacopo Foschi, a little-known 16th-century painter whose work deserves greater study. His *Immaculate Conception* is in the chapel immediately opposite and his *Transfiguration* is in the south transept.

The second cloister is a beautiful work by Bartolomeo Ammannati (c. 1565): its unusual design incorporates a portico of three arches in the centre of each side. It is now part of a military barracks, but the cloister and chapel are usually open to the public on a few days every year. Off the cloister is the Cappella Corsini with tombs—dating from the Gothic to the Baroque period—of various members of this famous Florentine family, many of whom held high ecclesiastical office, including Lorenzo, who became Pope Clement XII: his tomb bears his bust by Gherardo Silvani (1731).

The refectory

Open 10.30–1 except Mon; T: 055 287 043. Entrance to the left of the church, at no. 29.
The refectory is the only part of the 14th-century convent to survive. Above a fresco of the *Last Supper* (almost totally ruined) is a huge *Crucifixion* (also damaged), both of them painted c. 1360–65. They are attributed to Andrea Orcagna and his *bottega*, which probably included his brother Nardo di Cione. A partial restoration, after years of neglect, revealed one of the most dramatic scenes of the Crucifixion in 14th-century Florentine painting.

The **Fondazione Salvatore Romano** is also displayed here. This collection of sculpture, left to the city by the Neapolitan antiquarian Salvatore Romano in 1946, includes a *Madonna and Child* attributed to Jacopo della Quercia, and a fountain attributed to Ammannati. On the end wall, the two damaged fragments of bas-reliefs showing two Bishop Saints were found in Padua and are thought to be works by Donatello from the church of the Santo. In the centre of the room are an angel and *Virtue* (or a caryatid), both fine statuettes by Tino da Camaino.

SANTA MARIA DEL CARMINE & THE BRANCACCI CHAPEL

Map p. 398, A3–A4

Open 10–5; Tues, Sun and holidays 1–5. Entrance through the cloisters. There is a combined ticket with Palazzo Vecchio. Visitors should book in advance (T: 055 276 8558) but if you are on your own you can often go straight in. Only 30 people are allowed in at a time.

The church of Santa Maria del Carmine (which was never given a façade) is famous for its frescoes by Masaccio in the Brancacci Chapel. A Carmelite convent was founded here in 1250 and the first church begun in 1268.

MASACCIO & THE BRANCACCI CHAPEL

The frescoes of the *Life of St Peter* were commissioned by Felice Brancacci, a rich Florentine silk merchant and statesman, c. 1424. The design of the whole cycle may be Masolino's, and he worked on the frescoes together with his pupil Masaccio. Masaccio seems to have assumed full responsibility for the frescoes after Masolino departed for Rome in 1428. Later that year Masaccio himself broke off work abruptly for an unknown reason, and left for Rome, where, by the end of the year he was dead, aged only 27. Brancacci was exiled from Florence in 1436 as an enemy of the Medici, and the cycle was only completed some 50 years later by Filippino Lippi (c. 1480–85), who carefully integrated his style with that of Masaccio, possibly following an earlier design. This is a moving example of how subtly Renaissance artists were able to 'complete' earlier works of art. In 1690, the chapel was saved from demolition through the efforts of the Accademia del Disegno and Vittoria della Rovere, mother of Cosimo III. In the 18th century the church was devastated by fire, and the lunettes and vault of the chapel, probably frescoed by Masolino, were destroyed.

The frescoes by Masaccio were at once recognized as a masterpiece, and profoundly influenced the Florentine Renaissance. All the major artists of the 15th century came here to study the frescoes, which combine a perfect application of the new rules of perspective with a remarkable use of chiaroscuro. 'Masaccio ... like Giotto a century earlier ... (was) a great master of the significant, ... endowed to the highest degree with a sense of tactile values, and with a skill in rendering them. In a career of but a few years he gave to Florentine painting the direction it pursued to the end.' (Bernard Berenson). The frescoes were restored in 1983–89, when it was found that an egg-based substance had been applied to the surface in the late 18th century, causing mould to form and obscuring the colour. Today the superb colouring and details of the landscapes can once again be appreciated.

The frescoes

Upper row

Entrance arch: Masolino, *Temptation of Adam and Eve*.

Right wall: Masolino, *St Peter, Accompanied by St John, Brings Tabitha to Life* and *St Peter Heals a Lame Man* (with a charming view of Florence in the background). The figures on the left and some details in the background may be by the hand of Masaccio.

Right of the altar: Masaccio, *St Peter Baptising*.

Left of the altar: Masolino, *St Peter Preaching*.

Left wall: Masaccio, *The Tribute Money*, perhaps the painter's masterpiece. Three episodes are depicted in the same scene: in the centre, Christ, surrounded by the Apostles, outside the gates of the city is asked by an official (with his back to us) to pay the tribute money owing to the city. Christ indicates a lake to St Peter, and (on the left) Peter is shown extracting the money from the mouth of a fish at the side of a lake. The scene on the right shows Peter handing over the tribute money to the official. The head of Christ has been attributed by some scholars to Masolino.

Entrance arch: Masaccio, *Expulsion of Adam and Eve from Paradise*, one of the most moving works of the Renaissance: it is known to have been painted in just four days, and shows the artist's remarkable skill in depicting the human figure (recalling also classical sculpture). The poignant figures are charged with great emotion.

Lower row

Entrance arch: Filippino Lippi, *Release of St Peter from Prison*.

Right wall: Filippino Lippi, *Saints Peter and Paul Before the Proconsul* and the *Crucifixion of St Peter*.

Right of the altar: Masaccio, *St Peter and St John Distributing Alms*.

Left of the altar: Masaccio, *St Peter, Followed by St John, Healing the Sick with his Shadow*.

Masolino: *Temptation of Adam and Eve.*

Left wall: Masaccio, *St Peter Enthroned with Portraits of Friars*, his last work; the next half of this panel was begun by Masaccio and finished by Filippino. It shows *St Peter Bringing to Life the Emperor's Nephew* (the faces executed by Masaccio are more strongly illuminated; Filippino's figures are, in contrast, flatter and stand as if in shadow).

Entrance arch: Filippino Lippi, *St Peter in Prison Visited by St Paul* (to a design by Masaccio).

During restoration work, fragments of frescoes attributed to Masaccio—including two heads and part of the scene with *St Peter Healing the Sick with His Shadow*—were found behind the 18th-century altar (since removed). The lovely altarpiece, the *Madonna del Carmine*, known as the '*Madonna del Popolo*', is the earliest of the huge *Maestà* painted for churches in the city (*see p. 88*), and one of the very few works of this date not removed to a museum. It was probably made around 1270 for the high altar of the first church, but was already in this chapel by 1460. Once attributed to Coppo di Marcovaldo, it is now thought to be by the anonymous Master of Sant'Agata.

The church and convent

Church open 9–12 & 4.30–6. The rooms off the cloister can also be seen by appointment on Mon and Sat.

There are interesting frescoes detached from the cloister buildings from various periods between the 14th- and the late 16th centuries (by Giovanni da Milano, Starnina, Alessandro Allori and Filippo Lippi). Lippi, despite the fact he was a friar, was the father of Filippino, who worked in the Cappella Brancacci, and was one of the most famous Florentine painters of the Renaissance—a rare example of both father and son excelling as major artists of their day. Filippo is immortalized in a poem by Browning, who lived near the Carmine at Casa Guidi (*see p. 279*). The poem takes the form of a monologue in which the jovial artist admits his lack of vocation but explains how the convent gave him the opportunity to observe human nature and human physiognomy which served him so well as a painter. His patter evidently wins the favour of the night watchmen who catch him revelling late at night in the streets (which since the early 14th century had been illuminated by lanterns). Filippo was born in 1406, close to the church in Via dell'Ardiglione, the little street to the left of the façade (worth exploring to see the simple house, just beyond the archway, which bears a plaque). In the second refectory, known as the Sala Vanni, is the *Supper in the House of the Pharisee* by Francesco Vanni.

The huge wide interior of the church was rebuilt in an undistinguished late Baroque style in 1782. The best thing in it is the sumptuous Chapel of Sant'Andrea Corsini, commissioned in 1675–83 by Bartolomeo and Neri Corsini from Pier Francesco Silvani in honour of their ancestor Andrea Corsini, who died in 1374 and was canonised in 1629. It is one of the most important Baroque works in Florence, with a ceiling by Luca Giordano (1682) and marble and silver reliefs by Giovanni Battista Foggini.

Another wing of this huge convent can be seen in Via della Chiesa (off Via de Serragli), formerly used by the Albergo Popolare (no. 68), built in 1930 as a hospice for the poor (and, with 125 beds, still used to house those in need).

SAN FREDIANO

Borgo San Frediano gives its name to a district typical of this part of the city, with numerous artisans' houses and workshops. At its far end is **Porta San Frediano** (*map p. 398, A3*). This gate, and the adjoining stretch of wall with crenellations, which runs from the Torrino di Santa Rosa on the banks of the Arno, is the best-preserved part of the last circle of medieval walls built by the Comune in 1284–1333. The gate and its high tower, built in 1324 (perhaps by Andrea Pisano), protected the road to Pisa. It preserves interesting ironwork, and its huge wooden doors, decorated with nail heads, with their old locks. The city's emblem—an iris—is carved in stone high up on the tower. At no. 4 Via Lorenzo Bartolini is the **Antico Setificio Fiorentino**, a silk weaving factory which was moved here in 1786. Twelve artisans still use the 17th- and 18th-century hand looms and late-19th-century machinery to produce exquisite silk fabrics which are hand-dyed and woven to traditional designs. There is a show-room (*open Mon–Fri 9–1 & 2–5*) but the factory itself can only be visited once a year (usually on the last weekend in November).

Borgo San Frediano itself passes the bare stone exterior of the large church of **San Frediano in Cestello**, which has a rough-hewn façade facing the Arno. The church was rebuilt in 1680–89 by Antonio Maria Ferri, and its fine dome is a conspicuous feature of this part of the city. Inside, all six side chapels have good frescoed decoration in the domes, spandrels and lunettes, carried out at the end of the 17th and the beginning of the 18th centuries by Florentine painters (including Giovanni Camillo Sagrestani, Matteo Bonechi, Alessandro Gherardini, Antonio Domenico Gabbiani, Pier Dandini and Antonio Franchi) who also executed the altarpieces. The church also preserves a polychrome wooden statue of the *Madonna and Child* by the 14th-century Pisan or Florentine school.

In Piazza del Cestello is the Granaio di Cosimo III, a grain store designed in 1695 by Giovanni Battista Foggini and now used as a barracks. From the piazza, there is a view across the river of Ognissanti and its bell-tower, with the campanile of Santa Maria Novella behind. The diagonal stone dyke in the Arno here was built to serve the watermills on the river.

Via Santo Spirito (*map p. 398, B3*), has a number of interesting palaces, including Palazzo Manetti (no. 23) which has a 15th-century façade. This was the home of Sir Horace Mann in 1740–86, while serving as English envoy to the Tuscan court. His famous correspondence with Horace Walpole provides a remarkable picture of 18th-century Florence. In 1740 Walpole stayed nearby at Mann's guest-house, the Casa Ambrogi (one of the old houses at the south end of Ponte Vecchio which were destroyed in 1944), together with the poet Thomas Gray during their tour of the Continent.

The stretch of the river between Ponte Santa Trìnita and Ponte Vecchio is the only place where there is no Lungarno, since houses directly front the water. Borgo San Jacopo is an ancient road which led out of the old city. The church of **San Jacopo sopr'Arno** (*open Tues and Thurs 5–6; T: 055 210 139*) is preceded by an old portico of three arches, possibly dating from the 11th century, transported here in 1529 from a demolished church. San Jacopo (which had a river gate) is now used for concerts and exhibitions. In the interior the Romanesque columns were exposed in the 1960s, at a time when the Baroque was not in vogue, and when it was thought important to reveal the oldest parts of the building. Despite this, the Baroque design of 1709 and the painted decoration from the early 18th century have survived.

On the corner of the pretty Via Toscanella is the Torre Marsili di Borgo (no. 17), which has an *Annunciation* from the della Robbia workshop and two angels above the door.

WALK EIGHT

AROUND THE OLTRARNO

When Cosimo I moved his household to Palazzo Pitti in 1549, Florence gained what was in effect a royal residence, and noble families built *palazzi* for themselves nearby. The streets described here still preserves some of this courtly flavour.

From the south end of Ponte alla Carraia, **Via de' Serragli**, a long straight road, first laid out in the 13th century, leads away from the Arno past a number of handsome 17th–18th-century palaces. Beyond the crossroads with Via Santa Monaca it is lined with simple, low medieval houses, in a local shopping area. It crosses Via della Chiesa, in which a house at no. 93 bears a plaque recording the death here of Walter Savage Landor in 1864. He was a famous poet in his day and had lived from 1829 to 1835 in the Villa Gherardesca at San Domenico below Fiesole: his extravagant, opinionated personality made him one of the best known foreign residents in Florence. He returned to live in the centre of Florence at the end of his life, befriended by Robert Browning who lived nearby at the Casa Guidi (*see p. 279*).

Via del Campuccio skirts the garden wall of **Giardino Torrigiani**. This is the biggest private garden in Florence, with fine trees (usually open a few days each year, although a corner of the garden can be seen from the nursery at 146 Via de' Serragli). It was created by Pietro Torrigiani (1773–1848) and encloses a stretch of town walls built by Cosimo I. The fantastic neo-Gothic tower was built by Gaetano Baccani in 1821 as an astronomical observatory. The gardens are decorated with 19th-century sculptures by Pio Fedi, a pupil of Lorenzo Bartolini, whose former studio at no. 99 Via de' Serragli still has sculptures by him outside.

Via de' Serragli ends at Piazza della Calza, named after the Convitto della Calza, with an attractive asymmetrical loggia. The Convitto was first built as a hospital (in 1362), and later became a convent. It was restored in 2000 as a home for retired prelates, a hostel for visiting churchmen and pilgrim groups, and a conference centre. In the refectory there is a *Last Supper* by Franciabigio and on the walls pretty frames with frescoes by 18th-century Florentine artists including Tommaso Gherardini and Giuseppe Zocchi. In another room there is a polychrome stucco bas-relief, a 15th-century copy of Donatello's *Madonna de' Pazzi* and a 15th-century wooden Crucifix.

From the car park in the lane between the 14th-century city walls and the garden wall of Giardino Torrigiani you can go through a small gate in the walls and up the steps to the walkway along the top and into the Porta Romana guard-house over Via Romana.

Porta Romana is a well-preserved gate built in 1328 to a design by Andrea Orcagna. On the inside face, the keystone of the arch is decorated with the iris of Florence, sculpted in marble in 1331 by Giovanni Pisano. In the lunette is a fresco by the Florentine school of the *Madonna and Child Enthroned with Saints* dating from the early 14th century. Outside the gate is an incongruous colossal statue called *Dietro-fronte* ('back to front'; 1981–84), apparently a woman with a stone block on her head, by Michelangelo Pistoletto. He gave it to the Comune and it was set up here in the 1980s, where it has remained, despite the protests of local residents.

From here **Via Romana** leads back down towards the river. On the left is the simple 14th-century church of San Felice, altered in the mid-16th century when it was taken over by the Dominicans. The Renaissance façade and the sanctuary are almost certainly by Michelozzo (1457). In the interior, the first half of the nave contains a closed gallery supported by eight columns and a pretty vault, added as a nuns' choir in the mid-16th century. On

the west wall are early-18th-century funerary monuments. Over the high altar is a large Crucifix, almost certainly by Giotto, which is in very good condition. In the nave are remains of a fresco of the *Pietà* attributed to Niccolò di Pietro Gerini (interesting for its unusual iconography), and a terracotta group of the same subject dating from the early 17th century. There is also an altarpiece by Ridolfo Ghirlandaio, son of Domenico, and a lunette fresco of the *Virgin of the Sacred Girdle* (late 14th-century Florentine). In the chapel to the left of the presbytery is an altarpiece composed of paintings by different hands and of different periods: in the centre the *Madonna and Child* is by Rossello di Jacopo Franchi (early 15th century), while the two saints (by Pier Francesco Foschi), and the *Pietà* (by the Maestro di Serumidio) date from a century later.

On the north side the seventh altar has a fresco by Giovanni da San Giovanni (the angels are by Volterrano) and the sixth altar has a triptych by Neri di Bicci beneath a frescoed lunette of the 14th century. The triptych on the first altar is by a follower of Botticelli (known as the Master of Apollo and Daphne). In the adjoining convent there is a *Last Supper* painted by Matteo Rosselli in 1614.

On Via Romana is Palazzo Torrigiani, built in 1775 by Gaspare Maria Paoletti as a natural history museum, the largest collection of its kind in Italy. It is known as **La Specola** from the astronomical observatory founded here by Grand Duke Peter Leopold. Here, in 1814, Sir Humphrey Davy and Michael Faraday used Galileo's 'great burning glass' to explode the diamond. On the third floor is the **Zoological Museum** (*open 9–1; closed Wed*), with anatomical models in wax (around 1,400 of them), made in 1775–1814 by Clemente Susini and others, and including a life-size figure of a man, '*lo scorticato*'. In the 19th century these were one of the great 'sights' on Florentine tourists' itineraries. The Tribuna di Galileo on the first floor, with elaborate marble and mosaic decorations, was commissioned by Leopold II in 1841.

On the opposite side of Via Romana is the charming little **Oratorio di San Sebastiano 'dei Bini'** (*open Fri, Sat & Sun, 3–6*), with works by Giovanni Biliverti, Baccio d'Agnolo, Pier Francesco Foschi, and others attributed to the early 16th-century Maestro di Serumidio, Baccio da Montelupo, Leonardo del Tasso, and Filippino Lippi.

Via Maggio leads down towards the river. Its name (from Maggiore) is a reminder of its origin as the principal and widest street of the Oltrarno. It was opened soon after Ponte Santa Trìnita was first built in 1252, and it became a fashionable residential street after the grand dukes moved to Palazzo Pitti in the 16th century. It now has numerous elegant antique shops. The palace at no. 8 was built in the 15th century by the Ridolfi and acquired in 1619 by Count Camillo Guidi, secretary of state for the Medici. On the first floor is the **Casa Guidi**, an apartment rented in 1847 by Robert Browning and Elizabeth Barrett Browning after their secret marriage in 1846 (*open April–Nov Mon, Wed, Fri 3–6; T: 055 354 457*). The apartment can be rented for short lets from the Landmark Trust, which is based in the UK (*T: 44 1628 825 925*).

THE BROWNINGS IN FLORENCE

Robert Browning and Elizabeth Barrett Browning lived in the Casa Guidi until Elizabeth's death in 1861 (she is buried in the English Cemetery, *see p. 179*). The living room, dining room and study have been restored as far as possible to their appearance when the Brownings lived here. There is also a good library of works by and relating to the Brownings. The Brownings' son Pen was born here in 1849 and purchased the house after his father's death in 1893. Since 1993 the apartment has been owned by Eton College and is leased to the Landmark Trust.

Both Brownings wrote much of their most important poetry here, including Elizabeth's *Casa Guidi Windows* and *Aurora Leigh*, and Robert's *The Ring and the Book*. Robert's stay here also inspired him to write poems about the Florentine painters Fra Filippo Lippi and Andrea del Sarto, and the statue of Ferdinando I in Piazza Santissima Annunziata (*The Statue and the Bust*). Elizabeth took an active interest in the cause of Italian Independence from Austrian rule. The Brownings were mostly confined to the Casa Guidi because of Elizabeth's delicate health, and visitors from abroad would call on them here.

Bianca Cappello.

Farther on is Palazzo Corsini Suarez (or Commenda di Firenze; no. 42), named after Baldassare Suarez of Portugal who acquired the palace in 1590. It was built in the late 14th century and reconstructed in the 16th, partly by Gherardo Silvani. It is now the seat of the Archivio Contemporaneo Alessandro Bonsanti, a branch of the Vieusseux Library (*see p. 210*), and conserves the papers of the artist and writer Alberto Savinio (1891–1952), the playwright Eduardo de Filippo (1900–84), and the writers Pier Paolo Pasolini (1922–75) and Vasco Pratolini (1913–91). It has a pretty courtyard.

Palazzo Ridolfi (no. 13), built in the late 16th century (attributed to Santi di Tito), stands just beyond Palazzo di Cosimo Ridolfi, a small palace built at the beginning of the 15th century. The numerous narrow old streets on the right lead up to Piazza Pitti.

Opposite is the **Palazzo di Bianca Cappello** (no. 26), with good graffiti decoration attributed to Bernardino Poccetti (c. 1579). The house was built by Grand Duke Francesco I for the beautiful Venetian girl Bianca Cappello, who was first his mistress and then his wife.

Farther down on the left is **St Mark's Anglican church**, in part of the ground floor of Palazzo Machiavelli. It is a Tractarian–Byzantine–Renaissance fantasy created by the Florentine resident John Roddam Stanhope Spencer in 1877–79. The pre-Raphaelite decoration, designed in detail by Spencer, survives virtually intact, including the bronze lamps, stencilled walls and fittings. A chalice incorporates the engagement ring of Holman Hunt's wife, donated to the church following her death in childbirth in 1866 (Stanhope Spencer was a disciple of Holman Hunt), and the treasury and vestments have been carefully preserved. The large painting of *St Michael Archangel* by Giuseppe Catani Chiti, was commissioned by Sir Thomas Dick Lauder (d. 1919) who lived in Florence.

Founded in 1870 by Anglo-Catholic zealots led by the Rev. Charles Tooth, St Mark's is traditionally High Church. The Anglican liturgy is still celebrated here (with traditional Tractarian pomp and splendour) every Sunday morning at 10.30 (*services also at 9am on Sun, 6pm on Thurs, and 8pm on Fri*). The church and palace (the parson's residence) can usually be visited on request in the mornings (*10–12*).

Palazzo Machiavelli (nos 16–18) once belonged to a branch of the great statesman's family. It was divided in two in the 19th century (as the façade shows) but the interior is well preserved, having been bought by the Anglicans in 1877–1905.

FORTE DI BELVEDERE
& SAN MINIATO

San Miniato can be reached directly from Stazione Santa Maria Novella and Porta Romana on bus 12 to a request stop at the foot of the steps (just before Piazzale Michelangelo). It can also be reached by the steps from Porta San Niccolò (map p. 399, F4). If you have time, the following route on foot is highly recommended (bus 13 can then be taken back to Porta Romana and Stazione Santa Maria Novella).

From Piazza dei Rossi (*map p. 397, A4*) the narrow **Costa San Giorgio** winds up the hill towards Forte di Belvedere. At the junction with Costa Scarpuccia (a beautiful road leading downhill to Via de' Bardi) is the church of San Giorgio sulla Costa (or Spirito Santo), used by the Romanian Orthodox community (*open only for a service at 10.30 on Sun*). It has one of the best Baroque interiors in Florence (by Giovanni Battista Foggini; 1705). The altarpieces are by Tommaso Redi, Jacopo Vignali and Passignano, and on the ceiling is the *Glory of St George* by Alessandro Gherardini. The high altar is also by Foggini. The church contains a rare mechanical organ of c. 1570 by Onofrio Zeffirini.

Farther up the street is the house (no. 19) purchased by Galileo for his son Vincenzio. To the left is the Villa Bardini (*entrance at no. 8, to be opened shortly*) with a huge park which extends down the hillside to Palazzo dei Mozzi.

The pretty Costa San Giorgio continues up between the high walls of rural villas to **Porta San Giorgio**, which still has a fresco by Bicci di Lorenzo. Dating from 1260, it forms part of the walls built to protect the Oltrarno in 1258, and is the oldest gate to have survived in the city. On the outer face is a copy of a stone relief of St George (the original is preserved in Palazzo Vecchio), thought to have been made in the same year as the gate. The entrance to Forte di Belvedere is here.

FORTE DI BELVEDERE
Map p. 398, C4

This is a huge fortress designed by Buontalenti (probably using plans drawn up by Don Giovanni de' Medici) in the shape of a six-pointed star. It was built by order of Ferdinando I in 1590, ostensibly for the defence of the city, but in reality to dominate it. It is open for contemporary art exhibitions and it is only then that you can visit the ramparts, which provide the very best view of Florence (*for information, T: 055 200 1486*). The handsome Palazzetto at the centre of the fortress has a loggia and two façades, one facing the city and the other facing south.

A pretty walk

Via di San Leonardo leads out of Florence beyond the fortress. It is one of the most beautiful and best-preserved roads on the outskirts of Florence (but beware of cars), leading through countryside past villas and their gardens and between olive groves behind high walls. Some of the pretty incised decoration on the plaster of the walls survives. A short way along on the left is a handsome building (no. 13) with outside steps and a dovecote tower. This was the residence from 1919 to 1970 of Timothy and Leolyn Spelman, who left it to the Johns Hopkins University of Baltimore. It is now the Charles S. Singleton Center for Italian Studies. The gate in front of the villa was designed by Cecil Pinsent. Beyond, preceded by a charming little garden with four cypresses, is the church of **San Leonardo in Arcetri** (*open for services at 5 or 6pm on Sat, and 8–11am on Sun and holidays; at other times ring at no. 25*). This was founded in the 11th century and contains a pulpit of the early 13th century, removed from the church of San Pier Scheraggio, with beautiful bas-reliefs. The paintings date from the 15th century: the high altarpiece of the *Madonna and Child with Saints* by Lorenzo di Niccolò; the *Madonna of the Sacred Girdle with Saints* and an *Annunciation with Angels and Saints* (decorating a tabernacle), both by Neri di Bicci; and the damaged painting of *Tobias and the Angel* by the Master of San Miniato.

The road continues past a house on the right (no. 64) where a plaque records Tchaikovsky's stay in 1878, to Viale Galileo.

From Forte di Belvedere to San Miniato

Via di Belvedere, a picturesque country lane with olive trees, follows the straight line of the city walls. These were built in 1258, reinforced in 1299–1333, and again in the 16th century. Even though greatly reduced in height, this is the best stretch of fortifications to survive in Florence. The road descends steeply with a fine view of the defensive towers and the tall Porta San Niccolò beyond. At the bottom is **Porta San Miniato**, a simple 14th-century arch in the wall. The doors, which were torn from their hinges in the Arno flood of 1966 and swept far downstream, were found and reinstalled here 30 years later after restoration. A road leads straight uphill from the gate, and a short way up on the left begins the stepped Via di San Salvatore al Monte. Lined with cypresses, this ascends the hill past the wall of a little rose garden (*open May and June*), and an area reserved for the cats of the city. It ends at the busy Viale Galileo, from where a monumental flight of steps leads up past a cemetery (1839) to San Miniato al Monte.

SAN MINIATO AL MONTE
Beyond map p. 399, E4

Open 8–12 & 2.30–6 (winter); 8–12 & 2–7 (summer).
The finest of all Tuscan Romanesque basilicas, with a famous façade, San Miniato is one of the most beautiful churches in Italy. Together with the Baptistery and San Lorenzo, it was the most important church in 11th-century Florence. Its position on a green hill above the city is incomparable. The stunning view from the terrace takes in the walls climbing the hillside to Forte di Belvedere on the left. Looking across the

Arno, you can see Palazzo Vecchio, the small dome of the Cappella dei Principi, the white roof of the Baptistery, the Campanile and the towers of the Badia Fiorentina and the Bargello, with the Duomo behind. On the right, just above the trees can be seen the west end of Santa Croce and its campanile. In the distance, the Villa della Petraia with its tower is prominent at the foot of Monte Morello.

History of San Miniato al Monte

The deacon Minias was a member of the early Christian community from the East who settled in Florence. A legend even suggested he was an Oriental prince, the son of the King of Armenia. He is thought to have been martyred c. 250 during the persecutions of the Emperor Decius, and buried on this hillside. The present church, built in 1013 by Bishop Hildebrand, is on the site of a shrine protecting the tomb of St Minias. The Benedictine Cluniac monastery, founded here at the same time by the Holy Roman Emperor Henry II, was one of the first important religious houses in Tuscany. In the 17th century it was used as a hospital, and later as a poorhouse. In 1924, the Olivetan Benedictine monks returned here: they still live in the monastery and look after the church which has been extremely well restored over the years.

The Exterior

The façade, begun c. 1090, is built of white and dark-greenish marble in a geometrical design reminiscent of the Baptistery. Above the exquisite little window in the form of an aedicule is a 13th-century mosaic (remade in 1861) of *Christ Between the Virgin and St Minias*, the warrior-martyr. In the tympanum, supported by two small figures in relief, the marble inlay repeats the motifs of the pavement inside. It is crowned by an eagle with outstretched wings standing on a bale of cloth, emblem of the Arte di Calimala (the cloth-importers guild), who looked after the fabric of the building.

The Interior

The superb interior, built in 1018–63, survives practically in its original state. Its design is unique in Florentine church architecture with a raised choir above a large hall crypt. Many of the capitals of the columns came from Roman temples in the city. The pavement is composed of tomb-slabs, except for the centre of the nave which has seven exquisite marble intarsia panels (1207), designed like a carpet, with signs of the Zodiac and animal motifs. The decoration on the inside of the upper part of the nave walls, in imitation of the façade, was carried out at the end of the 19th century, when the open timber roof, with polychrome decoration, was also restored.

At the end of the nave is the **Cappella del Crocifisso**, an exquisite tabernacle commissioned by Piero il Gottoso from Michelozzo in 1448. It is superbly carved and ingeniously designed to fit a setting that was built some 400 years earlier. It was made to house the venerated Crucifix which is said to have bowed approvingly to St John Gualberto (*see p. 207*) when he pardoned his brother's assassin; the painted panels of the doors of the cupboard which protected the miraculous Crucifix are by Agnolo Gaddi (1394–96). The enamelled terracotta roof and ceiling are the work of Luca della Robbia. The inlaid coloured marble frieze bears the emblem of Piero de' Medici (whose arms also appear on the back of the tabernacle). The copper eagles on the roof are by Maso di Bartolomeo.

On the outer stone walls of the aisles are a number of frescoes: the earliest date from the late 13th century and are by the steps up to the choir on the north side (*Virgin Annunciate* and a fragment of a Nativity scene). The *Madonna Enthroned with Six Saints* in the southwest corner of the nave is by Paolo Schiavo (1436) and the huge figure of St Christopher next to it dates from the 14th century or earlier. In the north aisle are two detached frescoes (a *Madonna and Child with Saints* and a *Crucifixion with Seven Saints*) by Mariotto di Nardo. The fine painted Crucifix, thought to date from c. 1285, shows *Christ Triumphant*, and although the face of Christ has been severely damaged, the rest of the decoration survives, with Christ blessing in the disc of the *cimasa* and two angels below and on the two terminals. On either side of the figure of Christ are the mourning figures of the Madonna and St John, and at the bottom of the Cross the *Denial of St Peter*. While recognizing that this work is one of the most important of its time, art historians have not so far identified with certainty the name of the painter.

Built onto the north wall of the church is the **Chapel of the Cardinal of Portugal**, the funerary chapel of Cardinal Jacopo di Lusitania, who died in Florence at the age of 25. It was begun in 1460 by Antonio Manetti, Brunelleschi's pupil (who also worked on the church of Santo Spirito), and finished, after his death in the same year, probably under the direction of Antonio Rossellino. It incorporates some of the best workmanship of the Florentine Renaissance. The exquisitely carved tomb of the Cardinal is by Antonio Rossellino (1461–66). The ceiling has five medallions (1461) by Luca della Robbia. These represent the Cardinal Virtues and the Holy Ghost, against a background of tiles decorated with classical cubes in yellow, green and purple, and are among the masterpieces of Luca's enamelled terracotta work. The altarpiece of *Three Saints* by Antonio and Piero del Pollaiolo (1466–67) was replaced by a copy when the original was moved to the Uffizi. The frescoed decoration of this wall, including two angels, is by the same artists. Above the marble bishop's throne on the west wall is a painting of the *Annunciation* by Alesso Baldovinetti (1466–73), who also frescoed the Evangelists and Fathers of the Church in the lunettes beside the windows, and in the spandrels.

Steps lead up to the raised **choir** which has a beautiful marble transenna dating from 1207, and pulpit, also faced with marble. The lectern is supported by an eagle above a carved figure standing on a lion's head, a rare example in Florence of figure sculpture of this date used to decorate an architectural feature. The low columns in the choir have huge antique capitals.

The **apse** (*light at the top of the stairs on the right*) has a beautiful inlaid blind arcade with six small Roman columns between opaque windows. The large apse mosaic representing *Christ between the Virgin and St Minias with Symbols of the Evangelists* (1297) was first restored in 1491 by Alesso Baldovinetti. The Crucifix behind the simple Renaissance altar is attributed to the della Robbia. The carved and inlaid stalls date from 1466–70. To the right of the apse is an altarpiece by Jacopo del Casentino showing St Minias and scenes from his life.

The **sacristy** (1387) lies to the south of the apse. It is covered with frescoes by Spinello Aretino; in the vault are the Evangelists and in the lunettes the *Life of St Benedict*, one of Spinello's best works (restored in 1840). There is also a polychrome bust of St Minias (wearing a crown) attributed to Nanni di Bartolo, two della Robbia statuettes, and stalls like those in the choir. In the lunette above the little door is a *Pietà* recently attributed to Giovanni da   Piamonte (1470–72). Just outside the sacristy, on the walls of the choir there are some very early frescoes of saints (13th century).

The 11th-century **crypt** beneath the choir has beautiful slender columns, many of them with antique capitals. The original 11th-century altar contains the relics of St Minias. The small vaults are decorated with frescoes of saints and prophets against a blue ground by Taddeo Gaddi.

On the west wall of the church, there is the simple tomb of the poet Giuseppe Giusti (1800–50) and a monument to the Tuscan artist Giuseppe Bezzuoli (1784–1855) by Emilio Santarelli (returned here in 2000 after it had been allowed to be removed to the cemetery of the Porte Sante in 1964, when works of this period were out of vogue).

The fine **cloister** of the Benedictine monastery (*admission only by special permission*), on the right side of the church, was begun c. 1425. On the upper loggia, damaged fragments of frescoes in *terraverde* are recognized as some of the most interesting works known by Paolo Uccello, illustrating scenes from monastic legends with remarkable perspectives and a beautiful figure of a woman. The *sinopie* are preserved in a room off the cloister. One of the frescoes dates from the 16th century, and is signed by Bernardo Buontalenti. On the lower walk is a fragment of a sinopia attributed to Andrea del Castagno.

The Bishop's Palace and Porte Sante

On the right of the façade is the crenellated Bishop's Palace, with attractive twin windows. This dates from 1295, when it was used as a summer residence by the bishops of Florence from the 14th–16th centuries. In later centuries, it was used as a barracks and hospital, and was restored in the 20th century.

The massive stone campanile replaced one that collapsed in 1499; it was begun after 1523 from a design by Baccio d'Agnolo, but was never finished. During the siege of Florence (1530) Michelangelo mounted two cannon here, and protected the belltower from hostile artillery by a screen of mattresses.

The *fortezza* originated in a hastily improvised defence-work planned by Michelangelo during the months preceding the siege. In 1553, Cosimo I converted it into a real fortress with the help of Francesco da Sangallo, Tribolo and others. The walls now enclose a large monumental cemetery, called the **Porte Sante** (*entrance on the left of the church*), laid out in 1854 by Niccolò Matas, and finished by Mariano Falcini in 1864. Surrounded by cypresses it has numerous neo-Gothic chapels and well-carved tombs. Collodi (Carlo Lorenzini), author of *Pinocchio*, is buried here, as well as the writer Vasco Pratolini (1913–91) and the painter Pietro Annigoni. Near the entrance is the tomb of the sculptor Libero Andreotti (1875–1933), with a striking bronze of the *Resurrection*.

PIAZZALE MICHELANGELO

Near San Miniato, in a grove of cypresses on the side of the hill, is the church of **San Salvatore al Monte**, a building of gracious simplicity by Cronaca, which Michelangelo called his *bella villanella* (his pretty country maid). The interior, which now has a rather gloomy abandoned feel about it, has an open timber roof. On the west wall is a bust by Andrea Ferrucci of Marcello Adriani, a chancellor of the Florentine Republic, who died in 1521. On the north side are small 16th-century stained glass windows: the one over the south side door is attributed to Perugino. There are two terracotta groups of the *Deposition*, one attributed to Santi Buglioni, and the other (over the north door) attributed to Giovanni della Robbia. In the sanctuary are two early 15th-century paintings, one of the *Pietà* attributed to Neri di Bicci, and the other of the *Madonna Enthroned* by Giovanni dal Ponte.

Viale dei Colli is the name given to the sequence of three avenues lined with fine trees and public gardens—Viale Michelangelo, Viale Galileo and Viale Machiavelli—which form a spectacular roadway 6km long, laid out by Giuseppe Poggi in 1865–70. It is one of the most panoramic drives near Florence, following a winding course from Piazza Ferrucci via Piazzale Michelangelo and the steps below San Miniato, to Porta Romana. The Viale is followed by bus 12 and 13.

As a central feature, Poggi created **Piazzale Michelangelo**, a contrived viewpoint, with a balustrade surrounding a huge terrace from which there is a remarkable panorama of the city. He also designed the monument to Michelangelo here, which consists of bronze reproductions of some of his famous marble statues in the city including the *David*, and the Palazzina del Caffè (now a restaurant). Today the terrace is little more than a coach park, always crowded with tourists. The view takes in the entire city as well as its surrounding hills, and beyond—on a clear day—you can see as far as the plain of Pistoia and the peaks of the Apennines. On the extreme left are the olive fields on the hillside below Forte di Belvedere (on the skyline), and the city walls descending to Porta San Niccolò. The view down the Arno centres on Ponte Vecchio. On the other side of the river, Palazzo Vecchio can be seen, as well as the top of Orsanmichele, the dome of the Cappella dei Principi (San Lorenzo), the Campanile and cupola of the Duomo, with the stone towers of the Badia and Bargello in front. Nearer at hand is the huge church of Santa Croce and the green dome of the synagogue. Straight ahead is the hill of Fiesole.

A delightful **Iris Garden** below the terrace is open in May (*entrance on the right of the balustrade*). On the hillside are some 2,500 varieties of iris; a red iris on a white ground is the symbol of Florence. An international competition has been held here annually since 1957.

ENVIRONS OF FLORENCE

FIESOLE & ENVIRONS

Fiesole is the best known place in the environs of Florence. The little town sits on a hill with splendid views of the city—best from the approach road and from the highest part of the hill around the convent of San Francesco. It is also interesting for its Roman theatre, Etruscan walls, Duomo, and small museums, all sited close together off the main piazza. There are lovely walks in the vicinity, including the beautiful old road up from the hamlet of San Domenico di Fiesole. Both places can also be reached from Florence on foot by a number of old country roads with charming views (notably Via di Barbacane and Via delle Forbici).

How to get there

Bus no 7, which leaves every 20 minutes from Stazione Santa Maria Novella (east side) and Piazza San Marco, goes to Fiesole via the hamlet of San Domenico, with a journey time of about 30 minutes. The main road to Fiesole (followed by the bus) is Via di San Domenico which ascends the hillside with a beautiful view of Fiesole and its villas. A double curve precedes San Domenico.

SAN DOMENICO DI FIESOLE

San Domenico di Fiesole is a little hamlet within the Comune of Fiesole. The **church of San Domenico** (*open 8.30–12 & 4.30–6*) dates from 1406–35; the portico (1635) and campanile (1611–13) were added by Matteo Nigetti. In this convent Fra' Angelico first entered the religious order (after 1437 he moved down to the convent of San Marco). The painting he made for the high altar of the church is preserved here, although it is now in a side chapel (there is a light on the right): the *Madonna Enthroned* is surrounded with angels and three Dominican saints in their black-and-white robes (Dominic, Thomas Aquinas, and Peter Martyr) with St Barnaba (included to honour a wealthy patron of the convent called Barnaba degli Agli). Formerly a late-Gothic triptych with a gold ground, it was altered in 1501 when it was enlarged at the top and the architectural background and landscapes were added by Lorenzo di Credi, and the frame was redesigned (the paintings of saints are by a follower of Lorenzo Monaco). The panels of the predella are copies; the originals are in the National Gallery, London.

The side chapels have Renaissance arches in *pietra serena* and some of the altarpieces have handsome Mannerist frames. The fine chancel designed by Giovanni Caccini and the gilded wooden tabernacle by Andrea Balatri both date from the first years of the 17th century. On the south side there is a wooden Crucifix dating from

The hills of Florence south of the Arno, with Torre del Gallo on the skyline.

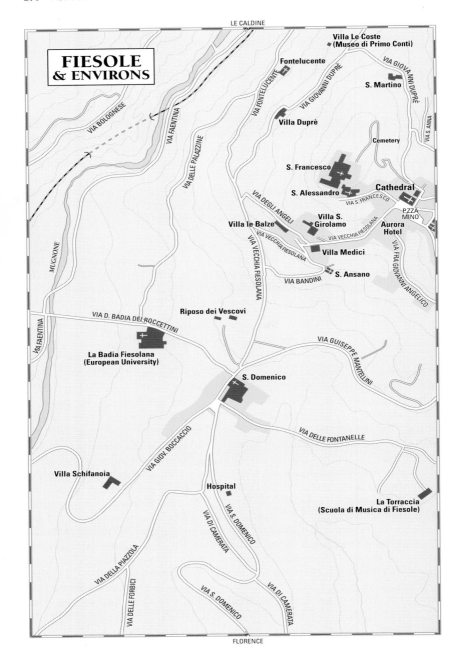

LE CALDINE

FIESOLE & ENVIRONS

Villa Le Coste
(Museo di Primo Conti)

Fontelucente

VIA FONTELUCENTE

VIA GIOVANNI DUPRÈ

VIA GIOVA NNI DUPRÈ

S. Martino

VIA BOLOGNESE

VIA FAENTINA

VIA DELLE PALAZZINE

Villa Duprè

Cemetery

VIA S. ANNA

S. Francesco

S. Alessandro

Cathedral

VIA DEGLI ANGELI

VIA S. FRANCESCO

P.ZZA
MINO

Villa le Balze

Villa S.
Girolamo

Aurora
Hotel

VIA VECCHIA FIESOLANA

VIA VECCHIA FIESOLANA

Villa Medici

VIA FRA GIOVANNI ANGELICO

MUGNONE

VIA BANDINI

S. Ansano

VIA FAENTINA

VIA D. BADIA DEI ROCCETTINI

Riposo dei Vescovi

VIA GUISEPPE MANTELLINI

La Badia Fiesolana
(European University)

S. Domenico

VIA GIOV. BOCCACCIO

VIA DELLE FONTANELLE

Villa Schifanoia

Hospital

La Torraccia
(Scuola di Musica di Fiesole)

VIA S. DOMENICO

VIA DI CAMERATA

VIA DELLA PIAZZOLA

VIA DELLE FORBICI

VIA S. DOMENICO

VIA DI CAMERATA

FLORENCE

PIAN DI MUGNONE

S. Martino

VIA RIORBICO

VIA A. COSTA

VIA BASTIANINI

VIA S. ANNA

VIA DELLE MURA ETRUSCHE

VIA DEL BARGELLINO

VIA FRANCESCO FERRUCCI

STRADA DEI BOSCONI

Roman Theatre
& Museum

Museo
Bandini

P.ZA DEL
MERCATO

VIA MARINI

VIA PORTIGIANI

Etruscan Tombs

VIA GRAMSCI

VIA G. MATTEOTTI

Borgunto

Cathedral

P.ZA
GARIBALDI

P.ZZA
MINO

Aurora
Hotel

Town Hall

SM Primerana

VIA F. POETI

Camping site

FIESOLE

VIA GIUSEPPE VERDI

VIA BELVEDERE

VIA SANT'APOLLINARE

S. Apollinare

VIA ADRIANO MARI

VIA CORSICA

VIA MONTE CECERI

VIA FRA GIOVANNI ANGELICO

Villa S. Michele
Hotel

VIA GIUSEPPE MANTELLINI

MONTE CECERI

Pensione Bencistà

La Torraccia
(Scuola di Musica di Fiesole)

VIA BENEDETTO DA MAIANO

N

0   400 yards

0   400 metres

Villa Temple Leader

S. Martino
a Maiano

IL SALVIATINO   PONTE A MENSOLA & SETTIGNANO

the mid-14th century and a painting of the *Crucifixion* attributed to Jacopo del Sellaio and a *Baptism of Christ* by Lorenzo di Credi.

On the north side there is an *Annunciation* by Jacopo da Empoli (1615) and an *Epiphany* by Giovanni Antonio Sogliani (completed by Santi di Tito).

There are only a few monks left in the convent now, and it is not always easy to gain access to the little chapter house (*ring at no. 4, right of the church*). This contains a beautiful fresco of the *Crucifixion* by Fra' Angelico (c. 1430) and a detached fresco (with its sinopia) of the *Madonna and Child*, also attributed to him. In the orchard is the Cappella delle Beatitudine (1588), with frescoes by Lodovico Buti.

Walks from San Domenico

The pretty Via delle Fontanelle leads southeast from San Domenico, passing the grounds (left) of **Villa Sparta** with a long avenue of cypresses leading to a garden designed by Cecil Pinsent. From 1905–49 Pinsent designed or restored over 20 villas and gardens, mostly for British or American residents in the hills around Florence, thus contributing in great measure to the preservation of the splendid countryside here. For much of this time he worked in partnership with the architect Geoffrey Scott, best known as the author of *The Architecture of Humanism*. Some distance farther on is **La Torraccia**, a large villa with a loggia where Walter Savage Landor lived from 1829 until 1835, and now the seat of the Music School of Fiesole, founded in 1974. It has a fine park and a charming little Italianate garden, partly redesigned by Landor (*sometimes open; T: 800 414 240 or 055 597 8373*).

In Via Boccaccio, which also starts at San Domenico, is the 15th–16th-century **Villa Schifanoia** (*occasionally opened by the Comune di Fiesole, T: 800 414 240 or 055 597 8373*), with a pretty garden, which since 1989 has been used by the European University Institute; and **Villa Palmieri**, the garden of which, with fine lemon trees grown in pots, was the scene of one of the episodes in Boccaccio's *Decameron*.

The **Badia Fiesolana**, in Via della Badia dei Roccettini, was the cathedral of Fiesole until 1025. Its lovely position is traditionally associated with the spot where St Romulus was martyred in the reign of the emperor Domitian. A certain Donatus, thought to have been an Irishman, was elected to the bishop's see when he stopped here on his return from a pilgrimage to Rome, and was canonized after his death in 876. The church was rebuilt in the 15th century under the direction of Cosimo il Vecchio, who founded a library here with the help of Vespasiano da Bisticci. The European University Institute was established by the member states of the European Community in the conventual buildings in 1976, and since then it has gained a high academic reputation. Some 500 PhD students from all over the European Union come here to study every year, carrying out research in Law, Economics, History and Civilization, and Social and Political Sciences.

The rough stone front of the church (*open 9–5.30; Sat 9–12*) incorporates the beautiful façade of the smaller Romanesque church with inlaid marble decoration. The interior, entered through the 15th-century cloister, has an interesting plan derived from Brunelleschi (begun in 1456). The side chapels have handsome round arches in *pietra serena* by Francesco di Simone Ferrucci. The east end, also decorated with *pietra serena*, has an elegant inscription to Piero de' Medici (Il Gottoso, father of Lorenzo the Magnificent) and the date of 1466. The high altar in *pietre dure* (1612) was designed by Pietro Tacca. From the charming terrace in front of the church, the view extends beyond cypresses and olives to Florence.

FIESOLE

Fiesole is a charming little village with a population of 15,000 inhabitants. It occupies a magnificent position on a thickly wooded hill overlooking the valleys of the Arno and the Mugnone. It has always been a fashionable residential district, much favoured by foreigners in the 19th century, when its beautiful hillside was enhanced by fine villas surrounded by romantic gardens and stately cypress groves. An Etruscan city, its foundation precedes that of Florence by many centuries, and, with its own local government, it is still proudly independent of the larger city. It is crowded with Florentines and visitors in summer when its position (295m) makes it one of the coolest places in the neighbourhood.

HISTORY OF FIESOLE

Excavations have proved that the hill was inhabited before the Bronze Age. The site of *Faesulae*, on a hilltop above a river valley, was typical of Etruscan settlements. Probably founded in the 6th or 5th century BC, it became one of the chief cities of the Etruscan confederacy. It is first mentioned in 283 BC, when its inhabitants, in alliance with other Etruscans, were defeated by the Romans at Lake Vadimone. With the Roman occupation it became the most important town in Etruria, but the barbarian invasions led to its decline. In 854, the county of Fiesole was merged with that of Florence. After a decisive battle in 1125, in which only the cathedral and the bishop's palace escaped destruction, Florence finally gained control of Fiesole.

The bus terminates in **Piazza Mino da Fiesole**, the spacious main square of the town, named after the Renaissance sculptor (1429–84) of the same name. Born at Poppi in the Casentino, Mino made Fiesole his home and left some of his best works in its cathedral (*see below*). At the top end the old Palazzo Pretorio, now the town hall, which has a loggia decorated with the coats of arms of many *podestà*, stands next to the quaint porch of **Santa Maria Primerana**. This little church, rebuilt in the 16th-17th centuries contains a 14th-century painted Crucifix, a bas-relief with a self-portrait in profile of Francesco da Sangallo, and a Crucifix with the *Madonna and Saints* by Andrea della Robbia. The sanctuary contains a highly venerated painting of the

Madonna dating from around 1255, in a Gothic tabernacle, and damaged frescoes by Niccolò di Pietro Gerini.

Sadly the square is now more or less inaccessible: the municipality initiated major building work here in 2004, to create more office space, and this threatens to destroy the piazza's simple and hospitable late-19th century aspect, as well as modify the distinctive slope of the hillside. The new project also at first ignored the fact that—inevitably—there were important remains of the centre of the Roman city just below the surface. The equestrian monument (1906) records the meeting between Vittorio Emanuele II and Garibaldi at Teano in southern Italy in 1860, when the handshake between the king and popular hero symbolized the unification of Italy.

The Cathedral of San Romolo

Open 7.30–12 & 3–5 or 6.
The cathedral was founded in 1028, and enlarged in the 13th and 14th centuries, but heavily restored in 1878–83. The tall bell-tower of 1213 (the crenellations were added later) is visible from Florence and the surrounding hills.

The bare stone interior, with a raised choir above a hall crypt, is similar in plan to San Miniato al Monte. The massive columns have fine capitals (some of them Roman). Above the west door, there is a garlanded niche containing a statue of St Romulus (San Romolo), Bishop of Fiesole, by Giovanni della Robbia (1521). The handsome high altar in grey-green and white marble dates from 1273.

Stairs lead up to the choir, preceded by a 19th-century balustrade made by a skilled local stonemason. On the right is the little Cappella Salutati, which has vault frescoes of the Evangelists by Cosimo Rosselli, and two of Mino da Fiesole's best sculptures: the tomb of Bishop Leonardo Salutati (1465) with a fine portrait bust, and an altarpiece. Over the high altar stands a splendid large painted altarpiece by Bicci di Lorenzo (c. 1440), with the *Madonna and Child and Saints Alexander, Peter, Romulus and Donatus*. It was donated to the church by Bishop Benozzo Federighi just before his death in 1450. The apse is frescoed by Nicodemo Ferrucci (late 16th century). In a chapel on the left is a marble altarpiece by Andrea Ferrucci (1493).

The crypt (coin-operated light) has four little columns with interesting primitive capitals. Behind the screen, surrounding the altar of St Romulus, are four marble columns with charming antique Ionic capitals. The vault was painted in the 15th century in lapis lazuli with stars. In the apse is a marble reliquary urn. The lunettes (late 15th century) are frescoed with stories of St Romulus. Roman remains can be seen below the pavement. The granite font is the work of Francesco del Tadda (1569). A small chapel contains an early 13th-century painting of the *Madonna and Child Enthroned* (the *Madonna del Soccorso*), showing the influence of Byzantine icons.

The hill of San Francesco

Between the seminary (1697) and the bishop's palace (1675) Via San Francesco, a very steep paved lane, climbs up the hill. At no. 4 is the entrance to the **Cappella di San Jacopo** (*open Sat, Sun and holidays 10–5 or 7; combined ticket with the Roman*

Theatre and Museo Bandini). This was a 14th-century oratory attached to the bishop's palace. It houses an early 15th-century fresco of the *Coronation of the Virgin* attributed to Bicci di Lorenzo (the lunette of the *Apostle St James the Greater* was painted by Antonio Marini in 1853). The chapel now houses a collection of goldsmiths' work from the diocese of Fiesole, including 13th and 14th-century processional Crosses, a 15th-century mitre decorated with enamels, a 16th-century crozier, and 17th- and 18th-century church silver.

The lane continues up past (right) a public park (*described below*) and a terrace on the left planted with ilexes, where there are two war memorials. From here there is a splendid view of Florence with the Duomo standing out in the middle. Above, beside another viewpoint, is the **church of Sant' Alessandro** (*open only twice a year for services, and closed at other times unless exhibitions are being held here*). It was heavily restored in 1814 and again after 1957. Traditionally thought to be on the site of an Etruscan and Roman temple, it was probably founded in the 6th century. The Romanesque church was altered in the 16th and 18th centuries. The bare basilican interior is remarkable for its *cipollino* marble columns with Ionic capitals and bases from a Roman building. An oratory off the left aisle (light on right) contains an altarpiece of the *Assumption* by Gerino da Pistoia (showing the influence of Perugino) and 16th-century Mannerist frescoes of the life of the Virgin.

Beyond (left) the church of Santa Cecilia at the top of the hill (345m), is the site of the Etruscan and later Roman acropolis, where the convent buildings of **San Francesco** (*open 9–12 & 3–6 or 7*) now stand. The church dates from c. 1330 and was restored in neo-Gothic style in 1905–07, with an attractive little rose window. The choir arch is attributed to Benedetto da Maiano. Over the high altar, there is a *Crucifixion and Saints* by Neri di Bicci. On the south side (first altar), the *Marriage of St Catherine* by Cenni di Francesco is surrounded by paintings of the early 19th century. On the second altar there is an *Immaculate Conception* by Piero di Cosimo. On the north side (first altar) is an *Adoration of the Magi* by the school of Cosimo Rosselli, and (second altar), *Annunciation* by Raffaellino del Garbo.

In the Franciscan friary, there are several charming little cloisters, some remains of the Etruscan walls, and a missionary museum (*open 10–12 & 3–5*) of Eastern *objets d'art* with a remarkable miscellany of objects (mostly unlabelled). The museum contains a particularly interesting Egyptian collection (including a statuette thought to represent the wife of Rameses II) and works from China (including bronzes and Ming and Qing vases). The convent also owns a collection of 16th–17th-century ceramics including apothecary jars and tableware. From the piazza outside, a gate leads into a public park with an ilex wood, through which shady paths lead back downhill to the main square.

Roman Theatre and Museo Civico

Open 9.30–7; winter 9.30–5; closed Tuesday in winter; T: 055 59477. Discount for students and over 65s. Combined ticket includes entry to the Museo Bandini (see p. 297) and the Cappella di San Jacopo (see above). There is a café in the grounds.

From Piazza Mino, the street behind the apse of the cathedral leads to the entrance to the Roman theatre and archaeological excavations, and the Museo Civico which contains the Costantini collection of Greek vases.

From the terrace above the theatre there is a good comprehensive view of the excavations in a plantation of olive trees, backed by the Mugnone valley and the dark cypresses of the hill of San Francesco. The excavations were begun in the 19th century, and several of the edifices were arbitrarily restored in 1870–92.

The Roman theatre, built at the end of the 1st century BC, was enlarged by Claudius and Septimius Severus. The cavea, which was partly dug out from the hillside (the sides are supported on vaults), is 34m across and held 3,000 spectators. The seats on the right side are intact; the others have been restored with smaller blocks of stone. Plays and concerts are performed here during a festival held every summer.

To the right of the theatre are the Roman baths (reconstructed in 1892), probably built in the 1st century AD and enlarged by Hadrian. In front are three rectangular swimming baths. The chambers near the three arches (reconstructed) consist of the hypocausis, with circular ovens, where the water was heated, the calidarium with its hypocaust, and the tepidarium. In front of the arches is the palestra, and behind them the frigidarium. A small terrace here provides a fine view of a long stretch of Etruscan walls (4th–3rd century BC; reinforced in the Roman and medieval periods), with a gateway, which enclosed the city. On the other side of the theatre (to the northwest) is a Roman temple (1st century BC), with its basement intact, and, on a lower level, remains of an Etruscan temple (4th or early 3rd century BC), both of them approached by steps. Nearby are copies of the two original altars from the temples (the larger one is Roman). In this area a Lombard necropolis (6th–7th century AD) has also been excavated. There is a stretch of Roman road near the theatre.

Museo Civico

The museum was built in 1912–14 and the exterior is an idealized reconstruction of the Roman temple. Its collection was founded in 1878 and is now being re-evaluated in the light of new excavations. Under the portico, there is a fragment from the frieze of the Roman temple.

Ground floor: The first five rooms contain a topographical collection from Fiesole and its territory, including Bronze Age artefacts, the well-preserved *Stele Fiesolana* (5th century BC) with reliefs of a funerary banquet and dancing and hunting scenes, Etruscan and Roman urns, a marble frieze from the Roman theatre, and the so-called bronze *She-wolf* (in fact the torso of a lioness), which was found on the probable site of the centre of the Etruscan Roman city.

Upper floor: Two rooms on this floor display part of the Antiquarium Costantini, a splendid collection of Greek vases donated to Fiesole in 1985 by Alfiero Costantini. This includes Corinthian vases (7th century BC) and models of animals (including deer, a hedgehog and a ram's head used for perfumes), and fine Attic black-figure amphorae. The exquisite red-figure vases (late 6th century BC) include one with Theseus and the minotaur, and another signed by Hermonax (460–450 BC), and one with the figure of Eros, attributed to the Pan Painter (480 BC), and one with a female head. There is also a black-figure water jar with a banqueting scene, a two-handled cup in brown impasto, and Bucchero ware. The pottery from Puglia includes an unusually shaped pitcher (late 8th- or early 7th century BC), red-figure vases, a pair of large water jars (320–310 BC), and a red-figure amphora attributed to the Baltimore Painter, of the same date. The collection also includes Gnathian vases from Taranto, and black-glazed pottery.

The three other rooms on this floor contain the so-called antiquarium, made up of various collections donated to the museum, and a coin collection. Another room displays a torso of Dionysius, a Roman copy of the early Imperial period of a Greek original, and Roman marble heads.

Museo Bandini

Opening times as for the Roman Theatre and Museo Civico, above. Entrance opposite.
The small Museo Bandini houses a collection of 13th–15th-century Florentine paintings which belonged to Angelo Maria Bandini (born in Fiesole in 1726), and which was left by him at his death in 1803 to the Diocese of Fiesole.

Bandini was the first librarian of the Biblioteca Marucelliana and later of the Biblioteca Laurenziana. The attractive little building that houses the collection was designed by Giuseppe Castellucci in 1913.

At the bottom of the stairs are two terracotta busts of Apostles attributed to Pietro Francavilla—the museum has eight more. The paintings are arranged chronologically in two rooms on the first floor. They include a 13th-century Tuscan Crucifix attributed to Meliore; works by Bernardo Daddi, Taddeo Gaddi and his son Agnolo, Nardo and Jacopo di Cione, Giovanni di Bartolomeo Cristiani, Bicci di Lorenzo, and his son Neri di Bicci, and Lorenzo Monaco. There is also a case of Byzantine ivories including one with the Archangel Gabriel (11th–12th century).

Walks near Fiesole

Against the hill of San Francesco is a large section of the Etruscan walls, and another stretch of the walls can be seen by following Via Giuseppe Verdi from Piazza Mino. Via Belvedere, with superb views, continues uphill to Via Adriano Mari which skirts the walls along the eastern limit of the Etruscan city. From here Via Montececeri (also with magnificent views) leads across to the extensive **woods of Montececeri**, once owned by Temple Leader (*see p. 300*), which up to 1929 was used as a quarry for *pietra serena*. The bare slopes and disused quarries were then planted with oak, conifers, cypresses and pines. There are some lovely (signposted) paths here with views extending to Settignano and beyond. At the highest point (410m) a memorial stone records Leonardo da Vinci's flying experiments which he carried out here.

The lovely old road (Via Vecchia Fiesolana) which descends steeply to San Domenico passes the **Villa Medici** (*entrance at no. 2 Via Fra' Giovanni di Fiesole*). This is privately owned, but the garden is willingly shown, usually on weekdays (8–1: T:

055 59417, or specially opened; T: 800 414 240 or 055 597 8373). It was begun around 1453 for Giovanni de' Medici, the cultivated son of Cosimo il Vecchio who predeceased his father. It could be that Giovanni asked his close friend Leon Battista Alberti for help with the plan and that the work was carried out by the architect Antonio Ciacheri Manetti. Its design, the core of which survives to this day, was innovative in that it opened onto a panorama and was intimately connected to its garden by a series of terraces. It later became the favourite retreat of Giovanni's nephew, Lorenzo the Magnificent, and Angelo Poliziano and Pico della Mirandola, together with members of the Platonic Academy, frequently met here. The villa, enlarged in the 17th and 18th centuries, was bought in 1862 by the painter and collector William Blundell Spence, and in 1911 by Lady Sybil Cutting (wife of the architect Geoffrey Scott), whose daughter Iris Origo (1902–88), the historian and biographer, made additions to the garden, which is one of the earliest of the Renaissance, built on several terraces on the steep hillside with a superb view of Florence. It is at its best after Easter. Cecil Pinsent worked on the box-edged geometric garden on the lower terrace in 1915.

Opposite the garden wall of Villa Medici, at no. 26 Via Vecchia Fiesolana, is the little garden entrance to **Villa Le Balze**, beyond which can be glimpsed one of the garden 'rooms' created by Cecil Pinsent for the American philosopher Charles Augustus Strong. The villa was built for him by Geoffrey Scott in Renaissance style in 1913. It was left by his daughter to Georgetown university in 1979 and the garden is usually open on certain days of the year *(for information T: 055 599 478).*

The old road continues steeply downhill and there is a breathtaking view of the whole of Florence beyond a row of venerable cypresses. Further downhill, at no. 62, is the **Riposo dei Vescovi** *(privately owned, but sometimes opened specially; T: 800 414 240 or 055 597 8373).* This was the halting place in the 16th century for the bishops of Fiesole on their way up the hill from their residence in Florence. Dutch and Swiss owners in the late 19th century carried out alterations in an eclectic Jugendstil and neo-Gothic style, which were continued by the Dutch painter W.O.J. Nieuwenkamp (1874–1950) when he bought the house in 1926. The splendid Romantic park with numerous cypresses covers the hillside all the way down to Via delle Palazzine.

Another lovely old road can be explored from Via Vecchia Fiesolana: Via Giovanni Dupré. It leads up to a fork with Via Fontelucente, an even narrower old road which descends left to the **church of Fontelucente**, built over a spring, in a beautiful isolated spot above the Mugnone valley. The lovely Via delle Palazzine leads from here to the Badia Fiesolana *(see p. 292).* The very peaceful Via Dupré continues with a view across the valley towards Via Bolognese, where the hillside was disfigured by new houses in the 1950s. Villa Dupré (no. 19) was the home of the 19th-century sculptor Giovanni Dupré, one of the most famous Italian sculptors of his day.

The road from here climbs uphill to the 16th-century **Villa le Coste** (no. 18), where the painter Primo Conti (1900–88) lived. The Museo di Primo Conti in the garden *(open 9–1, except Sun and holidays)* contains a representative collection of Conti's works, which was left to the Comune. The painter is buried here in a chapel of 1702, decorated with episodes from the life of St Rosalia, attributed to Francesco Botti. The road curves to the right round the hill, and from the hamlet of San Martino, with the campanile of the cathedral of Fiesole prominent ahead, it is a short way back past the Roman theatre to Piazza Mino.

MAIANO

The pretty Via Benedetto da Maiano (unfortunately busy with traffic) diverges from the main Florence road below Fiesole. The bus can be taken downhill from Piazza Mino to the request stop here. It passes the entrance to the **Pensione Bencistà**, a hotel which has always been favoured by English visitors. It was formerly called Villa Goerike and was where the painter Arnold Böcklin (1827–1901) lived and died. His famous *Island of the Dead*, with its tall cypresses, is thought by some to be inspired by the English Cemetery in Florence, where his baby daughter lies buried.

At a crossroads is the little group of houses called **Maiano**, the home of the brothers Benedetto and Guiliano da Maiano (1442–92 and 1432–90), who were well known sculptors and architects. The church of San Martino a Maiano (*open Wed 4.30–7, or ring at no. 6*) is of ancient foundation and was restored by John Temple Leader (*see p. 300*). The choir is decorated with *pietra serena*. Above the west door, in its original frame, is a *Madonna and Child with St John and Two Saints* by Giovanni Battista Naldini. A farm (produce for sale) now occupies the Benedictine monastery. A road continues uphill for a few hundred metres past two *trattorie* and disused *pietra serena* quarries (now visited by rock climbers), with fine views. A marked path leads from the end of the road to Monte Ceceri.

Via del Salviatino runs from the crossroads down to Florence. It passes the gate of the Villa di Maiano (left) or Villa Temple Leader (now Corsini), with its tower. Privately owned, the villa is used for receptions (*sometimes shown by previous appointment; T: 055 599 600 or 055 598 631, or opened specially; T: 800 414 240 or 055 597 8373*). It was restored in 1850–63 by Felice Francolini for John Temple Leader, as his residence.

The road continues downhill with a view of Fiesole from a hairpin bend. It then skirts the garden wall with cypresses of Villa il Salviatino (entrance at no. 21), the 16th-century home of Alamanno Salviati, surrounded by a thick wood of ilexes.

CASTEL DI POGGIO & VINCIGLIATA

East of Fiesole, beyond Borgunto, the attractive Via di Vincigliata diverges right along a ridge round the north shoulder of Monte Ceceri through magnificent woods. Opposite a semicircle of cypresses is the entrance (at no. 2) to the Villa al Bosco di Fontelucente (now Peyron) or **Villa di Bosco** (*privately owned, but sometimes shown by previous appointment, T: 055 59223, or specially opened, T: 800 414 240 or 055 597 8373*). The villa was acquired by the Peyron family in 1914 when the exterior was restored by the architect Ugo Giovannozzi. After it was severely damaged in the last war, the garden was redesigned and carefully replanted.

Just beyond the villa there is a superb view of Florence. The road climbs to a fork; on the left a road leads to Montebeni and Settignano; and to the right the road continues past the gate (right; no. 4) to **Castel di Poggio** (*the park and interior are sometimes shown by appointment, T: 055 59174*).

Rebuilt in the late 15th century by the degli Alessandri, one wing was added in 1820 when the garden was transformed into an interior courtyard. It was restored again in 1922. The views in every direction are breathtaking, looking over unspoilt hillsides of woods and fields.

The road now descends, lined with magnificent cypresses planted by Temple Leader, to the **Castello di Vincigliata** (*privately owned, but used for receptions and shown by appointment, T: 055 599 556, and sometimes opened specially, T: 800 414 240 or 055 597 8373*). John Temple Leader was a wealthy entrepreneur who came to live in Florence in 1850 and remained here until his death in 1903. He acquired many farms and villas between Settignano and Fiesole, and numerous stone quarries which he closed down and planted with woods. He wrote biographies of Sir Robert Dudley and Sir John Hawkwood, and contributed generously to the funds spent on the new façade of the Duomo. During his lifetime the castle, which he used as a museum of medieval and Renaissance works of art, was one of the most important 'sites' of Florence, and he was visited here by numerous distinguished travellers. The castle was built in 1031, but destroyed by Sir John Hawkwood in 1364. Hawkwood (*see p. 41*) was in the service of Pisa at the time. It is said that the *condottiere* had led his troops to Florence, but finding the city too strongly defended, had turned his sword on properties in the surrounding hills instead. The castle was a complete ruin when Temple Leader acquired it in 1855. He appointed a local architect Giuseppe Fancelli to rebuild the castle in neo-Gothic style, with the help of skilled stonemasons from Settignano and the painter Gaetano Bianchi.

PONTE A MENSOLA

Bus 10 leaves every 20 minutes from Stazione Santa Maria Novella and Piazza San Marco to Settignano via Ponte a Mensola, with a journey time of 30 minutes.

The village of **Ponte a Mensola** lies at the foot of the hill of Settignano. In Via Poggio Gherardo is the park of the **Villa di Poggio Gherardo** (*no admission*), traditionally thought to be the setting for the earliest episodes in Boccaccio's *Decameron*. In 1888, it was purchased by Janet and Henry Ross: Janet, an expert on Tuscan villas and Tuscan food, died here in 1927. Off the approach road to Settignano from the centre of Florence, there is a big sports centre and a football museum. Farther downhill is the sports ground of Campo di Marte with the Stadio Comunale, a remarkable building (1932) by Pier Luigi Nervi, altered and enlarged for the World Cup games in 1990.

San Martino a Mensola

This 9th-century Benedictine church is in a beautiful position above the village of Ponte a Mensola (*open 4.30–6 and Sun at 10.30; at other times ring at the priest's house under the portico on the right*). It was founded by St Andrew, who is thought to have been a Scotsman and archdeacon to the bishop of Fiesole, Donato, who in turn was probably from Ireland. It is preceded by a 17th-century loggia. The 15th-century campanile was damaged by lightning in 1867.

The graceful 15th-century interior replaced the Romanesque church (remains of which have been found beneath the nave). It was restored in 1857 by Giuseppe Fancelli and again in 1999. The sanctuary is preceded by a beautifully carved arch in *pietra serena* with two pretty little tabernacles. On the high altar is a triptych of the *Madonna and Child with the Donor and Saints* (the donor is Amerigo Zati) by a follower of Orcagna (1391), known, from this painting, as the Master of San Martino a Mensola. The other painted altarpieces are particularly fine and include a triptych by Taddeo Gaddi, an *Annunciation* by a follower of Fra' Angelico, and a *Madonna and Four Saints* by Neri di Bicci.

In the pavement, a stone marks the burial place of St Andrew. The church preserves a wooden casket decorated with fine paintings, which formerly contained the saint's body, and his wooden reliquary bust which dates from the end of the 14th century.

Villa I Tatti

House and garden not open to the public, but shown to scholars with a letter of presentation, by previous appointment (in small groups usually on Tues and Weds afternoons). T: 055 603251. Main entrance 26 Via Vincigliata.

The little by-road leads from the church across a bridge over the Mensola to a group of houses by the garden entrance to Villa I Tatti. The locality was known as 'Tatti' at least as early as the 15th century. The house was acquired by John Temple Leader in 1854, and by Bernard Berenson, the pioneer scholar of the Italian Renaissance, in 1905.

The villa contains Berenson's library and photographic library as well as his exquisite collection of Italian paintings (including works by Domenico Veneziano, Sassetta, Michele Giambono, Cima da Conegliano, Luca Signorelli, Bergognone and Lorenzo Lotto) and a small but choice selection of Oriental works of art.

The lovely Italianate garden (*admission as above*) was laid out by Cecil Pinsent in 1911–15, in imitation of an early Renaissance garden. The terraces are planted with symmetrical parterres and descend the steep hillside surrounded by high hedges of cypresses. Beyond the garden, which is beautifully kept, is a small ilex wood.

Corbignano

In Via di Corbignano, a peaceful old country lane, is **Villa Boccaccio** (no. 4; rebuilt), once owned by the father of Giovanni Boccaccio, who probably spent his youth here.

Above the charming little hamlet of Corbignano is the Oratorio della Madonna del Vannella (1719–21; *open for a service on the last Sun of the month, otherwise T: 055 604*

418). The fresco of the *Madonna and Child*, believed by Berenson to be an early work by Botticelli, was for centuries venerated by the stonemasons and sculptors of Settignano. The road ends at the cemetery of Settignano (*see below*).

From Ponte a Mensola the main road continues up to Settignano, winding across the old road; both have fine views of the magnificent trees on the skyline of the surrounding hills. The main road passes the conspicuous neo-Gothic building known as the Mezzaratta by Adolfo Coppedè (1920) and (right) Villa Viviani where Mark Twain finished *Pudd'nhead Wilson* in 1892.

GIOVANNI BOCCACCIO

The birthplace of the celebrated author Giovanni Boccaccio (1312–75) is uncertain: perhaps Certaldo, a small Tuscan town, or even Paris, where his Florentine father had mercantile interests, but he lived most of his life in Florence. His *Decameron* (1348–58) is a brilliant secular work which established him as the father of Italian prose, and which had a great influence on European literature (including Chaucer). The book is a collection of tales told by seven ladies and three gentlemen who decide to leave the centre of Florence in order to escape the plague of 1348; they spend ten days in the garden of a villa in the surrounding hills recounting stories to each other. The Villa di Poggio Gherardo and the villa now known as Villa Palmieri are both thought to have been settings for some of the earliest episodes, and other places in the environs of Florence near Fiesole are associated with the book. Boccaccio acted as ambassador for Florence after 1350, and was a close friend of the poet and the first great humanist Petrarch (1304–74) and of Dante.

SETTIGNANO

Settignano (178m), a peaceful village on a pleasant hill, is little visited by tourists. It has narrow, picturesque lanes and many fine villas surrounded by luxurious gardens. Delightful country walks can be taken in the vicinity. It is known for its school of sculptors, the most famous of whom were Desiderio (1428–64) and the Gamberelli brothers (known as Antonio and Bernardo Rossellino, 1427–79 and 1409–64).

The bus terminates in the piazza. The **church of Santa Maria** stands here, built in 1518 and reconstructed at the end of the 18th century. It contains a charming group of the *Madonna and Child with Two Angels* in white enamelled terracotta, attributed to the workshop of Andrea della Robbia. The 16th-century organ was reconstructed in 1908 and has been restored. The pulpit was designed by Bernardo Buontalenti. In the dome above the high altar is an *Assumption of the Virgin* by Pier Dandini. On the north side, the second altar has a painted terracotta statuette of St Lucy attributed to

Michelozzo, surrounded by frescoes of 1593.

The numerous narrow lanes in and around Settignano, mostly with splendid views over unspoilt countryside, are well worth exploring on foot. From the right of the church, Via Capponcina leads downhill to Via dei Buonarroti-Simoni and **Villa Michelangelo** (no. 65; *no admission*), where Michelangelo spent his youth (a charcoal drawing of a triton or satyr, attributed to him, was found on the kitchen wall, and was detached and restored in 1979). Farther downhill, surrounded by a garden with cypresses and pine trees, is **Villa la Capponcina** (no. 32), where Gabriele d'Annunzio lived in 1898–1910 and where he wrote most of his best works. From here you can continue on foot downhill to Via Madonna delle Grazie, which continues as a foot-path which crosses a bridge (opened in 2004) over the Mensola to reach the hamlet of Ponte a Mensola.

The narrow main road of Settignano (Via San Romano) continues from the piazza and Via Rossellino soon diverges right to the **Villa Gamberaia** (no. 72). This has a famous garden considered one of the most representative of Tuscany, immaculately maintained and with remarkable topiary. It is privately owned, but open to the pub-lic (*open 9–6 & 9–7 in summer; ring the bell; T: 055 697 205*). It was laid out in 1717 by Andrea Capponi. The famous parterre garden survives with cypress, yew and box hedges designed around a fountain (the beds were replaced by pools at the beginning of the 20th century). From the terrace, there is a wonderful view beyond olive groves to Settignano on its ridge and the Duomo beyond. An ilex wood surrounds the gar-den as well as ancient cypresses and pine trees. There are two elaborate grottoes and a fine collection of azaleas.

PIAN DE' GIULLARI

Best reached on foot from Ponte Vecchio via Costa San Giorgio and Via di San Leonardo (see p. 281).

The beautiful old country road beyond Forte di Belvedere, Via di San Leonardo (*described on pp. 281–82*), traverses Viale Galileo and continues uphill. Via Viviani leads past the garden wall of **Villa Capponi**, bought in 1928 by Henry and Esther Clifford, who entertained numerous well-known Americans here. The beautiful gar-den (*which can sometimes be seen by previous appointment; T: 055 223 465*) preserves its 16th-century character and is at its best from the end of April until June and in September. Cecil Pinsent designed the swimming pool on the lowest terrace. Via del Pian de' Giullari soon meets Via Torre del Gallo named after the conspicuous **Torre del Gallo**, rebuilt in medieval style by the antiquarian Stefano Bardini in 1902. In the picturesque little village of Pian de' Giullari stands **Villa di Gioiello** (no. 42), the house where the aged Galileo lived from 1631 until his death in 1642. The 16th-cen-tury house and farm, with a loggia overlooking its lovely gardens, are owned by the state (*for admission ask at the Observatory of Arcetri, part of Florence University's* Institute

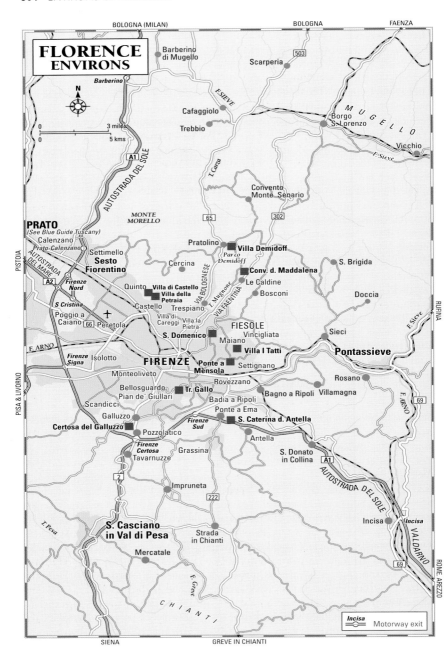

FLORENCE ENVIRONS

of Astronomy, which is close by). Beyond are several more lovely country roads, which provide beautiful, peaceful walks. Via San Matteo in Arcetri passes the rebuilt convent where Galileo's daughter Suor Maria Celeste lived as a nun, before her death in 1634 at the age of 33. One hundred and twenty-four remarkable letters from her to Galileo survive. In the other direction from Pian de' Giullari (signposted for Santa Margherita a Montici) the old road continues past **Villa Ravà** (no. 71), purchased by Francesco Guicciardini in 1527, who wrote his famous *History of Italy* here. Guicciardini shared Machiavelli's view that only strong and ruthless government would lead to political survival. He was employed by two Medici popes, Leo X (1513–21) and Clement VII (1523–34). His *History of Italy* gives a merciless analysis of many rulers, including those whom he had served.

Beyond several more villas, the road continues through open countryside, leaving the locality of Pian de' Giullari, and climbs up to the church of **Santa Margherita a Montici** (*open Sun 10–12.30*). This has a distinctive crenellated campanile and occupies a splendid position, with views of the two valleys of the Arno and Ema. The church contains two paintings by the Master of Santa Cecilia, one of which, *St Margaret and Scenes from her Life*, is thought to date from before 1300. Also in the sanctuary is a ciborium by Andrea Sansovino.

MONTEOLIVETO & BELLOSGUARDO

Bus 12 from Piazza Santa Maria Novella to Viale Raffaello Sanzio (for Monteoliveto) and Piazza Torquato Tasso (for Bellosguardo). Also bus 42 (nine times a day) for Bellosguardo (going on to Marignolle) from Porta Romana.

Both Monteoliveto and Bellosguardo can be visited on foot from the Oltrarno. They are lovely residential districts with some large villas where a number of writers stayed in the 19th century. There are superb views of Florence from the road up to Bellosguardo and delightful walks nearby.

Monteoliveto

On the south bank of the Arno, near Ponte della Vittoria, is the thickly wooded hill of Monteoliveto. It is reached via Viale Raffaello Sanzio and (right) Via di Monteoliveto. The **church of San Bartolomeo** (*open 9–1; for admission, ring at no. 72a*), was founded in 1334 by monks from the convent of Monteoliveto Maggiore in Tuscany, and rebuilt in the 15th century; it has been restored several times since.

The west wall and triumphal arch have good frescoes by Bernardino Poccetti. On the second altar on the south side there is an *Assumption of the Virgin* signed and dated 1592 by Domenico Passignano, below which is a little reliquary case with a charming 18th-century figure of the Virgin as a baby. On the high altar, the *Entry of Christ into Jerusalem* is a copy by Il Poppi of an altarpiece by Santi di Tito. The domed sanctuary and triumphal arch are interesting works which show the influence of Leon Battista

Alberti and Francesco da Sangallo. On the left wall there is a fresco fragment (with its sinopia opposite) of the *Last Supper* by Sodoma. The first altarpiece on the north side is by Domenico Passignano and his follower Fabrizio Boschi, and the second altarpiece is by Simone Pignone. There are also six 18th-century *scagliola* altar-frontals.

The road ends in front of an entrance to the **Villa Strozzi** (*open daily 9–dusk*). This has a beautiful wooded park with fine views of Bellosguardo. Owned by the Comune of Florence since 1974, it is now used by a school of design. There are two other entrances, one on Via Pisana and one on Via Soffiano.

Bellosguardo

The adjoining hill, with cypresses and pine trees to the south, is aptly called Bellosguardo. Numerous illustrious visitors to Florence, including many writers in the 19th century, stayed in the lovely villas here. It is approached from Piazza San Francesco di Paola.

In the piazza stands the church of **San Francesco di Paola** (*open for services only*). This was built by the Minims, the friars of San Francesco di Paola, in 1593, and has early 18th-century decorations and a detached fresco of the *Madonna del Parto* by Taddeo Gaddi. To the right of the church is the gloomy Villa Pagani, with a tower built by Adolfo Coppedè in 1896.

Via di Bellosguardo climbs uphill to a little walled public garden behind a hedge, with a few pines and cypresses. Here is the Villa dello Strozzino, a fine Renaissance villa with a pretty loggia at one corner. On the right, the extremely narrow (and picturesque) Via Monteoliveto leads to the ancient little church of San Vito (*open for a service on Sun mornings*) with a pretty porch. The interior was remodelled in 1662.

Via di Bellosguardo continues uphill with a superb view back of Florence, and, on the right beside a group of pine trees, is **Villa Brichieri-Colombi** (no. 20). This was owned by Isa Blagden in 1849–73, and she was often visited here by the Brownings. Henry James wrote *The Aspern Papers* here in 1887. The old road narrows and a sharp turn left (Via Roti Michelozzi) ends at **Torre di Bellosguardo**, well restored as a hotel, with a delightful garden and magnificent views of Florence. Adjoining it (entrance from Piazza di Bellosguardo) is the **Villa dell'Ombrellino**, ostentatiously restored in 1988 as a trade centre and used for conferences and receptions. The villa was rented by Galileo in 1617–31 before he moved to Arcetri. In 1924 the villa was bought by Colonel George Keppel and his wife Alice, a glamorous hostess best known as the mistress of King Edward VII. Their daughter, the writer Violet Trefusis, was an intimate friend of Virginia Woolf and Vita Sackville-West; she lived here in the 1950s and '60s, entertaining numerous international celebrities at grand receptions.

Piazza di Bellosguardo has a few trees and at no. 6 stands the **Villa Mercedes**, also known as Villa Belvedere al Saraceno, by Baccio d'Agnolo with a charming courtyard. It is thought that Henry James took this villa as a model for the 'Villa Pandolfini' in his first novel *Roderick Hudson*, published in 1875, and also as the residence of Gilbert Osmond in *The Portrait of a Lady*. Via San Carlo leads downhill out of the piazza towards the conspicuous tower of **Villa di Montauto** where Nathaniel Hawthorne stayed in the 1850s. It provided the setting for the castle of Monte Beni in his novel *The Marble Faun* (1860).

From Piazza di Bellosguardo, Via Piana continues past more luxurious villas ending at Via di Santa Maria a Marignolle. The road to the left leads to **Villa la Colombaia**, with a closed-in loggia, which is now a convent school. Florence Nightingale was born here in 1820. She was the first person ever to be called Florence, from the city of her birth. From here the lovely old Via delle Campora can be followed back downhill to Porta Romana.

THE CERTOSA DEL GALLUZZO

Bus 37 leaves Piazza Santa Maria Novella (every 20 minutes) and there is a request stop below the hill of the Certosa. Journey time about 30 minutes.

The Via Senese begins at Porta Romana; from here it climbs and then descends through Gelsomino to Galluzzo, passing (right) the thick cypresses of the Cimitero Evangelico degli Allori. Formerly, this was a cemetery only for Orthodox Greeks, but since 1878 it has been a cemetery for non-Catholics. At Galluzzo, beside the Ema, a road just before the piazza diverges right and ascends behind the Certosa to Villa i Collazzi, a beautiful Mannerist villa built in 1560. The garden has fine trees, including cypresses, oaks and ilexes, and there is a parterre on a terrace below the villa.

Certosa del Galluzzo

Open 9–11.30 & 3–5.30 (winter 3–5); closed Mon; T: 055 204 9226. Tours are conducted by the monks about every half hour.

Beyond the village of Galluzzo, immediately to the right of the road on the Colle di Montaguto, stands the Certosa. This historic monastery, remarkable for its peaceful atmosphere, is interesting for its architecture as well as its frescoes by Pontormo. The monks' cells, the church and the Gothic Palazzo degli Studi can be seen on the edge of the hill. It was founded in 1342 by the Florentine Niccolò Acciaioli. In 1958, the Carthusians were replaced by Cistercians, their first reappearance in the area since their expulsion by the Grand Duke 176 years before. There are now only 7 monks here.

From the entrance, a long flight of steps ascends to the upper floor of the **Palazzo degli Studi**, which was begun by Niccolò Acciaioli as a meeting place for young Florentines to study the liberal arts. Five frescoed lunettes of the Passion cycle (severely damaged) by Pontormo (1522–25) are exhibited here—they are among his most important works and were detached from the Great Cloister. They were painted when he came to live in the monastery in order to escape the plague in Florence in 1522. Behind the Crucifix, which dates from 1350–60, are five oil paintings by Jacopo Chimenti, known as Empoli, which are excellent copies of Pontormo's lunettes showing their original appearance. Also here is a fresco by Empoli of the *Sermon on the Mount*, detached from the top of the stairs, and another copy by him of a work by Pontormo, this time his *Supper at Emmaus*, now in the Uffizi. An adjoining room displays 16th–17th-century works, including paintings of the Apostles by Orazio Fidani (1653).

The spacious courtyard dates from 1545. The 16th-century façade of the **church** is by Cosimo Fancelli. The interior is divided into two parts: the monk's choir has fine vaulting (covered in the 17th century with frescoes by Orazio Fidani) and good 16th-century stalls. On the east wall is a fresco by Bernardino Poccetti (1591–92).

The visit continues through the extensive conventual buildings, entered through a door on the left wall of the church. Here the **colloquio**, reserved for conversation with visitors, has interesting 16th-century stained glass, and beyond is a charming little cloister reconstructed in the late 16th century by Giovanni Fancelli. Off it is the **chapter house**, with the pavement tomb of Leonardo Buonafede, which has an expressive effigy by Francesco da Sangallo (1550), and a good fresco of the *Crucifixion* by Mariotto Albertinelli (1506). A door leads out into the secluded **Great Cloister**, decorated with 66 *tondi* containing white majolica busts of saints and prophets, by Andrea and Giovanni della Robbia. In the centre is a well of 1521 and the monks' cemetery, still in use. One of the monks' cells, at the beginning of the right walk, may be visited; they each have three rooms, a loggia and a little garden. Most of the cells have a fresco over the door, and a little window through which food was passed.

The **church of Santa Maria** was built in 1404–07 (the stained glass window is by Niccolò di Pietro Gerini) but remodelled in 1841. Beneath the lay brethren's choir is a chapel (*closed at present*) with the magnificent tomb-slab of Cardinal Agnolo II Acciaioli, now thought to be the work of Francesco da Sangallo. There are three more beautiful pavement tombs of the Acciaioli family and the Gothic monument to the founder, Niccolò Acciaioli (d. 1365).

THE MEDICI VILLAS OF CAREGGI, LA PETRAIA & CASTELLO

Bus 14C from Via de' Martelli or Stazione Santa Maria Novella (right side) to the Villa di Careggi (the penultimate request stop before the terminus). No. 28 for Sesto Fiorentino runs from Stazione Santa Maria Novella (right side): the second 'Castello' request stop is the one for La Petraia, and the last 'Castello' request stop is the one for Villa di Castello. Although you should definitely take a bus to cross the uninteresting northern suburbs of Florence, there are pretty country walks in the hills behind Careggi, La Petraia, and Castello.

Villa Medicea di Careggi
Open 8–6, Sat 9–12; closed Sun and holidays; T: 055 427 9755.

Careggi has given its name to the main hospital of Florence. At the top of the hill, beyond the buildings of the hospital at no. 17 Viale Pieraccini (request-stop), in a well-wooded park, is the villa itself. This was one of the most important Medici villas, but only a few painted decorations from the early 17th century survive and most of the rooms are used as administrative offices.

History of the villa

The 14th-century castellated farmhouse, owned by Tommaso Lippi, was acquired by Giovanni di Bicci de' Medici in 1417 for use as a suburban residence. His son Cosimo il Vecchio returned here after his exile in Venice in 1434, and employed Michelozzo to enlarge the villa and add a loggia. It became the literary and artistic centre of the Medicean court, and is traditionally taken as the meeting place of the famous Platonic Academy, which saw the birth of the humanist movement of the Renaissance. Among the members who met in the gardens here were Marsilio Ficino, Angelo Poliziano, Pico della Mirandola, and Greek scholars including Gemisthos Plethon and Argyropoulos, who came to Florence after the fall of Constantinople. Cosimo il Vecchio, Piero di Cosimo, and Lorenzo the Magnificent all died in the villa. It was burnt after the expulsion of the Medici at the end of the 15th century, but renovated by Cosimo I who commissioned works from Pontormo (now lost) to decorate it. In the early 19th century it was owned by Lord Holland, who sold it to Francis Sloane in 1848. Sloane (1795–1871) trained as a geologist but came to Florence as a librarian c. 1824. He made a lot of money through his management of copper mines near Volterra for the Lorraine grand duke Leopold II, and became a public benefactor who made significant contributions towards the work on the new façades of the Duomo and Santa Croce. Sloane restored the villa and partly transformed the garden. It became a nurses' home in 1930, and is now used partly as administrative offices by the hospital of Careggi, and partly for meetings and lectures.

Tour of the villa

The courtyard, which incorporates parts of older buildings and has an ancient well, has composite capitals with acanthus leaves designed by Michelozzo. Off it, on the ground floor, is a room with early 17th-century frescoed lunettes. In a garden loggia there is a fresco by George Frederic Watts, painted in 1844–45 while Watts was staying here as a guest of Lord Holland. The subject is the murder of Pietro Leoni, Lorenzo the Magnificent's doctor—who, legend says, was thrown into the well in the courtyard, accused of failing to save Lorenzo's life. He had attempted to cure his patient's uricaemia with a philtre of powdered emeralds.

A 16th-century staircase leads up to the first floor. A little studio used by Cosimo II's brother Carlo de' Medici in the early 17th century has a vault fresco with *grottesche* by Michelangelo Cinganelli. The delightful corner loggia, with columns on three sides, overlooking the garden, has a charming ceiling frescoed with birds and *grottesche*.

Near the custodian's office on the ground floor is an interesting underground cellar, dating from the early 17th century, with a barrel vault painted with a trellis and birds, a worn majolica floor, and a grotto decorated with shells.

Part of the garden survives, laid out c. 1617 probably by Giulio Parigi, with laurel hedges and ilex groves. It was altered in the 19th and 20th centuries when the palm trees, cedars, and sequoia were planted. The orangery dates from the mid-19th century. Some paths with pebble mosaics survive.

The Villa della Petraia

Open 9–dusk; except second and third Mon of month; the villa closes 1 hour before dusk; T: 055 451 208. Combined ticket with the Villa di Castello gardens. Refreshments available.
Villa della Petraia, standing on the site of a 14th-century castle of the Strozzi, was rebuilt in 1575 (preserving the tower of the castle) for Grand Duke Ferdinando I by Buontalenti. In 1864–70 Vittorio Emanuele II lived here, and in 1919 Vittorio Emanuele III presented it to the state.

The garden

The beautiful lower garden was designed in the late 16th century for Ferdinando with symmetrical parterres on terraces descending from the moat in front of the villa which served as a fishpond as well as a cistern for irrigation (it is now full of goldfish and carp). It was altered in the 19th century under the influence of Victorian taste, but dwarf pear trees and persimmons have recently been replanted in this part of the garden, and the meadows of wild flowers (particularly beautiful in early spring) are left uncut as they were in the days of the Medici grand dukes. The fine hedges throughout the garden are planted with libernum, laurel and box.

On the upper terrace of the garden, on either side of the villa, from which there is a fine view, pots of orange and lemon trees are put out around Easter time (taken in in the winter). The beautiful fountain by Tribolo and Pierino da Vinci, with a bronze statue of *Fiorenza* by Giambologna, has been replaced by a very fine copy, and the original has been removed to the inside of the villa. On the other side of the villa is a charming symmetrical *giardino segreto*, a 1991 recreation of the way it would have looked at the turn of the 16th and 17th centuries. This had rare plants such as asparagus, artichokes and tulips. The little garden is at its best from late February to April. A magnificent park, with ancient cypresses, extends behind the villa to the east. The park and gardens are beautifully maintained.

The villa

The villa is shown on request (ring the bell). The 16th-century courtyard was covered with a glass roof and given a Venetian floor and chandelier so that it could be used as a ballroom by Vittorio Emanuele II. The decorative frescoes beneath the two side loggias, illustrating the history of the Medici family, are by Volterrano (1636–46); those on the other two walls have late 16th-century *grottesche* by Cosimo Daddi. In two rooms off the courtyard are temporarily displayed the bronze group of *Antaeus and Hercules* by Ammannati (1558–59), removed from a fountain in the garden of Villa di Castello, and four bronze putti from the same fountain. Another room displays two paintings by Crescenzio Onofrio and Alessandro Magnasco, and two sculptures of gladiators (also removed from the garden of Castello where they have been replaced by copies), one by Domenico Pieratti and the other an antique Roman work integrated by Pieratti.

On the other side of the courtyard is the splendid Sala Rossa hung with tapestries: four of them are 18th-century Flemish works from Parma and the other was made in Florence in the 17th century. The huge 19th-century carpet was restored *in situ*. There is a collection of clocks here and in the following rooms. In the chapel (1682–95), with frescoes attributed to Pier Dandini or Luigi del Moro, is a painting of the *Madonna and Child* by Pier Francesco Fiorentino, and an altarpiece of the *Holy Family* by the school of Andrea del Sarto.

The private apartments on the first floor are decorated in Neoclassical style. In the corridor is a remarkable long Chinese silk scroll painting of the *Port of Canton* (1765). In a room off the loggia is exhibited the original bronze statue of *Fiorenza* (Florence wringing the water of the Arno and Mugnone from her hair) by Giambologna, removed from the fountain in the garden. The bedroom of the 'Bella Rosina', wife of Vittorio Emanuele II, decorated in blue damask, has the best early 19th-century Piedmontese furniture. The Salotto Giallo, with yellow walls in the style known as 'retour d'Egypte', has French chairs, and a travelling desk made in Lucca, all in Empire style. In the chapel are frescoes by Cosimo Daddi and a copy of Raphael's *Madonna dell'Impannata* (the original is in Palazzo Pitti, *see p. 118*). The billiard room is a remarkable period piece, with chintz furniture, hung with 17th-century paintings by Francesco Curradi, Passignano, and two by Matteo Rosselli acquired by Cardinal Carlo de' Medici. There is a remarkable collection of late 19th- or early 20th-century parlour games and mid-19th-century alabasters, including intricate globes.

Villa Il Bel Riposo and Villa Corsini

In Via della Petraia is Villa 'Il Bel Riposo', with a 19th-century castellated tower in medieval style, where Carlo Lorenzini (Collodi) lived while writing *Pinocchio*. This famous children's book was first published in 1880. Lorenzini took part in the Risorgimento and worked as a journalist and for the Prefecture of Florence. Opposite is Villa Corsini (*open Wed & Sat 8.30–5.30, Sun 8.30–2*) rebuilt for Filippo Corsini in 1698–99 with a Baroque façade by Antonio Ferri. The Medici grand dukes lent the villa to Sir Robert Dudley (the son of Sir Robert Dudley, Earl of Leicester, Queen Elizabeth I's favourite), who was a naval engineer and administered the port of Livorno: a plaque records his death here in 1649. Inside the villa are displayed some sculptures from the Archaeological Museum of Florence, including a huge statue of the sleeping Ariadne, which is a Roman copy of a Greek original of the Pergamene school; a colossal bust of Hercules; and a very damaged marble lion, a Greek original of the 5th century BC. There are plans to open the first floor also and the lovely garden, partly dating from the 16th century with box hedges and lemon trees and a fountain by Tribolo.

The Medici Villa di Castello

Admission to the gardens only, 9–dusk; closed second and third Mon of the month; T: 055 454791. Combined ticket with the Villa della Petraia.

In front of Villa Corsini, Via di Castello leads in five minutes to Villa di Castello. Although the fountains have been altered and some of the statues removed over the centuries, this is the Medici garden which perhaps best preserves its 16th-century appearance, and it was the model for all subsequent Italianate gardens. It is still of the greatest botanical interest, especially for its magnificent tubs of citrus trees.

History of the villa

The villa was acquired by Giovanni and Lorenzo di Pierfrancesco de' Medici, Lorenzo the Magnificent's younger cousins, in 1476. Here they hung Botticelli's famous *Birth of Venus*. Botticelli's *Primavera* and *Pallas and the Centaur* were also later brought here (and all the pictures remained in the house until 1761). The villa, inherited by Giovanni delle Bande Nere, was sacked during the siege of 1530 (*see p. 30*), but restored for Giovanni's son, Cosimo I, by Bronzino and Pontormo. It was bought by the state in 1919, and drastically 'restored' and transformed in the early 1970s as the seat of a national research council and of the Accademia della Crusca, founded in 1582 for the study of the Italian language. The first edition of the institute's dictionary dates from 1612.

The garden

Cosimo I employed Tribolo in 1541 to design the garden. The fountains were laid out on a central axis intended to celebrate the establishment of the Medici family as absolute monarchs in Tuscany. This was altered in the 18th century when the great marble fountain by Tribolo (assisted by Pierino da Vinci) was moved to its central position: formerly it was the fountain closest to the villa, and the crowning bronze figures of *Hercules and Antaeus* by Ammannati (1559–60) represented the triumph of Hercules (or Cosimo) over Vice. Since its restoration this has been temporarily exhibited in the Villa della Petraia (*see above*), while the exquisitely carved base, some 6m high, has been carefully restored in one of the garden buildings here and a copy (the largest of its kind ever made in Italy) will be installed *in situ*.

The fountain which used to be in the centre of the gardens, and which represented Florence as chief city of the grand duchy, no longer exists, although the crowning figure of *Fiorenza* is now in the Villa della Petraia. The third element, beneath the terrace, was the elaborate grotto (well preserved), also probably designed by Tribolo, full of exotic animals and encrusted with shell mosaics and stalactites, and lined with natural stone taken from real grottoes. The huge basin on the left has beautifully carved decorations thought to be by Tribolo. Giambologna's bronze birds, now in the Bargello, were removed from here. In the floor and round the walls are water spouts: visitors (who were 'locked in' by a gate) were regularly surprised by a thorough drenching from their hosts.

From the upper terrace, backed by woods, there is a good view. Here, surrounded by an ilex wood, or *bosco*, inhabited by numerous birds, is a colossus representing Appennino rising out of a pool and feeling the cold, by Ammannati.

The garden is at its best from April to June, and when the magnificent collection of citrus trees, in some 1,000 terracotta tubs, are put out in the gardens for the summer. The trees make up one of the most important collections of its kind in the world, with over 100 varieties including some that are ancient and unique. Some of the plants are 300 years old. Some citrus trees are still grown outside at the top of the garden, and there is a fine collection of azaleas. In the beds surrounded by low box hedges, tulips, daffodils and bluebells flower in March.

On the right is the charming little *giardino segreto* (*opened on request*), created in the late 17th century by Cosimo III, where an unusual variety of cream-coloured Indian jasmine grows (in flower from July to October). The box hedges were replanted ten years ago and some classical varieties of antique rose were reintroduced. The lower area of this little garden has about 400 varieties of aromatic and medicinal herbs which were known to have been cultivated here in the 16th century (including some 20 varieties each of thyme and of sage). The garden is beautifully maintained and the four gardeners take care not to use chemical fertilizers.

MUSEO STIBBERT,
VILLA LA PIETRA & VILLA DEMIDOFF

Museo Stibbert

Open Mon, Tues and Wed 10–2; Fri, Sat and Sun 10–6; closed Thurs. Tours begin every 30 minutes and last 1 hour; T: 055 486 049. The Japanese collection has been closed since 1988, but there are plans to open it for pre-booked visits while restoration of the upper floor proceeds. There is a little café on the ground floor with a few tables in the garden. Bus 4 from Piazza Unità Italiana to Via Vittorio Emanuele II.

The museum and its collection

The museum was created by the Englishman Frederick Stibbert (1838–1906) in his home here. Born in Florence to an Italian mother and English father, Stibbert inherited a great fortune, and became a collector, traveller, artist—and, in 1866, a Garibaldian hero. He bequeathed his museum to the British Government, which then passed it on to the city of Florence. He built this huge, rambling villa (incorporating part of an earlier building) in 1878–1905, with one part designed as a museum, and the other as his residence. The exterior of the building is covered with a miscellany of decorative details.

The 57 period rooms were designed for Stibbert's eclectic collection: heavily decorated and bizarre in atmosphere, they are crammed with an extraordinary variety of objects. The paintings are generally of most interest for the costume of their sitters, but they include good works by Luca Giordano and Alessandro Allori, as well as some earlier works in the Sala delle Bandiere, named after the Sienese Palio flags which decorate the ceiling. The collection of costumes includes that worn by Napoleon Bonaparte at his coronation as King of Italy in 1805.

Stibbert's particular interest and field of study, however, was armour and costume, and his collection is famous for its Japanese armour—the best collection in Europe (particularly notable for the arms and armour of the Edo period), and its superb Asiatic armour, much of it Turkish and used for the first time by Sultan Selim I at the end of the 15th century. A huge neo-Gothic hall is filled with a cavalcade of fully armed horses and knights of the 16th century, with six soldiers wearing 16th-century Asiatic armour. Another room displays a 15th-century *condottiere* mounted on his steed, and there is tournament and battle armour dating back to Etruscan and Roman times, and one of the finest collections of spurs in existence.

The charming little Art Nouveau fumoir was created in 1890 and entirely decorated with ceramics from the Ulisse Cantagalli workshop. Cantagalli carried out a lot of work in Florence for the English community, and his ceramics show the influence of William Morris and William de Morgan.

Several rooms have Neoclassical frescoes by Luigi Ademollo, which already decorated part of the house before Stibbert bought it.

The park and neighbouring gardens

Also created by Stibbert, the park of Museo Stibbert (*open 9–dusk daily except Thurs*) is landscaped in Victorian style and planted with conifers. It is in the process of restoration. Near the house is a Gothic terrace with a Venetian well-head and Gothic architectural fragments. Farther downhill, on a lake, is an Egyptian temple, perhaps designed by J.B. Papworth, guarded by lions and sphinxes. The orangery was designed by Giuseppe Poggi, and the terracotta statues were probably produced in the Cantagalli workshop.

The public park of **Villa Fabbricotti**, with ilexes, cypresses, limes, elms, laurels and cedars of Lebanon, adjoins the grounds of the Museo Stibbert (*entered from Via Federico Stibbert and at no. 48 Via Vittorio Emanuele II*). The villa was restored in 1864 and leased to the British Consul, who arranged for Queen Victoria to stay here in 1894.

At the other end of the long Via Vittorio Emanuele II is the entrance to the **Giardino dell'Orticoltura** (*open daily*), a horticultural garden created in 1859, but now greatly altered. The splendid greenhouse built by Giacomo Roster in 1880 is usually open when excellent flower shows are held here in spring and autumn. The gardens are divided by the railway line; the entrance to the upper gardens is in Via Trento; these gardens have a crescent of pine trees, and a delightful fountain created in 1990 in the form of a huge snake-dragon.

Villa La Pietra

Garden and villa open by appointment. There are also two open weeks a year—for information T: 055 5007210. Bus 25 from Stazione Santa Maria Novella.

From the Museo Stibbert the lovely old Via di Montughi leads uphill to emerge on the Via Bolognese, the old Roman road to Bologna, in front of the gate of Villa La Pietra (no. 120), surrounded by fields of olives on its huge estate, and preceded by a splendid long avenue of cypresses above pink China rose-bushes.

The **villa** was built in the 1460s for the Sassetti (Francesco Sassetti was manager of the Medici bank under Lorenzo the Magnificent), and sold to the Capponi in 1545. In 1907 Arthur Acton's wealthy American wife Hortense Mitchell purchased the property. It was the birthplace and residence of their son, the aesthete and historian Sir Harold Acton (1904–94), one of the most famous Anglo-Florentines of the last century, who was made an honorary citizen of Florence in 1986. He bequeathed the villa to New York University and it is now used as a branch campus which takes undergraduate students, as well as a conference centre. The villa, which contains one of the most interesting private collections of works of art in Florence, including a notable group of early Tuscan paintings, has been carefully conserved, and the rooms are still fully furnished as they were in the Actons' day.

The beautiful **garden**, a successful imitation of a 16th-century Tuscan garden, was created by the Actons: it is now being restored and replanted so that in a few years time it will regain the appearance it had at the height of its splendour in the late 1930s. It is a green garden, on a very large scale, in which some 200 17th-century allegorical statues, some by Orazio Marinali (who produced much of statuary for the Palladian villas around Vicenza), are a special feature. The garden was designed to be viewed from the upper terrace and the house, and is laid out in 'rooms' on different levels. The planting is predominantly box, yew, cypress and ilex, with hedges of cypress and ilex, and low box edging with clipped bay trees. There is a green theatre and good topiary, and a *boschetto* of laurels. The very high terrace attached to the house has cascades of banksia rose and wisteria. The charming walled kitchen garden, or *pomaria*, is decorated with shell mosaic. This was part of the original Renaissance garden, and its pear trees and box and myrtle hedges have been replanted. The beds along the walls have viola and iris and yellow roses. Here orange and lemon trees are kept in pots, and two huge Portugal laurels grow in front of the orangery built in the 1650s. The 57-acre estate includes four boundary villas.

Villa Demidoff

Open March–Oct Sun and holidays 10–7; April–Sept Thurs, Fri, Sat, Sun 10–8; T: 055 409 427. No dogs. Bus 25 from Stazione Santa Maria Novella. Journey time about 40 mins.
Farther out of Florence, the Via Bolognese follows the long ruined walls of the huge park of Villa Demidoff, the main entrance of which is at Pratolino. Some 17–18 hectares of the splendid, well-kept park belong to the province and are open to the public. The park is one of the most beautiful open spaces near the city, and its fields and woods make it a lovely place to picnic. There is a café-restaurant in one of the farm buildings. The most remarkable sight is Giambologna's colossal statue of *Appennino* (1580): the giant is pressing down the head of a monster (water used to gush out of its mouth). This is almost the only survival from the famous garden created here by Buontalenti for Francesco I, the villa of which was demolished in 1824. Paolo Demidoff, son of Nicola, a Russian emigré from St Petersburg, built his residence in 1872 in the service wing of the Medici villa, and his descendants lived here until 1955.

APPENDIX

These buildings (listed alphabetically) are described in brief since many of them are not open regularly to the public and are either of less importance than those described in the main body of the guide or are outside the historic centre of the city.

CHURCHES, ORATORIES & CONVENTS

Fuligno (Cenacolo di)
Map p. 398, C1.
Entrance at no. 42 Via Faenza. Open Mon, Tues, Sat 9–12 or when the custodian is available; ring any bell; T: 055 286 982.
The ex-convent of Sant'Onofrio (or Fuligno) was founded here in the early 14th century, and part of the present building dates from 1420. After its suppression in the 19th century, a beautiful fresco of the *Last Supper* was discovered in the refectory. At first attributed to Raphael (whose bust was set up here at that time), it was later thought to be by the hand of Perugino. Recent studies have suggested that Perugino designed the work while he was in Florence in the last decade of the 15th century but that it was executed by a member of his *bottega*, perhaps Giovan Maria di Bartolomeo, called Rocco Zoppo. It is in very good condition. In the background is a lovely landscape with the *Agony in the Garden*.

Gesù Pellegrino
Map p. 399, D1.
Via San Gallo.
Rebuilt in 1588 by Giovanni Antonio Dosio with a fresco cycle (1590) and three altarpieces by Giovanni Balducci (Il Cosci). In the nave is the tomb-slab of the Pievano Arlotto (1400–84), rec-

tor of the church, and subject of a famous painting by Volterrano (*see p. 116*). The inscription reads (in translation): 'This tomb was ordered by the Pievano Arlotto for himself and for whoever wishes to enter it'.

Holy Trinity
Map p. 399, E1.
26 Via Micheli.
Since 1967 this has been owned by the Waldensian Community. The Waldensians, who originated in the south of France c. 1170, were condemned by the Lateran Council in 1184 and fled to northern Italy where they settled, especially in the district around Turin. An Anglican church, built by Domenico Giraldi, was founded here in 1846. The present neo-Gothic building, with stained glass windows, was designed in 1892 by the English architect G.F. Bodley. The choir screen and wooden stalls, also by Bodley, were made in Florence in 1902 by the workshop of Mariano Coppedè.

Montedomini (ex-Convent of)
Map p. 399, F4.
Via dei Malcontenti.
This huge hospice for the elderly (now partly used by the University), is on the site of a 15th-century hospital, later

used by two Franciscan convents of closed orders (Montedomini and Monticelli). The buildings were redesigned as a hospice in the early 19th century by Giuseppe del Rosso, and it became a Pia Casa di Lavoro (workhouse), and was further enlarged in 1860. It incorporates a church consecrated in 1573 with a vault painted by Agostino Veracini in the 18th century. A wing of the hospice, used from 1894 to 1938 as a military hospital, has painted decorations by Galileo Chini.

Russian Church
Beyond map p. 398, C1.
Via Leone X. Open for services (sung mass) on the third Sunday of the month and on major church festivals.
The church was built with funds raised from the large Russian colony in Florence (which included the wealthy Demidoff family) and consecrated in 1904. Throughout most of the 19th century, Florence was a fashionable place to spend the winter for many aristocratic Russian families. The architects of the fine building came from Russia, and the pretty majolica decoration on the exterior was carried out by the Ulisse Cantagalli workshop. It is now a national monument owned by the Russian Orthodox community of Florence.

St James's Church
Map p. 398, A1.
9 Via Bernardo Rucellai. Open for services, admission on request in the morning.
The neo-Gothic American Episcopal church (1908–11). It has a good stained glass by Italian craftsmen, including a rose window by Ezio Giovannozzi.

Sant' Agata
Beyond map p. 399, D1.
110 Via San Gallo.
The façade (1592) is by Allori, who also painted the high altarpiece of the *Marriage at Cana* (in a handsome frame). Other paintings are attributed to Lorenzo di Credi, Lorenzo Lippi and Neri di Bicci.

Sant'Agnese (Istituto)
Map p. 399, D1.
79 Via Guelfa.
Now an old people's home run by the Compagnia del Bigallo (*see p. 60*), with a pretty little Baroque chapel (early 18th century; frescoes by the school of Sagrestani).

San Barnaba
Map p. 398, C1.
Via Guelfa.
The 14th-century portal bears a della Robbian lunette. The pretty interior was remodelled in 1700 and there is a Baroque organ above the nuns' choir.

San Carlo dei Lombardi
Map p. 397, B2.
Via Calzaiuoli.
Dating from 1349–1404, this has a severe (much ruined) façade, and in the unattractive interior there is a *Deposition* by Niccolò di Pietro Gerini.

Sant' Egidio
Map p. 399, D2–E2.
Via Bufalini.
The church of the hospital of Santa Maria Nuova, founded in 1286 by Folco Portinari (believed to be the father of Dante's Beatrice), and still one of the main hospitals of Florence. The

entrance is beneath an unusual portico (1574–1612) by Bernardo Buontalenti. In the interior, dating from around 1420, are remains of Portinari's tomb and a splendid high altar with a ciborium in *pietre dure* dating from 1666. A door to the right of the church (*usually kept closed; admission through the hospital buildings*) leads into a cloister, the oldest part of the hospital, with a *Pietà* by Giovanni della Robbia. To the left of the church, in another old courtyard, is the tomb-slab of Monna Tessa, the servant of Portinari, who persuaded him to found the hospital. In the offices of the Presidenza, above (*opened on certain days of the year or by appointment*), are a *Madonna and Child* by Andrea della Robbia and detached frescoes of Martin V consecrating the church, by Bicci di Lorenzo (with its sinopia), and the same pope confirming its privileges, by Andrea di Giusto (repainted).

Santa Elisabetta delle Convertite
Map p. 398, B4.
Via de' Serragli (corner of Via del Campuccio).
This small deconsecrated church is now used as a hall for concerts and lectures. It was next to a convent founded in the 14th century for destitute girls and converted prostitutes. The interior preserves a beautiful triumphal arch (1494) which shows the influence of Brunelleschi, and a frescoed ceiling with the *Glory of St Mary Magdalen* by Alessandro Gherardini (1703). Frescoes have been discovered in the nuns' choir with stories of martyrs, almost certainly by Bernardino Poccetti.

San Filippo Neri
Map p. 397, C3.

Piazza San Firenze.
San Firenze, a huge Baroque building, now occupied by the law courts, designed by Francesco Zanobi del Rosso (1772–75) is flanked by two church façades designed by Ferdinando Ruggieri (1715). The church of San Filippo Neri (left), by Gherardo and Pier Francesco Silvani (1633–48) has an unusually tall interior, decorated in 1712–14 (the ceiling was painted by Giovanni Camillo Sagrestani). The law courts are to be moved out of Florence to a vast building near Novoli, designed by Leonardo Ricci and still under construction, though its towers, much higher than any other building in the vicinity of the city, have already irreparably altered the view of Florence and its surroundings.

San Francesco dei Vanchetoni (Oratorio di)
Map p. 398, B2.
17 Via Palazzuolo. The custodian lives next door and sometimes shows it on request.
Owned by the Comune and often used for concerts, the oratory was built in 1602 by Giovanni Nigetti, with a vestibule and façade by Matteo Nigetti (1620). The ceiling frescoes are by Pietro Liberi, Volterrano, Cecco Bravo and others. The chapel behind the altar contains a 16th-century Crucifix, and the charming sacristy has inlaid cupboards.

San Giovanni di Dio
Map p. 398, B3.
Borgo Ognissanti.
Built by Carlo Marcellini (1702–13) next to the ex-hospital of San Giovanni di Dio, founded in 1380 by the Vespucci family (closed down in 1982). It was enlarged in 1702–13 by Carlo

Marcellini to incorporate the Vespucci house on this site, including the birthplace of Amerigo (*see p. 204*). In the fine atrium (1735) are sculptures by Girolamo Ticciati.

San Giovannino dei Cavalieri
Map p. 399, D1.
66 Via San Gallo.
Preceded by an unusual vestibule with original cupboards. In the tribune, surrounded by worn frescoes by Alessandro Gherardini (1703), is a large *Crucifixion* by Lorenzo Monaco. At the end of the right aisle is an *Annunciation*, a painting by the Master of the Castello Nativity. On the right wall is a worn fresco of *St Michael Archangel* by Francesco Granacci. In the left aisle is a *Nativity* by Bicci di Lorenzo, and a *Coronation of the Virgin* by his son, Neri di Bicci. On the west wall is the *Birth of the Baptist* by Santi di Tito and the *Beheading of the Baptist* by Pier Dandini.

San Giovannino degli Scolopi
Map p. 397, B1.
Via de' Martelli.
This little church was begun in 1579 by Ammannati, who designed the second chapel on the left as his burial place (1592). The fourth chapel on the right was built in 1692–1712 for Grand Duke Cosimo III. The altarpiece of the *Preaching of St Francis Xavier* is the best work of Francesco Curradi. The vault fresco is by Pier Dandini and the stucco angels by Girolamo Ticciati. The first chapel on the left has angels, *Jacob's Dream* and the *Fall of Lucifer*, by Jacopo Ligozzi. The altarpiece is by Alessandro Allori. The confessionals date from the late 17th century.

San Giuseppe
Map p. 399, F3.
Via di San Giuseppe. Open 5–7; Weds also 9.30–12.
Built in 1519 to a design by Baccio d'Agnolo. The portal dates from 1852 (thought to be based on a design by Michelangelo). The oratory with pretty graffiti decoration and the elegant campanile (designed by Baccio d'Agnolo) both date from 1934.

The handsome interior has pretty frescoes by Sigismondo Betti in the centre of the vault and in the choir (1754), with architectural perspectives by Pietro Anderlini. The organ, with its original mechanism, is by the workshop of the Agati of Pistoia (1764). On the south side, the first chapel has a 16th-century lunette (left side) and an unusual funerary monument by Odoardo Fantacchiotti (1854). The second chapel was decorated in 1705. The damaged triptych attributed to Taddeo Gaddi and the 14th-century carved wooden Crucifix both belonged to the Compagnia di Santa Maria della Croce al Tempio. The third chapel has frescoes by Luigi Ademollo (1840), and on the altar is a *Nativity*, an early work by Santi di Tito. Above the high altar, inlaid with a floral decoration in *pietre dure* in 1930, is a painted Crucifix by the early 15th-century Florentine school. The 17th-century stalls and 16th-century paintings in octagonal frames complete the decoration of the choir. On the north side, the third chapel (left wall) contains an *Annunciation* attributed to the Maestro di Serumidio; the second chapel has an early 16th-century copy of the fresco of the *Madonna del Giglio* (formerly in the tabernacle outside the church) and a painted Crucifix attributed to Lorenzo Monaco. The first chapel (left wall) has *San Francesco di Paola Healing a Sick Man* by Santi di Tito and, on the altar, a polychrome wooden Crucifix of the 17th century and two later figures.

San Jacopo tra i Fossi
Map p. 399, E3.
Via de' Benci.
Now the Evangelical church, it has a fine 18th-century ceiling incorporating a painting by Alessandro Gherardini.

Santa Maria dei Candeli
Map p. 399, F2.
Borgo Pinti.
Redesigned by Giovanni Battista Foggini in 1704, it has a ceiling fresco by Niccolò Lapi.

Santa Maria degli Angeli
Map p. 399, E2.
39 Via degli Alfani.
Remodelled in 1676, the church is now used for lectures. The unusual interior has a barrel vault with frescoes by Alessandro Gherardini and stuccoes by Vittorio Barbieri and Alessandro Lombardi. In the former refectory is a *Last Supper* (1543) by Ridolfo del Ghirlandaio. The cloister on the right of the church has graffiti decoration and lunettes by Bernardino Poccetti, and busts attributed to Caccini and Francavilla. Off the cloister is a little chapel (1599) with a fresco in the dome by Poccetti who probably also painted the altarpiece. There are also sculptured medallions attributed to Caccini and Francavilla.

Santa Maria della Croce al Tempio
Map p. 399, E3.
Via di San Giuseppe.
This little church (deconsecrated) contained frescoes attributed to Bicci di Lorenzo, detached for restoration.

Santa Maria a Ricorboli
Beyond map p. 399, F4.
Via Fortini.
In a chapel in the north aisle is a very late, damaged *Madonna and Child* by the hand of Giotto.

San Niccolò al Ceppo (Oratorio di)
Map p. 397, C2.
5 Via Pandolfini.
Built in 1561 for a confraternity founded in the 14th century (now used for concerts). In the vestibule are two oval paintings of saints by Onorio Marinari (1695) and a trompe l'œil ceiling by Giovanni Domenico Ferretti (c. 1735). The statue in stucco of the *Madonna and Child* is by Camillo Camillani (1572). The Oratory has 17th-century wooden benches and a frescoed ceiling by Ferretti, Pietro Anderlini and Domenico and Francesco Papi. The altarpiece of the *Crucifixion* is by Francesco Curradi, and on the walls are a *Visitation* and *St Nicholas with Two Members of the Confraternity* by Giovanni Antonio Sogliani (1517–21). The *Crucifixion with St Nicholas of Bari and St Francis* is by Fra' Angelico. Outside on the corner of the street (Canto alla Badessa) is a tabernacle with a 16th-century fresco of the *Annunciation* by Giovanni Balducci.

San Niccolò sopr'Arno (or San Niccolò Oltrarno)
Map p. 399, E4.

Via di S. Niccolò. Open 8–10.30 & 5.30–7.
Founded in the 11th century and rebuilt at the end of the 14th. Several interesting frescoes were found beneath the 16th-century altars during restoration work after the 1966 flood. In the chapel at the end of the south side, there is a fresco of St Ansano, attributed to a little-known painter Francesco d'Antonio, together with its sinopia. A door (not always open) leads into the sacristy, which contains a *Madonna della Cintola*, a beautiful fresco of the late 15th-century Florentine school (attributed to Baldovinetti), within a *pietra serena* tabernacle by the *bottega* of Michelozzo. Beneath it is a 14th-century triptych attributed to an unknown artist named the Master of San Niccolò from this work. The triptych of the *Madonna and Saints* is attributed to Bicci di Lorenzo. Also here are two small paintings of St Michael and St Gabriel Archangel by Il Poppi. The painted altarpieces in the church are by artists born in the mid-16th century (Empoli, Il Poppi, Alessandro Fei, Alessandro Allori, and Giovanni Battista Naldini). There is also a wooden Crucifix by Michelozzo.The precious organ by Dionisio Romani dates from 1581.

San Paolino
Map p. 398, B2.
Via Palazzuolo.
Founded in the 10th century, it has a bare façade. The interior was rebuilt in 1669 by Giovanni Battista Balatri, and is interesting for its 17th–18th-century paintings. On the south side, the first chapel contains two Albizi funerary monuments attributed to the *bottega* of Giovanni Battista Foggini, which incorporate two skeletons. In the second

chapel, there is an *Annunciation* by a follower of Giovanni Antonio Sogliani and two paintings by (left) Francesco di Antonio Ciseri (1891) and (right) Volterrano. The south transept has a polychrome marble altar and an altarpiece of the *Death of St Joseph* by Giovanni Domenico Ferretti. On either side of this are the *Marriage of the Virgin* by Vincenzo Meucci and the *Rest on the Flight* by Ignazio Hugford. In the Sanctuary is the *Ecstasy of St Paul* by Francesco Curradi. The north transept has a marble altar by Girolamo Ticciati, and another altarpiece by Francesco Curradi. In the first chapel (left wall) is *Christ in the Garden* by Tommaso Gherardini and (right wall), the *Adoration of the Magi* by Giovanni Domenico Ferretti. The pretty 18th-century confessionals have *tondi* painted by Ottaviano Dandini.

San Salvatore al Vescovo
Map p. 397, B2.
Piazza dell'Olio.
Incorporated in the huge Palazzo Arcivescovile, partially reconstructed by Giovanni Antonio Dosio in 1584 (the façade was rebuilt in 1895 when the piazza was enlarged). The church interior was entirely frescoed in 1737–38 with quadratura by Pietro Anderlini, and an *Ascension* in the vault by Vincenzo Meucci. The frescoes in the apse and dome, and the monochrome figures of the Apostles, are all by Giovanni Domenico Ferretti. The little Romanesque façade of the earlier church can be seen in Piazza dell'Olio.

San Salvi (Convento di)
Beyond map p. 399, F3.

16 Via San Salvi. Open 8.30–1.50; closed Mon; T: 055 238 8603.

The conventual buildings of the Vallombrosan abbey of San Salvi contain a celebrated fresco of the *Last Supper* by Andrea del Sarto—known as the Cenacolo di San Salvi (*see opposite*)—and a small museum of 16th-century works. The long gallery, with fine vaulting, is hung with some interesting large 16th-century altarpieces, all of them labelled, including works by Franciabigio, Michele di Ridolfo del Ghirlandaio, Vasari, Il Poppi, and Empoli. In the room at the end, there are beautifully carved reliefs by Benedetto da Rovezzano from the tomb of St John Gualberto formerly in the nearby church of San Michele a San Salvi (*see below*), and willfully damaged during the Imperial siege of 1530 (when Holy Roman Emperor Charles V sent an army to Florence to reinstate the Medici), when most of the heads were defaced.

Two rooms, one with a lavabo by Benedetto da Rovezzano, and the other with a huge fireplace which served the convent kitchen, contain paintings by contemporaries or followers of Andrea del Sarto, including Giuliano Bugiardini (*Madonna and Child*), Franciabigio, Pontormo, Giovanni Antonio Sogliani, Maso di San Friano, Raffaellino del Garbo (*Annunciation* and the *Madonna Enthroned between Saints*).

The Refectory contains two more works by Andrea del Sarto: a very ruined fresco of the *Annunciation* detached from the Sdrucciolo di Orsanmichele, and a *Noli me tangere* from the convent of San Gallo.

San Michele a San Salvi is a 14th–16th-century church entered through a charming late 14th-century cloister (the small upper loggia was added in the 15th century). At the entrance to the chapter house there is a relief of *St John Gualberto and two Vallombrosan Monks* by Benedetto da Rovezzano. The church has ceiling frescoes by Vincenzo Meucci, and a chapel off the south transept (now used as a sacristy) with interesting remains of early 15th-century frescoes in *terraverde* and a statue of a female saint attributed to Andrea Orcagna.

Santo Stefano al Ponte

Map p. 397, B3.
Via Por Santa Maria.

In a secluded little piazza, this is a very old church, first built in 969, but severely damaged in the Uffizi bomb explosion in 1993 (*see p. 86*). The handsome Romanesque decoration of the façade dates from 1233. The interior (restored and now used as a concert hall) was altered by Ferdinando Tacca in 1649. It contains altarpieces by Santi di Tito and Matteo Rosselli, a painting by Jacopo di Cione, and a bronze altar frontal of the *Stoning of St Stephen* by Ferdinando Tacca. At the elaborate east end, the altar steps (removed from Santa Trìnita) are a remarkable Mannerist work by Buontalenti (1574). Beneath is a large crypt.

San Tommaso d'Aquino (Oratorio di)

Map p. 399, E2.
8 Via della Pergola.

Built in 1567 to a design by Santi di Tito, who also painted the high altarpiece with the Crucifix and St Thomas.

ANDREA DEL SARTO'S 'CENACOLO DI SAN SALVI'

The Refectory of the Convento di San Salvi contains Andrea del Sarto's celebrated *Cenacolo di San Salvi* (1511–27), a masterpiece of Florentine fresco which is remarkable for its colouring and dramatic movement. Each Apostle is beautifully painted; Judas is shown seated on the right of Christ and St John on the left. The austerity of the setting is relieved by the charming detail of two servants observing the scene from a balcony above. This is perhaps the most famous fresco of the *Last Supper* in Italy, after that by Leonardo da Vinci in Milan. It is extremely well preserved, as the Convent of San Salvi was a closed order and remained inaccessible until the early 19th century. The *tondi* of saints and the *Trinity* on the intrados were the first part of the fresco to be painted (the *grottesche* are by del Sarto's collaborator Andrea di Cosimo Feltrini).

Scalzo (Chiostro dello)
Map p. 399, D1.
69 Via Cavour. Usually open Mon, Thurs and Sat 8.30–2; T: 055 2388604.
This charming little early 16th-century cloister has very fine frescoes in monochrome by Andrea del Sarto (1510–26). They depict the life of St John the Baptist, but the scenes were not painted

in the narrative order of the story, and two of them were painted by Franciabigio when Andrea left for France—though he returned to complete the cycle. Above the scenes, Andrea del Sarto also painted the decorative friezes.

To the right of the door are *Faith* (c. 1523); *Angel Announcing the Birth of the*

Baptist to St Zacharias (1523); *Visitation* (1524); *Naming of the Baptist* (1526); *Blessing of the Young St John Before Leaving for the Desert* (by Franciabigio, 1518–19); *Meeting of Christ with the Young St John* (Franciabigio, 1518–19). The scenes on the end wall are almost totally ruined. They are *Baptism of Christ* (c. 1507–08) and the *Preaching of the Baptist* (1515); *Baptism of the Multitude* (1517); *Capture of the Baptist* (1517); *Dance of Salome* (1521); *Beheading of the Baptist* (1523). On the entrance wall is the *Banquet of Herod* (1523). The terracotta bust of St Antoninus dates from the early 16th century.

LIBRARIES

Archivio di Stato
Map p. 399, F3
Viale della Giovine Italia.
The Florence National Archives has been housed since 1989 in a new building designed by Italo Gamberini near Piazza Beccaria. Founded in 1582, the archives date back to the 8th century, and provide scholars with a wealth of information on the political and economic history of the city.

Archivio Storico del Comune di Firenze
Map p. 399, E2.
33 Via dell'Oriuolo.
The 18th-century Palazzo Bastogi houses the archives of the Comune of Florence, established by Peter Leopold in 1781 (the documents cover the period up until 1960). The main hall has Neoclassical stuccoes and painted decoration.

Biblioteca Marucelliana
Map p. 399, D1.
43–47 Via Cavour.
Founded by Francesco di Alessandro Marucelli (1625–1703) and opened to the public in 1752 in the present building built by Alessandro Dori (the reading room retains its 18th-century book-cases, and the holdings now number over 300,000 volumes). It is particularly rich in works on Florence.

Biblioteca Nazionale
Map p. 399, E4.
Piazza Cavalleggeri.
The most important library in Florence. The main building was erected in 1911–35 by Cesare Bazzani. The National Library was formed from a collection bequeathed by Antonio Magliabechi (d. 1714), the librarian of the Palatina and Laurenziana libraries, and was first opened to the public in 1747. The Biblioteca Palatina-Medicea (1711) and the library of Ferdinand III (1861), together with several monastic collections, were later additions. It includes an important collection of material relating to Dante and Galileo. It became a copyright library for books published in Italy in 1870. In 1966, nearly a third of the library's holdings was damaged when the Arno flooded, and a restoration centre here is still salvaging and conserving the books.

Biblioteca Riccardiana
Map p. 399, D2.
14 Via de' Ginori. Open weekdays 8–2;

closed Easter week and the last half of Aug. Housed in a 17th-century wing of Palazzo Medici-Riccardi, this was founded by Riccardo Riccardi and opened to the public in 1718. It is a fine example of a private library, with a delightful reading room frescoed by Luca Giordano. The original bookshelves contain illuminated manuscripts and incunabula.

British Institute
Map p. 398, B3.
9 Lungarno Guicciardini.
Palazzo Lanfredini, by Baccio d'Agnolo, has bright graffiti decoration (restored). On part of the ground floor and first floor are the library and the office of the director of the British Institute of Florence. A non-profit making independent institution, this was founded in 1917 by a group of Anglo-Florentines—including Edward Hutton, G.M. Trevelyan, Lina Waterfield, Gaetano Salvemini, Arthur Acton, and Aldo Sorani—and received a Royal Charter in 1923. Its role is to maintain a library of English books in the city, and to promote British culture in Italy and Italian culture to English-speaking visitors. The Lending Library (with about 50,000 volumes, the largest collection of English books in Italy) was named after its benefactor Harold Acton in 1989 (who, on his death in 1994, bequeathed the premises to the Institute). It can be used for a small fee and retains the atmosphere of a 19th-century general browsing library. The reading room has comfortable armchairs and English newspapers. The collection includes books on Italian art, history, music and numerous 19th-century novels (many of them obscure works). It has been augmented over the years by the donations of Anglo-American residents in Florence. Public lectures are also held here on most Wednesdays of the year (usually at 6pm). The Institute runs a language school and courses in art history at no. 2 Piazza Strozzi (*map p. 397, A2*).

Istituto Geografico Militare
Map p. 398, B1.
10 Viale Strozzi. Open Mon–Fri 9–12.
This institute (on Via Battisti) has a remarkable cartographic library with works up to 1862 and an archive (maps from 1863–1963). The later material, principally maps made after 1963, is kept in a splendid building on Viale Strozzi, where they are also on sale.

SPECIALIST MUSEUMS

Gipsoteca (Istituto d'Arte)
Beyond map p. 398, B4.
Porta Romana. Admission by appointment at the art school.
This art school just outside Porta Romana, in the former royal stables, and surrounded by a park, once part of the Boboli Gardens (but now used as a car park), owns a remarkable Gipsoteca, a museum of plaster-casts of numerous famous antique and Renaissance sculptures, including many by Donatello and Michelangelo. They were mostly made at the end of the 19th and the beginning of the 20th centuries by Giuseppe Lelli; his son left them to the Institute

in 1922. The collection is arranged in a splendid hall. Nearby is a building known as Le Pagliere, which serves as a deposit for restored sculptures from the Boboli Gardens.

Museo Diocesano di Santo Stefano al Ponte

Map p. 397, B3.
Santo Stefano al Ponte. Not open regularly. For information, T: 055 225 843.
Opened in 1996 to display works of art removed here for safe-keeping from churches in the diocese, some of them now deconsecrated. The museum contains some interesting Tuscan works of art from the 14th–15th centuries. The most important works are in the sacristy. The *Madonna and Child* by Giotto (from the church of San Giorgio alla Costa, dated 1295–1300) has been heavily restored after damage in 1993. Also here are two *Madonnas* by Domenico Michelino; a bust of the Blessed Davanzati by Pietro Tacca; an *Annunciation*, a *Madonna* and a triptych by the Master of the Madonna Straus; an *Annunciation* by Bicci di Lorenzo; *St Julian* by Masolino (c. 1420); and an exquisite predella with the *Adoration of the Magi* by Paolo Uccello (c. 1437). The carved wooden group of the *Lamentation* is by the *bottega* of Orcagna (1360–65), and the reliquary bust of San Cresci by Bernardo Holzmann (to a design by Giovanni Battista Foggini).

Museo Fiorentino di Preistoria

Map p. 399, E2.
21 Via Sant'Egidio. Open 9.30–12.30 except Sun; T: 055 295 159.
A museum of prehistory founded in 1946 and exhibited in three large rooms.

The material is well labelled and arranged chronologically and geographically. The lower hall is dedicated to Italy, and includes a human skull of the Palaeolithic era found at Olmo near Arezzo in 1865; the upper hall displays material from Europe, Africa and Asia, including an interesting collection from the Graziosi expedition to the Sahara.

Museo di Firenze com'era

Map p. 399, D2–E2.
24 Via dell'Oriuolo. Open 9–2 except Thurs; T: 055 261 6545.
A small (rather disappointing) museum with maps, paintings and prints of the city in the ex-Convento delle Oblate. There is a 19th-century copy in tempera of the *Pianta della Catena*, an engraving of 1470 (now in Berlin), and the first topographical plan of Florence drawn by Stefano Bonsignori in 1584 for Grand Duke Francesco I. It makes use of an ideal perspective from an elevated viewpoint, and the city is represented using extremely accurate planimetric measurements. The charming series of lunettes of the Medici villas are by the Flemish painter Giusto Utens (1599). There are maps of Florence from the 17th- to the 19th centuries, and views of the city by Thomas Patch and Giuseppe Maria Terreni, and engravings by Telemaco Signorini of the Mercato Vecchio in 1874 before its demolition. The fine series of engravings (1754), with views of the city and villas in the environs, are by Giuseppe Zocchi. The elevations and sections of the Duomo, Baptistery and Campanile published by Sgrilli in 1755, were drawn by Giovanni Battista Nelli (1661–1725), who made the first measured survey of these buildings for the

Opera del Duomo. The famous *Fiera of Impruneta* was engraved by Jacques Callot in 1620. In the hall to the left of the entrance are prehistoric and Roman finds from excavations in the city and a model of the Roman town.

On an upper floor is the **Collezione Alberto della Ragione**, a good collection of 20th-century Italian art left to the city in 1970 by Alberto della Ragione (*open only by previous appointment on Sat; T: 055 276 8224 or 055 276 8558*). It includes mostly representational works by Arturo Tosi, Carlo Carrà, Giorgio Morandi, Ottone Rosai, Gino Severini, Mario Sironi, Felice Casorati, Giorgio de Chirico, Arturo Martini, Virgilio Guidi, Massimo Campigli, Filippo de Pisis, Lucio Fontana, Marino Marini, Carlo Levi, Mario Mafai, Scipione, Giacomo Manzù, Corrado Cagli and Renato Guttuso.

Also here are 58 paintings by Ottone Rosai (1895–1957) left to the Comune in 1963, and 12 paintings by de Pisis formerly part of a collection owned by the Florentine writer Aldo Palazzeschi.

Museo di Geologia e Paleontologia
Map p. 399, E1.
4 Via La Pira. Open 9–1 except Mon and Sun; T: 055 275 7536.
The largest and most important geological and palaeontological collection in Italy. It includes material from the grand-ducal collections: vertebrates, skeletons of mammals from the Lower Pleistocene period in Tuscany, a gallery of invertebrates and plants, and a research section.

Museo di Mineralogia e Litologia
Map p. 399, E1.
4 Via La Pira. Open Mon–Fri 9–1, second Sun of month 9.30–12.30; T: 055 275 7537.
Includes samples of minerals and rocks from Elba, the Medici collection of worked stones, and a huge Brazilian topaz weighing 151kg (the second largest in the world).

Museo Nazionale di Antropologia ed Etnologia
Map p. 397, C2.
12 Via del Proconsolo. Open 9–1 except Thurs, Sun and holidays; Tues also 3–5; T: 055 239 6449.
Housed in Palazzo Nonfinito, begun in 1593 by Buontalenti, but left unfinished, hence its name. The great courtyard is attributed to Cigoli. The collection was founded in 1869 by Paolo Mantegazza, and was the first museum of its kind in Europe. It is still the most important ethnological and anthropological museum in Italy. Its collection, displayed in charming old-fashioned show-cases (although it is not very well labelled), covers Africa (notably Ethiopia, Eritrea, Somalia and Libya); North Pakistan (a rare collection of material relating to the Kafiri); South America (including mummies from Peru, collected in 1883) and Mexico; Asia (Melanesia, Sumatra—including the Modigliani collection c. 1880—Tibet and Japan, with the Fosco Maraini collection of Ainu material); and artefacts from the Pacific Ocean, probably acquired by Captain Cook on his last voyage in 1776–79.

Museo della Porcellana di Doccia
31 Viale Pratese, Sesto Fiorentino. Bus 28 from Stazione Santa Maria Novella. Open Wed–Sat 10–1 & 2–6; T: 055 420 7767.
Next to the Ginori porcelain factory in

Sesto Fiorentino, a northern suburb of the city, in a fine modern building (by Piero Berardi, 1965). Contains a large, well displayed collection of porcelain made in the famous Doccia factory founded by Marchese Carlo Ginori in 1735. The exhibit includes some of the earliest porcelain painted by Carlo Wendelin Anreiter von Zirnfeld of Vienna, and the first models by Gaspero Bruschi and Massimiliano Soldani. The firm, known as Richard-Ginori since 1896, continues to flourish. Across the road, in a warehouse, Ginori seconds can be purchased.

Museo della Storia della Fotografia (Alinari)
Map p. 398, C1.
15 Largo Alinari. Open Mon–Fri 9–1.
The headquarters of Fratelli Alinari, founded in 1852 and famous for its

black and white photography, particularly its documentation of Italy's art and architecture. A small museum illustrates the history of the firm.

Osservatorio Ximeniano
Map p. 397, B1.
6 Piazza San Lorenzo.
The building is part of the convent of San Giovannino, built for the Jesuits by Ammannati in the mid-16th century. An astronomical observatory was founded here in 1756 by the Jesuit Leonardo Ximenes. A museum (founded in 1888) has instruments used by Ximenes and his successors, a telescope built in 1861, and maps of Tuscany drawn by Giovanni Inghirami in 1830, as well as two important libraries. A meteorological observatory was installed in 1813, and since 1889 it has been an important seismological institute.

PALACES

15th-century palaces

Palazzo Antinori-Corsini
Map p. 399, E3.
6 Borgo Santa Croce.
The beautiful courtyard dates from the end of the 15th century.

Palazzo Gondi
Map p. 397, C3.
2 Piazza San Firenze.
A very fine palace built c. 1489 by Giuliano da Sangallo with a pretty little courtyard (now occupied by a florist). It was completed (and the façade on Via de' Gondi added) with great care by Giuseppe Poggi in 1872–84.

Palazzo Pazzi-Quaratesi
Map 397, C2.
10 Via del Proconsolo.
Handsome palace attributed to Giuliano da Maiano (1458–69). The Pazzi coat of arms (removed from the exterior) is displayed in the vestibule which leads to a pretty courtyard (with good capitals). The Pazzi, one of the oldest Florentine families, organized a notorious conspiracy against the Medici in 1478 (*see p. 241*). Francesco de' Pazzi, who was wounded, hid here before being seized by the mob and hung from a window of Palazzo Vecchio.

Palazzo Spinelli
Map p. 399, E3.
10 Borgo Santa Croce.
Built in 1460–70, this has good graffiti decoration on the façade and in the courtyard. Numerous other 15th-century palaces were decorated in this way.

16th-century palaces

Casa Morra
Map p. 399, E3.
8 Borgo Santa Croce.
This house belonged to Giorgio Vasari and still contains frescoes by him. His contemporary the painter Federico Zuccari (who collaborated with him on the frescoes on the cupola of the Duomo) built his studio on Via Giuseppe Giusti (*see p. 178*).

Casino Mediceo
Map p. 399, D1.
57, Via Cavour.
Now occupied by law courts, this was built for Francesco I by Bernardo Buontalenti (1568–74), and used by the duke as a studio for his scientific studies. Buontalenti carried out numerous other commissions in Florence, and was involved in projects for the Uffizi, Palazzo Vecchio and the Boboli Gardens, and also designed farmhouses in the countryside close to the city.

Fortezza da Basso
Map p. 398, B1.
Admission only when exhibitions are in progress.
This huge pentagonal fortress, designed by Antonio da Sangallo the Younger, is of the first importance in the history of military architecture. The exterior wall in brick and *pietra forte* is still intact. Sangallo's keep on Viale Strozzi incorpo-rates the medieval tower of Porta Faenza. The fortress was erected by order of Alessandro de' Medici in 1534 to strengthen his position in the city as first Duke of Florence (he had been brought to power by the armies of the Holy Roman Emperor in 1530), and as a refuge in times of trouble. It became a symbol of Medici tyranny, and Alessandro was assassinated here by his cousin Lorenzaccio in 1537. It was very soon obsolete as the grand dukes had lit-tle need to defend themselves. Ever since it has been something of a white ele-phant—used at various times as a prison, an arsenal and barracks. After years of neglect and discussion about its future, it became an exhibition centre in 1967. The area within the walls was bru-tally transformed when a huge prefabri-cated steel building covered with alu-minium was built in 1978, and another (circular) one in 1987. A long 19th-cen-tury building has been used since 1966 as a restoration centre (with a scientific laboratory) for paintings, frescoes, and works of art in wood and paper, by the Opificio delle Pietre Dure (*see p. 164*). An adjacent building was restored in 1999 as an extension to the centre, but other buildings are now derelict.

Archaeological finds, including Roman material, have been made here. Public gardens have been laid out on the glacis.

The Fortezza is used as a venue for the

Mostra dell'Artigianato (an old-established exhibition of artisan's work from all over the world), and the prestigious 'Pitti' fashion shows, both held annually, and numerous other trade fairs.

Palazzo Ginori

Map p. 399, D2.
11 Via de' Ginori.
Attributed to Baccio d'Agnolo—as an early work dating from around 1520.

Palazzo Mannelli-Riccardi

Map p. 397, A1.
4 Piazza Madonna degli Aldobrandini.
This has a painted façade, but it is now very ruined. The front of the house is adorned with a bust of Ferdinando I by Giovanni dell'Opera.

Palazzo Mellini-Fossi

Map 399, E3.
20 Via de' Benci.
One of the first of many palaces in Florence to have its façade decorated with frescoes. The delightful mythological scenes of *Perseus and Andromeda* date from 1575. By the beginning of the 20th century only traces of them survived, but they were beautifully restored in 1996 by the Fossi family, who still live here.

Palazzo Neroni

Map p. 399, D2.
7 Via de' Ginori.
This palace, with pronounced rustication, is where Diotisalvi Neroni lived before his exile as an enemy of the Medici in 1466. Neroni was a leading figure in Florentine politics in the turbulent period following Cosimo il Vecchio's death in 1464. Together with other noble Florentines, he tried to exclude

Cosimo's son Piero from holding office but failed when a popular assembly called for his banishment. This was a significant moment in the consolidation of the (hereditary) power of the Medici. Next door (no. 9) is Palazzo Montauto, with remains of 15th-century graffiti and two ground-floor windows attributed to Ammannati.

Palazzo Niccolini

Map p. 397, C1.
15 Via dei Servi.
Designed in 1548–50 by Baccio d'Agnolo, who built a number of fine palaces in Florence in the 16th century, some of the best of which are on Via Tornabuoni (*see p. 208*). Its beautiful façade is typical of Florentine palaces of this period. The small courtyard has graffiti decoration, and in the garden beyond is an elaborate double loggia, probably by Giovanni Antonio Dosio.

Palazzo Pandolfini

Map p. 399, D1.
74 Via San Gallo.
Built in 1516–20 as a villa on the outskirts of the town for Bishop Giannozzo Pandolfini, it is still owned by the Pandolfini family. It is the most important architectural work known by Raphael, although executed by Giovanni Francesco and Aristotile da Sangallo. The handsome classical inscription records the bishop. When the *portone* is open the pretty garden façade can be seen. It has a terrace on the first floor, and a big garden (redesigned in the 19th century).

Palazzo dei Pucci

Map p. 397, C1.
Via dei Servi.

Bartolomeo Ammannati, famous as the architect of Ponte Santa Trìnita and the courtyard of Palazzo Pitti, is also thought to have designed several palaces in Florence. This, at the Canto di Balla, the site of an old postern gate in the medieval walls, is one of the largest palaces in the city, named after the old-established Florentine family who still live here. Emilio Pucci was a famous fashion designer in the 20th century. The central part of the long façade dates from the 16th century, and is in part attributed to Ammannati; the wings on either side are 17th-century extensions. On the corner is the worn Pucci coat of arms by Baccio da Montelupo.

Palazzo Taddei
Map p. 399, D2.
15 Via de' Ginori.
Built by Baccio d'Agnolo for the merchant Taddei who commissioned the tondo from Michelangelo which now bears his name and is owned by the Royal Academy, London. Raphael, while staying here as a friend of the family in 1505, saw and copied the tondo (the plaque is on the wrong house).

17th-century palaces

Palazzo Castelli (Marucelli)
Map p. 399, D1.
10 Via San Gallo.
Gherardo Silvani built numerous palaces in the city in the 17th century. This, built around 1630, is one of his best. The elaborate doorway is flanked by two grotesque satyrs sculpted by Raffaello Curradi. The coat of arms above was set up by its later owner Emanuele Fenzi (1784–1875), a banker who financed the Florence–Livorno railway.

Palazzo Guicciardini
Map p. 397, A4.
15 Via Guicciardini.
This palace was reconstructed by Gherardo Silvani in 1620, on the site of the residence of Luigi di Piero Guicciardini, Gonfalonier of Justice, which was burnt down during the 1378 revolt against the government by the Ciompi (cloth-workers). The great commentator on Florentine affairs Francesco Guicciardini was born here in 1483. On his retirement from political life in 1530, he wrote his famous *History of Italy*. Part of the façade has remains of graffiti decoration. In the courtyard is a large stucco relief of *Hercules and Cacus* attributed to Antonio Pollaiolo. Beyond can be seen the little garden, created in the 17th century but replanted in 1922. On the wall are numerous ancient reliefs. Casa Campiglio nearby, where Machiavelli lived and died in 1527, has been destroyed. Guicciardini and Machiavelli, both great statesmen and writers, who had served different causes, became close friends at the end of their careers.

Palazzo degli Orti Oricellari
Map p. 398, B2.
Via degli Orti Oricellari. Open only on certain days of the year.
Now owned by a bank, this palace contains a fresco by Pietro da Cortona. The Orti Oricellari were famous as a Renaissance *selva*, or forest: all that survives of this today is the colossal 17th-

century statue of *Polyphemus* by Antonio Novelli (an extraordinary sight which can also be seen in winter, when the trees are no longer in leaf, from outside the garden in Via Bernardo Rucellai).

Palazzo Panciatichi-Ximenes
Map p. 399, E2–F2.
68 Borgo Pinti.
Sebastiano di Tommaso Ximenes bought the building in 1603, and employed Silvani to restructure it (the façade dates from this time). Modifications in c. 1720 include the atrium, a handsome double stair, and interior courtyard.

Palazzo Rinuccini
Map p. 398, B3.
39 Via Santo Spirito.
Built by Cigoli and enlarged by Ferdinando Ruggieri. It incorporates a delightful little 16th-century theatre. The other Palazzo Rinuccini on this street (no. 41) was built by Pier Francesco Silvani (with a coat of arms on the corner of Via de' Serragli by Giovanni Battista Foggini).

18th-century palaces

Palazzo della Gherardesca
Map p. 399, F1
99 Borgo Pinti.
Built by Giuliano da Sangallo in the 15th century (with interesting bas-reliefs in the courtyard), but enlarged in the 18th century by Antonio Ferri. It has an attractive 19th-century garden in the English Romantic tradition. The small Neoclassical temple was designed by Giuseppe Cacialli in 1842.

Palazzo Martelli
Map p. 397, B1.
8 Via Zannetti.
This historic palace may perhaps be opened to the public as a museum illustrating the history of the Florentine noble families. There is a tabernacle on the exterior of its modest façade, which contains a *Madonna and Child with St John* attributed to Mino da Fiesole. The palace was left by the last member of the Martelli family to the Curia Vescovile in 1986 on condition that it was preserved as a gallery, and it has since been acquired by the state, together with the Martelli coat of arms by Donatello, which is now kept in the Bargello Museum (*see p. 220*).

A house was acquired here in 1520 by the Martelli family, who up until the mid-15th century had been one of the richest merchant families in Florence and close friends of the Medici. Roberto Martelli (1408–64) was an important patron of Donatello. After 1819, the interior was decorated in Neoclassical style. It retains the atmosphere of a discreet patrician family house, and contains one of the most important private collections left in Florence, formed by Marco di Francesco Martelli in the 1640s (and augmented by the Roman collection of Abbot Domenico Martelli, d. 1735). It includes two good works by Beccafumi, a tondo by Piero di Cosimo (dated 1510), and a painting by Salvatore Rosa. The main room and chapel have frescoes by Vincenzo Meucci (1738–39), and on the ground floor is a room decorated by Niccolò Contestabile (1759–1824).

19th-century palaces

Palazzo Borghese
Map p. 399, F3.
110 Via Ghibellina.
This grandiose pile, with its Neoclassical façade by Gaetano Baccani (1822) was built in less than a year by Camillo Borghese, husband of Pauline Bonaparte (sister of Napoleon I), for a party to celebrate the second marriage of Ferdinand III. The elaborate period rooms (now used by a club; admission sometimes granted) include the Galleria and Salone degli Specchi which are heavily decorated with chandeliers and gilded mirrors.

Palazzo Vivarelli-Colonna
Map p. 399, F3.
30 Via Ghibellina.
The seat of the Assessorato alla Cultura (the city's cultural department). The interior is interesting for its early 19th-century frescoes by Angiolo Angiolini and Francesco Nenci. The little walled garden, which is open to the public on some days, was laid out in the early 18th century, with an elaborate Baroque wall fountain in the form of a grotto with shells added in the 19th century, and a painted background. On the top of the walls are terracotta eagles, vases and putti. The central fountain, decorated with an eagle and serpent, is surrounded by Renaissance parterres, with beds marked out in *pietra serena*.

Villino Trollope
Map p. 398, C1.
Piazza dell'Indipendenza.
The piazza was laid out in 1869 as the first of the 19th-century squares in Florence. At the north corner stands the Villino Trollope, where Fanny Trollope lived from 1849 until her death in 1863. Her son Anthony wrote *Doctor Thorne* here in 1857. In 1887, Thomas Hardy stayed in a *pensione* in the building.

20th-century palaces

Art Nouveau Houses
Beyond map p. 399, F2.
Via Scipione Ammirato.
There are two fine houses here: the Villino Broggi-Caraceni (no. 99) built in 1911, and the Villino Ravazzini (no. 101) dating from 1907–08. They are both by Giovanni Michelazzi with ceramic decoration by Galileo Chini, and are the best examples of their period in Florence. There is another house of the same date by Michelazzi at no. 26 Borgo Ognissanti (*map p. 398, B2*).

In the southern district of the town, at nos. 9 and 13 Via Giano della Bella (*map p. 398, A4*), there are two more well preserved Art Nouveau villas.

Palazzo dei Congressi
Map p. 398, B1.
3 Via Valfonda.
An international conference centre opened in 1964 on the site of a Contini-Bonacossi villa. Its park was created in 1871 by the French poet Alphonse Lamartine.

Villa il Tasso
Beyond map p. 399, F4.
30 Via Benedetto Fortini. Open to scholars by prior arrangement.
This is where the art historian Roberto Longhi lived from 1930 until his death in 1970. It is now the seat of the

Fondazione Longhi. Longhi's collection of paintings includes works by Caravaggio and Guido Reni. The oldest part of the house dates from the late 15th century, but Longhi added a library wing in 1939.

STREET TABERNACLES

There are numerous little street tabernacles all over the city, each with a painted or sculpted image, and many of these are still honoured daily with flowers and candles. Some are described in the guide; others are listed below. The earliest, **14th-century tabernacles**, include: the *Madonna and Child* on the corner of Via Faenza and Via Nazionale (in an 18th-century tabernacle; *map p. 398, C1*); the fresco of the *Madonna and Child with Saints* in a stone tabernacle on the corner between Via del Porcellana and Via Palazzuolo (*map p. 398, B2*); the fresco in the tabernacle on the corner of Borgo Pinti and Via Alfani (*map p. 399, E2*); and the fresco of the *Madonna* in a fine tabernacle in Piazza Piattellina, just out of Piazza del Carmine (*map p. 398, A3*). On the corner between Via del Leone and Via della Chiesa (*map p. 398, A4*), a modern glass tabernacle protects a fresco of the *Madonna Enthroned with Angels*, a 1958 copy of a painting by Giottino, detached and removed in 1943.

15th-century tabernacles include the large Tabernacolo delle Cinque Lampade (of the five lamps), on the corner of Via de' Pucci and Via Ricasoli (*map p. 397, C1*), with a fresco by Cosimo Rosselli. At no. 39 Via Panicale

(*map p. 398, C1*) there is a fresco in a niche by the circle of Botticelli. A tabernacle in Via Sant'Antonino (on the corner of Piazza Unità Italiana; *map p. 398, C2*) contains an enamelled terracotta *Madonna and Child* by Andrea della Robbia, and in Via Pietrapiana (corner of Via de' Pepi; *map p. 399, E3*), there is a tabernacle with a fine relief of the *Madonna and Child* attributed to Donatello. On the corner of Via San Giovanni and Borgo San Frediano (*map p. 398, A3*) is a tabernacle with a 15th-century *Madonna and Child with Angels*.

16th-century tabernacles include the one at no. 77 Via Porta Rossa (*map p. 398, C3*) with a *Crucifix between Saints*, attributed to Giovanni Battista Naldini, and in Via Taddea (*map p. 399, D1*) the *Crucifixion* by Giovanni Antonio Sogliani. The large tabernacle at no. 27 Via Giusti (*map p. 399, E1*) contains a *Resurrection of Christ* by Alessandro Fei. In the 1520s Giovanni della Robbia executed the huge enamelled terracotta tabernacle above a fountain in Via Nazionale (*map p. 398, C1*), as well as the statuette of St Ambrose high up on the corner of Via de' Macci and Borgo La Croce (*map p. 399, F1*).

In Via delle Conce, named after the old tanneries, now converted into flats, a tabernacle in *pietra serena* (1704) on the corner of Via dei Conciatori (*map. p. 399, F3*) contains a copy made c. 1920 of an early 16th-century painting of the *Madonna and Child* from the church of San Giuseppe.

There are two frescoed early **17th-century tabernacles** by Giovanni da San Giovanni: one of the *Madonna* in Via Faenza (*map p. 399, C1*), and anoth-er showing *Senator Girolamo Novelli Displaying Acts of Charity to Prisoners* in Via Ghibellina (*map p. 399, F3*). On a corner of Via Cimatori (*map p. 397, C3*), at the Canto alla Quarconia, lit by a wrought-iron lamp, there is a fresco of the *Madonna and Child Appearing to St Filippo Neri* by Alessandro Gherardini, one of the last tabernacles to be erected in the centre of the city.

THEATRES

Teatro Comunale
Map p. 398, A2
Corso Italia.
This is the most important concert hall in the city, with a seating capacity of 2,100. The disappointing interior was rebuilt in 1961. The annual music festival known as the Maggio Musicale is held here from May to July.

Teatro Goldoni
Map p. 398, B4.
Via Santa Maria.
This little theatre (420 seats) was reopened in 1998 (having been closed for over 21 years). It has a charming interior with a circular vestibule and horseshoe auditorium, decorated at the beginning of the 19th century by Giuseppe del Rosso.

Teatro della Pergola
Map p. 399, E2.
18 Via della Pergola.
On the site of a wooden theatre erected in 1656 by Ferdinando Tacca (famous for the comedies performed here), the present theatre dates from the 19th century. Gordon Craig, actor and stage designer and son of Ellen Terry, was director here in 1906.

Teatro Verdi
Map p. 399, E3.
Via Ghibellina.
Founded by Girolamo Pagliano and built by Telemaco Bonaiuti, this huge theatre was opened in 1854. The largest cinema screen in Italy was installed here after 1966. It is also used for theatre and concerts, and is the seat of the Orchestra Regionale Toscana.

PRACTICAL INFORMATION

PLANNING YOUR TRIP

When to go

The most pleasant time to visit is May, or October and November when the temperature is often still quite high. Spring can be unexpectedly wet and cold until well after Easter. The most crowded periods of the year are from Easter to June and in September. The winter in Florence can be cold, though it is the best season to visit the major museums, as January, February and November are the only time the city is comparatively empty of visitors. The changeable climate of Florence is conditioned by its position in a small basin enclosed by hills. It can be extremely hot and oppressive in July and August. In August the city is empty of Florentines, and numerous shops, bars and restaurants close down for the whole month.

Health and insurance

British citizens, as members of the EU, have the right to claim health care in Italy if they have the E111 form available from post offices. There are also a number of private holiday health insurance policies, certainly advisable for visitors from outside the EU. Keep the receipt (*ricevuta*) and medical report (*cartella clinica*) to present to your insurer if you have to make a claim.

Disabled travellers

All new public buildings are obliged by law to provide access and specially designed facilities for the disabled. In the annual list of hotels in Florence published by the APT, hotels which are able to provide hospitality for the disabled are indicated. Information on facilities for the disabled on trains and at railway stations can be obtained from Stazione Santa Maria Novella, T: 055 235 2275. The disabled are entitled to a *carta blu* which gives a discount on the fare. Trains equipped to carry wheelchairs are listed in the railway timetable published by the FS (Ferrovie dello Stato, the Italian State Railways), available at newsstands. The city bus service provides facilities for wheelchairs on certain lines; for information, T: 800 424 500; www.ataf.net. There are free parking spaces for disabled drivers. Even though the kerbs of many pavements have recently been redesigned to facilitate wheelchair use, many pavements are too narrow, making the historic centre a difficult place to move around. For more information see www.tour-web.com/accessibleitaly

Maps

The Italian Touring Club publishes excellent maps, indispensable to anyone travelling by car in Italy. They include the *Grande Carta Stradale d'Italia* on a scale of 1:200,000, divided into 15 sheets. These are also published in three volumes as the *Atlante Stradale d'Italia*; the volume entitled *Centro* covers Florence and Tuscany. These maps can be purchased from Italian Touring Club offices and at many booksellers.

GETTING AROUND

Airports

The nearest international airport is at Pisa (T: 050 500 707), 85km west of Florence. There is a railway station in the airport (tickets are bought in the air terminal) which has a direct train service to Florence which takes 1 hour (via Pisa central and Empoli). Since the trains are infrequent and do not run late at night there is also now an efficient bus service run by Terravision (T: 3299074779; www.lowcostcoach.com). There are town buses (no. 7; every 15 minutes) from the airport to Pisa central station where there are other train services to Florence. Taxis for the centre of Pisa are also available (or T: 050 541600). For return flights from Pisa, there is an air terminal (T: 055 216 073) at Santa Maria Novella Station in Florence (on platform no. 5, near which the airport trains depart), which is open from 6am–4.30pm. Luggage can be checked in here for all flights except Ryanair, and boarding cards obtained (not later than 15 minutes before the departure of the airport train).

The small airport of Florence (Amerigo Vespucci at Peretola, T: 055 315 874 or 055 373498), a few kilometres north of Florence, has some flights from Europe (including London Gatwick operated by Meridiana, and Amsterdam, Barcelona, Brussels, Frankfurt, Munich, Paris and Vienna), as well as internal domestic flights. Shuttle bus (Volainbus) every 30mins from the arrivals terminus to the SITA bus station next to the railway station of Santa Maria Novella in about 20mins. Tickets can be bought on board. Taxis are also usually available (otherwise T: 055 4798, 055 4390). For baggage lost and found, T: 055 308023.

Bologna airport also has direct flights from London. It is at Borgo Panicale, 7km northwest of the city. There is an excellent bus service (Aerobus) every 20 minutes to Bologna station in about 10 minutes. This runs from the station 5.55am–11.30pm and from the airport 8.30am–11.45pm. There are trains from Bologna station (on the main Milan–Rome line) which take 60–75 minutes to Florence.

By car

Roads in Italy

Motorways (*autostrade*) charge tolls according to the rating of the vehicle and the distance covered. There are service areas (open 24 hours) on all motorways. Most motorways have SOS points every 2km. Motorways are indicated by green signs and normal roads by blue signs. At the entrance to motorways, the two directions are indicated by the name of the most important (not the nearest) town, which can be momentarily confusing. The Autostrada del Sole (A1) which runs down the centre of Italy between Milan, Florence, Rome and Naples is narrower than some of the more recently built motorways and carries very heavy traffic including numerous lorries, especially between Bologna and Florence. Driving on this road is easier on Sundays, when lorries are banned. *Superstrade*, dual carriageways, do not charge tolls. They do not usually have service stations, SOS points, or emergency lanes.

Driving in Florence

The centre of Florence is closed to private cars (except for those belonging to residents) from Monday–Saturday 8.30–6.30 (and also usually at night in summer), except on holidays. The limited traffic zone (ZTL) includes virtually all the area within the Viali and the Oltrarno and is now controlled by electronic devices. There are heavy fines for cars found within this area without authorization and they are sometimes towed away. Access is allowed to hotels within the limited traffic zone, but cars can only be parked outside hotels for a maximum of one hour (and must display a card supplied by the hotel). Access is also allowed for disabled drivers (and well-signposted parking places are reserved for them in a number of streets). On certain days of the year, the whole of Florence is closed to traffic (10–6.30) in an attempt to combat pollution. However, visitors arriving in Florence on those days are sometimes allowed access. For information T: 800 831 133.

Parking

There are very few large car parks with long-term parking near the centre of the city. The large underground car parks beneath Piazza Stazione (*map p. 398, B2*) and the Parterre (north of Piazza della Libertà; *beyond map p. 399, E1*) are both open 24 hours. There is a large car park along the inside of the walls between Porta Romana and Piazza Tasso (entered from Piazza della Calza; *beyond map p. 398, A4*). The car park beneath the Mercato Centrale (San Lorenzo; *map p. 398, C2*) is open 24 hours, but since it is used by shoppers at the central market the tariff is prohibitively expensive after the first one and a half hours from 7–2. The car park near the market of Sant'Ambrogio (*map p. 399, F3*), open 24 hours, is used by shoppers in the morning (cheap rate limited to two hours).

A number of streets and *piazze*, and some of the Viali (the avenues forming a ring road around the centre of Florence) also now have pay parking (blue lines), operational from 8am–8pm (purchase a ticket to be displayed on the windscreen from automatic machines). Other parking areas (white lines) are usually reserved for residents only (you have to check the signs placed at the beginning and on the same side of the street). Florence also has a number of garages (Via Nazionale, Via Ghibellina, Borgo Ognissanti, and in some hotels).

Accidents

In the event of an accident, the traffic police can be called (T: 055 577 777). The headquarters of the Automobile Club d'Italia (ACI) is at 36 Viale Amendola; for emergency breakdown service, dial 116 (in Florence, T: 055 524 861).

If your car is towed away, it will probably be taken to 16 Via Circondaria, Rifredi (T: 055 308 249), where it can be retrieved after the payment of a heavy fine (be sure to remember the number of your car licence plate so you can identify your vehicle). The local municipal police (Vigili Urbani, T: 055 212 290) who wear blue uniform in winter and light blue during the summer, and helmets similar to British policemen, are usually helpful.

By train

Stazione di Santa Maria Novella (*map p. 398, B1*) is the main station for all services of the state railways, and it is very close to the centre of the city. It has a restaurant, a left-luggage office, a bank and a tourist information office with hotel booking facilities (*see below*). The station is well served by buses (*see below*) and taxis, and there is an underground car park.

By bus

Although buses provide the best means of transport in Florence now that the city centre has been closed to private traffic, they tend to be crowded and it is usually worthwhile walking instead of waiting for a bus, especially as the centre (within the Viali or avenues forming a ring road around Florence) is so small. The town bus service is run by ATAF, which has an information office under the bus shelter on the east (right) side of the Stazione Santa Maria Novella (*map p. 398, B1*) open daily 6.30am–8pm. For information, T: 800 424 500 or look on www.ataf.net.

Electric buses

The small electric buses follow four interesting circular routes through the historic centre and are well worth taking once for the ride, especially if you are on your first visit to Florence. There are four lines (A, B, C and D) which cross the historic centre (and some pedestrian zones) on circular routes. They run Monday–Saturday every 10 or 15 minutes from 7 or 8am to 7 or 8pm (line D also runs on Sundays), and their routes are indicated at each bus stop.

A from Piazza Stazione in front of the Stazione Santa Maria Novella (*map p. 398, B2*) to Via Tornabuoni and then north via Piazza dei Ciompi to Piazza Beccaria car park (*beyond map p. 399, F3*).

B from Piazzale Vittorio Veneto at the Cascine (*beyond map p. 398, A2*) along the Arno as far as the car park of Piazza Piave (*map p. 399, F4*).

C connects Piazza San Marco (*map p. 399, D1*) with Sant'Ambrogio and Santa Croce and terminates on the other side of the Arno near Ponte Vecchio at the end of Via dei Bardi (*map p. 398, C4*).

D from Piazza Stazione in front of the Stazione Santa Maria Novella (*map p. 398, B2*) across Ponte Vespucci and then traverses the Oltrarno as far as Piazza Ferrucci (*beyond map p. 399, F4*).

Tickets

Tickets can be bought at machines at some bus stops, or from tobacconists, newspaper kiosks and some bars. There are various types of ticket which vary in price: a ticket for unlimited travel on any bus for 60 minutes (there is a slightly cheaper multiple ticket valid for four rides); a ticket valid for 3 hours; and for 24 hours. There are also tickets valid for two days, three days and seven days. Monthly season tickets are also available, including a student ticket. You have to stamp your ticket at automatic machines when you board the bus, and if you are found travelling without a valid ticket you are liable to a heavy fine. At night (from 9pm–6am) you can purchase a ticket from the driver of the bus.

As in other large cities, you should always beware of pickpockets on buses, and it is advisable to avoid very crowded buses by waiting for the next one.

By taxi

Taxis (painted white) have fare meters. The fare includes service, so tipping is not necessary. They are hired from ranks or by telephone: there are no cruising taxis. There are ranks at the Stazione Santa Maria Novella, Piazza Santa Maria Novella, Piazza San Marco, Piazza Santa Trìnita, Piazza del Duomo, Piazza della Signoria, Piazza della Repubblica, Porta Romana, and elsewhere. For Radio taxis, T: 055 4390, 055 4798, or 055 4242. A supplement is charged for night service and luggage.

Twelve horse-drawn cabs survive in the city (in 1869 there were 518). From Easter to early October they can be hired in Piazza Duomo or Piazza della Signoria, and you should agree the fare before starting the journey.

By bicycle

The Comune of Florence usually rents bicycles for the day (8.15–7.30 except Sundays and holidays) from certain car parks. You have to leave a valid document and return the bike to the place from which you hired it before 7.30pm. For further information, contact Firenze Parcheggi, T: 055 503 021.

There are also private bike-hire firms which have mountain bikes, including Alinari, 85 Via Guelfa, T: 055 280 500 and Florence by Bike, 120 Via San Zanobi, T: 055 488 992.

TOURIST INFORMATION

Tourist offices in Florence

The main information office of the Agenzia per il Turismo di Firenze (APT), is at 1 (red) Via Cavour (*map p. 399, D2*), T: 055 290 832 or 055 290 833, infoturismo@provincia.fi.it, www.firenzeturismo.it. It is open Monday–Saturday 8.30–6.30; in summer it is also open on Sunday 8.30–1.30. Up-to-date information is supplied here, as well as a (free) list of hotels, a map, opening times of museums and current exhibitions. The office also supplies free advice to visitors in difficulty or with complaints. There are subsidiary APT information offices at Amerigo Vespucci airport in Florence, and at 29 (red) Borgo Santa Croce (*map p. 399, E3*). There are also often mobile units in Piazza della Repubblica and at the Oltrarno end of Ponte Vecchio.

There is another information office (*map p. 398, B2*) run by the Comune of Florence at no. 4 Piazza Stazione Santa Maria Novella in a vaulted hall once part of the convent of Santa Maria Novella. www.comune.fi.it

The information office in Fiesole is at 3 Via Portigiani, T: 055 598 720.

A hotel booking office (ITA), which makes reservations on arrival, is open (8.30–7 except Sun) at the Stazione Santa Maria Novella, and on the motorway approaches to Florence, and at Pisa airport.

ACCOMMODATION

Information
The APT of Florence produces an annual publication—available free from their offices—that lists all the hotels in Florence and their charges.

Hotels
There are five official categories of hotels in Italy from the luxury 5-star hotels to the most simple 1-star establishments. These categories are based on the services offered (television in each room, telephone, and minibar) and often do not reflect quality. In Florence, ★★★ and ★★★★ hotels are not always on a par with hotels with the same designation in other large European cities.

It is essential to book well in advance in summer, at Easter and in September and October; you are usually asked to send a deposit or leave a credit card number to confirm the booking. You have the right to claim the deposit back if you cancel the booking at least 72 hours in advance.

Prices
Every hotel has to declare its prices annually. Prices change according to the season and can be considerably less in off-peak periods. For tax purposes, hotels are, by law, required to issue an official receipt (*ricevuta fiscale*) to customers; you should not leave the premises without one.

In all hotels, service charges are included in the rates, so tipping is not necessary. You should beware of extra charges added to the bill. You should also be cautious about arranging to hire a car and driver with the hotel porter: everyone involved expects to take a large cut, and a day in Florence spent in this way is bound to cost you a great deal and is hardly ever worthwhile.

Breakfast
Breakfast (*prima colazione*) can be disappointing and costly. By law it is an optional extra charge, although a lot of hotels try to include it in the price of the room. When booking, always specify if you want breakfast or not. If you are staying in a one-, two- or three-star hotel, it is usually a good idea to go round the corner to the nearest *pasticceria* or bar for breakfast. In some of the more expensive hotels, good buffet breakfasts are now provided, but even here the standard of the 'canteen' coffee can be poor: you can always ask for an espresso or cappuccino instead.

Prices per double room per night
★★★★★ €450–€700
★★★★ €275–€350
★★★ €140–€180
★★ about €100
★ €50–€75

The listing below is a selection of the best hotels in each category.

★★★★★ HOTELS

Westin Excelsior (*map p. 398, B2*). 3 Piazza Ognissanti, T: 055 27151, www.westin.com/excelsiorflorence
A hotel since 1863, it is now part of the Westin hotel group. 168 rooms heavily furnished, and some with terraces with good views. The public rooms and restaurant also have gloomy décor.

Grand Hotel Villa Medici (*map p. 398, A2*). 42 Via il Prato, T: 055 238 1331, F: 055 238 1336, www.sinahotels.it
Typical of the 1960s with 103 rooms, but rather more pleasantly and simply furnished than the other 5-star hotels in the centre. The small swimming pool is in a little garden at the back.

Helvetia e Bristol (*map p. 398, C3*). 2 Via de' Pescioni, T: 055 26651, F: 055 288 353, www.charminghotels.it
Elegant but small enough (52 rooms) to be cosy with it. Beautifully furnished, with superbly appointed rooms and marble bathrooms. The small restaurant serves good snacks and full meals.

★★★★ HOTELS

Berchielli (*map p. 398, C3*). 14 Lungarno Acciaiuoli and Piazza del Limbo, T: 055 264 061, F: 055 218 636, www.berchielli.it

An old-established hotel in the centre of Florence, decorated in Art Nouveau style. The 76 rooms are rather unimaginatively furnished. Most of the rooms overlook Piazza del Limbo or interior courtyards: those on the Arno have the better views but are noisier. Some rooms on the upper floors overlook a little terrace where breakfast is served in summer. No large groups.

Continental (*map p. 398, C3*). 2 Lungarno Acciaiuoli, T: 055 272 622, www.lungarnohotels.com
An old-established hotel in the very centre of Florence, one of three bought by the Ferragamo family (the other two are the Gallery Hotel Art and the Lungarno). Despite the cramped lobby, it has pleasant public rooms on the first floor and a delightful roof garden where breakfast is served in summer. Some of the attractive rooms on the fifth and sixth floors have outstanding views over Ponte Vecchio. The five double rooms in the tower are particularly delightful. There are six comfortable single rooms. The rooms without views are quiet and tend to be a little larger. No large groups. Efficient management and pleasant staff.

Gallery Hotel Art (*map p. 397, A3*). 5 Vicolo dell'Oro, T: 055 27263, F: 055 268 557, www.lungarnohotels.com

This hotel is almost next door to the Continental and is under the same management. Opened in 1999 in a renovated, rather pokey building without much character, it has ultra-modern decor and exhibitions of modern art in the public rooms. The rooms tend to be small and rather too simply furnished; however, they are all quiet, and one of the penthouse suites on the seventh floor has a superb view. Restaurant. No groups.

J & J (*map p. 399, F3*). 20 Via di Mezzo, T: 055 263121, F: 055 240 282, www.jandjhotel.com
A 16th century convent which was sensitively converted into a delightful hotel in 1988. It has 20 large rooms which are particularly attractive, spacious and tastefully furnished—although there is no lift. It is tucked away on a very quiet road in a pleasant district with lots of good restaurants. Family run, with friendly staff.

Lungarno (*map p. 398, C4*). 14 Borgo San Jacopo, T: 055 27261, F: 055 268437, www.lungarnohotels.com
This is the third hotel owned by the Ferragamo family (*see above*). It is in a modern building near the Ponte Vecchio which was built following the destruction of this area in the Second World War. The public rooms are comfortable, and the staff friendly. The rooms have balconies directly on the Arno. Convenient for those with a car as it has its own garage.

Monna Lisa (*map p. 399, E2*). 27 Borgo Pinti, T: 055 247 9751, F: 055 247 9755, www.monnalisa.it
In a lovely old palace on a quiet street, with attractively furnished and spacious public rooms and a delightful large garden at the back. The 35 rooms (no lift), with small bathrooms, are rather poky and less well furnished.

★★★ HOTELS

Annalena (*map p. 398, B4*). 34 Via Romana, T: 055 222 402, F: 055 222 403, www.hotelannalena.it
Opened as a pensione in 1919 in an old convent, much frequented by the British. An attractive building with high ceilings and furnished in a pleasant old-fashioned style. The 20 rooms all have bathrooms and are quiet, some on a long terrace which overlooks a pretty garden.

Beacci Tornabuoni (*map p. 398, C2*). 3 Via Tornabuoni, T: 055 212645, F: 055 283594, www.bhotel.it
Set on Florence's smartest street, an old-established hotel where many well-known Anglo-Americans have stayed. On the top floor of two adjoining palaces, it has an old-fashioned atmosphere, and a lovely roof terrace where breakfast and dinner are served. Some of the 28 rooms are very spacious. Particularly friendly, courteous service.

Della Signoria (*map p. 398, C3*). 1 Via delle Terme, T: 055 214 530, F: 055 216 101, www.hoteldellasignoria.com In a characterless post-war building near Ponte Vecchio, the 27 rooms are on five floors, and breakfast is served on a terrace. No groups.

Hermitage (*map p. 397, A3*). 1 Vicolo Marzio, T: 055 287 216, F: 055 212 208, www.hermitagehotel.com Efficiently run, with 28 very small rooms on five floors. Its special feature is a delightful roof garden with superb views.

Loggiato dei Serviti (*map p. 399, E1*). 3

Piazza Santissima Annunziata, T: 055 289 592, www.loggiatodeiservitihotel.it
In a lovely palace with vaulted rooms in the most beautiful square in Florence, converted with great taste into a small hotel (34 rooms). The simple furnishings and stone floors make it cool and pleasant, and the rooms have lovely city views.

Porta Rossa (*map p. 398, C3*). 19 Via Porta Rossa, T: 055 287 551, F: 055 282 179.
This is one of the historic hotels of the city which retains its Art Nouveau decorations from the first years of the 20th century. Spacious and old-fashioned, most of the rooms (not all with bathrooms) have high ceilings and are well furnished. No groups, so its charming character has been maintained.

River (*map p. 399, F4*). 18 Lungarno della Zecca Vecchia, T: 055 234 3529; F: 055 234 3521, www.hotelriver.com On the Arno, a little way outside the heart of Florence, but only about 10 minutes' walk from Ponte Vecchio. It has a discreet atmosphere, with 40 pleasant and spacious rooms: those at the back overlook a peaceful courtyard and are much quieter. There is a terrace on the second floor and a good breakfast is provided. Comfortable public rooms and friendly staff. No groups.

Torre Guelfa (*map p. 398, C3*). 8 Borgo Santi Apostoli, T: 055 239 6338, www.hoteltorreguelfa.com
This efficiently run hotel is set in a beautiful old 13th-century palace which has been well renovated. There are 12 quiet rooms, all with bathrooms, and most with air conditioning. Pleasant single rooms also. A lovely loggia is used for breakfast and there is a delightful living room. A 19th-century wooden stair leads up to the exceptionally high tower which has breathtaking views.

★★ HOTELS

Boboli (*map p. 398, B4*). 63 Via Romana, T: 055 229 8645, F: 055 233 7169.
A simple but pleasant hotel. The 18 rooms, with small bathrooms, are on three floors (no lift), only a few of which are on the back, but those on Via Romana have double glazing. Good views from the rooms on the upper floors.

Casci (*map p. 399, D2*). 13 Via Cavour, T: 055 211 686, F: 055 239 6461, www.hotelcasci.com
There are 25 quiet rooms, simply furnished, only two of which are on the noisy Via Cavour, and all of which have bathrooms. Friendly atmosphere.

La Scaletta (*map p. 398, C4*). 13 Via Guicciardini, T: 055 283028, F: 055 289562, www.lascaletta.com
An old-established family-run hotel on the top floor with a delightful roof terrace with views of the Palazzo Pitti and the Boboli Gardens. Of the 14 rooms, 12 have bathrooms; those on Via Guicciardini have double glazing.

Villani (*map p. 397, B2*). 11 Via delle Oche, T: 055 239 6451, F: 055 215 348, www.hotelvillani.it
A simple hotel on a top floor, very close to the Duomo. The 13 rooms, all with bathrooms, are very quiet and have wonderful views. Arrangement with the restaurant below.

★ HOTELS

Azzi (*map p. 398, C1*), 56 Via Faenza, T:

055 213806, hotelazzi@hotmail.com In a side street close to the station which has numerous small cheap hotels, and in a building which consists entirely of hotels. Despite this, it has 12 cosy, old-fashioned rooms, most of them on the back and totally quiet, three of them with their own bathrooms. There is one comfortable, spacious single room, and one with three beds overlooking a little garden. Breakfast is served at a communal table in a charming breakfast room, which has a door onto a terrace which is a cool place to sit on summer evenings. The pleasant young owner runs two more hotels on the upper floors of the same building and, if you specify your precise requirements, will take the trouble to give you the most suitable room. Takes small groups. No lift.

Bandini (*map p. 398, B4*). 9 Piazza Santo Spirito, T: 055 215 308, F: 055 282 761. An old, established hotel in a very fine palace in one of the loveliest squares in Florence. Unfortunately, it has become very run down in the last few years and is not as clean as it might be (partly because there are too many cats). The management can also be unreliable. Its special feature is a lovely loggia overlooking the piazza, and most of the rooms and the breakfast room have fine views. In a labyrinth of corridors and stairs, there are 12 rooms which vary in size; some are unusually large; five have bathrooms. There is a slightly spooky atmosphere presided over by a grey cat and its numerous relations.

Bretagna (*map p. 398, C3*). 6 Lungarno Corsini, T: 055 289618, F: 055289619, www.bretagna.it
In a very fine position in the centre of Florence, it has a charmingly old-fash-

ioned living room and dining room overlooking the Arno, with echoes of E.M. Forster. The 18 very simple rooms vary a great deal: some are more spacious than others; some are family rooms; some have their own bathrooms and some do not. They all have their own air conditioners, and one has its own tiny terrace. Only one room overlooks the Arno, but all the others are quiet. Takes small groups.

Brunetta (*map p. 399, E2*). 5 Borgo Pinti, T: 055 240 360, F: 055 247 8134.
A very pleasant, small family-run hotel on the third floor of a building set on a delightful, narrow old road in the town centre, with little traffic. The 11 rooms are spotlessly clean, but none of them have bathrooms (there are three communal bathrooms). Half of the rooms overlook Borgo Pinti and the others are totally quiet looking out over the roofs of Florence. One spacious single room. The hotel closes at midnight. No lift. At present, it doesn't have a licence for breakfast, but there are plenty of bars close by.

Fiorentina (*map p. 398, B2*). 12 Via dei Fossi, T: 055 219 530, F: 055 287 105. In a nice palace with a handsome entrance in a smart street. 16 rooms on two floors some with bathrooms. The rooms on the garden and inner courtyard are quieter than those on Via dei Fossi. Spacious breakfast room, friendly staff. Only takes visitors (no groups) from June or July to September, as the rest of the year it is completely occupied by students from American campuses studying in Florence.

Maria Luisa de' Medici (*map p. 399, D3*). 1 Via del Corso, T: 055 280048). An eccentric hotel with a weird atmosphere, crammed full of 17th-century paintings, sculptures and objets d'art, on the top floor of an 18th-century palace (no lift). Nine very quiet rooms, some of which can accommodate large families, two of which have bathrooms. An ample breakfast is served in your room.

Scoti (*map p. 398, C3*). 7 Via Tornabuoni, T: 055 292 128, www.hotelscoti.com
A very friendly family-run hotel with just 7 large rooms, two of them singles (none with their own bathrooms, although there are three bathrooms which are shared) on the second floor, all very quiet (not overlooking Via Tornabuoni). A charming frescoed main room, and old fashioned furniture. Breakfast, available on request, is served in your room.

HOTELS OUTSIDE THE CENTRE

All of these hotels have gardens, and are convenient if you have a car.

★★★★★ **Grand Hotel Villa Cora**. 18 Viale Machiavelli, T: 055 229 8451, F: 055 229 086, www.villacora.it. With restaurant and swimming pool.
★★★★ **Park Palace**. 5 Piazzale Galileo, T: 055 222 431, F: 055 220 517, www.parkpalace.com
★★★★ **Torre di Bellosguardo**. 2 Via Roti Michelozzi, T: 055 2298145, www.torrebellosguardo.com
A very elegant hotel in a beautiful villa with garden and swimming pool.
★★★★ **Villa Le Rondini**. 224 Via Bolognese Vecchia, T: 055 400 081, F: 055 268 212, www.villalerondini.it
With restaurant and swimming pool.
★★★★ **Ville sull'Arno**. 1 Lungarno Cristoforo Colombo, T: 055 670 971, F: 055 678 244, www.villesullarno.it

With swimming pool.
★★★ **David**. 1 Viale Michelangelo, T: 055 681 1695, F: 055 680 602, www.davidhotel.com

HOTELS IN FIESOLE

Fiesole is a particularly pleasant place to stay (especially in summer) and is within easy reach of Florence. It is convenient if you have a car, and there is an excellent city bus service which takes 20–30 minutes. All the following hotels have gardens and are in good positions.

★★★★ **Villa Aurora**. 39 Piazza Mino, T: 055 59100, F: 055 59587, www.auro-rafiesole.com
With restaurant.
★★★★ **Villa San Michele**.
4 Via Doccia, T: 055 567 8200, www.villasanmichele.orientexpress.com
A famous, established hotel in a lovely villa in a superb position, with a good restaurant.
★★★ **Bencistà**. 4 Via Benedetto da Maiano, T: 055 59163, pensionebencista@uol.it
An old-fashioned hotel with a charming atmosphere, which has been favoured for decades by British visitors, on the hillside below Fiesole.
★★★ **Villa Bonelli**. 1 Via Poeti, T: 055 59513, www.hotelvillabonelli.com

HOTELS IN THE ENVIRONS

Bagno a Ripoli
★★★★★ **Villa La Massa**. 6 Via La Massa, Candeli, T: 055 62611, F: 055 633 102, www.villamassa.com

Sesto Fiorentino
★★★ **Villa Villoresi**. 2 Via Ciampi, Colonnata, T: 055 443212, F: 055 442063, www.ila-chateau.com/villores

Pratolino
★★★★ **Demidoff**. 1556 Via della Lupaia, Vaglia, T: 055 505641, F: 055 409780, www.hoteldemidoff.com

YOUTH & STUDENT HOSTELS

Ostello per la Gioventù. Villa Camerata, 2 Viale Righi, T: 055 600 315, www.hostels-aig.org
This is the largest youth hostel in Florence and is set in a good position in a park at the bottom of the hill of San Domenico (220 beds). Bus no. 17 from the Stazione Santa Maria Novella (west side, Via Alemanni) via Via Cavour and Piazza San Marco (the service operates 5.30am–1.15am). Villa Camerata is also the regional headquarters of the Italian Youth Hostels Association. The cost of a bed (usually six in one room) includes breakfast (extra charge for lunch or dinner). Similar rates are available at two other hostels in the centre of Florence:
Santa Monaca. 6 Via Santa Monaca, T: 055 268 338, www.ostello.it
Archi Rossi. 94 (red) Via Faenza, T: 055 290 804, F: 055 230 2601.
Youth Residence Firenze 2000. 16 Viale Sanzio, T: 055 233 5558, F: 055 2306392, www.florencegate.it
Also has double rooms and a swimming pool.
Casa di Ospitalità per Universitari, Sette Santi. 11 Viale dei Mille, T: 055 504 8452; F: 055 504 7055, www.eidinet.com/7santi

HOSTELS (CASE PER FERIE)

Many hostels run by religious organizations are open to both young and old, and offer cheap if rather spartan accommodation. They often have restricted hours and early curfews, but are generally well run. They are all listed in the annual hotel list supplied by the APT. Among the most pleasant in the historic centre are:
Casa SS. Nome di Gesù. Francescane Missionarie di Maria, 21 Piazza del Carmine, T: 055 213 856, F: 055 281 835, benvenuti.fnn@tin.it
Istituto Gould Tavola Valdese. 49 Via de' Serragli, T: 055 212576, F: 055 280274, gould.reception@dada.it
Istituto Oblate dell'Assunzione. 15 Borgo Pinti, T: 055 2480582; F: 055 2346291.
Istituto Pio X—Artigianelli. 106 Via dei Serragli, T: 055 225044.

BED & BREAKFAST

This is a category on its own, for establishments which have only a few rooms. One of these is the **Villa Montartino**, 151 Via Gherardo Silvani, T: 055 223 520, www.montartino.com
Recently opened in a restored watchtower above the Ema Valley, it is in a lovely position surrounded by its own olive groves and vineyards. Not classified as a hotel since it only has a few bedrooms, but beautifully furnished and very comfortable (on a par with a ★★★★ star hotel). Meals can be ordered. Self-catering flats are also available. Lovely country walks can be taken near Arcetri.

FOOD & DRINK

Food in Florence, as in the rest of Italy, is generally good, but traditional local dishes have become more difficult to find, and Florentine cookery is now similar to that to be found all over the country. Traditional Florentine cuisine is characterized by the abundant use of olive oil (Tuscan olive oil is the best in Italy) and by some elaborate meat dishes which are cooked slowly (usually in a tomato sauce). The court of the Medici in Florence was famous for its banquets at which delicious food was served. When Caterina dei Medici married Henry II of France in the 16th century, she took with her to the French court her cooks (as well as her perfume-makers) which had a profound influence on French cuisine, though very few dishes which adorned the tables of the rich during the Renaissance have survived today. A seminal work (still in print) on Italian cookery (*La Scienza in Cucina e l'arte di mangiar bene*) was published in Florence in 1891 by Pellegrino Artusi (1820–1911) who came from Romagna to live in Piazza d'Azeglio in 1852. Some of the best items of traditional Florentine cuisine often served in the more simple Florentine restaurants are listed below.

The menu

HORS D'OEUVRES (ANTIPASTI)

Crostini, small pieces of toast or bread with a pâté made out of chicken livers, capers and anchovies.
Affettati usually include raw Parma ham, *salame* and *finocchiona* or *sbriciolona* (a delicious salami cured with fennel). In summer raw ham (*prosciutto crudo*) is served with melon or figs.
Pinzimonio, a plate of fresh raw vegetables (artichokes, fennel, celery and carrots) which are dipped in a dressing (usually oil and lemon).
Fettunta or *bruschetta*, served in the autumn: toast with garlic and oil straight from the press; if topped with hot black cabbage it is called *cavolo con le fette*.

FIRST COURSES (PRIMI PIATTI)

As in the rest of Italy, numerous pasta dishes are always served.
Ragù or *sugo di carne*, Tuscany is well known for this elaborate meat sauce cooked at length, made with minced meat, sausage, herbs and tomato which is used in pasta dishes.
Penne all'arrabbiata or *penne strascicate*, short pasta in a rich spicy sauce.
Pappardelle alla lepre, large flat noodles made with flour and egg with a rich hare sauce.
Fettuccine, ribbon noodles usually freshly made on the premises, often served with a meat sauce or with porcini mushrooms.
Minestrone, a thick vegetable soup with chopped vegetables (and sometimes pasta), the most famous first course produced in Florence. In winter, bread, cabbage and white beans are sometimes added to the soup and it is called *ribollita* or *minestra di pane*.
Panzanella, a cold salad made with bread, raw onions, tomatoes, cucumber, basil, oil and vinegar, often served in the summer.

Pappa al pomodoro, usually served hot or tepid, consists of tomato sauce, basil and bread.

Haricot beans and chick peas are a favourite winter dish; beans (*fagioli*) are cooked with sage and dressed with oil, or in a tomato sauce *all'uccelletto*.

MAIN COURSES (SECONDI PIATTI)

Meat in Florence is often stewed slowly for a long time in red wine and a tomato sauce: there are a number of variations generally known as *umido*, *stufato*, *stracotto* or *spezzatino*.

Bistecca alla fiorentina, a large T-bone steak which can be grilled in one piece and served to two or three people; although famous, this is not always easy to find.

Coniglio (rabbit) is often served in Florence, usually in *umido* or *alla cacciatora*, stewed in tomato sauce. The meat of rabbit and *faraona* (guinea fowl, almost always served roasted) is usually of better quality than chicken.

Arista, a joint of pork ribs cooked in the oven.

Ossobuco, stewed shin of veal.

Bracioline (veal escalopes) are also usually available (cooked in lemon or wine).

Trippa alla fiorentina, an unusual traditional dish, is tripe cooked in a tomato sauce and served with Parmesan cheese.

FISH (PESCE)

Fish is always the most expensive item on the menu but can be extremely good in specialist fish restaurants. Among the most succulent and expensive are *orata* (bream) and *triglie* (red mullet) usually cooked simply *arrosto* (roast) or *alla griglia* (grilled).

Fritto di pesce or *fritto misto di mare*, various types of small fried fish, almost always including *calamari* (squid) and *seppie* (cuttlefish), is usually the most inexpensive fish dish on the menu. Shellfish, often served cooked in white wine with garlic and parsley, includes *cozze* (mussels) and *vongole* (clams). These can also be served as a sauce for spaghetti.

Good fish dishes often to be found in simpler restaurants are *baccalà* (salt cod), usually cooked in tomato sauce, and *seppie in zimino*, cuttlefish cooked with spinach. *Zuppa di pesce* is a rich fish stew: if cooked with tomato sauce it is called *alla Livornese* (or *Caciucco*) since it is a speciality of Livorno.

VEGETARIAN DISHES

Porcini are large wild mushrooms and an expensive delicacy (only served in season). They are best grilled and are also often used as a sauce for pasta.

Melanzane alla parmigiana, aubergine cooked in the oven with a cheese and tomato sauce, is a good vegetarian main course.

Vegetable *tortini* are similar to omelettes and are good made with *carciofi* (artichokes) or *zucchini* (courgettes).

Insalata (salad) is the most popular vegetable dish; *insalata verde* is green salad (only lettuce), and *insalata mista* usually includes tomato and raw carrot.

Some restaurants in Florence serve excellent lightly fried vegetables, including courgette slices, artichoke hearts, courgette flowers, onions, tomatoes and sage.

In season, artichokes (served in a variety of ways), asparagus, courgettes and *gobbi* (a vegetable related to the artichoke) are usually good.

Fagioli all'uccelletto (see above) is also a vegetable dish.

Raw or cooked fennel (*finocchio*) is another typical Florentine vegetable.

DESSERTS (DOLCE)

Italians usually prefer fresh fruit for dessert and sweets are considered the least important part of the meal. In many simple restaurants and trattorie often only fruit is served at the end of the meal. The fruit available varies according to what is in season; strawberries (*fragole*) are good served with fresh lemon juice or red wine (rather than with cream). In summer, water melon (*popone*) is particularly refreshing. Fresh fruit salad (*macedonia*) is often good.

Biscotti di Prato are hard almond biscuits which you dip in a glass of Vin Santo or Morellino wine.

Castagnaccio, a traditional Florentine pudding, is a thin chestnut cake with pine nuts, rosemary and sultanas.

Schiacciata alla fiorentina, a plain cake.

Crostata, a fruit flan.

Zuppa inglese, a rich trifle sometimes offered in smarter restaurants.

Torta della nonna, a good pastry filled with custard and garnished with almonds. *Tiramisù* is a rich pudding based on mascarpone cheese, mixed with egg, chocolate, biscuits, and sometimes a liqueur.

Gelato (ice-cream) is also widely available, although is not usually home-made in restaurants.

CHEESE (FORMAGGI)

Bel Paese, a soft cheese made from cow's milk; it is rarely offered by restaurants.

Gorgonzola, a delicious strong creamy cheese made from whole cow's milk.

Grana, a type of Parmesan cheese produced in northern Italy.

Groviera italiano, Italian gruyère.

Mascarpone, a fresh rich cream cheese, usually used in desserts and not served on its own.

Parmigiano-Reggiano, usually the best quality Parmesan cheese made in the districts of Parma and Reggio Emilia.

Pecorino, a sheep's cheese, is almost always available, and in spring is eaten with fresh raw broad beans.

Wine

The cheapest wine is always the house wine (*vino della casa*), which varies a great deal, but is normally a drinkable *vin ordinaire*. The world-famous Chianti red wine is made from a careful blend of white and black grapes. Only wine produced from grapes grown in a limited area of the Chianti region, between Florence and Siena, can bear the label of the black rooster on a yellow ground in a red circle and be called *Chianti Classico gallo nero*. The other Chianti wines, some of which rival the Classico, include Chianti Colli Aretini, Chianti Colli Fiorentini, Chianti Colli Senesi, Chianti Montalbano and Chianti Rufina. The bright ruby-red Chianti is drunk younger than most French wines, and has between 11.5 and 13 per cent alcohol.

Other wines in Tuscany (where the red table wine is usually of better quality than the white) such as Vino nobile di Montepulciano, Vernaccia (white, from San Gimignano) and the celebrated Brunello di Montalcino are particularly good. Excellent red wine is also produced at Carmignano, near Florence, and around Lucca. Pitigliano, Montecarlo and the Val d'Arbia are good areas for white wine. Elba used to produce excellent wines (now hard to find), including Aleatico, a dessert wine. Vin Santo is an amber dessert wine (aged for a minimum of three years and with 17–18 per cent alcohol), produced in Tuscany and Umbria, similar in taste to an excellent sherry. It is often served with dry almond biscuits (*biscotti di Prato*) at the end of a meal.

Restaurants

There are numerous restaurants of all categories all over the city and a good inexpensive meal can be found with little difficulty. The selection below has been made taking the quality of the food as the main consideration, and places in the centre of the city have been preferred. Many of these are frequented mostly by Florentines. Apart from the famous restaurants in the most expensive category, others have been chosen for their food rather than for their surroundings or the service provided. You should expect the best restaurants to be crowded, often with a somewhat chaotic atmosphere and service which may seem rather slow or inattentive. In simple *trattorie* there is often a limited choice (and not always a menu), but don't let this put you off: the few dishes offered are often fresher and of higher standard than those in a restaurant where there is a lengthy menu. There are lots of places which serve excellent quick meals and snacks (*vinai, trippai, frigittorie*, and *rosticcerie; listed on pp. 358–59*): restaurants or bars which serve exclusively tourists, often with showy displays of precooked dishes, should be avoided. In the simplest *trattorie* the food is usually good, and considerably cheaper than in the more famous restaurants, though furnishings and surroundings can be a lot less comfortable. Most restaurants display a menu outside which gives you an idea of the prices: however, many simpler restaurants do not, and here, although the choice is usually limited, the standard of the cuisine is often very high.

Some restaurants still have a cover charge (*coperto*), shown separately on the menu, which is added to the bill, although this practice has officially been discontinued. Prices almost always include service, so always ask the waiter if the service charge has been added to the bill before leaving a tip, though is customary to leave a few Euro on the table as a sign of appreciation. For tax purposes, restaurants are now obliged to issue a receipt (*ricevuta fiscale*); you should not leave the premises without one.

Lunch is normally around 1pm and is the main meal of the day, while dinner is around 8 or 9. Very few restaurants in Florence stay open later than 11 or 11.30. It is acceptable to order a first course only, or to skip the first course and order only a main course. Many restaurants in Florence close down for part of August (or July), and throughout the year many are shut on Sunday (and Monday).

A selection of a few restaurants—divided into six categories according to price per person for dinner (wine excluded)—is given below.

★★★★★★   over €175 a head
★★★★★   around €100 a head
★★★★   around €40—€50 a head
★★★   around €30 a head
★★   around €15–€20 a head
★   around €10 a head

★★★★★★
Enoteca Pinchiorri. 87 Via Ghibellina (*map p. 399, E3*), T: 055 242 777. One of the most famous and expensive restaurants in Italy, which opened in 1974 and has managed to retain its reputation as probably the best luxury restaurant, despite some criticisms about its prices which scare away many Florentine gourmets. Run by Giorgio Pinchiorri and Annie Feolde, it has an exceptional selection of wines, arguably the best in Italy, and a remarkably creative cuisine. On the ground floor of a palace, it can seat about 80 people in two comfortable rooms, one with a balcony, and, in good weather, there are tables in the interior courtyard and in a loggia off it. There is a set menu for €175, but the minimum you can spend à la carte is around €200 a head (all prices exclusive of wine). Closed Sunday and Monday.

★★★★★
Harry's Bar. 22 Lungarno Vespucci (*map p. 398, B3*), T: 055 239 6700. A very elegant cocktail bar renowned for its impeccable service and formal old-fashioned atmosphere. Leo, the barman, produces superb cocktails, and you can also have just a club sandwich. In the restaurant, the food sometimes disappoints. A few tables are put out in the summer on the Lungarno. Closed Sunday.

Taverna del Bronzino. Via delle Ruote (*map p. 399, D1*), T: 055 495 220. One of the finest restaurants in Florence, which has maintained an extremely high standard for many years. Elegant and comfortable with impeccable service, the cuisine is creative and very good: one of the best places for fish. Closed Sunday.

★★★★
Il Cibreo. 8 Via Andrea del Verrocchio (*map p. 399, F3*), T: 055 234 1100. This is one of the best-known restaurants in Florence, especially famous in North America, and has been recommended in all the restaurant guides to Italy for many years, so it is best to book well in advance. It has a rather unusual atmosphere with informal service, and you are not given a menu. It seems, oddly, to be more like an Italian restaurant in North America rather than an Italian restaurant in Italy. It is an expensive place to eat, and lacks an expert wine waiter. Bear in mind that on the menu outside service is included, but this is not specified on your bill. It has a simpler one-room trattoria next door in Via dei Macci, which has the same chef, but a reduced menu, and costs half (★★). You can also eat a plate of the same food across the street at the pleasant **Caffè del Cibreo**. This has tables out-

side, but even here the prices are in the ★★★ category. Closed Sunday and Monday.

Don Chisciotte. 4 Via Ridolfi (*map p. 398, C1*), T: 055 475 430. Set in a rather unattractive street, near Piazza dell'Independenza, this is a restaurant which has acquired a good name for reliability and therefore has a devoted clientele and is almost always busy. It is a little bit pretentious and without much style, though the food is good (it specializes in fish), if rather expensive. Closed Sunday and Monday morning.

Oliviero. 51 Via delle Terme (*map p. 398, C3*), T: 055 212 421. A comfortable restaurant with great charm and excellent service. Its atmosphere is reminiscent of the 1950s and 1960s. It has a well-known chef and is a little cheaper than the other restaurants mentioned in this category. Closed Sunday.

Orient Express. 9 Borgo Allegri (*map p. 399, E3*), T: 055 246 9028. Traditional cooking of a very high standard. Closed Sunday.

★★★

Acqua al Due. 40 Via Vigna Vecchia (*map p. 397, C3*), T: 055 284 170. Opened about 20 years ago, this restaurant is one of the very few in the city that stays open until late (1am). Frequented by actors and theatre-goers, it has good pasta dishes, and the steak is served in an original way. Open evenings only (no closing day).

Alla Vecchia Bettola. 32 Viale Ariosto (*map p. 398, A3*), T: 055 224 158. A typical Florentine trattoria on the edge of the Oltrarno, although its setting is not very attractive. The food is usually adequate and you can eat outside.

Closed Sunday & Monday.

Beccofino. 1 Piazza degli Scarlatti (Lungarno Guicciardini; *map p. 398, B3*), T: 055 290 076. Run by a Scottish proprietor (who also runs Baldovino, *see p. 355*), this restaurant serves a modern variety of Tuscan food. Beccofino has an excellent selection of international wines, which can also be ordered just by the glass. There is a reduced menu in the wine bar (★★). Closed Monday.

Cavallino. 28 Piazza della Signoria (*map p. 399, D3*), T: 055 215 818. A long-established and reliable restaurant in Piazza della Signoria, the main square of Florence, with tables outside. Its splendid setting is without equal. Closed Wednesday.

Il Cavolo Nero. 22 Via di Ardiglione (*map p. 398, B4*), T: 055 294 744. Set in a delightful little side street, this is a pleasant restaurant, with creative and well-presented international cuisine. It has the atmosphere of an English or French restaurant rather than a traditional Tuscan establishment. You can eat outside in summer in an internal courtyard. Closed Sunday.

Cocco Lezzone. 26 Via del Parioncino (*map p. 398, C3*), T: 055 287178. This has also had a good name for many years as a typical Florentine trattoria, and the food has maintained a high standard. However, it lacks atmosphere and is not a particularly attractive place. On the plus side, the service is extremely fast and you can have a very quick meal here if you wish. Closed Sunday and Tuesday evening.

Domani. 80 Via Romana (*map p. 398, B4*), T: 055 221 166. An excellent fish restaurant which serves a superb variety of Japanese and Italian cuisine. It is one of the best places to eat in Florence and is very good value, despite the fact the setting is rather anonymous and without much character. It is very well attended by the Japanese. Closed Sunday and Monday.

Latini. 6 Via Palchetti (behind Palazzo Rucellai; *map p. 398, B–C3*), T: 055 210 916. This has been famous for decades as a typical Florentine trattoria with long, crowded tables and Tuscan cuisine, and a bustling atmosphere. However, its fame has meant that there are usually long queues of tourists on the street outside, and the food is no better than numerous other restaurants in the same price range. Closed Monday.

Mamma Gina. 36 Borgo San Jacopo (*map p. 398, C3*), T: 055 239 6009. A famous Florentine trattoria, now rather lacking in character. Closed Sunday.

Osteria dei Benci. 13 Via dei Benci (*map p. 399, E3*), T: 055 234 4923. Opened by a law student at Florence university, this is modelled on a typical Florentine trattoria, and has a youthful following. It serves good Tuscan food, specializing in meat (excellent raw ham and Florentine steaks). Very good desserts. Closed Sunday.

Osteria del Caffè Italiano. 11 Via delle Stinche (*map p. 399, E3*), T: 055 289 368. Opened in 1998, this is housed on the ground floor of one of the best preserved medieval palaces in Florence. Its atmosphere recreates that of a typical Florentine trattoria and it is run by the same proprietor as the Caffè Italiano in Via della Condotta. Unfortunately, since it has been discovered by tourists, the quality of the food and the service has lowered and the prices risen. It has a few tables outside in summer in the narrow old Via della Vigna Vecchia, round the corner. It also has a wine bar, where you can just have a snack. Closed Monday.

Osteria di Santo Spirito. 16 Piazza Santo Spirito (*map p. 398, B4*), T: 055 238 2383. This used to be a typical Florentine osteria but it has been transformed and given a somewhat more trendy atmosphere, similar to a London or Parisienne restaurant. However, the food is good and there are tables outside in one of the loveliest squares in Florence. Open every day.

Paoli. 12 Via dei Tavolini (*map p. 397, B2*), T: 055 216 215. At the heart of the historic centre, this is a very old restaurant in a fine vaulted room with mock Renaissance decorations and frescoes. It serves traditional, if rather unimaginative, Florentine fare. The tables are rather close together but there is a nice atmosphere, and service and cover price are included, making it good value. Popular with tourists. Closed Tuesday.

La Pentola dell'Oro. 24 Via di Mezzo (*map p. 399, F3*), T: 055 241 821. A club (membership by previous appointment; annual subscription) run by Giuseppe Alessi, a scholar of Renaissance cuisine who produces excellent traditional Tuscan dishes. This is a place in a category all of its own, with an extraordinarily imaginative menu, and a consistently high standard of cuisine. You eat downstairs in a cool cellar. The restaurant is frequented by Florentines and Italians serious about their food. Genuine local wine. Family run, with Alessi's wife in control in the kitchen, and his son sharing the management.

Perseus. 10 Viale Don Minzoni (*beyond*

map p. 399, F1), T: 055 588 226.
Situated in a noisy street outside the
historic centre, this fairly new restaurant is favoured by the young and has a
pleasant, lively atmosphere. It serves
very good meat and has tables outside
in the summer. Closed Sunday.
Quattro Leoni. Via Toscanella (1 Via
Vellutini; map p. 398, C4), T: 055 218
562. This was once a simple, cheap
trattoria, but it has now been livened
up and serves traditional Tuscan cuisine, with good meat. Tables outside.
Closed Wednesday at lunchtime.
Trattoria del Carmine. Piazza del
Carmine (map p. 398, A3), T: 055 218
601. An established typical Florentine
trattoria. A pleasant place to eat outside
in summer. Good Tuscan food and
homemade sweets. Closed Sunday.
'Il Troia' (Trattoria Sostanza). 29 Via
Porcellana (map p. 398, B2), T: 055 212
691. Founded in 1869, this has maintained the character of a genuine
Florentine trattoria perhaps more than
any other restaurant in the city. It has
sober furnishings and a marble bar at
the entrance. Set in a dark narrow side
street, it can sit only about 40 people in
one long, narrow room with marble
tables (some of which you share). Some
elderly locals come here for lunch every
day (and their napkins are kept for
them). It has a restrained, distinguished
atmosphere, with professional service. It
serves traditional Tuscan fare and is particularly famous for its T-bone steaks
(bistecca alla fiorentina). You are expected to eat a full meal; no credit cards;
the trattoria is closed at weekends—
rules which suggest that tourists are not
as welcome as they might be. It is
always advisable to book in the

evenings. Closed Saturday and Sunday.
Vino e Carpaccio. Via Pier Capponi
72a (map p. 399, F1), T: 055 500 0896.
Set outside the historic centre, this is an
unusual restaurant with a very limited
menu. The food is cooked by a
Sardinian chef and is good—the fish is
particularly fresh. As the name suggests,
it also specializes in a great variety of
carpacci. The desserts are excellent. The
restaurant is lined with hundreds of
wine bottles, any of which you are
invited to chose (you can also try them
by the glass). The only criticism is that
it is a little bit over priced. Closed
Saturday lunch and all day Sunday.

★★
Antico Ristoro di' Cambi. 1 Via
Sant'Onofrio (map p. 398, A3), T: 055
217 134. This began as a vinaio in the
heart of the popular district of San
Frediano in the Oltrarno and it retains
the atmosphere of a traditional
Florentine osteria, always busy and with
a fast turnover. It serves excellent classic Tuscan dishes, including good steak
and tripe. Even though large, it can be
difficult to find a place and is not some-
where you can linger over your meal;
the tables can also be crowded. There
are lots of tables outside in the charming little Piazza dei Tiratoio. Closed
Sunday.
Baldini. 96 Via il Prato (map p. 398,
A2), T: 055 287 663. A popular place
to eat for many years and the cooking is
sound traditional Tuscan fare. Closed all
day Saturday and Sunday evening.
Baldovino. 22 Via San Giuseppe (map
p. 399, E2), T: 055 241 773. Run by the
same Scotsman as Beccofino (see p.
355), this has an international feel since

numerous foreigners work here. Traditional Tuscan food and good Neapolitan pizzas (that is, the thicker variety). It also has a wine bar close by where you can just have a snack. Closed Monday.

Benvenuto. 16 Via della Mosca (*map p. 397, C4*), T: 055 214 833. An established and reliable trattoria, with standard Tuscan cuisine. Closed Sunday.

Borgo Antico, 6 Piazza Santo Spirito (*map p. 398, B4*), T: 055 210 437. A typical Florentine trattoria in one of the most attractive squares in Florence. It has tables outside in summer and is also a pizzeria. No closing day.

Ciao Bella. 18 Piazza del Tiratoio (*map p. 398, A3*), T: 055 218 477. A pizzeria owned by a Sicilian, with a German wife. Cheap and friendly but without much character. At night, when it is frequented by a young clientele, only pizza is served; though during the day, other dishes are available. Closed Tuesday.

Diladdarno. 108 Via de' Serragli (*map p. 398, B4*), T: 055 225 001. A pleasant traditional Florentine trattoria, where you usually share a table. The food is adequate and there is a small garden where you can eat outside during the summer. Closed Monday.

Le Mossacce. 55 Via Proconsolo (*map p. 399, D3*), T: 055 294 361. In a central street close to the Bargello museum, this has been open for many years, and serves good quality food of a consistently high standard at very reasonable prices. Very crowded and reservations are usually not accepted, but the service is extremely fast. No credit cards. Closed Saturday and Sunday.

Pandemonio. 50 Via del Leone (*map p. 398, A3*), T: 055 224 002. A little-known restaurant with good food. Closed Sunday.

Ruggero. 89 Via Senese (*just beyond map p. 398, A4*), T: 055 220542. A typical family-run Florentine trattoria of reliable standard, a little way out of the city beyond Porta Romana. Closed Wednesday.

Da Sergio. 8 Piazza San Lorenzo (*map p. 399, D2*), T: 055 281 941. Family-run trattoria only open for lunch behind the market stalls outside the church of San Lorenzo. This has been a good, simple place to eat for many years, although perhaps a little more expensive than other restaurants in this category. Closed Sunday.

Lo Skipper. 70 Via degli Alfani (*map p. 399, E2*), T: 055 284 019. An unusual restaurant located at the end of a short arcade and so not visible from the street. It is run by a nautical club which offers free membership for a year. Every month the menu changes and follows a certain theme, such as Greek, Mexican or Italian regional food. Simple, authentic ingredients. Closed Saturday lunch and Sunday.

Al Tranvai. 14 Piazza Tasso (*map p. 398, A4*), T: 055 225 197. Good cheap food. The atmosphere is friendly and there are some tables outside. At lunch, the clientele is mostly local, while in the evening it is favoured by the young and foreigners. Closed Saturday and Sunday.

★

I Fratellini. 27 (red) Via Ghibellina (*map p. 399, E3*). This grocery shop serves good meals at lunchtime only. It has no name outside but is run by the Bigazzi family. Chickens are roasted in an open fire and traditional Florentine dishes are served to locals who live or work in the area. Closed Saturday and Sunday.

La Casalinga. 9 Via dei Michelozzi (*map p. 398, B4*), T: 055 218 624. One of the best simple, cheap places to eat in Florence, just out of Piazza Santo Spirito. Run by a very friendly family, and often quite hectic at lunch-time when it is full of builders, foreign students and tourists. Closed Sunday.

Mario. 2 Via Rosina (Via Sant'Orsola; *map p. 398, C1*), T: 055 218 550. Open only at lunchtime and set in a side street close to the market of San Lorenzo. Always crowded with stall-holders and locals, a few tiny wooden tables and stools, efficient service and traditional Tuscan food for very reasonable prices. A favourite cheap eating place in Florence, and just the answer if you need a quick, substantial meal. Closed Sunday

Da Nerbone. Inside the Mercato Centrale di San Lorenzo (*map p. 398, C1*), T: 055 219 949. A good cheap place to eat inside the busy central food market of Florence where the stall-holders eat as well as discerning Florentines. Closed Sunday.

Pruto. 9 Piazza Tasso (*map p. 398, A4*), T: 055 222 219. Cheap tourist menu for lunch, although the service is slow. The fish is usually good. Tables outside in the summer. Closed Monday.

Sabatino. 2 Via Pisana (*just beyond map p. 398, A3*), T: 055 225 955. This became established many years ago in Borgo San Frediano as one of the most typical cheap places to eat in Florence. It has recently moved to just outside Porta San Frediano, but retains the

same atmosphere and is run by an extremely friendly family. It is frequented by elderly Florentines who live near by and go there most days for lunch, as well as builders and artisans who work in the area. Well worth a visit. Closed Saturday and Sunday.

VEGETARIAN RESTAURANTS

Il Vegetariano di Ambrosini. 30 Via delle Ruote (*map p. 399, D1*), T: 055 475 030. This is perhaps the best vegetarian restaurant in Florence.

Il Sedano Allegro. 20 Borgo La Croce (*map p. 399, F3*), T: 055 234 5505.

Gauguin. 24 Via degli Alfani (*map p. 399, D2*), T: 055 234 0616.

WINE BARS (ENOTECHE)

Pane e Vino. 70 Via San Niccolò (*map p. 399, E4*), T: 055 247 6956. In a lovely old road close to the Arno, this has a rather unusual atmosphere, open only in the evening. It has one of the very best selections of wine in the city and you can also eat well here. Closed Monday.

Le Volpi e l'Uva. 1 Piazza de' Rossi (Piazza Santa Felicita; *map p. 397, A4*), T: 055 2398132. A pleasant little wine bar where you sit at the counter (only open in the evening until 8), with a very fine selection of wines and interesting food (including a very wide range of cheeses), and usually good sweets. Closed Sunday.

Fuori Porta. 10 Via Monte alle Croci (*beyond map p. 399, E4*), T: 055 2342483. This is located outside Porta San Miniato, with outdoor tables in a particularly pleasant and peaceful area of the city. A delightful wine bar with very fine wines which you can also order by the glass, and good simple snacks. It is considered the best wine bar in town by numerous young Florentines. Closed Sunday.

VINAI

These are traditional Florentine wine bars which sell wine by the glass and good simple food. Many of them have closed down in the last few decades, but the few that are left are well worth seeking out, as they have a very special atmosphere and are much loved by the Florentines. The *vinaio* at no. 70 Via Alfani (*map p. 399, E2*), and the one in Via della Chiesa (corner of Via delle Caldaie; *map p. 398, B4*) both have seating; others are no more than 'holes in the wall' but have excellent snacks (as well as a good selection of wines) which you eat standing on the pavement: **Cantina Ristori** (Antico No), 6 Volta di San Piero (*map p. 399, E2*); **Donatello**, Via de' Neri (corner of Via de' Benci; *map p. 399, D4*); **Fratellini**, 38 Via dei Cimatori (*map p. 397, B3*); and the *vinaio* at no. 25 Piazza Castellani (*map p. 397, C4*).

SNACKS

Mariano. 19 Via Parione (*map p. 398, C3*). Very good sandwiches made to order, with especially good cheeses and cakes, and wine by the glass. Also a grocery store efficiently run by a friendly family, it has an elegant local Florentine clientele, with a few tables. Open from 8–3.30, and 5–8.

More elegant (and more expensive)

snack bars where you can order a light meal include the **Caffè Italiano**, 56 Via della Condotta (*map p. 399, D3*), T: 055 288 950, and **Boccadama**, 25 Piazza Santa Croce (*map p. 399, E3*). **Procacci** in Via Tornabuoni (*map p. 398, C3*), T: 055 211 656, is famous for its truffle sandwiches, and also has an unusual selection of cheeses.

Snack bars open late include **Du Monde**, 103 Via San Niccolò (*map p. 399, E4*), T: 055 234 4953 and **Eskimo**, 12 Via dei Canacci (*map p. 398, B2*).

RESTAURANTS IN THE ENVIRONS

These are mostly reasonably priced, and many have tables outside.

Maiano
La Graziella (T: 055 599 963; closed Tues), **Le Cave di Maiano** (T: 055 59133).

Settignano
Osvaldo (T: 055 603972, in Ponte a Mensola); **La Capponcina**, 17 Via San Romano (T: 055 697 037).

Bagno a Ripoli
L'Acquacheta (pizza and fish, open till late; T: 055 696 054); **Donnini**, Via di Rimaggio (T: 055 630 076).

Arcetri
Omero. 11 Via Pian de' Giullari (T: 055 220 053).

Galluzzo
Da Bibe. 1 Via delle Bagnese, Ponte all'Asse (T: 055 204 9085).

Serpiolle
Strettoio. 7 Via di Serpiolle (T: 055 425 0044).

Cercina
Ricchi. T: 055 402 024.
Trianon. T: 055 402 007.

Sesto Fiorentino

Dulcamara Club. 2 Via Dante da Castiglione (T: 055 4255 021).
Olmo
Le Quattro Strade (Il Pratone). 335 Via Faentina (T: 055 548920, closed Mon); **La Torre di Buiano** (T: 055 548 836);

Casa del Prosciutto. 58 Via Bosconi (T: 055 548 830); **Da Mario alla Querciola**. 428 Via Faentina (T: 055 540 024).
Pratolino
Villa Vecchia. Vaglia (T: 055 409 476).

Snacks (spuntini)

For a slice of pizza and other hot snacks go to a *rosticceria* or *tavola calda*. Some of these have no seating and sell food to take away or eat on the spot. They sometimes also sell *calzoni* (a pizza 'roll' usually filled with ham and mozzarella) and *crocchette* (minced meat or potato croquettes), grilled chicken and pasta dishes. The one at 48 Via di Sant'Antonino, off Via dell'Ariento by the San Lorenzo market, is particularly good as it serves the locals and those who work at the market. The bakery (Forno Sartoni) at 34 Via dei Cerchi (*map p. 397, B3*) has excellent pizzas and buns.

Friggitorie are small shops which fry snacks (sweet and savoury) on the spot and sell them over the counter to customers in the street. Though favoured by Florentines, many have closed down in the last few years. However, one particularly good one that is still open is Friggitorie No. 34 at 48 Via di Sant'Antonino (*map p. 398, C2*) which sells doughnuts (*ciambelle* and *bomboloni*), rice fritters (*frittelle di riso*), and *coccoli* (simple fritters made with water, flour, yeast and salt). It also sells pizza and *schiacciato* (flat bread topped with oil and salt). Friggitoria Rossi, in Via dell'Albero (*map p. 398, B2*), is also worth trying and sells *arrancini di riso* (rice balls fried in breadcrumbs, filled with butter and cheese or meat) and *polpettine di patate* (potato croquettes).

Trippai sell tripe, a Florentine speciality, in sandwiches from barrows on street corners. Good *trippai* include those in: Via dell'Ariento (*map p. 398, C1–2*), Piazza de' Cimatori (Via Dante Alighieri, *map p. 397, B3*), Via dei Macci (corner of Borgo la Croce, *map p. 399, F3*), Piazza del Porcellino (Mercato Nuovo; *map p. 397, B3*) and outside Porta Romana (*beyond map p. 398, A4*).

Cafés

Cafés (bars) are open all day. Most customers choose to eat and drink standing up—you pay the cashier first, and show the receipt to the barman in order to get served. In almost all bars, if you sit at a table you are charged considerably more—at least double—and are given waiter service (you should not pay first).

Well-known cafés in the city, all of which have tables (some outside) include Rivoire in Piazza Signoria; Le Giubbe Rosse and Gilli, both in Piazza della Repubblica; and Cibreo, 5 Via Andrea del Verrocchio (*map p. 399, F3*). A café specializing in tea is La Via del Tè, 22 Piazza Ghiberti (*map p. 399, F3*). In Settignano, try Caffè Desiderio, at 5 Piazza Tommaseo.

Caffèlatte, 39 Via degli Alfani (near Via della Pergola), open 8–midnight, except Sunday, is a particularly delightful little café (*map p. 399, E2*). It is set in an old dairy with its original furniture and counter, and serves delicious organically grown vegetarian snacks made on the premises. Reasonable extra charge for table service.

Other busy cafés include Le Colonnine, Via dei Benci (corner of Corso Tintori, *map p. 399, D4*), and Caffetteria Piansa, 18 Borgo Pinti (*map p. 399, E2*). The Chalet Fontana is a pleasant, comfortable café outside the historic centre on the corner of Via San Leonardo and Viale Galileo, with a garden in the summer.

Cake shops (pasticcerie)

Pasticcerie also almost always function as cafés. By far the best cake shop in Florence is Dolci e Dolcezze, 8 Piazza Beccaria (*just beyond map p. 399, F3*), but it is certainly not cheap, and has no seating. Other old-established cafés well known for their cakes, pastries and confectionery, include Rivoire on Piazza della Signoria (famous for its chocolate); Robiglio on Via dei Servi and Via Tosinghi (*map p. 399, D2 and p. 397, B2*); Giurovich, Viale Don Minzoni (*beyond map p. 399, F1*); Gambrinus, Via Brunelleschi; (*map p. 398, C2*); and Scudieri, Via Cerretani (*map p. 398, C2*). Less famous but now also very popular with Florentines is Patrizio Cosi, 11 Borgo degli Albizi (*map p. 399, E3*). The Forno Sartoni, 34 Via dei Cerchi (*map p. 399, D3*), sells exceptionally good simple cakes (as well as pizzas), at reasonable prices. The Pasticceria Alcedo Falli in Fiesole (29 Via Gramsci) also makes particularly good cakes and pastries.

Ice-cream

Some of the best ice-cream shops in Florence include Vivoli, 7 Via Isola delle Stinche (*map p. 399, D–E3*); Perchè no?, 19 Via dei Tavolini (*map p. 397, B2*); and Veneta, 7 Piazza Beccaria (*just beyond map p. 399, F3*).

Outside the centre of Florence, the following ice-cream shops are particularly good: Badiani, 20 Viale dei Mille and Cavini, 22 Piazza delle Cure (*both beyond map p. 399, F1*). In the environs of the city are La Fattoria di Maiano, 3 Via Cave di Maiano, and Villani, 8 Piazza San Domenico (San Domenico di Fiesole).

Chocolate

Excellent chocolate in numerous different forms is sold at Rivoire, Piazza della Signoria. Delicious Dutch chocolate (together with other Dutch specialities) is sold at very reasonable prices at L'Olandese Volante, 44 Via San Gallo (*map p. 399, D1*). Another chocolate specialist is Vestri, 11 Borgo degli Albizi (*map p. 399, D3*) where chocolate made in Tuscany can be bought in both liquid and solid form.

Picnics

Excellent food for picnics can be bought at delicatessens (*pizzicherie*), grocery shops (*alimentari*) and bakeries (*fornai*). Sandwiches (*panini*) are made up on request, and bakeries often sell good individual pizzas, rolls and cakes. In the autumn, many bakeries sell *schiacciata all'uva*, a delicious bready dough topped with fresh black grapes and cooked in the oven. *Pan di Ramerino* is a bun with rosemary and raisins (traditionally made during the Easter season, but now usually available all year round).

Fritelle di San Giuseppe are fritters made with rice, eggs, milk and lemon rind; *cenci* are simpler fritters.

MUSEUMS, GALLERIES & MONUMENTS

There is now an excellent telephone booking service for the state museums of Florence (T: 055 294 883; Mon–Fri 8.30–6.30, Sat 8.30–12.30) which, for a small extra charge, allows you to enter at a specific time without having to queue (you collect and pay for the ticket at the museum just before the booked time of entrance).

Hours of admission are given with individual entries. Opening times vary and often change without warning, so those given in the text may not be completely accurate. An up-to-date list of opening times is always available at the APT offices, but even this can be inaccurate. To make certain the times are correct, it is worth telephoning first. Ticket offices close half an hour (45 minutes at the Uffizi) before closing time.

Sometimes state museums are closed on the main public holidays: 1 January, Easter Day, 25 April, 1 May, 15 August and Christmas Day, but at Easter and Christmas they now usually have special opening times; for up-to-date information, ask at the APT.

Museum Week (*La Settimana dei Musei Italiani*) has now become established as an annual event (traditionally in late November or early December but for the last few years in March). Entrance to most state-owned museums is free during the week, and some have longer opening hours, while private collections may be specially opened. For information on state museums throughout Italy, toll free T: 800 991 199; www.beniculturali.it.

For a week, usually in late spring, the scientific institutes in the city are opened to the public and special exhibitions, lectures and tours held (a week known as the *Settimana della Cultura Scientifica*).

On 18 February each year there are celebrations in honour of Anna Maria Luisa de' Medici (on the anniversary of her death), who left the Medici art treasures to the people of Florence in 1737, and there is free entry to all state and municipal museums in the city on that day.

There are a number of organizations for safeguarding and restoring monuments in Florence, which arrange visits and lectures throughout the year. The following have an annual membership subscription: Amici dei Musei Fiorentini, 39 Via Alfani (T: 055 293 007); Associazione Dimore Storiche Italiane, 17 Borgo Santi Apostoli (T: 055 212 452); Fondo per l'Ambiente Italiano (FAI), 18 Borgo San Frediano (T: 055 214 595); Amici di Palazzo Pitti, Palazzo Pitti (T: 055 265 8123). The regional headquarters of Italia Nostra is at 9 Viale Gramsci.

There is free admission to all state-owned galleries and monuments for British citizens over the age of 65 (take your passport for proof of age and nationality). EU students between the ages of 18 and 26 are entitled to a reduction (usually 50 per cent). State museums are free during Museum Week.

CHURCHES & CHURCH SERVICES

The opening times of churches vary a great deal; those of the major churches have been given in the text. Some of the most important churches (Santa Croce, Santa Maria Novella, San Lorenzo) now charge an entrance fee and stay open 9.30–5 and are well illuminated. Others usually close at midday and do not reopen until 4 or 5, and a few are open only for services. Sometimes there are coin-operated lights for altarpieces and frescoes. A pair of binoculars can be especially useful to study details. You may not be allowed into some churches if you are wearing shorts or have bare shoulders; in the Duomo you will be given a paper tabard to cover yourself. In the text the terms north and south refer to the liturgical north (left) and south (right), taking the high altar as the east end.

Roman Catholic services

On Sunday and, in the principal churches, often on weekdays, Mass is celebrated up to midday and from 6 until 7 in the evening. Confessions are heard in English on Sunday at the Duomo, San Lorenzo, San Marco, Santa Trìnita, Santa Croce, Orsanmichele, and San Miniato al Monte.

Church festivals

On saints' days, Mass and vespers with music are celebrated in the churches dedicated to the saints concerned. The feast of the patron saint of Florence, St John the Baptist (24 June), is a local holiday and special services are held. On Easter Day the Scoppio del Carro is held in and around the Duomo (see opposite).

Non-Catholic churches and places of worship

Anglican: St Mark's, 16 Via Maggio.
American Episcopalian: St James, 9 Via Bernardo Rucellai.
Lutheran: 11 Lungarno Torrigiani.
Waldensian: 26 Via Micheli.
Greek Orthodox: 76 Viale Mattioli.
Russian Orthodox: 8 Via Leone X.
Jewish Synagogue: 4 Via Farini.

FESTIVALS

Scoppio del Carro

Held on Easter Day, this is the most famous traditional religious festival in Florence and has taken place for centuries. It is held in and around the Duomo at 11am. An ungainly, tall wooden carriage known as the *Brindellone* (which dates from 1764; restored after the flood in 1966), covered with fireworks, leaves its huge garage on Il Prato around 9, and is drawn by two pairs of white oxen (dressed for the occasion) through the streets of Florence to the main door of the Duomo, accompanied by a procession and band. Inside the cathedral, a 'dove' (nowadays nothing less than a rocket) is lit by the archbishop at the high altar and sent along a wire through the cathedral to ignite the bonfire of fireworks on the carriage (after which it returns to the high altar). The great dramatic explosion, which lasts several minutes, is accompanied by the ringing of the cathedral bells. The origin of this festival appears to go back to the Florentine capture of a war carriage from Fiesole in 1152. Later, richly decorated triumphal carts were constructed to convey the holy symbol of fire through the streets on religious festivals. Formerly, the mechanism of the 'dove' was less sophisticated and was sometimes not successful; if it failed to ignite the carriage it augured a poor harvest.

St John's day

St John (San Giovanni) is the patron saint of Florence. St John's Day is 24 June, a local holiday celebrated with fireworks at Piazzale Michelangelo at 10pm.

Calcio Storico Fiorentino

This is a 'football' game in 16th-century costume held in three heats during the latter part of June (one game always takes place on 24 June), usually in Piazza Santa Croce. The teams represent the four quartiere of the city: Santa Croce (*azzurri*; blue); Santa Maria Novella (*rossi*; red); Santo Spirito (*bianchi*; white); and San Giovanni (*verdi*; green). Tickets are sold at Box Office (*see p. 367*), or can be purchased a few days before the game at the Chiosco degli Sportivi near the arcades beside the post office in Via Pellicceria. The more expensive tickets are for numbered places: the team supporters (sometimes rowdy) choose the cheaper seats on the stands at the two short ends of the piazza. There are no seats in the shade.

At about 5.30, there is an exhibition of flag throwing and then a long procession in period costume through the centre of Florence enters the arena accompanied by drummers and led by the gonfalons (standard bearers) of the city. The various historic figures, bands, representatives and players of the four districts (who throw flowers to their supporters) are announced as they enter the arena. Some figures are mounted and a bullock (once the prize for the winning team) traditionally takes part in the ceremony. It takes about 40 minutes for the whole procession to enter the piazza and after *la grida* and the presentation of arms everyone except the players runs out of the arena. The 27 players of each team are presented by name and a cannon shot signals the start of the game. During the game, which is played with few rules and considerable violence, a *caccia* or goal (when the ball is sent into the low net along one of the short sides) is announced by two cannon shots fired from the steps of Santa Croce.

Festa della Rificolona

On 7 September, the eve of the Birth of the Virgin, the Festa della Rificolona is celebrated by children carrying colourful paper lanterns through the streets (especially in Piazza Santissima Annunziata). Some children now carry pea-shooters with which they try to destroy the lanterns. The name is a corruption of *fierucolone*, the name the Florentines gave the peasant women from the surrounding countryside who came to Florence carrying lanterns for the ancient traditional festival to honour the Virgin at Santissima Annunziata.

Festival of the Annunziata

On 25 March, the festival of the Annunziata, a fair is held in Piazza Santissima Annunziata when homemade sweet biscuits are sold from stalls. A *Fierucola del Pane* is also held here on 8 December.

Festa del Grillo

On Ascension Day (in May), there is a large fair in the Cascine where crickets were traditionally sold in little cages: since 1999 this has no longer been allowed, but the fair still takes place and is a lively event for children.

SHOPS & MARKETS

ANTIQUE SHOPS

There are numerous antique shops in Via Maggio (*map p. 398, B–C4*) and the small streets leading to Piazza Pitti, as well as in Via dei Fossi, (*map p. 398, B2–3*) and Borgo San Jacopo (*map p. 398, C4*).

ARTISTS MATERIALS

Shops selling artist's materials include **Rigacci**, 51 Via dei Servi (*map p. 399, D2*) and **Zecchi**, 19 Via dello Studio (*map p. 397, C2*).

BOOKSHOPS

Shops specializing in English books include: **Paperback Exchange**, 31 Via Fiesolana (*map p. 399, E2*); **BM Bookshop**, 4 Borgo Ognissanti (*map p. 398, B3*); and **McRae Books**, Via de' Neri (*map p. 399, D3*). The largest book-shops in Florence (which also stock English books) include **Feltrinelli**, 30 Via de' Cerretani (*map p. 398, C2*); **Feltrinelli International**, 12 Via Cavour (*map p. 399, D2*); **Edison**, Piazza della Repubblica (*map p. 398, C3*); and **Libreria Martelli**, Via Martelli (*map p. 399, D2*). Bookshops specializing in art history include: **Salimbeni**, 14 Via Palmieri (*map p. 399, E3*) and **Art & Libri**, 32 Via dei Fossi (*map p. 398, B3*).

CERAMICS

Italian pottery is sold at **Sbigoli**, 4 Via Sant'Egidio (*map p. 399, E2*). The shop called **Ceramica Artistica Migliori**, 39 Via dei Benci (*map p. 399, E3*) makes good copies of classic Italian majolica. **Andreini**, 63 Borgo degli Albizi (*map p. 399, E3*) also sells majolica. Shops specializing in kitchenware, ceramics and glass include **La Ménagère**, 8 Via dei Ginori (*map p. 399, D2*), and **Bartolini**,

24 Via dei Servi (*map p. 399, D2*). Richard Ginori ceramics are sold at 17 Via dei Rondinelli (*map p. 398, C2*), although much cheaper seconds can be found in **Sesto Fiorentino**, at the warehouse next to the Doccia porcelain museum.

CLOTHES

The smartest fashion shops in Florence are in Via Tornabuoni and Via della Vigna Nuova (*map p. 398, B–C3*). There are other elegant clothes shops in Via Calzaioli, Via Strozzi, Via Calimala, Via Roma, Via Guicciardini, Lungarno Acciaioli and Lungarno Corsini. Wellmade leather shoes at reasonable prices are sold in numerous shops in the centre of Florence. Gucci and Ferragamo, both in Via Tornabuoni, are famous for their shoes. Less expensive but good quality shoes are sold at Cresti (several branches). Italy has notably few department stores: the best known in Florence are La Rinascente, Piazza della Repubblica and Coin, Via dei Calzaioli. There are several branches of the chain department stores called Upim and Oviesse in Florence. Silk ties and scarves are sold in many shops and in the markets at reasonable prices. An old-established shop specializing in smart childrens' clothes is **Anichini** at 59 Via del Parione (*map p. 398, C3*).

FABRICS

Fabrics can be found at the **Arte della Seta**, 45 Via dei Fossi (*map p. 398, B2*). Exquisite hand-woven silk is made and sold at the **Antico Setificio Fiorentino**, 4 Via Lorenzo Bartolini (*map p. 398,*

A3). **Lisa Corti Home Textile Emporium**, 58 Via de' Bardi (a delightful little shop at the foot of Ponte Vecchio) and 95 Via San Niccolò (*map p. 399, E4*) sells lovely and unusual fabrics (including velvet, organza and muslin) for home furnishings as well as clothes and accessories all from exclusive designs by Lisa Corti.

HATS

Hats can be bought from **Borsalino**, 40 Via Porta Rossa (*map p. 398, C3*), and models for hats at **Bini**, 5 Piazza Santo Spirito (*map p. 398, B4*). Lovely straw hats can still be found on some stalls at San Lorenzo market. Other articles in straw (including baskets) are sold at **Martini**, 6 Via Santa Verdiana (*map p. 399, F3*).

JEWELLERY

This is another speciality of Florentine craftsmen: the shops on Ponte Vecchio and its immediate vicinity have superb displays. Some of these specialize in pearls, silver, gold or semi-precious stones. Artisans who repair jewellery (or make it to order) have their workshops in the Casa dell'Orafo close by.

LEATHER

Florence is well known for its leather goods (handbags, purses, belts and jackets) which are sold in the open-air markets of San Lorenzo and the Porcellino (Mercato Nuovo; *map p. 397, B3*), and from the stalls in Via dei Gondi (*map p. 397, C3*). There are also numerous shops specializing in leather, including

Grazia Gori, 64 Via Faenza (*map p. 398, C1*) and **Bojola**, 25 Via Rondinelli (*map p. 398, C2*). The large leather 'factories' in the district of Santa Croce cater mostly for tour groups and their guides. Gucci and Ferragamo, both in Via Tornabuoni, are famous for their fashion handbags.

SOAP & PERFUME

Very fine soap and perfumes are made at the **Farmacia di Santa Maria Novella**, 16 Via della Scala (*map p. 398, B2*), as well as at numerous *erboristerie* in the town (including Palazzo Vecchio, Dott. Di Massimo, 9 Via Vaccereccia, *map p. 397, B3*).

STATIONERY

Another speciality of Florence is its fine marbled paper, used to decorate stationery such as albums, boxes and picture frames. The best known shop is **Giulio Giannini**, 37 Piazza Pitti (*map p. 398, C4*). Other shops include **Il Papiro**: several branches, including 24 Piazza Duomo, 13 Via dei Tavolini (*map p. 397, B2*), and 55 Via Cavour (*map p. 399, D1*), **Il Torchio**, 17 Via dei Bardi (*map p. 398, C4*). A less well-known shop which has excellent hand-made products made on the spot by a family of artisans (also to order) is **Lo Scrittoio**, 126 Via Nazionale (*map p. 398, C1*). Another artisan, **Carlo Saitta** has his workshop at 28 Via dell'Agnolo (*map p. 399, E3*). Simple Florentine paper products are also sold in stationers' shops and in the open-air markets. A well-known stationery shop is **Pineider** (13 Piazza della Signoria and 76 Via Tornabuoni).

Markets

The main food market in Florence is the **Mercato Centrale**, also known as the Mercato di San Lorenzo. It is located in a covered market building near the church (*map p. 398, C1*; open Monday–Saturday 7–1; also 4.30–7.30 on Saturday except in July and August); **Sant'Ambrogio** is another good produce market near the church of the same name (*map p. 399, F3*; open mornings only), where butchers and grocers have their shops in a market building, and fruit and vegetables are sold from stalls outside.

The biggest general market in Florence is in the streets near **San Lorenzo** where stalls sell clothing, leatherwork, cheap jewellery and shoes (generally of good quality and cheap in price) throughout the day every day (except Sunday and Monday from mid-November to mid-December, and in January and February). Another similar general market (straw, leather and lace) is the Porcellino (**Mercato Nuovo**; *map p. 397, D3*) open at the same times. There are also stalls in Via dei Gondi (*map p. 397, C3*) which sell similar goods at the same times as the markets mentioned above. At Sant'Ambrogio there is also a general market (new and second-hand clothing, hardware, household linens, shoes) open in the mornings (except Sunday). A very large general market is held every Tuesday morning at Le Cascine, where numerous bargains can be found.

The **Mercatino delle Pulci** or flea market (antiques and junk) is open weekdays in Piazza dei Ciompi (*map p. 399, E3*). On the last Sunday of every month an antique and junk market is held in and around this piazza.

A market (*Fierucola*) of organic food and hand-made products is held every third Sunday of the month in Piazza Santo Spirito (*map p. 398, B4*), and on the weekend preceding 7 September in Piazza Santissima Annunziata. On the second Sunday of the month, a market of artisans' work is held in Piazza Santo Spirito. Artigianato e Palazzo is an annual festival of handmade artisans' wares held for three days in late May or early June in the beautiful garden of Palazzo Corsini sul Prato (entrance at 115 Via della Scala, *map p. 398, A1*).

ENTERTAINMENT

Listings information

Concerts, theatre performances and exhibitions are organized throughout the year and are advertized in the local press and on posters. They are listed in *Firenze Spettacolo* which is published every month and sold at newsagents—a few pages of the main events are in English. Information can also be found at: www. firenzespettacolo.it.

An up-to-date list of exhibitions is printed every month by the APT, and monthly leaflets called Informacittà give news of current events (there is also a website: www.informacitta.net).

Tickets for many concerts and plays are sold at Box Office, 39 Via Alamanni (*map p. 398, B1*), T: 055 210 804, and 8 Chiasso de' Soldanieri (*map p. 397, A3*), just out of Piazza Santa Trinita, off Via Porta Rossa, T: 055 219 402. It is often possible to buy them at the theatre on the evening of the performance.

Music

The Maggio Musicale, an annual music festival (May–July) is held at the Teatro Comunale at 16 Corso Italia (*map p. 398, A2*). Chamber music concerts by musicians from all over the world are organized by the Amici della Musica January–April and October–December at La Pergola Theatre at 18 Via della Pergola (*map p. 399, E2*). The Orchestra Regionale Toscana hold concerts regularly at the Teatro Verdi (*map p. 399, E3*), and the Orchestra da Camera Fiorentina hold chamber music concerts (usually at Orsanmichele; *map p. 399, D3*). Concerts are often held in the courtyard of Palazzo Pitti and in the Giardino Botanico Superiore in the Boboli Gardens in summer (by members of the Maggio Musicale orchestra, for information, T: 055 290 838).

Florence has a number of historic organs including those in the churches of Santissima Annunziata, San Niccolò sopr'Arno, the Badia Fiorentina and San Giorgio alla Costa. Organ concerts are often held in winter.

The Estate Fiesolana is an annual festival of music, drama, and films held from the end of June to the end of August in Fiesole.

PARKS & GARDENS

The following gardens and parks are described in the text (with their opening times). Many are of the greatest botanical interest and also contain superb fountains and sculptural masterpieces. The most beautiful garden in Florence is the huge Boboli Garden, open regularly to the public. The botanical gardens are also of great interest. Just outside the centre of Florence are the famous Medici gardens at the Villa di Castello and the Villa La Petraia.

Public parks open daily in Florence include the huge Cascine, Villa il Ventaglio, Villa Fabbricotti, Villa Stibbert and Villa Strozzi. The lovely park of Villa Demidoff at Pratolino outside Florence is open from March–Oct on certain days of the week. There is a rose garden on Via di San Salvatore al Monte (entrance at 2 Viale Poggi) open from May–mid-June, and a particularly beautiful iris garden open in May below Piazzale Michelangelo. In the horticultural gardens there is a splendid 19th-century greenhouse. There are also shady gardens on either side of Viale Machiavelli.

Private gardens in the centre of Florence include Palazzo Corsini sul Prato which is now open on weekdays. Other gardens opened specially on a few days of the year include the Giardino della Gherardesca, Giardino Torrigiani, Giardino Corsi, the Orti Oricellari and the garden of Palazzo Vivarelli Colonna (*for information, contact the Comune; T: 055 262 5945*).

Two famous historic private gardens near Florence are at Villa Gamberaia (Settignano), which is open on weekdays, and Villa Medici (below Fiesole), open on weekdays by appointment.

Three beautiful gardens now owned and maintained by American universities are at Villa I Tatti (Harvard University), shown to visitors only with a letter of presentation and by previous appointment; Villa La Pietra (New York University) and Villa Le Balze (Georgetown University), which are both sometimes open to the public by previous appointment.

Other beautiful privately owned gardens on the outskirts of the city—only accessible with special permission—include Villa Capponi (Arcetri) and, near Fiesole, Villa Palmieri. A little further away are the gardens of Villa Corsi Salviati (Sesto Fiorentino) and Villa I Collazzi (Galluzzo).

ADDITIONAL INFORMATION

Banking services

Banks are usually open from 8.30–1.30, and 2.30 or 2.45–3.30 or 3.45 every day except Saturday, Sunday and holidays. They close early (about 11) on days preceding national holidays. The commission on cashing travellers' cheques can be quite high. Money can also be changed at exchange offices (*cambio*) and at travel agencies (but usually at a less advantageous rate), as well as at some post offices and main railway stations. Some hotels, restaurants and shops exchange money, but usually at a lower rate.

Consulates

British Consulate, 2 Lungarno Corsini (*map p. 398, B3*), T: 055 284 133.
American Consulate, 38 Lungarno Vespucci (*map p. 398, A2*), T: 055 239 8276.
The British, American, Canadian, Australian, Irish and New Zealand embassies are in Rome.

Crime and the police

There are three categories of policemen in Italy:

Vigili Urbani, municipal police who wear blue uniforms in winter and light blue during the summer; their headquarters are at 6 Piazzale di Porta al Prato, T: 055 328 3333.

Carabinieri, military police who wear a black uniform with a red stripe down the side of the trousers; their headquarters are at 48 Borgo Ognissanti, T: 112.

Polizia di Stato, state police who wear dark blue jackets and light blue trousers; the Central Police Station (Questura) is at 2 Via Zara (T: 055 49771).

Crime should be reported at once; if it is theft, it should be reported to to either the Polizia di Stato or the Carabinieri. A detailed statement has to be given in order to get an official document confirming loss or damage (*denunzia di smarrimento*), which is essential for insurance claims. Interpreters are usually provided. If you have legal problems, contact the APT office at 1 (red) Via Cavour.

Emergencies

For all emergencies, T: 113: the switchboard will coordinate the help you need.

First aid services (*Pronto Soccorso*) are available at hospitals, railway stations and airports. The most central hospital is Santa Maria Nuova, 1 Piazza Santa Maria Nuova (T: 055 27581). Large general hospitals on the outskirts of the town are: Careggi, Viale Morgagni; San Giovanni di Dio, Via Scandicci, Torregalli, and Santa Maria Annunziata, Via dell'Antella. Children's hospital: Meyer, 14 Via Luca Giordano.

A volunteer service (AVO) helps translate for non Italian patients in hospitals (T: 055 425 0126).

First-aid and ambulance emergency 24hr service, T: 118

Ambulance service (run by volunteers of the Misericordia, Piazza del Duomo) T: 055 212 222

Ambulance service (run by volunteers of the Fratellanza Militare) T: 055 215 555

Mobile coronary unit T: 055 283 394

Fire brigade T: 115

Road assistance T: 116

Internet centres

Internet Train has numerous branches in Florence open 7 days a week: 24 Via Guelfa (*map p. 399, D1*), 40 Via dell'Oriuolo (*map p. 399, E2*), 30 Borgo San Jacopo (*map p. 398, C4*), 36 Via de' Benci (*map p. 399, E3*), 9 Via Giacomini (*map p. 397, A2*), 1 Via

Zannoni (Via Panicale; *map p. 398, C1*), 11 Via del Parione (*map p. 398, B3*), and 6 Via Santa Monaca (*map p. 398, B3*), 33 Borgo La Croce (*map p. 399, F3*). There is also one in the underpass of the railway station of Santa Maria Novella.

Lost property

The central office of the Comune is at 19 Via Circondaria, T: 055 328 3942. To report the loss or theft of a credit card, call:

Visa T: 800 877 232
Mastercard T: 800 872 050
American Express : 055 238 2876

Newspapers and magazines

Free publications include *Chiavi d'oro*, issued every two months in Italian and English, which gives detailed practical information on Florence and lists concerts and exhibitions, usually available at the APT information offices and in hotels. *Turismonotizie* magazine is also issued every two months and distributed at the APT information office and in hotels.

Magazines with information about the city include *Firenze Spettacolo*, which comes out every month and can be bought at newsagents; this gives detailed information about events in Florence. *Vista* is a magazine in English on Florence and Tuscany.

Foreign newspapers can be purchased at most kiosks and the *New York Herald Tribune*, published in Bologna, carries news on Italy.

Opening hours

The large shops and department stores and shops in the centre of Florence are open all day (9.30 or 10–7.30), and are sometimes also open on Sundays, but many others close for three or four hours in the middle of the day and are closed on Sunday. As a general rule smaller shops and local stores are open Monday–Saturday except between 1 and 4, and on Monday morning for most of the year (in summer they usually close on Saturday afternoon and open on Monday morning). Hardware shops are usually closed on Saturday afternoon and open Monday morning. Local food shops usually open Monday–Saturday 7.30 or 8–1 & 5–7.30 or 8, but are closed on Wednesday afternoon for most of the year. The Standa supermarket in Via Pietrapiana (*map p. 399, F3*) is usually open on Sundays and holidays.

From mid-June to mid-September all shops close on Saturday afternoon. Government offices usually work weekdays 8–1.30 or 2.

Personal security

For all emergencies, T: 113. As in cities all over the world, pick-pocketing is a widespread problem in Florence. Don't carry valuables in handbags and take extra care on buses. You should also be careful when using a credit card to withdraw money from automatic teller machines. Cash, documents and valuables should be left in hotel safes and it's a good idea to make photocopies of all important documents in case of loss. Italian law requires everyone to carry some form of identification with a photograph: it is therefore best to keep your passport with you. Lost or stolen passports will be replaced by the British and American consulates in Florence (see above). They will also help British and American travellers who are in difficulty and will give advice in emergencies.

Pharmacies

Pharmacies (*farmacie*) are usually open Monday–Friday 9–1, 4–7.30 or 8. Some are open 24 hours a day, including those at the Stazione Santa Maria Novella, at no. 7 Via Calzaiuoli (*map p. 399, D3*), and at no. 20 Piazza San Giovanni. (*map p. 398, C2*) A few are open on Saturdays, Sundays (and holidays), and at night: these are listed on the door of every chemist.

Photography

Rules about photography vary in museums and churches, so it is always best to ask first for permission (the use of a flash is often prohibited).

Postal services

The head post offices are in 53 Via Pietrapiana (*map p. 399, F3*) and Via Pellicceria (*map p. 398, C3*) and they are open 8.15–7 (except on the last day of the month when they are open 8.15–midday); on Saturday they are open 8.30–12.30. Branch post offices are usually open Monday–Friday 8.15–1.30 (Saturday 8.30–12.30). There is a small post office in the Uffizi gallery.

Stamps are sold at tobacconists (displaying a blue 'T' sign) as well as post offices. There is a priority postal service (for which special stamps must be purchased) for Italy and abroad, which promises delivery within three days. CAI post is a guaranteed, but much more expensive, express postal service which gives you a receipt. At post offices there are special boxes for letters abroad.

Public holidays

The main holidays in Italy, when offices, shops and schools are closed, are as follows:

1 January	New Year's Day
25 April	Liberation Day
Easter Monday	
1 May	Labour Day
15 August	Assumption
1 November	All Saints' Day
8 December	Immaculate Conception
25 December	Christmas Day
26 December	St Stephen

In addition, the festival of the patron saint of Florence, St John, is celebrated on 24 June as a local holiday in the city.

Museums are usually closed on 24 June, Easter Sunday and 15 August, although sometimes some of the state museums remain open on these days. There is usually no public transport on 1 May and the afternoon of Christmas Day. For annual festivals, see above.

Street numbering

In Florence, the numbers of all private residences are written in blue or black, and those of all shops in red, so the same number often occurs in blue or black and in red in the same street.

Telephones

There are public telephones in kiosks, as well as in a few bars and restaurants. These are operated by telephone cards, which can be purchased from tobacconists displaying a blue 'T' sign, bars, kiosks and post offices. Numbers that begin with 800, called *numero verde*, are toll-free. Telephone numbers in Italy can have from seven to eleven numbers. All require the area code, whether you are making a local call or a call from outside Florence.

Directory assistance (in Italian) is available by dialling 12. International telephone cards, which offer considerable savings, are now widely available from the same outlets as above. At Il Cairo Phone Center, 90 Via de' Macci, near Sant'Ambrogio (open daily 9.30–9) you can make low-cost international phone calls.

Florence area code 055
Dialling UK from Italy (0044) + number
Dialling US from Italy (001) + number
Dialling Florence from Europe or the US (0039) 055 + number

Tipping

Most prices in hotels and restaurants include a service charge, and so tipping is far less widespread in Italy than it is in North America. Even taxi-drivers rarely expect more than a Euro or two added to the charge (which officially includes service). In restaurants, prices are almost always inclusive of service. In hotels, porters who show you to your room and help with your luggage, or find you a taxi, usually expect a few Euro.

GLOSSARY OF ART TERMS

Aedicule, small opening framed by two columns and a pediment, originally used in classical architecture

Albarello (pl. *albarelli*), cylindrical shaped pharmacy jars, usually slightly waisted and produced by numerous potteries in Italy from the 15th to the 18th century

Amorino (pl. *amorini*), a small cupid or putto

Amphora, antique vase, usually of large dimensions, for oil and other liquids

Antefix, an ornament at the eaves of the roof to hide the join between tiles

Antiphonal, choir-book containing a collection of antiphons—verses sung in response by two choirs

Apse, vaulted semicircular end wall of the chancel of a church or of a chapel

Archaic, period in Greek civilization preceding the Classical era: from about 750 BC–480 BC

Architrave, the lowest part of an entablature, the horizontal frame above a door

Arte (pl. *arti*), Guild or Corporation

Attic, topmost storey of a classical building, hiding the spring of the roof

Avello (pl. *avelli*), family burial vault

Badia, from *abbazia*, an abbey

Baldacchino, canopy supported by columns, usually over an altar

Basilica, originally a Roman hall used for public administration; in Christian architecture an aisled church with a clerestory and apse and no transepts

Bas-relief, sculpture in low relief

Biscuit (or bisque), fired but unglazed earthenware or pottery

Borgo, a suburb; a street leading away from the centre of a town

Bottega, the studio of an artist; the pupils who worked under his direction

Bozzetto (pl. *bozzetti*), sketch, often used to describe a small model for a piece of sculpture

Campanile, bell-tower, often detached from the building to which it belongs

Canopic jar (or vase), ancient Egyptian urn used to preserve the internal organs such as the liver and lungs, and placed in the tomb beside the mummy

Cantoria (pl. *cantorie*), singing-gallery in a church

Cappella, chapel

Capomaestro, director of works or masterbuilder

Cartoon, from *cartone*, meaning a large sheet of paper—a full-size preparatory drawing for a painting or fresco

Cassone, a decorated chest, usually a dower chest

Cavea, the part of a theatre or amphitheatre occupied by the rows of seats

Cenacolo, a scene of the Last Supper (in the refectory of a convent)

Chiaroscuro, distribution of light and shade in a painting

Ciborium, casket or tabernacle containing the Host

Cinquecento, Italian term for the 'fifteen-hundreds' i.e. the 16th century

Cipollino, onion marble; greyish marble with streaks of white or green

Cippus (pl. *cippae*), sepulchral monument in the form of an altar

Colloquio, Parlour in an ecclesiatic building for conversation or visitors

Commesso fiorentino, Florentine

mosaic, the art of working *pietre dure*, hard or semi-precious

Contrapposto, a pose in which the body is twisted. First used in classical statuary, it is characteristic of Michelangelo's sculpture and works by the Mannerist school

Corbel, a projecting block, usually of stone

Cornice, topmost part of a temple entablature; any projecting ornamental moulding at the top of a building beneath the roof

Crater (see krater)

Crenellations, battlements

Cupola, dome

Diptych, painting or ivory tablet in two sections

Dossal, a cloth hung behind the altar or at the sides of the chancel

Duomo, cathedral

Exedra, semicircular recess

Ex-voto, tablet or small painting expressing gratitude to a saint

Foresteria, guest-wing

Fresco (in Italian, *affresco*), painting executed on wet plaster (intonaco). On the rough plaster (arriccio) beneath, the artist made a sketch (or sinopia) which was covered little by little as work on the fresco proceeded. Since the intonaco had to be wet during this work, it was applied each day only to that part of the wall on which the artist was sure that he could complete the fresco (these areas, which can now often be detected by restorers, are known as *giornate*). From the 16th century onwards cartoons (*cartoni*) were used to help the artist with the over-all design: the *cartone* was transferred on to the *intonaco* either by pricking the outline with small holes over which a powder was dusted, or by means of a stylus which left an incised line on the wet plaster. In the 1960s and 1970s, many frescoes were detached from the walls on which they were executed and so the sinopie beneath were discovered (and sometimes also detached)

Gonfalone, banner of a medieval guild or commune

Gonfaloniere, chief magistrate or official of a medieval Italian Republic, the bearer of the Republic's gonfalone

Graffiti, design on a wall made with an iron tool on a prepared surface, the design showing in white. Also used loosely to describe scratched designs or words on walls

Greek cross, church plan based on a cross with arms of equal length

Grisaille, painting in various tones of grey

Grottesche (or grotesques), a style of painting or stucco decoration used by the ancient Romans and discovered in the 1490s in the Domus Aurea in Rome (then underground, hence its name, from 'grotto'). The delicate ornamental decoration, normally on a light background, is characterized by fantastical motifs with intricate patterns of volutes, festoons, garlands, and borders of twisted vegetation and flowers interspersed with small winged human or animal figures, birds, masques, griffins, and sphynxes. This type of decoration became very fashionable and was widely copied by late Renaissance artists

Hemicycle, a semicircular structure, room, arena or wall

Hypocaust, ancient Roman heating system in which hot air circulated under the floor and between double walls

Incunabula, any book printed before 1500

Intarsia, a decorative inlay made from wood, marble or metal

Intonaco, plaster

Intrados, underside or soffit of an arch

Kourai, from the Greek word for young man (*kouros*) used to describe standing, nude male statues in the Greek Archaic style

Krater, a large, open bowl used for mixing wines, especially in ancient Greece

Lantern, a small circular or polygonal turret with windows all round, crowning a roof or a dome

Latin cross, a cross with a long vertical arm, usually used to described the plan of a church

Lavabo (pl. *lavabi*), hand-basin usually outside a refectory or in a sacristy

Lavatorium, the Latin name for a room with large hand-basins (lavabi) in stone or marble outside a convent refectory where the rites of purification were carried out before a meal

Lekythos, an ancient Greek vase, tall and narrow-necked with one handle, used as a vessel for oil

Loggia, covered gallery or balcony, usually preceding a larger building

Lunette, semicircular space in a vault or ceiling, or above a door or window, often decorated with a painting or relief

Lungarno (pl. Lungarni), a road which follows the banks of the Arno

Maestà, representation of the Madonna and Child enthroned in majesty

Majolica (or Maiolica), a type of earthenware glazed with bright metallic oxides that was originally imported to Italy from Majorca and was extensively made in Italy during the Renaissance

Mandorla, tapered, almond-shaped aura around a holy figure (usually Christ or the Virgin)

Medallion, large medal; loosely, a circular ornament

Monochrome, painting or drawing in one colour only

Monolith, single stone (usually a column)

Niello, black substance (usually a compound of sulphur and silver) used in an engraved design, or an object so decorated

Oculus, round window

Opera (e.g. del Duomo), the office in charge of the fabric of a building (in this case the Cathedral)

Opus, tessellatum mosaic formed entirely of square tesserae (pieces of marble, stone or glass)

Pala, large altarpiece

Palazzo, palace, any dignified and important building

Palestra, a public place devoted to training athletes in ancient Greece or Rome

Pax, sacred object used by a priest for the blessing of peace and offered for the kiss of the faithful; usually circular, engraved, enamelled, or painted in a rich gold or silver frame

Pendentive, concave spandrel beneath a dome

Piano nobile, main floor of a palace

Pietà, representation of the Virgin mourning the dead Christ (sometimes with other figures)

Pietre dure, hard or semi-precious stones, often used in the form of mosaics to decorate furniture such as cabinets and table-tops

Pietra forte, fine-grained limey sandstone used as a building material in Florence, and often for the rustication of palace façades

Pietra serena, fine-grained dark grey sandstone, easy to carve. Although generally not sufficiently resistant for the exterior of buildings, it was used to decorate many Renaissance interiors in Florence

Pilaster, a shallow pier or rectangular column projecting only slightly from the wall

Pinnacle, a small turret-like termination crowning spires, buttresses and roofs

Pluteus (pl. *plutei*), marble panel, usually decorated; a series of them used to form a parapet to precede the altar of a church

Podestà, chief magistrate who ruled a medieval city with the help of a council and representatives from the corporations. He had to be someone who was not a Florentine, and was also a military leader

Polyptych, painting or panel in more than three sections

Portone main entrance (large enough for carriages) to a palazzo or villa

Predella, small painting or panel, usually in sections, attached below a large altarpiece, illustrating scenes of a story such as the life of a saint, or of the Virgin

Presepio, literally crib or manger. A group of statuary of which the central subject is the Infant Jesus in the manger

Pulvin, cushion stone between the capital and the impost block

Putto (pl. *putti*), figure sculpted or painted, usually nude, of a child

Quadratura, painted architectural perspectives

Quadriga, a two-wheeled chariot drawn by four horses abreast

Quadriporticus, rectangular court or atrium arcaded on all four sides, derived from the atriums in front of paleochristian basilicas

Quatrefoil, four-lobed design

Quattrocento, Italian term for the 'fourteen hundreds' i.e. the 15th century

Rood-screen, a screen below the Rood or Crucifix dividing the nave from the chancel of a church

Scagliola, imitation marble or *pietre dure* made from selenite

Scarsella, the rectangular recess of the tribune of the Florence Baptistery, first called by this name by the early 14th century chronicler Giovanni Villani. Now also sometimes used for the rectangular sanctuary in a church

Schiacciato, term used to describe very low relief in sculpture, where there is an emphasis on the delicate line rather than the depth of the panel (a technique perfected by Donatello)

Sinopia (pl. *sinopie*), large sketch for a fresco made on the rough wall in a red earth pigment called sinopia (because it originally came from Sinope, a town on the Black Sea). When a fresco is detached for restoration, it is possible to see the sinopia beneath, which can also be separated from the wall

Spandrel, surface between two arches in an arcade or the triangular space on either side of an arch

Sporti, overhang, or projecting upper storey of a building, characteristic of medieval houses in Florence

Stele (pl. *stelae*), upright stone bearing a monumental inscription

Stemma (pl. *stemme*), coat of arms or heraldic device

Stoup, vessel for Holy Water, usually near the west door of a church

Stucco (pl. *stucchi*), plaster-work

Tempera, a painting medium of powdered pigment bound together, in its simplest form, by a mixture of egg yolk and water

Tepidarium, room for warm baths in a Roman bath

Term, pedestal or terminal figure in human form, tapering towards the base

Terraverde, green earth pigment, sometimes used in frescoes

Tessera, small cube of marble, stone or glass used in mosaic work

Thermae, originally simply Roman baths, later elaborate buildings fitted with libraries, assembly rooms, gymnasia and circuses

Tondo, (pl. *tondi*) round painting or relief

Transenna, open grille or screen, usually of marble, in an early Christian church

Tribune, the apse of a Christian basilica that contains the bishop's throne or the throne itself

Triptych, painting or tablet in three sections

Triton, river god

Trompe l'œil, literally, a deception of the eye; used to describe illusionist decoration and painted architectural perspective

Tympanum, the area between the top of a doorway and the arch above it; also the triangular space enclosed by the mouldings of a pediment

Viale (pl. *viali*), wide avenue

Villa, country house with its garden

INDEX

Explanatory or more detailed references (where there are many), or references to places where an artist's work is best represented, are given in bold. Numbers in italics are picture references. Dates are given for all artists, architects and sculptors.

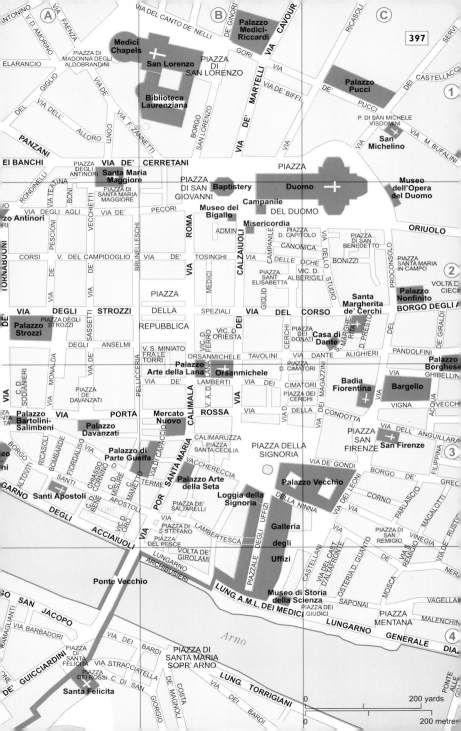

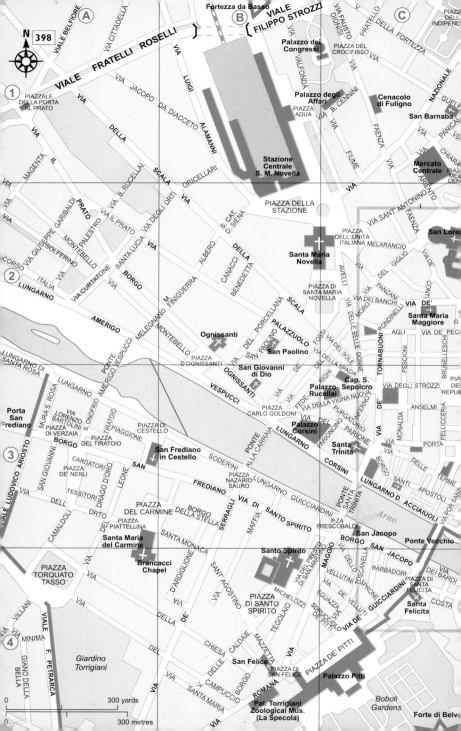

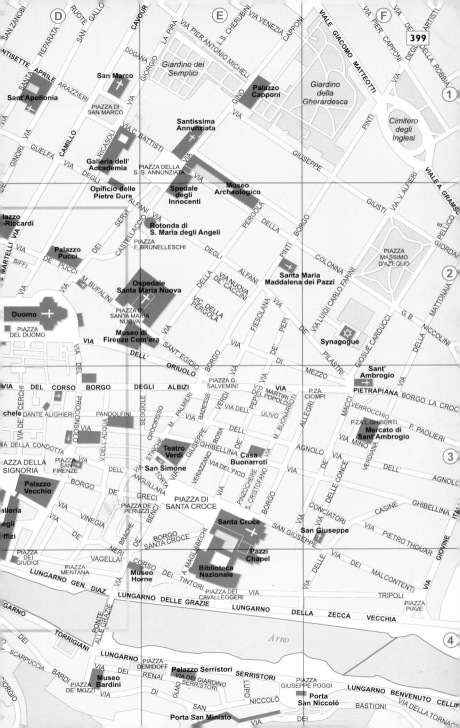

continued from p. 4

Editor-in-chief: Annabel Barber
Assistant editor: Judy Tither
Consulting editors: Charles Freeman, Nigel McGilchrist

The Florentine Renaissance: Nigel McGilchrist. Nigel McGilchrist was educated at Winchester and Oxford. He is an art historian who has lived in the Mediterranean—Italy, Greece and Turkey—for over twenty-five years, working for a period for the Italian Ministry of Arts and then for six years as Director of the Anglo-Italian Institute in Rome. He has taught at the University of Rome, for the University of Massachusetts, and was for seven years Dean of European Studies for a consortium of American universities. He lectures widely in art and archaeology at museums and institutions in Europe and the United States, and lives near Orvieto.

Historical sketch: Charles Freeman. Charles Freeman is a freelance academic historian with a long-standing interest in Italy and the Mediterranean. His *Egypt, Greece and Rome, Civilizations of the Ancient Mediterranean* (second edition, Oxford University Press, 2004) is widely used as an introductory textbook to the ancient world. His most recent book, *The Horses of St.Mark's* (Little Brown, 2004), is a study of the famous horses through their history in Constantinople and Venice. He leads study tours of Italy for the Historical Association and has recently been elected a Fellow of the Royal Society of Arts.

Design: Anikó Kuzmich
Maps: Dimap Bt.
Repro Studio: Timp Kft.
Architectural elevations: Michael Mansell RIBA & Gabriella Juhász
Floor plans and watercolours: Imre Bába
With special thanks to Richard Robinson

Photography:
Photo editors: Hadley Kincade, Róbert Szabó Benke
Annabel Barber: pp: 51, 61, 68, 72, 141, 147, 153, 167, 184, 203, 243, 271.
Bill Hocker: p. 288. Thomas Howells: p. 44.
Monica Larner pp. 3, 47. Phil Robinson: pp. 39, 55, 71, 255.
Polo Museale Fiorentino, Gabinetto Fotografico: pp. 73, 93, 96, 103, 121, 155, 221, 323.
The Bridgeman Art Library, London: pp. 110, 187, 192, 195, 244, 258, 274.

Printed in Hungary by Dürer Nyomda Kft, Gyula.

ISBN 1–905131–02–X